KT-417-841

ASCENT

ASCENT

A Life Spent Climbing on the Edge

CHRIS BONINGTON

SIMON & SCHUSTER

London · New York · Sydney · Toronto · New Delhi

A CBS COMPANY

First published in Great Britain by Simon & Schuster UK Ltd, 2017
A CBS COMPANY

3 5 7 9 10 8 6 4 2

Simon & Schuster UK Ltd
1st Floor
222 Gray's Inn Road
London WC1X 8HB

www.simonandschuster.co.uk
www.simonandschuster.com.au
www.simonandschuster.co.in

Simon & Schuster Australia, Sydney
Simon & Schuster India, New Delhi

A CIP catalogue record for this book
is available from the British Library

Hardback ISBN: 978-1-4711-5754-7
TradePaperback ISBN: 978-1-4711-5755-4
eBook ISBN: 978-1-4711-5756-1

Typeset in the UK by M Rules
Printed and bound by CPI Group (UK) Ltd, Croydon, CR0 4YY

To my mother Helen, Wendy
and Loreto

Contents

Introduction

Old Man

The Old Man of Hoy is the tallest sea stack in the British Isles but it started life as a promontory, a sheer band of red cliffs jutting out into the fierce tides of the Pentland Firth. Over time the sucking waves and wind hollowed out a tunnel in the sandstone that slowly expanded into a vast arch and then collapsed, leaving behind a slender tower, like a 400-foot needle, rising from the wild North Atlantic. It survives, for now, because it rests on a plinth of harder rock, a slender finger beckoning every climber who ever saw it. But in the wind you can feel it swaying, reminding you that nothing is for ever.

The Old Man was made for theatre. The clifftop opposite forms a perfect dress circle for an audience and the jumbled rocky isthmus that once linked it to the mainland are the uncomfortable stalls. Making my way down to the bottom, gingerly following a narrow twisting path slippery with wet grass, I was acutely aware of the dizzying space below my feet. The first time I came this way was almost half a century ago. Then I was thirty-two years of age, arguably in my prime. Now I was eighty, and every step was a struggle. Drizzle had been falling from the grey sky. Not for the first time in my life, I wondered what I was doing there.

It was Leo Houlding's idea. Leo is one of Britain's most talented young climbers and aged eleven had been the youngest person ever to climb the Old Man of Hoy. If we did it together, I'd almost certainly be the oldest. I was immediately attracted to the idea, but at the time was facing the greatest crisis of my life. My wife Wendy had been diagnosed with motor neurone disease in December 2012 and was in the final stages of this cruel illness. I couldn't leave her, certainly not to go climbing. She died on 24 July 2014. My grief was intense but climbing offered me the possibility of relief, almost an escape.

Going up to the Orkneys to climb the Old Man remained an attractive objective; it wouldn't be the first time I'd sought consolation in this wild and lonely place. In 1966, Tom Patey, one of the great characters of Scottish climbing and a dear friend, had invited me to join him in making the first ascent shortly after the tragic death by drowning of three-year-old Conrad, my first son. I think his aim had been similar to Leo's, to help me through my bewildering sense of loss. So I accepted Leo's invitation and in late August set out to climb the Old Man of Hoy once again.

In many ways, our lives had followed similar paths, both of us making a living through the sport we love, lecturing and filming our ventures. Yet even though Leo is almost young enough to be my grandson, I think we share the sheer joy in climbing. We had come to know each other through our association with the outdoor brand Berghaus; I have been their non-executive chair for twenty years, Leo is their highest-profile athlete. He has matured into an outstanding team leader, becoming an important international ambassador for British climbing while still retaining a wonderful warmth and sense of fun.

Our climb on the Old Man of Hoy would have a media dimension, for *The One Show*, the BBC TV magazine programme. They were sending a climbing presenter, Andy Torbet. The schedule was tight, just four days to get the Old Man climbed and filmed, whatever the weather, and it wasn't good. The first day was a recce while the crew rigged the route in preparation for filming. When I first climbed the Old Man live on television in 1967 for one of the BBC's most successful outside broadcasts, it had been a logistical extravaganza at the very limits of broadcasting technology. Now it was all done wirelessly with lightweight digital cameras and edited on computers.

One thing you can't change is the weather. It was raining hard now and there was a blustery wind as we plodded up the path to the top of the cliffs opposite the Old Man. I had plenty of time for doubts. For a start, I was horribly unfit; with Wendy's illness I hadn't had time for exercise, let alone climbing. In addition I had pulled something in my back just before leaving home while shifting some furniture. Was I up to it? Would I make a fool of myself in front of the cameras? Was it even possible to climb something like this at eighty?

The top of the Old Man came into sight, peeping over the cliff-top, and I felt a tide of memory rushing in, familiar faces from that broadcast so many years ago: Tom Patey, one of the greatest pioneers of Scottish mountaineering; Joe Brown, that rock-climbing wizard with his sly sense of humour and tombstone grin; Ian McNaught-Davis, Joe's ebullient, charismatic partner that day; and two from the next generation climbing a spectacular new route, the tyro Pete Crew and Dougal Haston, who would become a close friend and key member of my expeditions, enigmatic but hugely driven, all the way to the summit of Everest in 1975.

Soon Leo and I were standing on the edge of the cliff looking across to the Old Man: slender, somewhat menacing and very, very tall. There were group shots to take, and strategy to discuss. We were due to climb the following morning; the forecast was similar to what it had been for today, good in the morning but deteriorating. It was then I made my stand. I told the director there was no way I was prepared to try to climb it in those conditions and insisted on waiting another day. He wasn't happy but I stuck to my guns and it was finally agreed we'd spend the next day doing interviews and climb the day after.

The following morning dawned fine; we could certainly have climbed and filmed but I desperately needed that break. Being interviewed by Leo took my mind off things, exploring how my life had unfolded. Always at its core was the climbing: the great joy of movement on the crags, the challenge of wild and remote landscapes and the chances I'd taken both in the mountains and in my career. Even the little fill-in sequences, walking over the beach or hopping between the wave-smoothed rocks had a therapeutic quality. By the end of the day I had recovered my equilibrium.

Next morning it was cloudy again, with a light intermittent drizzle, but it wasn't too windy. We had no choice but to go for it and I felt ready. At the base of the tower, looming above us like a skyscraper, I took a deep breath: climbing shoes and harness on, waterproofs zipped up, feeling bulky and cumbersome, the radio mike emphasizing I was on show. Leo, cheerful and business-like, drifted up the first pitch. I had soloed this back in 1967 but when I started now I knew immediately my back wasn't right. Each move hurt, particularly when I bridged out, my legs wide apart. There was nothing to be done. I had to get on with it.

The second pitch is the crux and very daunting. It begins with an awkward traverse under a bulging overhang into the dark heart of the cliff's east face, moving from a place of security to having an unnerving void beneath your feet, the boiling sea a hundred feet below. It's what climbers call exposure, that thrilling mix of space and fear. The traverse ended below an overhanging crack too narrow for my body but too wide for my hands. I coped at first and despite my back was climbing reasonably well. Leo kept the rope tight, but it didn't do much to help. He'd also left a couple of slings in place at strategic points for me to pull on. Bless you, I thought, taking full advantage. It was only slightly cheating.

Filming a climb can be irritating; there are so many delays. Now I welcomed them since they allowed me a chance to rest and chat with old friends on the film crew. I had worked on several film projects with Dave Cuthbertson, universally known as 'Cubby', a brilliant rock climber who had refined his skills as a photographer and cameraman. He was doing the close-up work. We reminisced while Leo brought up Andy, our *One Show* presenter, and continued as Leo led the next pitch, quickly disappearing from sight.

I thought the climbing would now be relatively straightforward but the rock was wet and greasy and Leo had gone slightly off route, stuck in a high runner and traversed out to the right across a seemingly blank wall. I would now have to follow this traverse, with the promise of a swinging fall, like a pendulum, if I messed it up. To add to my trial, a fulmar chick was resting on a sloping ledge just above the start. The fulmar's method of defence is to puke a jet of fishy bile at whatever threatens it, including rock climbers, and it proceeded to empty its stomach at me as I struggled to find a way across.

We had another welcome rest below the final pitch, a steep corner that bristled with holds. It was the one I had led on the first ascent back in 1966, the easiest of all the main pitches but aesthetically the most satisfying with the great bonus that it led to the top of the Old Man. I had hoped to lead it, but realized I wasn't fit enough. Every move was now painful and I had the ominous feeling my back was about to get a lot worse.

There was another long but welcome delay as the filmmakers got into position for the final shots and then it was my turn to climb. I was glad of the rope above me, feeling slow and clumsy, but I managed without needing a tight rope, pulling over the top with a mixture of joy and tearful emotion. There was a hug from Leo, a pause while he brought up Andy, and then he produced a bottle of champagne from his rucksack. We toasted each other as the sun tried to break through and an Orkney ferry went cruising past. All the self-doubt was gone. The struggle and pain no longer mattered.

As I told the BBC interviewer, this business of getting old, in a way, is a bit of a pig. You're stiffer and you're slower; you can't quite achieve what you did before. What getting to the top of the Old Man of Hoy showed me was that one can at least go on doing something. In ten years, I reflected, I would be ninety: a sobering thought. It seemed unlikely I would still be able to climb something like this then. What I wanted was to make every single day of my eighties mean something, get out and climb and walk, enjoy my grandchildren, keep working and make life as rich and exciting as it possibly can be. That's what keeps you going.

PART ONE
Beginnings

Chapter One

Who Do I Think I Am?

How far are our personalities and the course of our lives shaped by the genes we inherit and how far by the environment in which we are brought up? I rather think it is a combination of the two, but with our genetic makeup having a very strong influence and those traits becoming visible from a young age. Looking back at my immediate ancestors, quite a few of them were undoubtedly adventurous in a variety of ways. They weren't great explorers or sportspeople, but they carved out a distinct life of their own.

On my mother's side, my grandmother, whom I knew as Nan and who played a major part in my early upbringing, was brought up a Catholic, the tenth child of a family of twelve. Her father, Timothy Doran, born in 1814 at Enniscorthy, County Wexford, went to Sydney as a young man, attracted by stories of fortunes to be made from the gold rush that started around that time. Until the gold rush, the majority of migrants had been convicts.

For Timothy, it was a step into the unknown, starting with the horrendous four-month voyage in a cramped sailing ship around the Cape of Good Hope and across the empty southern Indian Ocean, battened down in the hold for days on end, drinking brackish water and eating weevil-infested food. He spent twenty years in Australia but didn't talk about it; only scraps of family legend persisted. He spent most of his time in Sydney but ventured out to the lawless goldfields, where if he saw a shadow fall across his tent he shot first and only then went out to investigate.

One story suggests he was a fence for the armour-clad bushranger Ned Kelly, Australia's beloved outlaw, a Robin Hood who robbed the rich English cattle and sheep farmers encroaching on the land of small, mostly Irish homesteaders and was eventually hanged. There was never any mention of Timothy prospecting for gold; he was more likely a gold-mining 'sutler', selling provisions and implements, perhaps advancing money to prospectors and no doubt dabbling in the black economy of the time. Whatever the truth, when he returned to England in the early 1860s, settling in Liverpool, he had accumulated a modest fortune, bought a couple of houses and set up a chain of pawnbroker's shops.

When he met my great-grandmother Helen, then just nineteen, he knocked twenty years off his declared age, claiming to be thirty-one when they married in 1865. Helen had twelve children in twenty years and he gave all but two of them the middle name Sydney. Helen died in 1896 at only fifty, presumably from exhaustion. Timothy, born a year before the battle of Waterloo, died in 1903 at the grand old age of eighty-nine.

My maternal grandfather, Francis Storey, was also from Irish stock, albeit Protestant. His father, also Francis, my great-grandfather, was born and brought up in County Wicklow. He joined the Royal Irish Constabulary and then, also having an adventurous spirit, emigrated to Australia in 1865. More conformist than Timothy Doran, he joined the Australian Mounted Infantry and led an exciting, hard-riding life hunting down bushrangers and closing down shebeens. He claimed to have been one of the officers sent to arrest Dan Kelly, brother of Ned. Returning to England around 1881, he settled in New Brighton on the south bank of the River Mersey, a day-trippers' resort for the people of Liverpool where Francis built up a profitable shop called the Bon Marché opposite the pier. He also sat on the town council for many years, becoming mayor of Wallasey. I can remember my pride when in the late 1940s I sailed on a ferry named in his honour.

His eldest son, Francis Hubert, my grandfather, also had a nomadic disposition. He was training to be a doctor in Wrexham when he met Nan, my grandmother. They married but he didn't stick around, getting a job with the Colonial Service as a doctor in Nigeria. He'd come home every three years for six months but always seemed a stranger in an all-female household ruled by my grandmother, with two young daughters, Helen, my mother, and Thea. There was also Polly, Nan's younger sister, who never married, and a live-in maid. Francis was given early retirement in the mid 1930s, perhaps because of the quantity of whisky he consumed. He didn't stay home for long, getting a berth with the Blue Funnel Line as a ship's doctor, sailing the Atlantic convoys throughout the Second World War before retiring.

There were plenty of adventurous genes on my father's side. My paternal grandfather, Maximilian Christian Bonig, was born in Schleswig-Holstein in 1874. He always claimed to be Danish, since Schleswig and Holstein had been under Danish rule until Bismarck invaded in 1864. Holstein's population, however, was mainly German and my grandfather's relatives were all German. I assume it was because he ended up working for the British and became a British citizen that he changed the family name to Bonington.

Maximilian's family were farmers but life on the land didn't appeal; he ran away from home at the age of ten to join a sailing ship before being hauled back ignominiously. His parents eventually compromised and apprenticed him to a shipbuilder. Max knuckled down but still yearned for the sea. In 1890, aged sixteen, he went down to the docks to sign on as carpenter in a barque bound for Mauritius. It was the start of many adventures. He spent months at sea in a New Bedford whaler, was shanghaied aboard a Nova Scotia boat bound for the east coast of America with a blue-nosed, red-haired, one-eyed skipper and a mate who used a belaying pin to club the crew.

Aged twenty-one, he was mate on a schooner, but the ship ran aground near New Brunswick and Max was washed overboard. He was found unconscious on the sand. The rest of the crew took to the rigging but were found frozen to death the next day. After that he joined the United States Navy but his prospects seemed limited and missing home returned to Schleswig-Holstein. The sea soon lured him back. He found a ship bound for India, the ill-fated *Highland Glen*. Running flat out in the Roaring Forties, a freak wave washed Max overboard. He hung on to the foretopsail brace and was lifted back onto the deck as the ship heeled over. He left the ship at Calcutta, a fortunate decision, since it disappeared on its next voyage carrying kerosene to the West Indies.

Seeking more security, Max then got a job on the troop ship *Warren Hastings*, a state-of-the-art steamship with a metal hull that was claimed to be practically unsinkable. In January 1897, carrying a thousand troops and their families from Mumbai to Mauritius, the boat went off course in thick fog off the island of Réunion and struck a rock just after midnight. My grandfather was thrown out of his bunk and rushed on deck to find the bows of the vessel resting on a reef and thirty fathoms under the stern.

The ship was taking on water but the engineers stayed at their stations to keep the lights burning. If the watertight doors were shut, the vessel could be kept afloat long enough to get the passengers and crew off. With a few Indian lascars Max went below, barefoot and still in his pyjamas, working for nearly an hour in deserted gangways, shutting the heavy doors and screwing down the ports, gradually working his way aft. Then the lights flickered, the whine of the dynamos stopped and the scene was in darkness. Yet closing all those waterproof hatches worked. The crew got a line ashore and the women and children and then the troops escaped over the bows. Only two on board died.

Max was commended for gallantry and given the job of assistant harbourmaster at Port Blair, the principal town and centre of government in the Andaman Islands, then a colony formed on the same principles as Australia for convicts of both sexes from the Raj, prisoners released on 'ticket-of-leave' to work in the timber industry. The islands were covered in tropical rainforest and mangrove swamps and home to one of the oldest and most isolated human populations: the Negritos, dark-skinned and averaging four and a half feet in height. In Max's time, they presented a picture of life 30,000 years ago, hunter-gatherers who knew nothing of agriculture. When my grandfather arrived, there were only a few hundred left, the amiable coastal Negritos and a jungle tribe called the Jarawas who killed any intruder venturing into their hunting grounds.

Grandfather loved his new life, especially as he was in charge of shipbuilding, overseeing the construction of many vessels, some of them several hundred tons. In Port Blair he met Alice Parkinson, a pretty nineteen-year-old, whose dead father had been a sergeant major in the Royal Engineers. They fell in love and remained devoted to each other for the rest of their lives, marrying in 1908. Their first home was a wooden bungalow on Ross Island, in the harbour of Port Blair where the European officials lived. There were two clubs, one for senior officers, the other for juniors. In the evenings, white children, each with their *ayah*, played on the lawn. There were tennis courts, a library and even a bandstand, where convicts, dressed in smart white-and-blue uniforms, played in a brass band.

After seven years, Max moved to the forestry department, surveying every corner of the 3,000 square miles of the Andamans and Nicobars. I have a feeling he was happiest out in the jungle away from civilization and the social round of colonial life. He also became officer in charge of the Aborigines, looking after the friendly coastal tribes and doing his best to protect the tribes in the interior from contact with outsiders. Grandfather came nearer to understanding their minds than any other white man of that time. They trusted him and treated him as one of their own.

During the Great War, when he was in his early forties, Max was appointed to build and run a new settlement in the North Andamans to exploit the virgin forest there. Max picked a sheltered harbour called Stewart Sound. The Indian government was trying to encourage settlers so the population comprised mostly free people from the mainland. They lived under canvas, chopping down huge trees and draining mangrove swamps. Max and a medical orderly nursed those who succumbed to malaria or cholera. Elephants were imported from India to drag logs to the nearest tidal creek where they were lashed into rafts and towed to the newly built sawmill. The settlement thrived and thanks to Max's inspirational leadership was named Port Bonington. He was awarded the OBE when he retired in 1930, and later settled in Blackrock, Dublin, where he lived until his death in 1956.

His son, my father Charles, was born in 1910 on Ross Island, followed by two sisters, Marjorie and Lucy. Charles described in his unfinished memoir how he was cared for by a woman convicted of killing her husband: 'Her name was Chand Bibi, which in Hindustani means daughter of the moon; she was a short dumpy woman of about forty and her hair was turning grey; her brown face was crinkled and leathery, but in those early days, she was a second mother to me.'

Charles had an unusual early childhood. Aged eight, Max took him to the new settlement leaving his mother behind, saying that he'd be company for him since there were no other Europeans there. I have wondered if Max wanted to show his son, whom he obviously loved deeply, a different kind of world to that of Ross Island with its strict Edwardian values. 'My father was always a wonderful person to me;' my father wrote, 'he never beat me, but usually left that task to my mother. The next four years were the happiest of my life spent living in the North Andamans in the jungle camps. I spent all my time playing with the aboriginal pygmies ... out on the reef in their canoes – fishing, swimming and turtle hunting.'

When Charles was ten he was sent back to England to a strict Catholic prep school, where the cane was used for the slightest offence, and then Ampleforth, the Catholic public school. His parents came home for a long leave every three years, otherwise the children stayed with relatives. He then went up to Oxford where he met my mother. Mum had had a very different upbringing in Wallasey. She was quite a tomboy, preferring Meccano and Hornby train sets to dolls. Dark-haired and slim, she was handsome rather than pretty. Her sister, Dorothy, known as Thea, couldn't have been more different: a curly-haired blonde and very pretty, who played with dolls.

At the age of twelve, Mum started at Notre Dame High School for girls, was good at sport and increasingly successful academically. She was a rebel though, and fell foul of the school, which told her she would have to complete her two-year Higher School Certificate course in a year. She not only succeeded, she won three separate scholarships to Oxford to study English. She was the first girl from the school to go there.

Success undoubtedly went to her head. She partied a lot, discovered the joys of sex, went to very few lectures and fell in love with my father. He was even wilder than her and dropped out in his second year, returning to Burma, where his father got him a job with a timber company. Mum scraped through with a third-class degree, not bad considering how few lectures she attended.

After leaving Oxford, she persuaded Nan to sell her house in Wallasey and move down to London with her. Mum took a secretarial course and got a job as a shop assistant at a bookshop on Baker Street. She and Charles had kept up a warm correspondence and in early 1933 Max paid his fare back to England and gave him an allowance of four pounds a week. Charles and Mum were both very much in love, started to live together and slipped out to Kensington register office without telling their parents to marry. They moved into a small basement flat in Hampstead.

Even though she hadn't been to church since leaving school, Mum insisted on getting a blessing at the lovely little St Mary's Church in Hampstead. She became pregnant shortly afterwards and I was born on 6 August 1934 at the Elizabeth Garrett Anderson Hospital by Whitestone Pond, the highest point in London. She also had me baptized at the same little church with the name of Christian John Storey Bonington, maintaining her own family name.

The honeymoon didn't last long. It was the height of the depression and Charles couldn't get a job. My mother complained he was drinking too much and spending most of the day in bed. Money was short. Mum managed to get a part-time job with a successful romantic novelist called Berta Ruck, whose secretary had run off with her husband, the ghost-story writer Oliver Onions. Life became a struggle: caring for a baby, who cried through the night, struggling up the narrow steps with the pram, dropping me off at a local nursery each day and then returning in the late afternoon to a squalid flat.

Arguments escalated until, in a furious quarrel over money, Mum hit my father on the head with a poker. He dropped to the floor, unconscious, bleeding profusely. She dragged him to the bathroom and stuck his head under the old-fashioned geyser. Then, worried she'd killed him, Mum rushed out to the nearest phone box, her blouse and skirt covered in blood, leaving me fast asleep in the flat. She didn't dare return to the flat on her own so waited by the phone box till Nan arrived. When they got back, I was still fast asleep in my cradle and Charles was gone.

Mum took me to live with Nan, and Grandfather Bonington paid for Charles to travel to India. My mother didn't hear from him for several years. He remained in the Andaman Islands working for his father and then took off for Australia where he went walkabout across Queensland and New South Wales, worked a short stint on a Sydney newspaper, travelled plenty, made many friends and enjoyed the absence of responsibility he craved.

Back in England, Mum was also building a new life. While Nan took charge of me, she started working full-time, first as a copy typist then as secretary to the proprietor of a small advertising agency. Recognizing her talent with words, he promoted her to copywriter. Mum and Nan moved to a larger ground floor flat in Tanza Road with a big garden that backed onto the lower slopes of Parliament Hill on Hampstead Heath, settling into a comfortable routine. Mum's personal life also improved. She began an intimate relationship with an Australian journalist called Margo, while still sharing the Tanza Road flat with Nan.

My own memories of early childhood are disjointed: just stray, vivid images. My strongest, when I was probably three, was my first adventure. Playing with a little girl of around my age in the garden, we let ourselves out through the gate onto Hampstead Heath and were gone for a few hours. Nan was so worried she notified the local police. One of them found us playing together and took us back to Belsize Park police station where I spilt milk all over the inspector's desk.

I was an avid tree climber and attended a 'Health Kinder Garten' run by Mrs Kroemer who believed in unstructured outdoor play. Mum felt Nan was possessive and that I should have some discipline. I suspect there was an element of jealousy, handing over so much of my care while she went out to work to secure our financial survival. Yet Mum's career was going from strength to strength. She got a job as copywriter at the London Press Exchange, one of the top advertising agencies at that time.

I was blissfully unaware of the tensions between Mum and Nan or the tide of war about to engulf us. Mum on the other hand was riveted. She and Margo became increasingly politically aware, identifying themselves with the extreme left in the face of Nazi Germany's aggression and fascism in our own country. With the declaration of war, she was anxious to get me out of London and found a small boarding school called Pinewood at Goudhurst near Tunbridge Wells. Aged five, it took a little time for me to settle but eventually I was perfectly happy. With the fall of France and the threat of invasion, the headmistress, Miss Reid, decided to amalgamate the school with another, called Moorlands, near Kirkby Lonsdale in Westmorland. From an upstairs window, your eye followed a long winding drive, flanked with trees, to a view of the hills of the southern Lakes to the west and those of the Yorkshire Dales to the east.

During holidays, Nan came up and we usually stayed at a vegetarian guesthouse in Grasmere, Nan being a strict vegetarian. Mum would come up for short periods when she could get away from work. The impact of the Lakeland hills was more subliminal than anything else. Nan was essentially a suburban woman and never ventured into wild country. Our walks didn't go much further than the lower slopes of Fairfield, though I can remember a walk on a rainy day alongside what I think must have been the Sour Milk Ghyll in Easedale just out of Grasmere. It was wild, untamed country and I can still trawl its image from my memory. On another occasion I rowed Nan to the island in the middle of Grasmere and when she dozed off in the sun, I got back in the boat and explored, leaving her marooned. Given I couldn't swim and didn't have a life jacket, she was not best pleased.

My mother was once again in contact with my father, who was taken prisoner of war in November 1941. Having volunteered for the Australian Army at the outbreak of war, he was posted to Egypt, moved to a British regiment, was promoted and then volunteered for the newly formed Special Air Service, a tiny group of seven officers and sixty other ranks recruited by David Stirling, a charismatic young lieutenant with an outrageous plan. I suspect my father's unconventional past got him into the SAS, at thirty-two its eldest member.

The first operation was disastrous. Divided into five groups, each comprising an officer and ten men, they were to be dropped near two airstrips packed with Messerschmitt fighters near Tobruk. The weather was bad over the drop zone with high winds and poor visibility and as a result all their five aircraft missed it, landing the raiders miles away. Several were injured or killed in the process and only twenty-two made the rendezvous in the desert where the Long Range Desert Group picked them up.

My father's plane was shot up by a Messerschmitt and crash-landed. He had a badly shattered shoulder and was captured with the other survivors, spending the rest of the war in Germany. He joined in several escape attempts but never successfully. He wrote to me from his PoW camp, inspiring me to start hatching escape plans of my own. In a way, this proved my first expedition and exercise in leadership. I must have been eight at the time. I recruited three or four fellow escapees and scavenged bacon rinds at breakfast. Our greatest coup was stealing a fruit loaf bought for afternoon tea with prospective parents visiting the following day.

We slipped away at lunchtime and headed across the fields, stopping after an hour or so by the banks of a stream where we spent the rest of the afternoon playing. We ate the fruit loaf for tea and then began to think of where we'd sleep. There was a large tree by the stream. We could sleep in the branches to escape wild animals. It didn't take long to discover how uncomfortable that was. It was now getting dark and we drifted to the nearest road where a relieved but angry Miss Reid had been scouring the roads for us in her Morris Minor.

I was happy at Moorlands but my mother was concerned about the quality of my schoolwork. She felt I would do better closer to London where she could visit me more easily, choosing a progressive boarding school in Letchworth just north of London. It was vegetarian, which appealed to Nan, co-educational and didn't require a uniform. It was also much bigger and while I have no memories of it, I was bullied. The night before returning to school after a half-term holiday, my mother wrote in her diary: 'He looks well and heavier but his eyes seem sly and evasive. At night, his gallant pretence of happiness breaks down and he begs not to return to school.' My wish was granted. I stayed home but Mum was so concerned she took me to the Tavistock Clinic for psychological assessment. They didn't find anything drastically wrong and, to my mother's surprise, assessed my IQ at 143.

After I went to boarding school at the beginning of the war, Mum moved out of Tanza Road and set up home with Margo in a ground floor and basement flat on Downshire Hill, next to St John's Church. It had a back garden and an Anderson air-raid shelter for us and the other three tenants in the house: a sunken corrugated steel tunnel, covered in earth with room for two bunk beds. I was to get to know it well in the next year. The Blitz was over, but there were still regular night raids. Mum was so anxious about the shelter's impact on me that she read articles on how to distract children from the claustrophobia.

Things hadn't been easy for Mum. In 1943 she had been diagnosed with tuberculosis and spent time in a sanatorium. She had barely recovered when she decided to keep me at home. She chose a small co-educational prep about a mile away at the top of Hampstead Heath. Miss Miles, my new headmistress, asked if I had any questions.

'Yes please. Do you have discipline in this school?'

'We do – a kindly but firm discipline.'

'Then I'll come.'

It was a good choice and I quickly settled down, at the age of ten, walking to school by myself from the very start, making friends and enjoying lessons. But I was told I would no longer be seeing Nan. I didn't really understand why, but accepted it, as I think one does as a child, though I missed being taken out for treats and lunches at her flat in Roslyn Hill. Her queen of puddings with its meringue topping was a wonder.

'As the weeks go by,' Mum wrote in her diary, 'Chris grows plump again. Now that the over-close relationship with Nan has been ended, he seems to have sprung up, mentally and physically, like a retarded plant given new conditions. Every night, I dream of Nan. She stands in the dark room, rebuking me. But by day, I feel an immense relief and an absurd sense that I, too, have grown and gained in maturity.'

At home in Downshire Hill, Margo did all the cooking on top of her day job. She was now assistant editor of *Soviet Weekly News*, the Russian propaganda organ in the UK. I can't recall them being demonstrative in the love they felt for each other. Mum slept in the room on the ground floor linked to mine by double doors, the former sitting room of the house. Margo slept on a divan in our cosy kitchen-living room in the basement, looking out onto the garden. They had a cat called Maisky, named for the Russian ambassador.

In the evenings, after supper, we read Shakespeare plays, each of us taking different parts. Mum regularly read to me at night and made huge efforts for my birthdays and Christmas, finding Hornby train sets, lead soldiers and even an antique pistol. I felt comfortable with the family set-up, though must have been aware it was very different from that of my friends at school. This compounded my innate shyness and lack of social confidence. Mum describes how she admonished me for feigning a limp because I was frightened of another boy and didn't want to go to a birthday party where I might meet him.

'Sometimes you treat me as if I'm an old man of thirty,' I retorted. I was ten at the time.

'I guiltily realize,' Mum wrote in her diary, 'that I do expect considerable self-knowledge from him and apologize humbly. Unfortunately, such trivial incidents awaken my memory of Charles who so often evaded obligations by various subterfuges.'

My most vivid memory from this period was a German night raid, when we all retreated to the shelter in the garden. There was the roar of bombs detonating near by, the crackle of anti-aircraft fire and the more distant drone of bombers. I was both frightened and enthralled and wanted to get out of the shelter to see it all happen. The adults felt differently. There was a big thump alongside the shelter but no explosion followed. When at last the all-clear signal wailed, we emerged to find an unexploded incendiary bomb.

Approaching the end of my school year, Mum realized I had little chance of getting into a grammar. Determined to give me the best education she could, and earning a good deal as her career blossomed, she applied to our local public school, University College School, which had a junior branch that didn't require an entrance exam. Once there, you could move up into the senior school automatically. All I had to do was survive the interview with the headmaster, 'the alarming Dr Lake', as my mother described him. He was tall, very thin, white-haired with fierce dark eyes. Remarking on my name, I explained my Danish origins.

'Well, Christian, my young Dane, what is the capital of Denmark?'

'Belgrade, sir.'

I might not have known the answers to all of his questions, but I stood firm and looked him in the eye and never once glanced towards Mum for reassurance. I was accepted and soon settled down, making a few friends, though none of them close. I was conscientious in class but still behind and a terrible speller, something that worried Mum a great deal.

The war ended that summer and my father, released from his PoW camp, came back into our lives, much to my excitement: a father at last. He brought me an SS dagger and a two-dimensional brass model of a U-boat. Mum insisted on having the point of the dagger blunted so I couldn't stab myself or anyone else. My father tried to get back together with Mum, but she wasn't interested. After a couple of visits he no longer called; he would say he wanted to see me and then not show up. I remember vividly being hurt. He left to get on with his own life, eventually meeting Mary, who was to become his second wife and the mother of my half-brother and three half-sisters.

A year went by and Mum booked me into a holiday farm in Devon for the summer. I was now twelve and had met very few girls in the last two years, UCS being boys only. I can remember the thrill of having an illicit bath with one of the girls I met. There were riding lessons, and they had some ferrets, which were put under my care. At the end of a happy holiday I got the train back to Paddington but to my surprise Nan met me. I hadn't seen her for two years. She told me that Mum was ill in hospital and that I'd be staying with her until Mum recovered.

It's only since reading the notes for Mum's unfinished book that I learned the full story of what happened. She had been under intense pressure: the terrors of the Blitz, the challenge of bringing me up in conflict with Nan, and the stress of work. She had been promoted to running one of the agency's creative groups but with the return of male colleagues from the war there was fresh competition. Perhaps worst of all, Margo had fallen in love with a male colleague at work and as a result their relationship was in question.

'At work,' she wrote in her diary, 'my mind seems incapable of operation. My head feels as if it's stuffed with damp black cotton wool. I ring my doctor, but she is on her rounds. At lunch break, I call at her surgery but she has still not returned. I go home early.

Most of my actions are compulsive and have a ritual quality. When I wash up, I feel compelled to turn all the cups the other way round on their hooks. When Margo gets home, she persuades me to go to bed. She then rings Nan, who sends Father around. He sits beside me all night through the long hours of darkness, nightmarish with hallucination. In the morning, Margo has disappeared and I persuade Father to go home. Alone in the flat, I resolve on suicide. I close the kitchen window, block-up the key hole, turn on the gas and put my head in the oven.'

Fortunately Nan came round as soon as my grandfather had told her what was happening. She was just in time to switch off the gas and Mum was taken to hospital and sectioned. She was there for the next eighteen months. It's interesting how children accept what is happening to them. Nan's home was a first-floor flat in a big Edwardian house. I had a lovely room where I could play with my collection of lead soldiers, while Nan and Grandfather each had a very small bedroom. Nan contacted my father for financial support, since Mum was no longer working, to help with the fees at UCS, but he was starting afresh with a new family and strapped for cash.

I moved up to senior school, into the bottom stream, and life continued as normal. Then Mum was released from hospital. Her consultant had performed a lobotomy, a surgical procedure on the frontal lobe of the brain severing certain nerves to treat extreme depression. It had been successful, and while it removed some of her personal drive, in no way had it affected Mum's intelligence. She was, if anything, a kinder, warmer person.

There was no room for her in Nan's flat so she rented a bedsit nearby. She had lost her job with the London Press Exchange, and they wouldn't take her back, but she quickly found another job and naturally wanted to resume her role as mother so I moved into a corner of the bedsit. Her first problem was cooking. She had always had someone to do it for her: first Nan and then Margo. It was only after I complained that she took lessons. More importantly, she fed my huge appetite for reading, pointing me at the English classics: the Brontës, Jane Austen, Dickens and Thackeray, then the Russians: Tolstoy, Turgenev, Gogol, and French literature, Emile Zola's *Germinal* and Voltaire's *Candide*. Only recently have I come to appreciate how much I owe her and how great her love was for me.

Her relationship with Nan was now much better and I was able to enjoy both their affections. Money was tight but after a few months, through social services, we were able to get a fair-sized second-floor flat at a rent she could just afford, a few minutes' walk from Nan's and fifteen minutes from UCS. It must have taken great resilience. When she left hospital Mum spent some time looking for Margo, trying to find out where she was. She discovered that her married lover had returned to his family in the Soviet Union and Margo, in her grief, had taken her own life.

I was quite a timid child. There was a lad, a bit older than me, on the local milk round, who identified me as a little toff in my school uniform. He began threatening me so I started taking a long diversion to school to avoid him. Mum advised me to stand up and fight – even sending me to boxing classes – but I refused to go on with them, saying I didn't want to hit anyone, even a bully. I resigned myself to the longer walk. I was equally timid at games. Cricket bored me and I was frightened of the hard ball and I played truant to avoid rugby.

Put on report, I had to have a card signed off after every game. That pushed me into committing myself, throwing myself into tackling and mixing it in the rucks. I discovered the harder you played, the less you got hurt and suddenly found myself enjoying it. I lacked the ball sense and speed of reaction to become a good player, but as a wing forward ended up as captain of the third XV, the perfect niche for players of little skill but great enthusiasm.

In my second year at senior school I discovered a new boy with similar interests to mine. David was rather shy, no good at games, almost a caricature of the inky schoolboy, but I sensed we had lots in common. I invited him to tea and asked somewhat diffidently if he'd like to play with my toy soldiers; he was delighted and we became good friends. We were fascinated by military history, each of us building up our libraries from the second-hand book department at Foyles on the Charing Cross Road. I loved the museums too. My favourite was the United Services Museum in Whitehall, which had a huge scale model showing a crucial phase of Waterloo.

I was also keenly interested in current affairs and was left-wing, dating back to the Downshire Hill days when Mum and Margo were both active members of the Communist Party. Both had doubts after the end of the war, and Mum, after her breakdown, left altogether and returned to her Catholic faith. I actually joined the Young Communist League, something Mum said was very unwise. I went on demonstrations, for the excitement as much as anything else, but found the party meetings and the adults running them dull and rather dreary. As I became more aware of the millions who had been killed or imprisoned in the slave labour camps of Siberia, my disillusionment was complete.

Hampstead Heath had always been my childhood playground. From that first escape onto the Heath as a very young child, I explored its mysteries with a variety of friends: the woods and duelling ground of Kenwood House, the deciduous trees of the northern Heath, stretching down to Golders Hill and its deer park, swimming in the Hampstead Ponds, smoking my first and only cigarette in the dark vault under the viaduct at the age of nine. I still love wandering over it.

I extended my explorations to the London Docks, when they were still the greatest port in the world. On a Sunday, they were uncannily quiet, with cargo ships moored alongside the wharves, cranes silent, warehouses locked. I started cycling further afield, having saved up for a bike with dropped handlebars and a range of gears. I joined the Youth Hostel Association and spent weekends looking at castles as far afield as Dover. I became a bit of a wanderer, had one very good friend in David, was doing fairly well at school and seemed fairly happy. Yet I knew there was something missing, though I didn't yet know what that might be.

Chapter Two

A Passion Discovered

How does a life-changing experience start? With some, it's a single event; with others it creeps up on them over time. For me it was the latter. In the summer of 1951, I visited Grandfather Bonington, who, in the late 1930s, had retired to Ireland, perhaps mindful of his German birth and the fact that Éire would almost certainly be neutral in the coming war. I took a steam train from Euston bound for Holyhead and the ferry to Dún Laoghaire. Even the crossing to Ireland was an adventure, very different from going on the ferry from Seacombe across the Mersey to Liverpool, though even that I had always found exciting. This was the real sea and I was on my way to a foreign country. My grandfather's house was in Blackrock, a comfortable suburb on the south side of Dublin. From his back garden you could see the northern outliers of the Wicklow Mountains, nothing like as dramatic as those Welsh hills, but one particularly, the nearest, was a shapely grassy pyramid that had a real allure.

Grandfather, now in his late seventies, was very short, shrivelled by his years in the tropics, though you could still see how tough he had been in his prime; his shoulders were still broad, his chest deep and you could still feel the power of his personality. My grandmother had died a few years earlier, but his housekeeper Peggy fed us wonderfully well and he was full of energy, taking an active part in the community, was obviously well liked and worked hard in his garden and greenhouse. There were no other young people around, however, and my gaze strayed increasingly towards the hills. A few days before I was due to return I set out on my adventure, catching a bus to a point as close as I could to my objective and then finding my way, without a map, to the crest of the Little Sugar Loaf, 1,100 feet high, my first ever ascent of a mountain, small though it was.

On the way back home, this first glimmer of passion sparked into life as we rounded the coast of North Wales and passed Conway, with its magnificent castle built by Edward I to contain the truculent Welsh. Beyond it the mountains of the Carneddau stretch down to the sea. I gazed out of the carriage window, enthralled. There was something strangely exciting about the way the deep-cut, utterly desolate valleys wound their way into the mountains. There were no crags, just big rounded hills that gave a feeling of emptiness, of the unknown.

I stopped off in Wallasey to stay with my great aunt Polly. Nan's youngest sister, she had never married, worked in the post office until she retired, and lived in a lovely little first-floor flat. Once again, there were no young people to meet on our round of her elderly friends. At one of their homes, while they talked, I idly picked up a book of photographs of Scottish mountains and my imagination was suddenly jolted in a way I had never previously experienced. There were pictures of the Cairngorms, huge and rounded, the Cuillin of Skye, all jagged rock and sinuous ridges, but what struck me most was a picture taken from the top of Bidean nam Bian, towering above Glen Coe with the serried folds of hills and valleys merging into a blur on the horizon. To me it was wild, virgin country, yet just within my reach. I could imagine exploring these hills for myself. A book of Alpine or Himalayan peaks could never have had the same effect, for they would have seemed unattainable. I borrowed the book and spent the rest of the holiday examining every picture. I no longer planned imaginary battles but worked out expeditions through the mountains instead.

Once back at school I started to put my dreams into practice, determined to go and climb a mountain in the Christmas holidays. I had a sense of focused purpose that I don't think I had ever had before. First challenge was to find a partner. I persuaded a classmate, Anton, to join the expedition. Wales seemed more accessible than Scotland and the memory of those deep valleys still haunted me. What better objective than Snowdon, its highest mountain? We needed the right gear so I bought a pair of ex-War Department hobnailed boots from an Army Surplus Store. Anton made do with his school shoes. We both had our school macs. Mum and Anton's parents were amazing: they raised no objections at all, perhaps because in those days people did so little of that kind of thing and it never got in the newspapers. We set out in the New Year, hitchhiking up the A5 in the days before motorways and bypasses. We reached Llangollen just over the Welsh border that night and stayed in the youth hostel. We had chosen one of the hardest winters of recent years for our introduction to the hills and the following morning there was hardly any traffic on the road. We spent the entire day getting to Capel Curig in the heart of Snowdonia but it didn't matter, it was all so new and thrilling. Even the walks between lifts were exciting as the country got progressively bleaker and the hills, all clad in snow, got higher.

That night, in the youth hostel, Anton and I made our plans. We hadn't the faintest idea of what mountaineering would entail and looking around the common room at all the confident walkers and climbers, I felt very green. We huddled in a corner, very conscious of our complete ignorance; we didn't even look the part. I longed for a pair of proper nailed climbing boots, real climbing breeches and a well-darned sweater.

In the morning we set out for Snowdon, walking out of Capel Curig, past the Royal Hotel, now Plas y Brenin, the National Mountain Centre, and finally saw the mountain for the first time. Looking across a frozen Llynau Mymbyr, the three peaks of the Snowdon Horseshoe stood isolated seven miles away. To me they had all the grandeur of the Everest massif yet here was a challenge within our grasp. We got a lift all the way to Pen y Pass, gateway to Snowdon. We had a map and it showed a footpath all the way to the summit: this was known as the Pyg Track. Trouble was, it was concealed by snow and even worse the cloud had rolled in and more snow was beginning to fall. We were about to abandon our attempt when three climbers with ice axes strode past. They looked as if they knew what they were doing so we followed them.

Soon we had not the faintest idea of where we were as the snow whirled around us and we floundered up to our waists. My feet were numb; Anton was in an even worse state in his school shoes and kept slipping. The figures in front were fast-vanishing blurs in the swirling flakes. Above us loomed dark cliffs, below, a steeply dropping white slope merged into the cloud. Occasionally we got a glimpse of the dull black surface of Glas Llyn. Suddenly we were aware that everything around us was moving: we were being avalanched, sliding with increasing speed down a wide chute down the steepening slope. We had no idea of how dangerous our situation was or the consequences if we had gone over a cliff. We were tumbling down laughing and whooping until we came to a rest just above the frozen tarn. The experts also had been avalanched and we all plodded back to the road.

When we got back to the youth hostel that night, I was soaked, exhausted, but deliriously happy. I'd tasted the addictive elation of a brush with danger. Anton had a very different reaction and hitch-hiked home the next day, never to go into the hills again. I stayed on and the next day attempted to climb Glyder Fawr, but clouds rolled in and with a lack of confidence in either my map-reading ability or compass work, I retreated. The hostel was full so I checked into a little bed and breakfast, where fortuitously two proper climbers were staying. I'd been much too shy in the crowded hostel to join in any of the conversations, but this gave me the chance to listen and question. I had no idea that the sport of rock climbing even existed but talking to them, I knew instinctively that this was something I had to do.

Even so, back in London, how could I pursue it? There was no one at school who climbed, outdoor activities hadn't even been thought of, there were no climbing schools and precious few guides but, once again, I was in luck. My aunt Thea's lodger was a professional photographer and his assistant, with the promising name of Cliff, was a climber. He, very kindly, agreed to take me climbing on a sandstone outcrop called Harrison's Rocks near Tunbridge Wells. It wasn't at all like what I had imagined. You approached the cliff through woods and arrived at the top, finding yourself looking down a sheer vertical wall of sandstone between ten and fifteen metres high. Because the rock is so soft and friable, climbers rarely lead up it; the standard practice is to have the rope round a tree at the top and to belay from the bottom so you top-rope the climb. This makes the climbing very safe, meaning climbers can try harder routes without fear of injury, which is why the climbing at Harrison's was of a high standard.

There were plenty of climbs I could not get up, plenty of times when I began to fight, only to end up hanging in defeat on the rope being lowered to the ground. By the end of the day my fingers were like strips of limp rubber, incapable of opening a jam jar let alone bearing my weight. Every limb ached with weariness. But what a day! I felt in sympathy with the rock; I found my body somehow slipped into natural balance naturally, without any conscious thought on my part. There was not much exposure to worry about, with the crag being only thirty feet high, but what there was did not worry me. If anything, I found it stimulating. I knew I had found a pursuit I loved, that my body and my temperament seemed designed for it, and, most of all, that I was happy.

Until that day on Harrison's, I had never found a complete release in physical expression. Although I enjoyed rugger, I was always aware of my limitations, my instinctive fear of the ball, the slowness of my reactions. Even in the gymnasium, I was limited. I lacked the speed of reaction to control my limbs with quick precision and, perhaps as a result, I always experienced a jab of fear as I launched myself into a vault or handspring. This acted as a kind of brake, and I often landed badly or ended the exercise in an uncontrolled tangle of arms and legs. But even on that first visit to the rocks, I experienced none of these limitations; I was conscious only of feelings of confidence and intense enjoyment that I had never experienced before. I had discovered the passion that was to guide my life.

On the way back to London, I asked Cliff: 'Wouldn't you like to go climbing in Wales this Easter, just for a few days?'

'I wish I could, but I've got too much work to catch up on. I shall have a word with Tom Blackburn, though. I've done most of my climbing with him, he might take you.'

Cliff took me round to see Tom Blackburn that same week; I felt like an applicant for an important job, anxious to make a good impression and be invited to go climbing. Tom was a schoolmaster so he had a good holiday at Easter, but he was married with three children. Nevertheless, he promised to spend a few days in Wales with me immediately after Easter, and at least give me a grounding in climbing. I was delighted. It seemed almost too good to be true that he, a complete stranger, should be prepared to saddle himself with a schoolboy and complete novice to climbing, especially after a term of teaching boys like myself.

I did very little work at school for the rest of that term, but spent my entire time dreaming of the hills. I had a few pounds saved up and went into Blacks, one of the few climbing shops in London, to buy my first pair of boots, a magnificent pair bristling with clinker nails and a good two sizes too big. Cliff had given me an old hemp rope that was so worn it looked as if it had been used by the Victorian pioneers. My final item of equipment was an old school mac that Nan cut down to look like an anorak.

At last it was time to set out on my first real climbing holiday. I hitchhiked up to Ynys Ettws, the Climbers' Club hut in the Llanberis Pass where I was due to meet Tom Blackburn. As I walked along the track towards the hut, I felt shy, rather like a boy going to a new school. I wondered how many people I should find there, and what they would be like. I felt terribly conscious of my complete inexperience and hoped with all my heart that Tom Blackburn was already there. But there was no sign of him, only a telegram with the brief message: 'Children mumps hope arrive Thursday'.

The only other occupant was a man in his mid-twenties. He was sitting in the big kitchen-living room in front of a roaring fire. He was obviously a full-blooded climber, having a look of quiet ownership in the hut as if he were permanently installed, and in his talk showed that he had an intimate knowledge of the area, which indeed he did, for Tony Moulam was one of the leading rock climbers of that period. I don't imagine he was particularly pleased to find himself landed with a teenager, who had never been climbing before, but he was very patient with me, especially in answering all my questions, most of which were very naïve.

I spent the next few days wandering the hills on my own. The weather was consistently bad and Moulam, in spite of my broad hints, preferred to sit in front of the fire rather than take a young novice out on to the crags. When Tom Blackburn finally arrived I at last got on to a real crag and once the weather improved Tony joined us and took us up a couple of climbs that Tom, who hadn't climbed for some years, wouldn't have been able to lead. Then it was time for him to return to his mumps-ridden family. I nagged Tony into taking me up a climb and he chose *Crevice*, an awkward route near the hut. It was too hard for me, the only time I've been hauled up the climb and I arrived at the top exhausted, sobbing for breath. It was also useful, because I'd become overconfident and this showed me how much I had to learn.

That night, in front of the fire, I summoned up all my courage to ask Tony if there was any chance of joining the Climbers' Club, one of the senior climbing clubs in Britain, with a long and distinguished history dating back to the nineteenth century. I wanted to stay in this warm and comfortable hut, and, much more importantly, to belong, to feel part of the body of climbers. Tony must have been thoroughly embarrassed by my request; he talked about my youth, because I was too young to be allowed into the club, and the fact that I had only just started to climb.

'You know, Chris, there are a lot of lads, just like yourself, who start to climb with just as much enthusiasm. They're keen on it for two or three years and then they give it up and go on to something else. Whatever you think now, you might do the same. If you are still climbing in five years, that's when you should start thinking of joining the Climbers' Club.' I sat and listened in a state of dumb misery. It sounded like a sentence of eternal banishment. A few years later Tony told me that after our meeting at Ynys Ettws, he had thought I would either kill myself in the next few months or go on to do great things.

Next morning I set out on the next step of my odyssey. I planned to walk across the Glyders to reach the Ogwen Valley, stay in the Idwal Cottage youth hostel and find someone to climb with. It was a lovely sunny day with hardly a cloud in the sky. My disappointment from the previous night quickly vanished as I picked my way up the south slopes of Glyder Fawr, past Clogwyn y Grochan and Carreg Wasted, up steep grass and scrambly rock outcrops all the way to the top and then down to the col between Glyder Fawr and Y Garn, from where I picked up the steep and rocky path that goes down the side of the Devil's Kitchen, with its vertiginous deep-cut gully, waterfalls and vertical moss-clad walls deep in shade. It was wild and threatening, yet also alluring. Then down to the bottom to the shores of Llyn Idwal, where I stopped to examine the Idwal Slabs, a relatively easy-angled sweep of rock that was obviously climbed; I could see lines of scratched footholds snaking up the cliff, made by boot-nails. Could I follow one of those trails by myself, climbing solo? There was one line that followed a bit of a groove, was very well scratched and slightly more broken than the other lines. I sat and looked at it for a long time and then summed up the courage to try it in my clinker-nailed boots.

It was wonderful. There were plenty of holds for my hands and feet and I scrambled up, hardly noticing the drop below me until I reached a ledge stretching across the top of the slab. I felt a moment of elation and then wondered how the hell was I going to get down? Everything steepened above and I couldn't see an obvious way off up or down. I decided to retreat the way I had come. Climbing down, everything was more awkward and I was much more aware of the drop below, but I had no choice. I just had to keep going. When I reached the bottom, I felt the weight of fear lift with a huge sense of relief.

There were three other climbers at the bottom; they were a schoolmaster and two pupils, but the lads had had enough for one day and he asked if I'd like to do a climb. I confessed I was a beginner and had never led.

'Well, if you can solo up and down the *Ordinary Route*, you should be fine. I know just the route for us. We'll link three of the best but easiest routes on the crag: *Hope*, *Faith* and *Charity* combined.'

The teacher's name was Charles Verender, and he led the first pitch, brought me up and told me I'd have no difficulty on the second, my first ever lead. I creamed it, discovering the joy, indeed, euphoria of leading, of being first on the rope, of picking the route and knowing you had a significant distance to fall if you came off. This was in the days when you tied the climbing rope round your waist and had a couple of slings round your neck for running belays. Charles then led through and showed me the easy, but quite convoluted, way of getting off the crag. Better still he invited me to join them for the rest of their holiday. Like Tony and Tom, he was also a member of the Climbers' Club and his group were staying at Helyg, the club's Ogwen hut, a place rich in tradition.

Charles was an important mentor, not only in the way that he encouraged me to take the lead, but then to trust the care of one of his pupils to me, so that I then led throughout the holiday with the full responsibility of protecting and even instructing a beginner. That could not possibly have happened today. Both of us would need all sorts of certificates, which at sixteen I was probably too young to get anyway. In some ways Charles was my most important mentor; by the end of the holiday I was a competent leader and was sharing the lead with other Climbers' Club members. I had got my start.

Back in London, I climbed at every opportunity, at weekends

going to Harrison's Rocks for the day and getting to know other climbers. I had plenty of narrow escapes during that period, but in many ways these were the best days of all. Everything was strange and new, a constant process of discovery. Slowly working up through the grades, my first lead at 'Very Difficult', my 'Severe', the first trip to Scotland, the first iced-up gully on Tryfan – they were all tremendous adventures that had a freshness you only seem to experience in your teens, when the world seems newly made.

A year after my first visit to the Llanberis Pass, I returned with Dave Pullin, a friend of my own age, also still at school. We dossed under a boulder below Dinas Mot and climbed with all the fanaticism of youth, doing at least three climbs each day; I always felt cheated if I came off the crag before dark and never dreamt of spending the evening in the pub. Apart from anything else we couldn't afford it. We slowly worked our way through the Very Severes in the Llanberis guidebook and made our first timorous visit to the dark flanks of Clogwyn d'ur Arddu or 'Cloggy'. To us it was as frightening as the north wall of the Eiger.

Climbing now completely filled my life, not only when on the crags but back at home as well, where I read everything I could lay my hands on. At the same time, I realized that I had to find a career, and was now entering my final school term with A levels at the end of it. It had always been assumed I should go to university, and I was offered a place at University College, London to study my favourite topic: history. I now just needed to pass my exams, my other subjects being English and Latin.

After that I was not at all sure what I should do, but took it for granted that I should have to find some kind of conventional career. I thought of the Colonial Service, communism long abandoned. I was a keen reader of John Buchan, H. Ryder Haggard and Edgar Wallace, dreamed of being a district officer in the heart of Africa. Mum wisely questioned whether we'd have any colonies at all in a few years. Though I loved history and had just won the lower-sixth history prize, I couldn't see myself following an academic career either as a schoolteacher or going into further education. I was more focused on joining the university climbing club and having another three years of climbing before having to worry about a job.

I did work hard revising for my A levels because I really did want to get to university. All my classmates were heading for Oxford or Cambridge, but it would have put too hard a strain on Mum's finances. She was realistic; it was unlikely that I'd get a scholarship or bursary. I suffered from appalling exam nerves, even needing medication, but got through them and persuaded Mum to write me a sick note so I could hitch up to the Ogwen Valley for a long weekend. On the Monday, when I should have been back at school, I was climbing with a young Scottish climber, Mick Noon, a member of the Creagh Ddu Mountaineering Club, whose members worked in the shipyards of Glasgow and were famed for their toughness.

We headed for the Terrace Wall, halfway up the west face of Tryfan, a smooth wall about sixty metres high with some of the hardest routes of that time. We chose *Scars Climb*, which was then graded Very Severe and should have been well within my capability. It was certainly daunting: small finger- and toeholds, only a few minuscule spikes of rock on which to place the occasional runner. I just kept going until I reached a point where I was lying back on my fingers on a sloping edge of rock, with my feet pressed against a bit of a scoop, when first one foot slipped, then the other, and I was hurtling backwards in my first leader fall. I went about forty feet, all my running belays having pulled out, and banging my head on the way down, crunching my arm and leg on the rock, before I landed and rolled down the grassy slope at the bottom of the crag. I sat up, covered in blood and feeling dazed, but didn't seem to have broken anything.

There were plenty of people around and I was helped back down to the road without having to call for the mountain rescue team. Someone gave me a lift into Bethesda to be patched up by the local doctor. Next day, I hitchhiked home to London head bandaged and arm in a sling, a definite aid to getting lifts. After a couple of days convalescing at home, I was back at school with a note explaining that after recovering from a bad cold I had fallen off my bike. Mum was fantastic in the way she brought me up, never possessive or overprotective, giving me clear boundaries to work within. Until that fall, I didn't think I could fall off. It didn't put me off but it did show me I was fallible. I put my runners in with greater care, judged the outcome of pushing on more carefully and was now prepared to retreat.

A few weeks later I was fully recovered and set out for my odyssey to Scotland. This time I had a climbing partner, a first-year university student called Tony Taylor, a climbing mate from Harrison's. We hitched straight up to the Northern Highlands, which cast a spell more potent even than that of stern Glen Coe or the rugged Cuillin. It was the extraordinary sense of space, the perfect marriage of hills, sea and sky that enthralled me. We climbed to the full but had one day I'll never forget.

We had bivouacked under the vaulted arch of the ruins of Ardvreck Castle on a little peninsular jutting out into Loch Assynt. The next day we hitched to the village of Lochinver on the coast and began the long boggy walk in to Suilven. The mountain is a long whale-back, but approaching it from the west, head on, it looks like the whale's head, a broad sandstone pillar sitting on a plinth of Lewisian gneiss, some of the hardest and most ancient rock found in the Highlands which has guarded it from erosion over the millennia. Indeed *Suilven* is Norse for 'pillar', which from this angle, it appears to be. We were hoping to complete a climb on the buttress facing us.

Shouldering our heavy sacks, which contained our bivouac gear and clothing for the whole summer, we hiked up to the buttress and started climbing. Our route description was sketchy and I suspect we inadvertently completed a new route. I had exchanged my frayed second-hand hemp rope and nailed boots for a nylon hawser-laid rope and Vibram soles the previous summer. Like most sandstone, the strata were horizontal, with smooth, bulging vertical steps without any protection between each layer. There was no one to come to our aid in the event of an accident, no local rescue teams in those days. Working our way up the crag was challenging and committing yet hugely satisfying. We were the captains of our fate.

It was mid afternoon by the time we reached the top and started traversing the back of our whale, gazing around and down at the rolling sea of bog and lochans, broken by reefs of the light grey gneiss that forms this unique landscape. To the north and south were precipitous sandstone islands, Quinag to the north, and to the south, across the broad island-dotted reaches of Loch Sionascaig, rugged Stac Pollaidh. We planned to cross to it, after we had returned to pick up our rucksacks from the other end of the whale, skirting the shores of the loch all the way to the foot of Stac Pollaidh. There were no paths, no sign of other human beings, as we strode into the dark gloaming of the middle of the night. At last, desperately tired, after picking up a stalker's path to the east of Stac Pollaidh, we stumbled across a ruined bothy at dawn, having been on the go for twenty hours covering many miles over rough terrain with a climb and mountain traverse thrown in. Of all the climbing days I have had, this was among the most magical.

Tony had to go back to London so I hitched down to the Isle of Skye where I planned to stay in the Glenbrittle youth hostel for the rest of the holiday. The Black Cuillin, formed of hard rough gabbro, is the most rugged mountain range in Britain, stretching in a bristling spine of jagged peaks from the shores of Loch Scavaig in the south to the shapely pyramid of Sgurr nan Gillean at its northern end. It's a scramble to most of the summits and the Inaccessible Pinnacle on Sgurr Dearg is a proper climb, admittedly of only moderate difficulty, but an airy ascent nonetheless.

I teamed up with Betty, who was a little older than me and already at university where she had started climbing. There was no spark of romance, but we felt comfortable with each other and had a lot in common, quickly becoming friends; she was a good steady climber, able to follow me up anything I could climb and would lead through on easier ground.

Anxiety about my A levels was growing more insistent, as the date of the results grew close. I half expected to fail at advanced

Latin but was completely confident of English and history. Every time I got a letter from Mum I had to force myself to open it, fearing the news it might bring. We had come back from a brilliant day's climbing on Sgurr Alasdair, highest peak of the Black Cuillin, finishing with a wild scree run down its Great Stone Chute, taking huge leaps and landing in the loose stones, surfing them for a couple of seconds and then another leap down.

We got back in plenty of time to cook supper but a letter from Mum was waiting. I delayed opening it and went outside to be alone. I had a feeling of impending doom, and yet, at the same time, because I thought it was probably Latin, if I had failed, I was braced for the news. When I opened the letter and learned it wasn't Latin I'd failed, but English, a subject I had absolute confidence in, it was like being hit hard in the stomach. I just couldn't accept it, doubled up, couldn't stop sobbing. I didn't bother to go in for the meal but walked up the rolling grassy hillside behind the hostel. The sun was shining and the air had that soft translucence so special to the Western Isles. I sat in the warm grass, gazing out across Loch Brittle, towards the Outer Hebrides in the far distance, finding solace in that quiet beauty.

The holiday wasn't yet over. The weather was fine and there were climbs to do and so I put it out of my mind for the time being. The next day, Betty and I went climbing again as usual. It was only when I got home to Hampstead that the reality of having to face another year at school really sank in. All my friends had gone and I was being tutored on my own. Mum was quietly supportive, asked questions, discussed options but left me room to make my own decisions. I stuck it out till half-term but could stand it no longer. I decided do my national service, choosing the Royal Air Force with an eye to joining one of the RAF mountain rescue teams. I hadn't the faintest idea what I would do for a career when I was demobbed, but I did know I had discovered a passion that I would never lose. There was a wonderful release in planning all the climbing I could get in before I was called up.

Chapter Three

Mentors

When we came down that evening, there was a light on in Lagangarbh, the little climbing hut that stands at the foot of Buachille Etive Mòr in Glen Coe. John Hammond, a friend from London, and I had spent the last two days floundering through deep powder snow that completely covered the mountains. Being mid-week, we had seen no one else in the hills, a common experience in the 1950s. That had clearly changed. Three rough-looking climbers were sitting round the fire drinking tea: our tea. They ignored us, so John broke the ice.

'It's been a superb day, hasn't it?'

'Aye.'

'You're stopping here?'

'No, we're in the bothy by the road. It's free.'

The temperature in the hut was as chilly as it was outside. John took a closer look at the largest of the three, a wild-looking fellow with straw-coloured hair, high cheekbones and a thousand-yard stare. 'I've seen you before. Wasn't it in Chamonix last summer? You had a leg in plaster and your head in a bandage.'

'Aye, that'd be me.' He then told a convoluted story about climbing alone in the Chamonix Aiguilles and falling fifty feet. 'I was lucky to get away with it. But I only cracked my skull. We got pissed the same night and I tried to climb the church tower. The drainpipe came away when I was halfway up. That's when I broke my leg.'

I was still in awe of established mountaineers and quite content to listen. I guessed this must be Hamish MacInnes, already a legendary figure in Scottish circles though still only in his early twenties. Hamish had started as a schoolboy just after the war, cycling to Glen Coe from his home in Greenock, learning by trial and error. He'd done his national service in Austria, discovering aid climbing, hanging off pitons rather than the rock, on the steep limestone walls of the Kaisergebirge. He brought these tactics home to Scotland, hammering pegs into cliffs with abandon, earning himself the nickname 'MacPiton' and the displeasure of the Scottish Mountaineering Club. Hamish didn't care. He was the archetypal individualist and having started climbing with the working-class Creagh Dhu, wasn't bothered about offending the establishment.

'Where are you going tomorrow?' John asked at the end of the evening.

'Up the Rannoch Wall,' Hamish said, explaining they were after a first winter ascent.

'Perhaps we could follow you up?' John said.

A gleam hardened in Hamish's eye. 'You can, if you take the Gnomie with you.' 'Gnomie' was the youngest of the three, not yet a full member of the Creagh Dhu. He still had to complete his apprenticeship and was at the beck and call of the others. Climbing as a three was a nuisance, but not if it meant a first ascent we would never have managed on our own.

Next day we expected Hamish and his friends early but it was mid morning before they arrived and the Buachille was looking grim under a shroud of grey. There were flakes of snow in the air and the hut seemed warm and comfortable.

'The weather seems to be brewing up,' John said.

'It'll be all the more interesting,' Hamish replied. 'Anyway, better be off, it's dark at six.'

It's a long way to Rannoch Wall, right at the top of the mountain and we set off in single file. Hamish paused at a long slide of water ice we had to cross. 'Some *bampot* tried to solo this last week, came unstuck at the top. Landed down there. We had to shovel his brains back into his head; it was quite messy.' With that image in our minds, we started up Curved Ridge, an easy enough way up the mountain, but I wish I hadn't been too proud to get the rope out. It felt like eternity until Rannoch Wall came into view, bristling with overhangs and fluted ribs of blank rock. Below us was a gully shooting steeply down into blank space.

Hamish was planning to climb a route called *Agag's Groove*, popular in summer but now smothered in snow and ice. No one had climbed it in winter before. We listened to him singing an Irish rebel song, out of sight around the corner, while the rope inched slowly up and we huddled together, until the slack was taken in and it was time to move again.

We soon discovered why Hamish was pleased to be shot of Gnomie. He was achingly slow. My windproofs became sheeted in ice, like a white suit of armour, the clothes underneath soaked in sweat. I stared up at a blank wall with a rising sense of panic that I'd reached a dead end. Hamish and his partner had long since disappeared, but to my relief I heard a shout from below. They had reached the top and were now back down in the gully.

'Are you planning to spend the night out?' he yelled. 'Good bivouac practice for the north walls.'

I was not amused. 'Where the hell does it go from here?'

'Traverse left and you'll find a peg. There's a bit of ice that makes it a wee bit hard.'

It was awkward but I could see the peg twenty feet away and the holds Hamish had cleared. My hands were numb and I was shivering so hard I almost fell off, but once I reached the peg my confidence returned. John followed quickly but when Gnomie reached the peg, another shout floated up.

'Mind you get the peg out.' There was the sound of frenetic hammering from below.

'I can't get it out, Hamish. It's bent in the crack. My hands are frozen solid.'

'You're not coming up until that peg's out. A night out will do you no harm. Don't let him up, Chris.'

Bugger the peg, I thought, but Hamish was implacable. We waited, cursing and shivering, while Gnomie hammered away. There was a weak cry of triumph.

'I've got it, Hamish.'

Up came Gnomie and having coiled the ropes, frozen like wire, we stumbled down, grateful that Hamish had waited. By ourselves we would never have found the way.

So began my long friendship with Hamish MacInnes. The three Creagh Dhu disappeared that night, but at the end of the week, when John left for London, Hamish returned. The snow was still thick but as always he had 'a nice little problem' up his sleeve that would suit conditions: the first winter ascent of *Crowberry Direct*. I was already willing to follow him anywhere. I could hardly believe my luck to be climbing with one of Scotland's best. It was a frightening climb, the rock was covered in thin ice and Hamish had to take his boots off at one point to climb in his socks. It was a nervy moment, but Hamish announced that conditions were better than he feared.

'Tomorrow we'll go on the big-time stuff. *Raven's Gully*. It'll be the best route in the glen if we get up it.'

I had heard of Raven's, knew that Hamish had already been on it twice. The previous year a lad called Big Bill from the Creagh Dubh had stepped backwards off the top of the first overhang and fallen a thousand feet down the gully below. Hamish had thought him a goner, but the lad just got up and shouted up to them. The month before, he'd tried again but got benighted. Dressed in jeans with only a thin shirt under his anorak, he was in grave danger of freezing to death. He'd been rescued from above after someone saw his flashlight from the valley. When I saw the spot where he'd waited, jammed for eight hours without a rope, I began to understand how tough Hamish was. I was amazed at how little clothing he wore.

The gully was an imposing place, a deep-cut gash flanked by one of the most intimidating walls in Scotland. The first obstacle was a huge chockstone, site of Big Bill's fall, and I took a stance there, freezing in its lee as Hamish chipped ice off the wall to the side and clawed his way up. Worse was to follow. The back of the gully was running with water and we became soaked. Again, he had to take his boots off while the ice-cold water running down my neck diluted my enthusiasm. When I reached his last piton, the rope was running off at an angle. If I took it out and fell off, I would swing thirty feet into the bed of the gully.

'Use the holds, man. A swing won't do you any harm. That peg cost two bob.'

'I'll pay you for the bloody peg. I'm coming across.'

When I finally reached Hamish he was standing on a snow-ledge in his socks.

'Aren't your feet cold?'

'No, I can't feel them. I won't bother to put my boots on. I'll be needing socks again for the next pitch. It's a grand climb, isn't it?'

It seemed a miracle he wasn't frostbitten. My feet were like blocks of ice inside my boots and two pairs of socks. He allowed me to lead the next pitch so I got a good look at his bivouac perch from the month before, a chimney that looked like a bottomless coffin. Luckily I could climb to one side, up ground that had been too icy when Hamish last came this way. Soon we were both standing near the summit of the Buachaille, our wet clothes steaming in the sunshine. I was gloriously happy.

Soon after I got back from Scotland my call-up papers arrived and in early March 1953, I joined the Royal Air Force. At the back of my mind I held hopes of getting into the RAF's mountain rescue team, having spent a wild New Year's Eve with Johnnie Lees, one of the founding forces in mountain rescue, and his friends in the summit café on Snowdon. Because I had the right academic qualifications I was automatically put up for a commission and then passed the selection board. I was also offered the chance at a regular commission, in preference to simply fulfilling my national service. In want of a career, I agreed and chose the RAF Regiment, which sounded more interesting than one of the administrative branches.

'Why don't you want to be a pilot?' asked one of the officers on the Regular Commissions Board. I guessed, accurately, that not being interested in flying wasn't a good answer.

'I don't think I've got fast enough reactions, sir.'

'We've got experts paid to find out that sort of thing. I'll put you down as air crew.'

'Thank you, sir, I've always dreamed of flying.'

I didn't think it mattered much. I had absolutely no chance of passing the aptitude tests. But then I did and had to adjust my mind to the outlandish notion I was about to become a pilot.

First, though, I had to do my square-bashing at RAF Hednesford, in Cannock Chase. That Easter, I met up with Betty, the girl I'd climbed with the year before on Skye, in the Llanberis Pass, swapping leads on some classic routes, climbing *The Cracks* on Dinas Mot. It was a foul day, wet and windy, but poor weather was no excuse in those days.

On my last day of leave we did the Snowdon Horseshoe, starting up Crib Goch. The weather had turned good and Hednesford seemed another world. Coming down off Lliwedd we overtook another couple and Betty recognized the girl. She in turn introduced us to the tall gangly bloke with her, but I didn't catch his name. Then we started down the steep broad ridge at the end of Lliwedd. I've always been fast downhill, so was surprised to find the tall fellow right behind me. I sped up, taking giant leaps over the rocks and reached the bottom, still with a mile to go to the car park at Pen y Pass. The tall man was still on my heels but I went as fast as I could and just made it ahead of him. We stood there, hands on knees, gasping for breath.

'I had to hold back a bit,' he said finally. 'I've got a big race next week.' The penny dropped. The name I'd half-heard was Roger Bannister, already a famous runner in 1953. He made his first attempt on the four-minute mile that spring. I met him years later, having told the story many times, but he'd forgotten all about it.

After Hednesford, I transferred to the Royal Air Force College at Cranwell, between Lincoln and Grantham: not great country for a mountaineer. For the first two terms we did more basic training without going near an aircraft. Once we did start flying, my judgement about my own aptitude proved more accurate than that of the experts. I was hamfisted with the controls, completely incapable of judging distance and height in relation to my control of the aircraft. 'Yesterday we went flying for the first time,' I wrote to Nan. 'It's hard to imagine one will ever be able to control this marvellous machine as one would a bicycle.' Prophetic words. My instructor didn't even trust me on the ground after I almost drove my Chipmunk trainer into a petrol tanker.

I never enjoyed flying. I was like someone with an aversion to heights going climbing. Yet I hated the idea of failing and was painfully aware of being the only one in my group who wasn't judged competent to fly solo. When I was finally assessed by the chief flying instructor, I got the plane off the ground neatly and prepared to take the familiar circuit round the airfield: turn over the cricket pavilion, cut the engine at the clock tower and lower my flaps at the parade ground. But my instructor was cannier than that.

'We'll go for a bit of a run,' he said through the intercom. 'I'll take over for a bit.' Then he took me to another airfield and invited me to 'put her down there'. I was still 500 feet off the deck as I reached the end of the runway. On my next attempt I got it down to a hundred feet. I no longer cared about passing: that was now beyond me. All I wanted was for it to be over with me safely on the deck. On my third attempt, still several miles short of the airbase, I limped along at stalling speed fifty feet above the ground. When the runway finally appeared, I hauled back on the stick and cut the throttle. The aircraft thumped into the strip and bounced furiously from one wheel to the other.

A weary voice crackled through my headphones.

'I think I'd better take over.'

We roared away, back to Cranwell, my cheeks wet with tears. I had failed. My flying career was over. I was offered the chance of becoming a navigator or transferring to ground operations, but I wasn't comfortable with the technical side of navigation and couldn't bear the thought of a desk job. Yet I had enjoyed service life, had been happy at Cranwell, so opted to transfer to the army and applied to Sandhurst.

It was now midsummer, and since the Sandhurst term didn't start until September, I was in a happy limbo for two months, paid £3 a week with nothing to do; my only obligation was not to leave the country. I headed to Snowdonia and took up residence in a road-mender's hut beside the huge boulders at the foot of Dinas Cromlech, a popular doss for climbers.

At weekends we'd be crammed in like sardines, but the only other permanent resident was a wild character with a shock of red hair and a quick, wolfish grin. Ginger Cain was in a similar boat to me, in that we were both waiting for an interview: mine was with the Regular Commissions Board, his the Conscientious Objectors' Board. He couldn't understand why I would give up the feckless, irresponsible life we revelled in that summer. In retrospect, neither can I, except that I always felt the need of a steady career and security.

Happily, we both passed our respective boards in late July. I was going to be a soldier and Ginger was a fully fledged 'conchie': we went to the pub to celebrate. It was a grey summer and the routes were usually wet and slimy, so we spent a lot of time in the pub, more to chat up the girls working at the Pen y Gwryd than to drink. When the weather improved, we overcame our anxiety to try some of the routes of the legendary Rock and Ice, particularly those of the Manchester builder's mate Joe Brown, someone who had achieved an almost mystical status. We did his route *Sickle* on the cliff Clogwyn y Grochan, merely 'Very Severe' as opposed to 'Extremely Severe', except this was a Joe Brown Very Severe and consequently terrifying.

I didn't know Joe or any of the other members of the Rock and Ice club. They were a remote and mythical elite while I was on the fringes of the climbing scene, coming from the south and never having climbed on gritstone, the starting point for Joe and his partner Don Whillans. Taking on their routes felt like a step into the unknown. The best we managed that summer was *Surplomb*, another route on Clogwyn y Grochan. In those days you stood in a sling resting on a tiny flake of rock and then climbed a steep crack into a V-shaped groove that opened out as you gained height. At the top of this I was in a terrifying position, high above the ground with little protection, braced across the groove, needing to pull across and pivot on my toes. It was the hardest route I'd done, and our egos were only slightly dented when I learned Joe had made the first ascent in nailed boots during a snowstorm.

I spent the next two months being shouted at by Guards sergeant majors on the drill square of the Royal Military Academy, Sandhurst. I did have my own room, a great luxury, and six of us shared a servant. Ours was a confirmed snob. He delighted in telling me of the young gentlemen he had catered for in the past. 'They were a much better class, such nice young gentlemen, all from the best public schools. The Academy just isn't the same today,' he would say looking at me. My neighbour was more acceptable, having been to Winchester. He was going into the Scots Guards and would rush off to London for midweek deb parties or hunt balls.

I would like to have flitted off to deb parties and hunt balls and couldn't help envying this self-confident elite with their unspoken codes of what was and was not acceptable. Those of us with ordinary middle-class backgrounds aped their ways. I hid my unfashionable suit at the back of the wardrobe and acquired the Sandhurst leisure uniform: tight cavalry twill trousers, plain, coloured waistcoat and tweed jacket, with a second-hand bowler for trips up to London. Quite unconsciously, wanting to fit in, I added a public-school veneer to my north London accent.

Yet I loved Sandhurst, flung myself into everything with immense enthusiasm. The study of war had been my passion as a boy and now I was playing soldiers in the woods behind Camberley, like cowboys and Indians but with guns and thunder-flashes. 'I am so glad you like Sandhurst,' my grandfather wrote from Dublin. 'You know I felt relieved you left the air force. One hears of so many crashes these days.' He reminded me that my grandmother's family had representatives in the King's Own Scottish Borderers for 172 years. Family pride was restored.

I did well enough to be made an under officer – allowing me to wear a sword on parade – and passed out seventeenth out of around 500 in the order of merit. There was plenty of free time to go climbing and a small club of fellow climbers, one of whom was a very bright, highly amusing young man in my own platoon. Mike Thompson came from the northern Lakes and had a marvellous eye for an unclimbed line; we would dash down to the Avon Gorge and he would point me at blank pieces of rock.

Leaving Sandhurst, I chose to join the Royal Tank Regiment and was sent to Münster in north-west Germany. I quickly realized that two years spent learning to be an officer had done little to prepare me for handling a small group of men and three fifty-ton Centurion tanks. My predecessor had been likeable if a little lazy, but I tried too hard to correct things, often too proud to ask my sergeant's advice, too conscious of the pips on my shoulder. Sergeant Melville was a seasoned veteran and had fought in the desert and Italy. Thanks to my pig-headedness it took me a year to repair the damage I did in those first few weeks. It was fine for lecturers at Sandhurst to warn us of the dangers of familiarity, but sharing a mobile steel box with three other men required a different approach if you wanted their respect.

Being an armoured regiment, there was little chance of real action, unless the Russians invaded, in which case there would be rather too much. We trained in Germany for full-scale war. Imaginary atom bombs were detonated while we baked in our tanks pretending to avoid enemy fall-out, all hatches closed. It was a magnificent game, especially the big exercises, as we raced across country, our juggernauts smashing through walls, voices in my headphones relaying the state of battle. I would get terribly excited. We practised retreating a lot, and during one exercise half our tanks broke down, even before our Russian pursuers had fired a shot.

I had moments of triumph, leading a huge tank formation on a night march across the training area without getting lost. At the end of the exercise, near the former Nazi concentration camp of Bergen-Belsen, we had an American colonel over for dinner. He boasted about the amazing accuracy of their swanky new tanks, so I challenged him to a duel. At dawn, the gleaming new American tank arrived, their crew turned out impeccably. Our tank was just off exercise, covered in dents from bumping into things, and our crew was a scruffy national service mob. But we still beat them.

Despite the fun, I never felt like I belonged. There were no mountains close by and while I'd been able to escape to Wales during training, now it was almost impossible. Nor did I much like the regular army officers; they had different values and ambitions. As I explained to Mother: 'The British regular officer will rarely discuss serious military topics, but revels in garrison gossip and small talk.' We hardly saw anyone from other regiments, let alone the local German community. For female company, a large number of officers were chasing a smaller number of British nurses; it never occurred to them to ask the local girls out. Some of my fellow subalterns, especially those national service ones headed for university, had German girlfriends and improved their language skills as a result. I was too shy and dated one of the English nurses with whom I had my first physical relationship.

There could not have been a greater contrast with the free-and-easy relationships among mountaineers. If I'm honest, I felt quite lonely. I wrote to Hamish to see if he fancied climbing together in the Alps and when he sent me back a postcard suggesting we go to Switzerland to try the north face of the Eiger I was desperate enough to agree. I thought: this would be a good start to my Alpine career. In 1957 it had only been climbed twelve times and claimed fourteen lives. I should have laughed it off, because I hadn't yet been to the Alps.

When the train came round the back of a spur just outside Grindelwald and I saw the Eigerwand for the first time, deep in shadow, tier upon tier of dull grey ice and rock, on a scale grander than anything I had imagined, I felt afraid and heartily regretted agreeing to Hamish's plan. I was almost wholly ignorant of what sort of equipment I might need.

'Have you got a duvet?' Hamish asked.

'What's that?'

'A down-filled jacket. You can take a sleeping bag. How about a bivy sack?' More blank looks. Hamish produced a large plastic bag. We had no ice pitons, but managed to buy a couple. My anorak was more suited to a Sunday walk. Hamish's rucksack had fallen to bits so he borrowed my spare. Our only clue to the route was a postcard he'd bought that morning.

It was three years since I'd seen Hamish, during which time he had emigrated to New Zealand, done some new routes in the Southern Alps and then mounted a two-man Himalayan expedition. 'We had hoped to try Everest,' he explained. 'The Swiss in 1952 left big dumps of food all the way up to the South Col. It's a pity John Hunt and his boys got there first.' Instead they got to 22,000 feet on the neighbouring peak of Pumori. Hamish was undoubtedly a hard man, but I wasn't sure I was. I prayed for bad weather.

Unfortunately, it was a perfect morning so we completed our preparations and caught the train to Kleine Scheidegg, walking up from there to the base of the wall, which shoots straight up from Alpine pastures. One moment you're in lush grass, the next you're scrambling up the north face. We planned to get as high as possible on the easy stuff and start early next day on the difficulties. Or at least, Hamish was. I was hoping for rain. I'd never climbed with a rucksack before, and we were carrying forty pounds. Happily a thin scum of grey cloud appeared that evening, and I announced I was off. Hamish had to follow, no doubt cursing cowardly Sassenachs under his breath. Given good weather, I think we could have climbed it. Hamish certainly could, and I would have led on the rock pitches. But if the weather had turned, we would have been in desperate trouble. I was simply too ignorant to appreciate the risk I had taken.

Hamish's next target was another of the great north faces, the Walker Spur of the Grandes Jorasses. Holed up in bad weather at the Leschaux Hut, we had to concede it was out of condition. Hamish cooked up an alternative plan for a new route on a neighbouring peak, the Aiguille du Tacul. I marvelled at his patience, his ability to spend hours lying in his sleeping bag semi-comatose, guarding his reserves. I on the other hand paced around the hut anxiously as our food dwindled to nothing. We did our new climb, and while it wasn't hard or particularly good, I loved the feeling true exploration brings. There were no manmade limitations on us: we were free to choose our own route. Rattling across Germany on the train back to Münster, I was already dreaming of next summer.

Hamish had great plans. We moved into a shepherd's hut near Montenvers, high above the Chamonix valley. 'There will be less temptation to spend any money,' he said, 'and it's nearer the crags.' He seemed frighteningly gaunt, a thin goatee emphasizing his hollow cheeks, having spent the winter in the Himalaya looking for the yeti. I insisted on a practice route, so we climbed the west face of the Pointe Albert, Hamish shamelessly bashing out all the pitons he could to equip us for harder things. After that, he insisted on trying another new route, this time on the Pointe de Lépiney. 'Right up your street,' he promised. 'Rock all the way. Nothing's been climbed anywhere near it.'

When our objective came into view for the first time, I saw at once why it had never been climbed. A series of slabs 200 feet high ended at a colossal leaning tower of granite with a prominent overhang at around half height.

'We'll never get up that,' I told Hamish.

'It always looks a lot worse from below,' Hamish replied. Not this time: the climbing proved as taxing as it looked, and we ended up bivouacking beneath the overhangs, squeezing into a coffin-like recess at the back of a ledge. After a grim night we breakfasted on stale bread and weak tea and then I tackled the overhang, spraining an ankle when the wooden wedge I was hanging off popped out of its crack. I went straight back up and finished the pitch, but if anything the climbing above looked harder. With grey cloud creeping in we retreated, ending up on a tiny ledge, hanging off a piton under a waterfall. It was another fiasco and, even worse, I went down with a hideous cold.

I lay in my sleeping bag, crammed in the corner of our hut, nose running, while Hamish dreamed up hard new lines to try. 'Look, Hamish, you can stuff your new routes. I couldn't care less if it's the last great, unclimbed problem in the Alps. I just want to be sure of getting to the top of one or two good, standard climbs.' The argument went back and forth as I snuffled in my sleeping bag and the rain hammered down. At last we came to a compromise. 'I'll go on any route you name, provided it's been done before.'

Hamish thought it over. 'How about the south-west pillar of the Dru?'

This was, in 1958, among the hardest routes in the world, Walter Bonatti's masterpiece climbed solo over five days. Only four other parties had done it since his first ascent three years before. The plan excited and appalled me; it seemed a vast undertaking but the rock was reportedly good. My confidence was boosted by the arrival of two Austrians in the hut below ours. Walter Philipp, a mathematician studying in Vienna, already had a formidable reputation as a climber with first ascents in the Eastern Alps. His partner Richard Blach was only nineteen but also talented.

Approaching the foot of the Petit Dru, the rock glowed orange in the evening sun. We settled down to bivouac, quite cosy next to our roaring Primus stove. Just before dark I noticed two diminutive figures toiling up the moraine towards the boulders where we lay.

'That'll be Whillans,' said Hamish. 'I heard that he was asking about the pillar. We're going to have quite a party.'

I wasn't sorry to see him. I'd heard a great deal about Don's prowess as a climber. Three years before, he'd climbed the west face of the Petit Dru with Joe Brown, the fourth ascent overall. The figure in the lead was short and powerfully muscled, with a cloth cap on his head. He carried a vast rucksack with baguettes sticking out at right angles from under the lid. That was Don Whillans all right. The figure behind was just as short but more slender: Paul Ross, a leading Lakeland climber. We spoke briefly, Don weighing us up, before he carried on up the slope. 'See you tomorrow,' he called over his shoulder.

I barely slept, my mind careering between anticipation and fear. When the alarm went off at two, Walter muttered about the cloud and Hamish agreed we should wait for dawn to see what the weather was doing. Relieved, I fell into a deep sleep only to be shaken awake after what felt like a few minutes.

'Wake up, Chris! The clouds have cleared,' Hamish said. 'It's going to be a good day.'

Don had started late too; we spotted him beginning the dangerous couloir that led to a serrated ridge above our heads called the Flammes de Pierre. At first we climbed solo but while the angle wasn't steep, the holds were sloping and covered in gravel and I was mightily relieved when Hamish stopped to get the rope out. Then he started cutting steps with his ice axe, since only one of us had crampons. Don and Paul both had a pair so pulled away. I looked up at the pillar above us, glowing in the morning sun, longing to escape the icy prison of the couloir, but we had to be methodical. It was eleven-thirty before we reached the foot of the pillar.

Above our heads lay another 2,000 feet of hard rock climbing the like of which I'd never known before. The granite was cleaved into smooth cracks and grooves, sweeping up endlessly and dropping below into the steep gully we'd just climbed. Hamish brought up the rear, bashing out the pegs while I led, but after only 200 feet I was already weary. Could I keep this up? I heard shouts above and poked my head round a ledge to see Don and Paul resting in the sun, watching Richard crossing a huge overhang, standing in *étriers* clipped to pitons. When Don led it, he crossed the slab on his feet. Each move he made was calculated and apparently effortless. When it came to my turn, I felt the rock pushing me off balance.

'Did you go up here, Don?' I shouted, looking up a bottomless groove of rock with no sign of pitons or wedges.

'Aye.'

'Is it hard?'

'It's a bit strenuous.'

What followed was one of the hardest pitches I'd ever led. The crack widened and I couldn't jam my hands firmly. I shoved an arm into the back of the crack and levered myself out and up, but there was no rest and nothing to stand on. The rope dropped in a clean arc for fifty feet to my last piton. I would take a huge fall if I fell. Struggling to thread a small stone wedged in the crack, I started talking to myself, as I always do when in serious difficulty. I finally collapsed onto the ledge next to Paul.

'Did you like Don's little variation? The bugger went off route.' Then he pointed to another groove full of pitons and wedges.

I sat on the ledge wondering if there was going to be much more of this, but as the afternoon wore on I regained confidence. There were no more Whillans variations. Don shouted down. 'There's a ledge like a ballroom up 'ere.' He wasn't joking. When I pulled onto it he was heating a pan of snow over a gas stove. There was an hour or so before dark, but there wouldn't be another ledge like it. The Austrians climbed the next pitch, to speed us up next morning, and then we settled in. Just as darkness fell, there was a roar from the couloir below. We craned our necks over the edge to see tons of rock falling to the glacier, flashing sparks. There was a smell of sulphur in the air.

'Just as well that little lot didn't roll this morning,' Don said.

Then, as the silence deepened again, we heard the unmistakable whine of a stone falling from above. We ducked, there was a thud and we looked round to see Hamish clutching his head, blood gushing through the gaps between his fingers. Luckily I had a bandage in my rucksack, which eventually staunched the flow. The large ledge, we realized, was a death trap; we had no choice but to cram ourselves at the back of it, escaping the line of fire. I spent the night gazing longingly at the lights of Chamonix, frozen to the bone. People there were eating in restaurants, climbing into comfortable beds.

At dawn we hobbled round like old men. 'How are you feeling?' I asked Hamish.

'Bloody awful,' he said. 'I keep feeling dizzy but I think I'll be all right.' None of us wanted to retreat down that awful couloir, but I wasn't sure I could give Hamish the help he needed.

'Do you think it would be a good idea if you climbed with Hamish?' I said to Don. 'You'll be able to help him out better than I can. Paul and I can stay at the back and take the pegs out.'

'Fair enough,' Don agreed. 'We'd better get going.'

For the rest of the day Don nursed Hamish up the route, following Walter and Richard. Sometimes Hamish would slump on the rope but he kept going. Months later he was still experiencing dizziness. Yet despite the crisis, the climbing was superb, up a series of grooves, fingers jammed into cracks, legs framing the void. At noon, Paul and I caught Don and Hamish sprawled on a comfortable ledge watching Walter working his way up a bulging wall. 'I'm sure the route doesn't go that way,' Don said. 'Hold my rope, Hamish, I'll have a look round the corner.' Soon after he disappeared from view there was a shout of triumph. 'I knew it!' Don had got us back on route but it was too late to do anything more that day. I shared Don's plastic bivouac sack, wondering if we'd asphyxiate as Don smoked through the night.

'Better than freezing to death,' he said.

We reached the summit next day but still needed another bivouac before starting our descent. Through it all Don remained much as he was at the start, a tough, self-contained little man who would let nothing hurry him. I've no doubt it was Don and Walter who got us up that route. Climbing down, it was Don who took control. Hamish and I had recovered our strength but Richard was so exhausted he could barely speak. In Britain I had become used to being in control, climbing to my limits. Now I was uncertain and full of doubt; I hated this sensation of constant anxiety. Yet Don's self-confidence inspired me and I learned from it. My experience on the pillar taught me that however bad conditions got and whatever went wrong, I could extricate myself. I never again suffered the blind fear of unknown dangers. Fear was something I could reduce or banish through action. I had Don to thank for that.

PART TWO

Apprenticeship

Chapter Four

Abode of the Gods

Back in Germany, I grew increasingly disenchanted with life. 'At the moment,' I wrote to Mum, 'I am acquiring a hearty dislike for the army in general and tanks in particular. I don't think I have really got much of a vocation for peacetime soldiering. I think I shall try to take up climbing professionally. It's something I love, and I think I am good at, even if it does not lead very far. The army is certainly not a thing I am good at.'

She was not impressed: there was no such thing as a professional mountaineer. Not unreasonably, given her experience with my father, Mum wanted me settled in a respectable career, with all the security that implied. There was part of me that felt that way too. I have often felt I'm quite lazy, happy to drift along if the situation seems settled, which was quite easy to do in the army. On the other hand, life with the regiment was often intolerable. I had come up with all sorts of wheezes to maintain my interest. The previous winter I'd appointed myself regimental skiing officer despite not being able to ski, and managed to escape to the Alps for three months with six troopers where a group of Norwegian army instructors taught us how to langlauf. We did very well in our divisional patrol race, skiing with rifles as you do in a biathlon. We even beat one or two cavalry regiments, who, coming from the better public schools, had been skiing from childhood.

My commanding officer, Lt Col. R. G. 'Sniffy' Saunders, was an old-school tank man and impatient with my restlessness. He sent me on a signals course at Bovington, which I enjoyed, and when I came back I reorganized the regiment's communications, which I loved. But the day-to-day grind of life as signals officer was much less interesting. I couldn't stand teaching courses and hated the very notion of maintenance. I was fed up with the jobs I was being given and could see things only getting worse. Then, browsing through the routine orders in the squadron office, I came across a paragraph inviting applications for the job of instructor at the Army Outward Bound School at Tywyn in west Wales. I'd never heard of it, but assumed it was much the same as the civilian Outward Bound. The prospect of working in the mountains and teaching climbing was immensely appealing.

'You know, it won't be good for your career,' Sniffy warned me. He recommended a few more years in the regiment and then perhaps a junior staff job or secondment to the Trucial Oman Scouts, just about the only unit connected to the British army that was at the time doing any fighting. Even that didn't seem enticing: there would be a complete dearth of women and Oman's excellent climbing was then unknown, certainly to me. So I persevered, and eventually Sniffy let me go. I left the regiment in January 1959 and, while I didn't admit it at the time, knew in my bones I wouldn't be back.

Life in Tywyn was a revelation after Germany. Students were met off the train by the camp commandant, Lt Col. 'Fighting Jack' Churchill, often credited with the last use of a longbow in battle, having killed a German NCO with one in France in 1940. He was a dab hand with a broadsword as well and liked to play the bagpipes. He had a set with him now.

'Ah, you must be Bonington,' he said. 'I've got to see to this lot first. I'll see you in the mess.' By 'this lot' he meant the three ranks of young men now lined up outside the station, peering around at their new environment, somewhat bemused that no one was shouting at them as normally happens in such situations. Then, to the skirl of Jack's bagpipes, and a swirl of his kilt, the group marched off towards Morfa Camp.

The school had existed for only a year, put together, unusually for the army, with the co-operation of the entire staff. It was more typical that neither the commandant nor the chief instructor had any experience of Outward Bound training or elementary mountaineering before being assigned. The most experienced instructor was a commando called Mick Quinn; it was his enthusiasm and knowledge that made the school a going concern. There were two lieutenants and six sergeants each in charge of a patrol of ten students. We were all on first-name terms. The fact all ranks came together to debate policy, often fiercely, engendered a sense of unity not possible elsewhere in the army. The boys could put away their uniforms for the duration. Our brightest students came from the army's apprentice schools, where the courses were stimulating and demanding. Some of the boys from Junior Leaders' regiments were barely literate.

Each course lasted three weeks: the first involved fitness work, basic map reading and first aid, a bit of rock climbing and canoeing and then a night out camping. We stepped it up in the second week, climbing and hiking in Snowdonia, and then in the third did a mini-expedition, the students crossing forty miles of mountain country in three days on their own. 'Some of you, no doubt,' Ian Cooper, one of the sergeants, told that first batch of students, 'might have heard that Outward Bound builds character; well, I wouldn't try to build any of your characters in just three weeks, but what you can do is find out something about yourselves. You will do things that you never thought you could.' As a judgement of outdoor education, that seemed about right to me. The course was particularly good, I felt, for boys who were a little shy or not naturally good at sport, but were intelligent enough: rather like me, in fact.

The days passed quickly, teaching in the classroom, racing round the assault course or climbing on the sea cliff a mile or so from camp. I quickly discovered I was too interested in my own climbing to become a good teacher. I found it frustrating to take learners up the same easy climbs over and over again, and longed to escape onto harder routes. But for most of the boys the climbing was the highlight of the course, probably because it was exciting without being physically too arduous.

My two years with the Army Outward Bound also meant a return to the British climbing scene. I felt like Rip van Winkle waking from his long sleep. There were new faces in the pubs and the hills were much more crowded. More than that, there had been a shift in atmosphere. When I left for Sandhurst in 1955, the routes of Joe Brown and Don Whillans still engendered a superstitious respect. I remember trying *Cenotaph Corner*, the famous open-book corner on Dinas Cromlech, scuttling back down after the first few moves. By the summer of 1959, any number of people had done it. Confident I was as good as they, I cruised it; the route seemed to have sprouted holds in my absence. It wasn't that I was a much better climber. The mystery had evaporated, and now I discovered the real difficulty had existed between my ears.

Equipment had also changed. In 1955 we all wore very tight gym shoes but in 1959 I bought my first pair of 'PAs', the forerunner of the modern rock boot. They stuck to small wrinkles in the rock that a gym shoe would roll off. Protection was also improving. In 1955 I might place the odd sling over a flake of rock, but the basic principle that the leader must not fall was as true then as it had been before the Great War. Now I carried a pocketful of pebbles to insert into cracks, a practice that Joe Brown did much to perfect. Soon there would be metal wedges. The margin of safety was starting to widen.

That summer I climbed in the Dolomites, teaming up with Gunn Clark, then an engineer based in France, who I met at the campsite. Gunn had just made the first British ascent of the Walker Spur in the Grandes Jorasses with Robin Smith and he and I now made the first British ascent of the Brandler Hasse, a fearsomely steep route on the north face of the Cima Grande. It was one of the earliest hard ascents in the Dolomites done by British mountaineers and prompted something of a rush. Compared to this world of excitement and achievement, the army was starting to feel like a dead end. My regiment was now in Libya. I really didn't want to go to Libya.

Happily, I could put off contemplating my future for a while. I got an invitation for the following spring to join a joint-services attempt on Annapurna II in Nepal, at almost 8,000 metres one of the highest mountains then unclimbed. It was ten miles east of Annapurna itself, barely any higher but scraping over 8,000. Annapurna was the first peak of that magical altitude to be climbed in 1950. Our expedition would be a joint British and Nepali affair, the brainchild of two extremely senior generals, the recently retired Field Marshal Sir Gerald Templer and the head of the Indian army, General Kodandera Subayya Thimayya. The details, including the peak, were left to Jimmy Roberts, a Gurkha officer and military attaché in Kathmandu. Jimmy had been to Annapurna II in 1950 with Bill Tilman, the great man's last expedition, and wanted a return match. Four teams had tried it since, so it was clearly a plum.

So much of that first expedition to the Himalaya was a delight. In those days you took the boat, and in early 1960 I escaped the British winter on board the *SS Cilicia*, bound for India. The voyage was a dreamy interlude, full of lazing around and shipboard romances. From Mumbai, we travelled north by train, in a state of mild hysteria at the novelty of everything and our vast amount of supplies, before gathering as a complete team in Kathmandu at the end of February.

We were a disparate bunch. From the British contingent of six, only Dick Grant from the Royal Marines had been to the Himalaya before, although two of the others had some Alpine experience. Jimmy cast a cool eye over his charges. 'It is one of the weaknesses of an expedition of this sort,' he wrote afterwards, 'that there are too many cooks concerned in the production of broth. Each service must be given fair representation, numbers are forced up, and the final product tends to be a collection of individuals of varying experience rather than a balanced team.' I learned a lot from Jimmy.

If the team was unwieldly, we set great store by the nine Sherpas Jimmy had brought together, hardened veterans and almost all from the same village. Their previous experience covered every major peak in Nepal: Everest, Kangchenjunga and Makalu among them. Most had carried to more than 26,000 feet. They rather put us to shame.

This being the military, we were assigned a Sherpa each as our personal valet and on the first morning of our sixteen-day trek to base camp, the cheery presence of Tashi appeared at the entrance of my tent with a mug of steaming tea. It was a wonderfully clear morning and from the tent door I could see sharp green ridges and brown hills merging into a rampart of snow peaks across the entire northern horizon. I scrambled out of the tent to join Jimmy, who was gazing at the line of mountains with an expression something like ownership: this was his home.

'That's Himulchuli over there,' he told me, pointing to a distant pyramid of snow in the west, 'and that must be Annapurna II, though you can hardly see it.'

It was little more than a pimple, a hundred miles to the far west, but that moment was one of the most exciting of the expedition. I felt like a teenager again, seeing Snowdon for the first time. The first sight of your goal can be even more exhilarating than reaching the top: the scent of the future is in your nostrils. The days that followed were almost as exciting, with all the joy of a new experience, the constant change of scenery, the luxuriant sub-tropical green giving way to forests of pine and then the stony slopes and flat-roofed houses of the high mountains. The faces changed too, from the fine features of our Kathmandu porters, to the broader faces of the ethnic Tibetans inhabiting the high valleys.

Our destination was Manang, on the north side of the Annapurna massif that bars the village from the rest of Nepal. A rough jeep track reaches the village now, but in those days it was remote and rather lawless, swelled by the arrival of Tibetan refugees following the Dalai Lama's flight the year before. At one stage, locals sent us a demand for 2,000 rupees for various offences, including shooting bharal, which we didn't do, and smoking, which some of us did, commuted to fifty rupees if we paid up promptly. I think we settled on thirty.

The route itself was not particularly difficult, but it was long and committing. Being so early in the season we found ourselves ploughing through deep snow as we established camps towards a shoulder at 24,000 feet, below the summit mass of Annapurna IV, which we bypassed. From the shoulder we actually dropped down a little, traversing to the base of Annapurna II's summit ridge. It was mostly just hard work, but at least Dick Grant and I had the interesting role of route-finding. By the end of April we had established camp three, a palatial snow cave at 21,000 feet, still 5,000 feet short of the summit.

With us was Ang Nima, one of the Sherpas who had been on the successful 1953 Everest expedition. Since then he'd served in the British army as a mess waiter in Malaya. He would look at us rather disdainfully, as though he'd rumbled us in some way. Tashi was a complete contrast, always optimistic and constantly helpful. Then in his fifties, Tashi had worked for several of the pre-war Everest teams. 'Like' is too weak a word for what Dick and I felt about him: we loved him. Old enough to be our father, he spoilt us the entire time we were on the mountain. At the end of a long day, when we had slumped into sleeping bags, Tashi would be struggling with the Primus stove to make dinner.

At this stage of the expedition, I was feeling disheartened. I hadn't acclimatized well and was struggling to keep up; the only thing that kept me going was the fear that if I admitted defeat I'd be off the summit team. On our first attempt to reach the shoulder, we put up a tent at camp four and suffered miserably through the night. Next day, we turned back at 22,000 feet, still short of our objective, in the face of a vicious wind. Still feeling tired, I was only too pleased to turn and run. We bundled up our tent, stuffed it into the rucksacks and fled back to the snow cave. There we discovered

Jimmy had given the order for the whole team to withdraw to recuperate from the immense effort we'd put in so far and prepare for the final push.

After a couple of days, I was restless to return. The weather had come good and I started to panic that we'd miss our window. Jimmy stuck to his guns. Having brought us down he was determined to give us a good rest. It must have been a hard decision but one that showed his qualities as a leader. Afterwards, he admitted to gnawing doubts that he'd wasted the best weather of the spring.

Gathering us round in a semi-circle, pencils and notebooks in hand, as though in the field on a military exercise, we awaited his orders. There was something almost simian about Jimmy; he had the features of a wrinkled boy and when he got excited his voice became high-pitched. But he was tough. Ill for much of the climb, he didn't let that impact on the rest of us. Sketching out his assault plan, I breathed a sigh of relief when he confirmed my place on the summit bid, along with Ang Nima and Dick, who was in charge.

In the end, Jimmy's decision to delay worked out. We had six days of perfect weather as we moved back up the mountain and established camp five on the shoulder, just shy of 24,000 feet. Jimmy had told us to use oxygen above camp four and I found myself wholly invigorated. But then the weather broke, clouds building up overnight from the south. By morning a full-blown storm was rattling the tent. Dick suggested we traverse to the base of the summit ridge to dump the loads for camp six. Fighting through the wind, buried in cloud, I discovered I was enjoying myself, yet by the time we'd flogged back up the slope to camp five on the shoulder we both felt near defeat.

'I think we've had our spell of good weather,' I said to Dick. He was crouched over the Primus, trying to thaw out the regulating valve on his malfunctioning oxygen set. 'We should have come up earlier.'

'It's not that bad,' he said, more phlegmatic than I. 'We can sit it out for another couple of days.' I don't remember ever losing my temper with Dick, and if he felt frustrated with me, he never showed it, even when I spilt porridge on his sleeping bag. He was the kind of person who got on with everyone. I was worried about his oxygen set and suggested he get a replacement sent up. He agreed, but then added: 'I'll manage somehow.' He hadn't once complained that day, when he was struggling to breathe; I knew I couldn't have kept going under the same circumstances.

That night we slept well, with none of the tension before a big effort. We'd spent the day in our sleeping bags, waiting out the storm. When I woke, my brain and body dulled with hypoxia, it took me a moment to realize that the wind had dropped. I stuck my head out of the tent and saw a lot of high cloud coming from the north. I told Dick I was worried it might turn nasty later.

'Where did you say it was coming from?'

'The north.'

He sat bolt upright. It was the first time the weather had come from that direction. 'It might mean a change for the better,' he said.

'I hadn't thought of that. We might as well push on to camp six today.'

'Bugger that,' he said, 'we'll go for the summit.'

Having made the decision, the three of us were out of the tent door in double time and climbing by seven-thirty. The other Sherpas at camp five would bring up the tent for camp six behind us. Soon we were moving towards the summit ridge in bright sunshine, just below the crest, the jumbled jigsaw of a hanging glacier several thousand feet below our boots. Dick's oxygen was still not working well, so when we arrived at the summit ridge a couple of hours later he waved me into the lead. It was still 2,500 feet to the summit and something like a mile in distance.

Huge cumulonimbus clouds were building from the south while from the north the high cloud had thickened and was now washing across the ridge behind us. The weather felt ominous but we didn't consider turning back. We were fixed on the summit. A few hundred feet of hard snow led to a rock band like the loose tiles of a derelict house. There was no time for belays; we just took care not to touch anything. Past this obstacle was another ribbon of snow clinging to the crest and I led up that, the effort apparently endless, a slash of the axe, step up, the next gasping breath, on and on. I no longer glanced behind at the building cloud; I was looking instead for the summit, thought we were there, and then saw the ridge continuing, felt the sag of disappointment. When we did arrive, at a small cone of snow from which everything dropped away, I barely believed it.

It was a tremendously moving moment, perhaps because it was my first big unclimbed peak but more I think because we had worked so well together. We were cut off from the others by the flood of cloud around us, perched on our summit, marooned in space. It was four in the afternoon; we would do well to make camp before dark. That sensation of isolation hadn't left Ang Nima's mind for a moment.

'Down going, Sahibs,' he said.

From that moment the climb became a struggle. All elation left me. We would have taken any risk for the summit, but now I was running on empty. My oxygen ran out and I could barely keep moving let alone watch the rope. Then Dick was falling and before I could do anything I was pulled off my feet too and shot past him. Dick managed to catch himself and when the rope came taut stopped me as well. We carried on without a word but knew how close we'd come. When we finally reached the tent, Urkein and Mingma were there to hand us mugs of tea and I collapsed into my sleeping bag, overwhelmed with fatigue and anxiety. In the night, plagued with a sore throat and difficult breathing, I became convinced I was dying. I woke Dick up so he could share my last minutes. He assured me I'd be fine and rolled over.

Three days later, having descended to base camp, I still felt the same anxious sense of anticlimax, but cured it in an unexpected way. Having dismantled our camps in record time, Jimmy decided to take the expedition back to Pokhara on another route, heading north-west across the Thorong La, now a popular trek, through the pilgrim village of Muktinath and then turning south down the Kali Gandaki. There was a shortcut though, across the Tilicho passes and past the ice lake between them, a route taken by Maurice Herzog in 1950. Having read his account, I wanted to repeat the journey and asked Jimmy if he would let me go that way with Tashi. What followed was one of the most satisfying mountain experiences of my life.

The Sherpas had celebrated our joint success in the village with huge quantities of rakshi, the local homebrew. While we'd been climbing Annapurna II, Mingma and Urkein had nipped up Annapurna IV, the first all-Sherpa ascent anywhere. So Tashi left Manang nursing a colossal hangover and I soon drew ahead of him, stopping to read while he caught up. 'Sorry, sorry, Sahib,' he would say when he finally caught up. 'Rakshi no good.'

Slowly, all the tension and drama of the last weeks faded away and with the prospect of unknown country ahead of me, my mood lifted. Thanks to Tashi, stopping to gossip with the local women, buying pheasant eggs for our tea, I became more rooted in where I was, even though I understood not one word in ten. We slept that first night under the stars next to a small fire and next day crossed the wild, desolate pass to camp on the shore of the lake. We were only a dozen miles or so from the nearest human habitation, but with the high mountains above fringing the night sky it felt incredibly remote. I felt happier and more content than I had on the summit. When we crossed the second pass next day, I was sorry to leave the mountain solitude, once again part of an alien group in a strange land. But I felt wholly at peace.

Returning to Wales, I was confronted with a familiar problem: the cloud of confusion over my future. My posting to the Army Outward Bound School would end in a few months but I was done with regimental soldiering. As Sniffy Saunders had predicted, my posting to Wales had cost me; I'd been knocked back for promotion to captain. Other ideas occurred to me. I had written to the colonel of the Special Air Service, although not through the usual channels. For someone who loved service life but was an odd-shaped peg in a regimental hole, the SAS might have provided the answer. But it might also have proved awkward. No doubt my membership of the Young Communist League would have been flagged up during the necessary security checks; there was a lot of paranoia around in the 1950s. Anyway, I would have been required to kill people in a direct and personal way, very different from being in a tank. The SAS did write back to me suggesting I apply, but by then I had decided to leave the army.

I had been invited on another Himalayan expedition, this time a civilian one. Joe Walmsley was a well-known climber from the north-west; a few years before, he had led an attempt on Masherbrum, a difficult peak in the Karakoram. Don Whillans had been part of that team and come close to the summit: a superb effort. When I saw Joe at a Climbers' Club dinner that autumn, he told me he was gathering a team to try Everest's near neighbour Nuptse, more than 7,800 metres high. Don was part of his plans.

'Have you got everyone you want?' I asked him.

'Why, do you want to come along?' I barely thought about it: to hell with the army. It never occurred to me to ask for permission; I doubt they would give me any more time off. And while the army had sent me to Annapurna II, it was the wrong place to push a climbing career.

'Yes, if you've got room.'

It was time to start hunting for another job. Yet I was so used to the security the army offered that my instinct was to join another – any other – large organization. That's how I ended up as a margarine salesman.

I wrote to all the big companies and landed a preliminary interview with Unilever, which I passed with flying colours. Transferring to the corporate world didn't look so hard. Next was Unilever's selection board, a more intellectual version of what I'd done to get into Sandhurst. Instead of imaginary alligator-infested swamps we ran imaginary soap manufacturers. Having cleared this hurdle, I found myself in front of the managing director of Van den Berghs, an associate company that sold marge. On either side of him were two other directors.

'You strike me as being a drifter,' one of them said as an opener. 'First you tried the air force, then the army, now us.' I became somewhat pink-faced with indignation as I defended myself.

'Yes,' another director started up. 'But why choose marketing?' I came up with a spiel about using 'counter-marketing techniques' to acquire equipment for the Annapurna expedition.

'Sounds like begging to me. How do we know you're not going to shoot off on another expedition in a couple of years?'

'Nuptse will be my last expedition,' I promised. 'I realize I can't base my career on climbing all my life.' I wasn't sure about the company, but I convinced myself and they offered me a job. I would soon settle down to a long and prosperous career in commerce. And since I didn't have to start until September, I could have a marvellous swansong. After Nuptse, I could stop off on the drive home for a few weeks in the Alps.

A few weeks later, I was plodding up a steep snow slope towards camp six on Nuptse, just below the crux rock band at 24,000 feet. My breezy optimism had deflated somewhat. With me was Les Brown, a tall young climber from Stockport with a strong Alpine record. I liked Les and got on well with him, but the expedition had proved rather acrimonious. The night before he and I had squabbled, Les wondering why I'd promoted myself to the front of the queue when there were loads to be carried, me wondering why progress had been so slow while I'd been recuperating from illness at base camp. Joe Walmsley put a stop to our stupid quarrel but the expedition did feel a bit like every man for himself.

That evening we'd watched the pair in front, Dennis Davis and Tashi Sherpa, my great friend from the year before, go right to the foot of the rock band. As Les and I now gasped our way up to the top camp, I prayed they had found a way through it. If we could surmount this last obstacle, we should be in a position to reach the summit. They were still climbing when we arrived and so we hacked another platform for our tent and settled in to wait. It was a magnificent evening. We were at last creeping above the surrounding mountains. Ama Dablam's slender spire merged into the background peaks. To the west the rounded dome of Cho Oyu, an 8,000-metre peak, seemed not much higher than we were.

It was dark when Dennis got back to the tent. He was thinner than when I had seen him last, haggard with weariness, but there was a look of triumph in his eyes.

'We've got through the band. It doesn't look too bad beyond.'

'What was it like?'

'Nothing like as hard as we thought it would be.' Dennis had found a straightforward traverse that cut across the rock band with just one hard section, an iced-up chimney that had caused him trouble. I wondered aloud if we could dash to the summit from here.

'I don't know about that; it's a still a long way from the top.' Over the previous few weeks I'd come to have a grudging respect for Dennis. He was stringy and tough, with a bristling moustache and a relentless appetite for hard work. Over the past few days, throughout a period of bad weather, he had plugged away to push the route. But Dennis was also abrasive, couldn't let things go without throwing in a sarcastic barb. This moment was no exception. 'I was beginning to wonder what had happened to the rest of you: nothing much has been coming up for the last few days. I was thinking of pressing on with Tashi. It looked as if we should have to do the whole bloody lot ourselves.'

I suppose it was inevitable we would clash. Dennis was a stickler: precise in everything he did, a useful quality in his work as a site engineer. He was also obsessively tidy. Even in the tent at night he wouldn't relax until absolutely everything was organized. I was the reverse, rather indolent and happy to do the minimum to keep things going, comfortable in the squalor of an untidy tent and happy to eat off a dirty plate if it meant less effort expended. We had spent a week together forcing the route on the lower slopes of the mountain, nervy work traversing under tottering ice cliffs and up ice crests that barely seemed to be stuck to the rock beneath. By the end of it, as I wrote in my diary, I was ready to smash his face in. I'm sure he felt the same about me.

The team as a whole never gelled. This might have had something to do with Don's absence; he'd pulled out after a motorcycle accident. Most of the team had a connection to Don, like John Streetly, born in Trinidad, who had won a boxing blue at Cambridge. John was similar in size to Don, but of a very different temperament: likeable, dynamic, self-confident but sometimes difficult to read. Perhaps if Don had been there, then the chemistry might have worked. I know I came across as too pushy and self-absorbed; I hadn't been able to put aside my own prejudice and ambition for the sake of the team. But I was furious when a teammate warned Joe to keep a wary eye in case I tried to make off with expedition cash to fund my summer in the Alps.

At the time I was too dismissive of Joe's leadership. He was such a contrast to Jimmy the year before, who was very clear and decisive. Joe kept a much lower profile, perhaps overwhelmed by the personality clashes. In retrospect I realized he played a more patient game, quietly making sure supplies kept trickling up the mountain while allowing his team of egotistical civilians to sort themselves out. I didn't blame him when he told the newspapers on getting home that he wouldn't lead another expedition; at thirty-eight and with a young family he had other priorities. But even though we only ever reunited as an expedition once, thirty-five years later, we achieved a great deal.

The south face of Nuptse was an incredible challenge in 1961, ahead of its time in many ways. When we planned our climb of Annapurna's south face, the Nuptse ascent was a landmark by which to steer. Our route was ingenious but long, climbing a spur of rotten snow and ice that buttressed the face. At the top of this, it swung left through the rock band before traversing further left to a summit gully and the ridge to the top. That sounds amenable, but it was a gigantic undertaking. We needed a grand total of eight camps to reach the summit and ran out of rope to fix, resorting to some ancient lengths of hemp we acquired locally.

Despite the arguments and the scale of the climb, we persevered. Les and I took a turn in front above the rock band, cutting steps in the snow above camp seven. Dennis couldn't resist a dig. 'You couldn't have chosen a worse line,' he said, handing me a cup of tea when we got back to camp seven. We agreed that next day we would establish camp eight in the gully. Dennis and Tashi would cut steps while we followed with their tent and gear. The day after that they would push on up the gully, cutting more steps, in readiness for a big team push to the summit. Yet when Les and I, together with Jim Swallow and Pemba Sherpa, reached camp eight as per the schedule, Dennis and Tashi were still not back. By the time we had dug platforms in the snow for our tents, it was dark and there was still no sign of them.

'The bastard's gone for the top,' I said to Les. 'They'll have to bivouac if they don't hurry.' It was past eight o'clock when we finally heard their shouts.

'Did you do it?' I asked Dennis.

'Yes.'

'Bloody well done, you deserved it.' And I really meant it. Dennis had gone better than any of us and shown more determination as well. He already knew this would be the highpoint of his mountaineering life.

When we set out next morning, we found a line of steps so good we could take off the rope and climb solo. I pulled ahead of the others, with Pemba on my heels. The gully stretched endlessly in front of me; six steps, a rest, breathless in the snow. I was determined not to let Pemba overtake me, determined only to look at the snow in front of me and not glance up where I knew the top of the gully would only seem as distant as ever. I chided myself: ten steps this time. But I only managed eight before I leaned against the slope, panting for air.

Finally, the top of the gully was just above me, ten more slow steps and after two months of effort our whole world changed. Now we could look into the Western Cwm and across to Everest. My first impression was one of immense, boundless space, a sea of brown beyond the huge bulk in front of me, rolling hills flecked by the occasional peak of snow, reaching towards the distant horizon. There was no haze; each distant undulation was etched sharp in the cold thin air. The summit was a corniced cap of snow and Pemba and I collapsed on it, grateful the struggle was over. I couldn't imagine climbing another 3,000 feet to the summit of Everest without oxygen. And not once did it occur to me that a good chunk of my life would be spent on the black rocky triangle in front of me: the south-west face. It was the brown, arid plateau of Tibet that stuck in my memory.

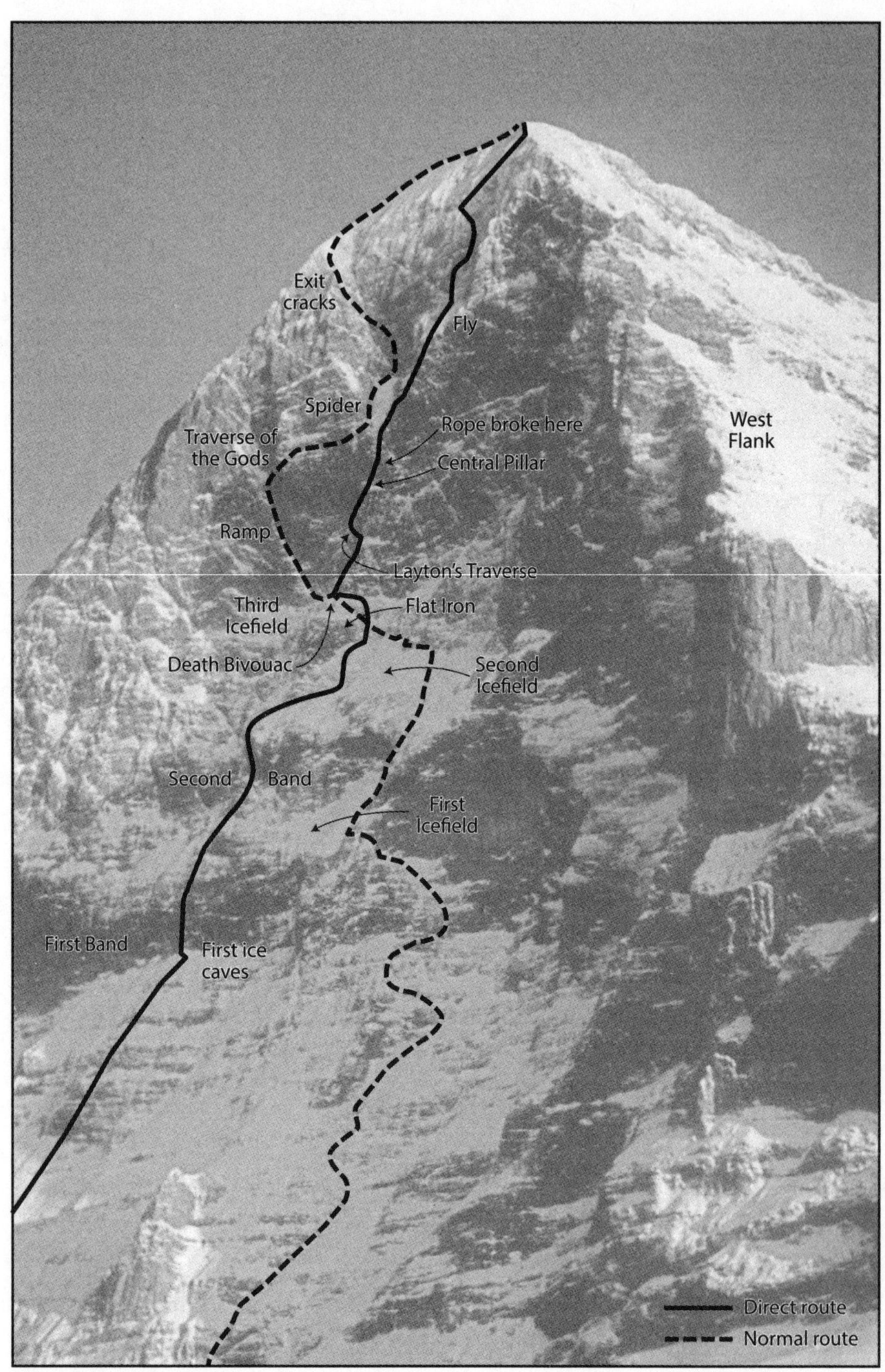

The north wall of the Eiger.

Chapter Five

A New Life

Don Whillans was watching me peeling potatoes, sitting outside our tent at Alpiglen, under the north wall of the Eiger.

'The trouble is, Chris, you're too greedy. You'll always crack before I do.'

Which of us did the cooking was a regular test of willpower, one I usually lost. We'd been living like this for two weeks, watching the face, waiting for conditions to improve. A day of stormy weather and heavy snow would knock our hopes back, the clouds would lift, optimism would soar, only for storm clouds to gather again as we were sorting our gear. It was monotonous, but I could feel the strength coming back after Nuptse and the long drive home.

I'd met Don in Chamonix after 7,000 miles of dusty roads, flies and punctures, all the way from Kathmandu. He had hitchhiked from Manchester in three days with a rucksack as tall as himself, determined to head straight to the Eiger. Doing an easier climb just to get fit wasn't part of his philosophy. I persuaded him to join me on a training climb on the Aiguille de l'M before heading to Switzerland, just to see how unfit I was. After getting stuck halfway up the wall, legs shaking, body heavy and useless, I had a clearer idea.

'You're climbing like a bloody nana,' Don shouted up.

At the top I told him I didn't think I'd ever been so unfit.

'You'll be all right. When Joe got back from Kangchenjunga he was nearly as bad. You can do your training on the face. By the time you get to the top you'll be fit – or dead!'

As the days ticked by, my resources dwindled. John Streetly had kindly offered to loan me twenty pounds, which boosted the ten quid I had left after Nuptse. 'It'll get yer used to civvy street,' Don said. 'You don't know how soft you've had it in the army.' But after weeks of eating potatoes fried, curried or boiled, I suggested we hitch to Lucerne to take up an offer I'd had to visit the Swiss climber Max Eiselin. 'He might be good for a decent meal.'

It took for ever to get a lift to Interlaken but once there a Volkswagen pulled up beside us before we could even raise a thumb.

'Do you want a lift?' the driver said. She was young, attractive, apparently unattached and from her accent, American. I manoeuvred myself into the passenger seat while Don sulked in the back with the rucksacks. 'I'm not going far, I'm afraid. Where do you want to get to?'

'Lucerne,' I said. 'But let's have a coffee before we press on.'

Thoughts of Lucerne went out of the window. Anne was tall and dark-haired, with a strength and warmth in her face that I found immediately attractive. From our first exchanges in the car I felt at ease in her company. She was in Europe studying French and having failed to persuade her to come to Lucerne, Don and I dossed outside her youth hostel under the stars. Next day we all swam in the Thunersee and then Anne returned to Geneva, dropping us back in Grindelwald with a promise to return.

A few days later we started up the face, climbing unroped up the easy ground at the bottom, the ledges covered in snow so we had to wear crampons. I felt none of the fear I'd experienced with Hamish five years before, knowing better what was ahead and having more faith in my own ability. I also had complete faith in Don. He left his sack at the foot of the Difficult Crack and spent an hour fighting his way up what was in effect a vertical skating rink. The Hinterstoisser Traverse was a near-vertical wall of snow.

'I wonder how long it'll take to clear.'

'It'll be some days yet, if at all,' Don said. 'Let's get back before the stones start coming down.'

Abseiling down we met four Polish climbers who had moved into our campsite a few days before. We'd rather kept our distance until now, but sharing the experience of the wall brought us together. One of the Poles had dropped his rucksack and so he and his partner came down with us. That afternoon in the Hotel des Alpes, enjoying a rare beer to celebrate our safe return, we were summoned to the telephone.

'Were you on the Eiger this morning?' There was no preamble, just someone shouting down the line. 'I'm from the *Daily Mail.*'

Next morning a Swiss freelance turned up in the cleanest climbing breeches I'd ever seen. 'Soft as shit,' Don concluded. It was my first experience of the media obsession the Eiger provoked.

'They all seem to want to get a story for nothing,' Don observed. 'I wonder how much they make out of it.'

'I don't see why we shouldn't make something of it ourselves,' I told him. 'The papers will make a story up even if we don't tell them anything, and God knows we need the money.' We were down to our last six pounds.

'Well, let's climb it first, then we can think about selling stories.'

That morning the Poles who had stayed on the wall returned to camp in a pathetic state, clothes sodden and equipment in disarray. We became friendly, to the immediate benefit of our diet. They were good cooks and had plentiful supplies from home. But after another fortnight, growing fat on Polish ham, the weather was no better.

'I think we're wasting our time here,' Don said. 'Do you know anything about that Central Pillar of Frêney?' I knew that it was in a remote position high on Mont Blanc and that Robin Smith had tried it a few years before. 'I fancy doing a good new route,' Don continued. 'It faces south so should come into condition quickly.' The Poles left as well. Two of them headed for the Matterhorn, another went home but Jan Długosz, who spoke the best English, asked if he could join us. Anne drove us to France in the Volkswagen.

The Central Pillar of Frêney had long been an obsession of the great Walter Bonatti and had a fearsome reputation. Earlier that summer, four of a party of seven he was leading perished in a bitter storm as they tried to retreat. We only knew the barest details of this terrible disaster. That anyone had survived it was largely thanks to Bonatti's great skill and his intimate knowledge of the mountain. Since then, another two Frenchmen had tried, and we went to see one of them, an instructor at the École Nationale called Pierre Julien. 'I know him quite well,' Jan told us. 'Why don't we ask him to join us?' We needed a fourth, and at the very least we might get some information. Julien told us he was too busy to come, but told us about the route, particularly the challenge above his high point.

'There are some cracks out to the left,' he warned us. 'You'll need some big wedges.' Walking back to the campsite we ran into Ian Clough, an English climber we knew who had just arrived from the Dolomites. Ian was from Baildon in Yorkshire and started his climbing life on the gritstone edges near his home. Like me, he had served in the RAF with the idea of joining their mountain rescue team. He had just done the first British ascent of a hard route on the Cima Ovest but you'd hardly know it. Ian was the most modest man I ever had the good luck to climb with; so many leading climbers have big egos, but Ian wasn't one of them. He seemed the perfect person to join us.

Several days later we caught the last cable car to the top of the Aiguille du Midi. Just as the doors were closing, three heavily laden climbers pushed their way on. I immediately recognized Pierre Julien. Jan muttered that the other two were René Desmaison and Yves Pollet-Villard, leading French alpinists.

'I don't think there's any doubt where they're going,' Don said. Julien threaded his way through the crush to speak to us.

'You go to Frêney?'

'Perhaps. And you?'

'Perhaps.'

At the top station, they took the small *télécabine* across the

Vallée Blanche to the Torino hut. None of us could understand why. It took them in the wrong direction.

'They've probably got a helicopter,' Don said. Julien had used one on his previous attempt, despite criticism that this was cheating. 'Anyway, there's nothing we can do about it.' We set off towards the col and its little bivouac hut.

The hut was heaving when we got there so we stayed outside to cook dinner. I couldn't help glancing across to the Grand Pilier d'Angle, the huge granite buttress that shoulders the bulk of Mont Blanc. You couldn't see our pillar but I could trace our route up to the Col de Peuterey. As I watched, a puff of smoke erupted high on the buttress and then mushroomed into a brown torrent of rocks that crashed into the glacier below, filling the cirque with an ear-splitting roar. The smell of sulphur reached us at the hut from a mile away. We would have to walk under this buttress in the dead of night. It felt like an omen.

None of us slept, we just lay there, wedged into the overcrowded sleeping platform of the hut. Finally it was time to go; we made coffee, shouldered our rucksacks and stepped out into the night. The sky was a deep black, glistening with stars, but it seemed warm to me. Don brushed aside my suggestion we switch routes.

'It's as settled as it ever will be.'

Once we left the familiar track to the Brenva face and committed ourselves to reaching the Col de Peuterey, gateway to the Frêney pillar, I began to relax. Don chopped his way up an awkward bulge of ice at the bottom of the couloir and then we climbed more quickly, each of us in our own pool of light. Four hours after setting out from the hut, we were on the col.

'There's no point going to the foot of the pillar before it's in the sun,' Don reasoned. 'Let's have a brew.' We crouched around the stove as sunlight crept down the pillar and Ian spotted a pair of climbers coming up behind us. We needed to get moving. Crossing the top of the Frêney glacier, we worked our way across the bergschrund, and began climbing. The rock was solid and warm to the touch, an almost sensual pleasure to climb as we picked a route up a series of cracks. Looking back down to the col, the two climbers were putting up a tent for the night and had been joined by two more pairs, presumably the French among them.

We were now 1,500 feet up the pillar, at the foot of its most striking feature, the smooth, 400-foot tower known as the *chandelle* or candle. Resting against the pillar was a pedestal of granite some fifty feet high. Bonatti and his group had sat out the storm on top of it and we found some sad relics of their ordeal: an empty gas cylinder, a cooking pot and some wooden wedges. Don used some of them forcing his way up to the overhang that we knew would form the crux section.

'I reckon this is as far as the others got,' he called down, before edging his way leftwards and then disappearing round a corner. The rope lay still in my hand for twenty minutes and then he reappeared. 'Bugger all round here.' He worked his way back rightwards until he was directly above me, spreadeagled across an overhanging prow, inching upwards imperceptibly. I longed for him to come down so I could put on my duvet and settle in for the night. It was bitterly cold.

'I think it'll go,' Don shouted and then threaded the ropes through his last piton to abseil down. It was typical of Ian to spend the night brewing up. Our legs grew stiff with cold but being so high the morning sun was quickly on us. Using Don's pegs from the night before, I soon reached a belay under the overhangs, looking straight down at the glacier 3,000 feet below. Don disappeared round the corner, leaning towards a corner on tension from the rope, pushing a tiny piton into a crack. He tapped it with his hammer but a glancing blow sent it spinning into the void. He tried again with another, and this one rang true. He was up.

Don suggested I stop a little below him and belay in a more comfortable spot. Then he climbed up to the roof, which jutted straight out for twelve feet and split on one side by a chimney. Don was struggling to get a peg into a crack in front of his nose, but he wasn't able to take his hands off the rock. Fifty feet above, his feet were skating off the rock.

'I'm coming off, Chris!' He fought on for a moment, and then arrived in a mass of flailing limbs, hanging upside down and looking into my face. I watched a flurry of banknotes and cigarettes drifting in space towards the glacier below.

'I've lost me 'at,' Don said. The loss of our cash worried me more.

'Are you all right?'

By way of reply, he lit a cigarette from his spare pack, hands trembling. Tired of standing in the cold, I offered to have a go. I had no illusions: if Don couldn't climb it free then I certainly couldn't. But I thought I might be able to engineer some aid. By now, the French team had caught us so I shouted down to Ian to ask if the new arrivals had anything.

'They say we can have some gear in a minute. They want to look at the other side first.'

Time dragged on. 'Have they made up their bloody minds yet?'

'They say we're on the wrong line. They need all the gear for themselves.'

'In that case, bugger them.' I managed to haul up some more slings, excavated some stones from the back of the crack, wedged them sideways, clipped slings round them and stood up in my *étriers*. From my new vantage point I could bang in a good peg. The chimney now narrowed into a slit and I had to arch myself out over a void that ended thousands of feet below and swing up on small handholds, heart in mouth, climbing with desperate speed. I reached a ledge and yelled with excitement: we were there. Don followed and took up a better stance just above me. Ian and Jan were still on the ledge where we'd bivouacked.

'You'd better prusik up on the rope,' Don shouted down. As they prepared to leave, Desmaison offered Ian some pegs and asked if he would tie off their rope above the overhang so they could follow in the morning. We found a small sloping ledge that just about took all four of us, but I no longer cared. We had done it. Next morning we climbed the last two pitches as two aircraft circled overhead taking pictures. Near the summit, a reporter jumped out of a helicopter to wait for us as we plodded up. He'd brought a flagon of red wine and some tins of fruit juice. Slightly tipsy, we set off on the long descent to Chamonix.

We met the French climbers for a celebratory champagne lunch, but I was already thinking of the next climb. I had four days left before starting at Van den Bergh's and the weather was perfect. Surely we had enough time for another route? But that would mean flying home, and I didn't have the fare. The French magazine *Paris Match* wanted our pictures, so I sold those on behalf of the team; *Le Dauphiné* also wanted an interview. It was obvious that for the right story there were deals to be done. That night I met a friendly Australian reporter for the *Daily Mail* called Desmond Zwar and over a bottle of wine agreed that in return for an exclusive they would meet our expenses and fly me home.

Time was critical, so next morning Anne drove us to Grindelwald. By late afternoon we were back in Alpiglen. The *Mail*'s photographer knew his business and wheedled us into a fierce embrace. 'Can't you make it a bit more personal than that? Let's have a bit of real passion.' The story ran under the headline 'A kiss before the Eiger', but the attempt was a bust. Don and I raced up to the Swallow's Nest bivouac feeling on top form but it was a warm night and the face was rotten with loose stones. Don, always attuned to the mood of mountains, knew the game was up, but I tried to persuade him to go a little further, under pressure from our newspaper deal.

'That's how half the accidents occur on the Eiger,' he said, 'with people pushing on just a bit further. We can come back next year.'

As I prepared to leave for home, fate intervened again. A tourist rushed up to us saying he had seen a climber fall from the Eiger. Not quite believing him, we thought we'd better go back to check. A self-important tourist was standing over a body shrouded with a blanket, which he lifted with a flourish to reveal what a long fall can do to a human. I saw in his excitement the voyeurism of the Eiger. At that moment I could have thumped him.

Several hours later, in a deserted airport lounge, I hugged Anne for the last time. We arranged to meet for Christmas in Paris but somehow it felt like a final goodbye. Five hours later I was standing outside a huge office block, scrubbed and shaved, dressed in a dark suit, watching a flood of men and women pouring into the building.

Quite what I was thinking when I became a management trainee I'm not sure. Part of it was the shadow of my upbringing. My mother certainly saw the value of a secure position. She was still working successfully as a copywriter for a top London agency and would use me occasionally in campaigns. I suppose the image of a bold young executive fresh from the mountains climbing the corporate ladder appealed to me at some level. But I had hated office work in the army and nothing changed about that in civilian life.

I spent six months as a trainee hearing innumerable lectures about other people's jobs and then was given one of my own, as a sales rep. Grocers relied on me to assess their margarine needs but somehow I always got it wrong. When shopkeepers discovered they had fifty surplus boxes of margarine, or ran out in the middle of the week, they were understandably angry. I managed to lose a dozen accounts in my first six months without managing to sign any new ones. By the end of my margarine career, I had whittled down my Friday visits to three clients. It did make getting away climbing easier.

That New Year of 1962 I was due to give a lecture and, late as always, stumbled into my compartment as the train began pulling out. My slides went everywhere, and a girl leaped up to help me. We got chatting, and I discovered she lived just round the corner from me on England Road. She and her flatmates were having a party on Twelfth Night and invited me along. She didn't mention that she had a friend who was looking for some adventure in her life and thought I might fit the bill. Her friend, Wendy Marchant, was small and dark and wore a little black dress; we sat and talked as though we had known each other for years. When we danced, she held me close; there was something kittenish about her, very sexy. I immediately felt I didn't want to be out of her company.

I discovered Wendy really did want more adventure in her life. Her father Les had been a Baptist minister, but had become disillusioned with organized religion and now worked as an illustrator. Her upbringing had been far from conventional but it was full of love and emotional security. At the age of twelve, at school in Brighton, she'd told her best friend she was going to marry an outdoor type: 'no nine to five person for me'. The idea I would spend the rest of my life selling margarine was no less appalling to Wendy than it was to me. Like her dad, she worked as an artist illustrating children's books, but she wanted to experience more of the world.

When her friend told her that an outdoor type was coming to the party, she had imagined a Canadian lumberjack, so my appearance, rosy-cheeked and boyish despite being twenty-eight, took an adjustment. I think what she responded to most was my enthusiasm and joy in life. I might have lacked the rugged looks – I doubt it was a coincidence that I grew a beard once I left Van den Bergh's, which I've never been without since – but those qualities I had in abundance. After that first night we were inextricably bound to each other: we married that May.

Wendy and I arrived at the register office together, a little late as I had rushed round my shops that morning. Mum and Dad were there, the first time they'd been together since 1946, when Mum had told him their marriage was definitely over; Wendy's parents, Les and Lily; my aunt and uncle, and two friends, Billy Wilkinson and Eric Vola, but no best man.

Having fallen in love, it was natural I should want to share my other passion. Soon after Wendy and I became engaged I took her climbing in the Peak District at a friendly gritstone crag called Froggatt Edge. She was keen but a little apprehensive as I tied a rope around her waist.

'Now, this route is only a Diff,' I told her.

'What's a Diff?'

'Difficult.'

'Couldn't we start with something easy?'

'Difficult is easy: I know it sounds contradictory. But anything easier than this would be a walk. We'll soon have you doing Very Severe.'

I bounced up the climb, reassuring her how easy she'd find it, but when it came to her turn she was tense and hugged the rock, as beginners often do. I'd found the climbing so easy I'd gone off route to make it harder; as a consequence the rope was running to one side and when I glanced at my belay, it didn't look as good as it ought to have been.

'For God's sake, don't slip: I'm not sure I can hold you.'

That was enough for Wendy. Quite reasonably, she panicked and lunged across the slab to grab my foot; with a big effort I managed to haul her onto the top of the cliff, but I'd blown it. It was the last time she ever went climbing. Yet she loved the wild and was happy to come with me, even if she just sat at the bottom. More importantly, she developed her own interests independent of me and then shared them, just as I did with her. That exchange would become part of the bedrock of our marriage.

Although she could be quite shy, once Wendy committed to something she pursued it as deeply as she could. As a child, her passion had been horses; she managed to find an ex-stunt pony that she could ride for free. Her parents nurtured this innate open-mindedness and curiosity; her father Les was equally curious and loved discussing alternative ways of seeing, encouraging me to look at the world afresh. Her mother Lily wrote short stories on her typewriter on the living-room table, which was covered in artwork. There was a huge sofa by the fire where they'd sing folk songs in the evening.

We tried to recreate a little of that life, taking a six-month lease on a furnished room in Hampstead from an elderly Austrian woman who glared in disapproval through the French windows at the chaos inside, the washing in front of the gas fire, Wendy bent over her drawings at the table, works in progress on the floor, every available space crammed with our possessions. 'They do not care,' she would complain, stomping up the stairs. 'They make my room untidy. They live like animals.'

I suppose it was ironic that marrying Wendy gave me the confidence to give up my job and take that first step into the insecure unknown. But she saw in me a profound lack of fulfilment, of frustration. I needed to be doing the thing that made me happy, which was climbing. I had to find a way to live my passion more fully. The previous autumn I'd been invited on an expedition to Patagonia, at the tip of South America, but in the first flush of my new career I'd turned it down. Now I asked for time off to go, knowing full well what the reaction would be. It duly arrived: 'Put as plainly as possible, the time has come for you to make up your mind whether you leave mountaineering or Van den Bergh's.'

There was no point waiting; if I was quitting then I should quit now. I already had plans to go back on the Eiger. I also had a good idea of the media's interest and the contacts to exploit it. There were plenty in the Alpine Club who looked down on this sort of thing but selling the story gave me the chance. Telling stories was in my genes. My father, after all, was a journalist; after a spell on *The Times* he edited *Power News*, house magazine of the nationalized electricity industry. My mother was a thwarted novelist. At heart, I loved telling stories. I signed a deal with the *Daily Express* and they came to photograph us setting out for Alpiglen on Don's bike.

By the end of July, I was at the bottom of the Eiger's Second Icefield, staring across its vast, stone-pocked expanse of grey ice, as Don quickly followed up the steps I'd cut. A stone whistled down from above, emphasizing our exposure. Conditions were no better than the year before, but this time we had pushed on a little further. The top of the Eiger had disappeared behind wet grey clouds. Stones zipped down with a high-velocity rip that made us want to be anywhere else. I said I thought a storm was coming.

'Aye, let's push off down,' Don said.

As we turned we saw two climbers coming towards us, shouting in German: they were Swiss guides. We shouted back in English.

'Two of your comrades are in trouble,' came the reply. 'Will you help us to rescue them?'

We turned back up the slope but had no idea who they were or what had happened; all we knew was that one was injured. We started across the icefield, cutting huge steps as we went, knowing we might be coming back this way with an injured man. Don said he could see someone, hundreds of feet away, and called up to him. The figure seemed not to notice, a distant blob of red against the sombre grey of dull ice, but he stopped on a small spur of rock thirty feet nearer to us.

We continued, listening to the falling rocks, but then there was a different sound, a sort of 'whoosh' that filled the face. I looked up and saw a man sliding down the ice and then catapult into space below. I laid my forehead against the ice and swore loudly and repeatedly as the shock washed over me. Was this the injured man? Or the figure in red? We hurried on, feeling horribly exposed, the Swiss guides long since vanished. One last rope length and I was only a few feet from him. As I turned to ask Don to move across a little, the climber spoke.

'It's all right, I can come over to you.'

I had never met Brian Nally before, but knew of him. With Tom Carruthers he'd made the first British ascent of the Matterhorn's north face. I did know his dead partner Barry Brewster, an intense but brilliant rock climber, just twenty-two years old. Nally told us Brewster had suffered a huge fall and been badly injured; he had watched over him until he died in the night. Nally appeared unaffected by his ordeal. His rope was badly tangled around his neck, but otherwise he seemed together.

'Are you going to the top? Can I tie on to you?'

My nerves were already stretched and his question made me snap.

'We've come to get you down, you bloody fool.'

'But why not go on up, now that you've come so far?'

'Your friend is dead. Do you realize that?'

Only then did the penny drop. Nally was in shock. My anger was wholly misplaced. He was like an automaton: he did what you asked but seemed incapable of thinking for himself. I stood there for twenty minutes untangling his rope while Don waited. Finally we could start down, the ice now running with water, the sound of falling stones almost continuous. As we reached its end, the storm broke and we were engulfed in a hailstorm, all three of us hanging from the same ice screw as the wind tore against our sodden clothing. Then, almost as suddenly, it stopped.

Don now demonstrated his genius once again. Now soaked through, we had to get off the mountain as fast as we could. As we abseiled down the Ice Hose, he calculated that this was the source of a stream he had seen from below. If we abseiled straight down, we wouldn't need to reverse the Hinterstoisser traverse and so reach the railway tunnel more quickly. It was an inspired piece of route-finding. If Anderl Hinterstoisser had known about it in 1936, he would not have frozen to death.

The press were agog at Brian Nally's fate. Two Swiss journalists hired a special train to fetch him down. Still in shock, he had his account bullied out of him. The newspapers cast him as a hapless victim and in a later edition of the *White Spider*, Heinrich Harrer suggested he and Brewster were not sufficiently competent. It was grotesquely unfair; both men had earned the right to be there. To make matters worse, he was presented with a huge rescue bill from the Swiss authorities. Their role was confined to collecting Brewster's body. Brian Nally became friends with Don, but developed an animus against me, suggesting that on the face I had asked him what newspaper he was with. It simply didn't happen. The situation was so extreme that any discussion of that sort would have been ridiculous. Even so, in the gossipy world of British mountaineering the story gained currency; it dogged me for years.

Both of us felt disgusted by what we had seen.

'I've had enough of the Eiger for this season,' he said that night in our hotel room. We escaped to Innsbruck, climbing rock routes in the Kaisergebirge and the Karwendel. By the end of August we were out of money. Wendy and Don's wife Audrey had to hitchhike home while we took the bike. On the way we stopped off in Switzerland, at the superb granite peaks of the Bregaglia, and in six hours dashed up the north face of the Piz Badile, once a serious climb but meat and drink to British climbers, even in the early 1960s.

Feeling strong and fit, and seeing how great conditions were in

Chamonix, I tried to persuade Don to stay on, but once he made a decision he rarely havered.

'Anyway,' he said, 'we haven't got any gear.' This was true: we'd given most of it to the girls to carry home. But I was reluctant to go home without having achieved something significant. Then I ran into Ian Clough, like Don also preparing to leave. It didn't take much to convince him to stay for one more route. I rushed around the few climbers left in town to borrow the gear I needed and next morning we set out for the Grandes Jorasses to try the famous Walker Spur.

That night we bivouacked a hundred feet up the route, one of several parties spending the night out, all enticed by the perfect conditions. We spent the next morning overtaking them, as one would on a busy main road, waiting for breaks in the traffic. Several times we ran into people I knew. It was like being in Wales. Then a dark cloud crept across the summit and the other parties began abseiling off. Ian and I didn't even discuss it. We just motored on, the cloud lapping around us, sure the weather would hold, in absolute harmony. With Don I deferred to his greater skill and wisdom but with Ian I felt like an equal. The route just flowed by, climbing at its addictive best. It was so good that when we reached the summit, rather than just go down, I persuaded Ian to traverse the length of the Grandes Jorasses, a huge outing ending at the Torino Hut.

Even then, my climbing fever hadn't left me. Lying in bed next morning, weary from our immense effort, I nudged Ian.

'Wake up – I've just had an idea.' He rolled over and ignored me. 'It's important. How about going for the Eiger?'

'Fuck off, tell me about it later,' he said and snuggled back down. Two hours later I tried again. He yawned. 'Might as well have a go, I've always wanted to do it but never had the right partner.'

Thirty-six hours later we were in Alpiglen sorting out our gear but my confidence was fraying. The weather seemed dicier than forecast and I was missing Wendy. There were bad omens everywhere, but I had fired up Ian now. As we scrambled up the first rocks I noticed bloodstains, a scrap of flesh and bone, but kept quiet in case I spooked him. He did precisely the same.

We stopped on a good ledge protected by an overhang below the Difficult Crack, the standard bivy spot where I had stopped with Hamish in 1957. It was almost dark when we noticed another party climbing towards us.

'Who are you?' Ian shouted down. The man in front replied in German but his companion called out in broad Scots.

'And who the hell do you think you are?'

It was Tom Carruthers, Brian Nally's partner on the Matterhorn the year before. His partner had sprained his ankle and so he had teamed up with his companion, an Austrian called Anton Moderegger. It seemed crazy to me: neither could understand what the other was saying.

We ate heartily and slept well, too well in fact, because it was dawn when we woke. Sounds of activity came from around the corner where Tom and Anton had spent the night.

'Come on, Ian,' I said. 'We want to be sure of getting away first.'

The Difficult Crack was free of ice and I swarmed up it. The Hinterstoisser too was in perfect condition.

'If we don't get up it this time, we never shall,' I told Ian.

'Don't count your luck too soon,' he muttered.

Yet our good fortune continued. The face held much less ice and where before we had laboriously cut steps we now rock-climbed quickly. At the Second Icefield I chose to go straight up, mostly on our front points, and traversed quickly along its crest, where it had come away from the rock above. Then, as though paying for our fast progress, we made a mistake, going off route and wasting an hour. That familiar sense of anxiety the Eiger provoked crept over us. Above was the Flat Iron, easy enough but horribly exposed to stone fall. We found the twisted piton Brian Nally had relied on to hold Barry Brewster's fall.

Looking down from the top of the Flat Iron, we were shocked to see the other two still at the far end of the Second Icefield. Instead of going straight up as we had, they were moving diagonally.

'If they don't hurry up they're going to reach the Flat Iron when the stones start.'

We shouted instructions but they were too far away to hear: two tiny ants on a sweep of grey ice. Their predicament made us feel the danger of our own situation and we pushed on with the climb. Ian cut steps up the steep Third Icefield but then we reached the Ramp, the narrow rock gully stretching leftwards up the face. We felt relieved with rock all around us, so much less exposed than the ice below. I bridged up a chimney, back against one wall, feet against another. It had been cold below but this work soon warmed us up. Ian got the tough pitch, chipping a thin skin of ice off the handholds, slow, painstaking work to reach the top of the Ramp. Somewhere up there was the start of the Traverse of the Gods, leading into the centre of the face to the icefield dubbed the White Spider.

There was a shout from above. Outlined against the cloud was a figure to our right. Were they in trouble? A rescue would be almost impossible. They were Swiss and grinned happily when we reached them. They didn't seem the kind of people you'd expected to meet on the north wall of the Eiger and were moving dreadfully slowly, having only managed 300 feet that day. It seemed too early to stop for a bivouac but that's what they were doing. I felt obliged to offer them our help but they seemed content.

'We are tired. We shall stay here and go on tomorrow.'

We crossed the rubble-strewn ledges of the traverse, clinging to the steep wall above, listening to the mournful tune of the cow horn at Kleine Scheidegg and the rattle of the railway far below. The sounds only emphasized our isolation. Nothing could help us here. At the end of the traverse I stuck my head round the corner to look up the White Spider but was greeted with the shriek of a falling stone. The afternoon bombardment had begun. We might have reached the top that day, but the risk wasn't worth it.

Our bivouac was not as comfortable as the night before but our clothes were dry and there was enough snow for drinks. We dozed and the night didn't drag as it often does. Next morning we raced to the top of the Spider but then lost our way in the Exit Cracks. The line we were on was so easy I became suspicious, and launched up an evil-looking groove almost bereft of cracks. At one point I had to bridge round a loose flake of rock, the rope dropping cleanly down to Ian sixty feet below, feet pasted to rock that was covered with a film of ice.

'You got your hard pitch,' he said, gasping for breath as he followed. 'Are you sure that was on the route? There should have been pegs on it.' It soon became apparent we'd come too far right. I'd been right first time. At least the climbing now felt like child's play; we took the rope off and raced towards the summit icefield. Looking down, I noticed the immense gulf below our feet, dropping away to the woods and valley thousands of feet below.

'I reckon we could do with the rope,' Ian said. I agreed wholeheartedly. We went to the top cautiously, full of gratitude for our good fortune. I have never been on a climb with such a grim atmosphere, partly from my own dark experiences, but also from its very structure, an amphitheatre that focuses all your fears. On the summit, in sunshine, we munched dried fruit and basked in feelings of joy and relief. Two hours later we were back in Kleine Scheidegg. Entering the hotel, the proprietor, Fritz von Almen, called us into his office.

'Could you tell me the names of the two climbers who were behind you?' We told him and asked him why, even though we could guess. 'I'm afraid I have bad news for you. They are dead.'

Tom Carruthers and Anton Moderegger had been caught out, he said, somewhere between where we had seen them and the top of the Flat Iron. I wondered if they couldn't just be out of sight, perhaps in the Ramp?

'No, I'm afraid not. I searched the lower part of the face with my telescope and was able to pick out their bodies.'

Even in the perfect conditions we'd enjoyed, the Eiger had made its claim.

Chapter Six

Making My Way

The impact of climbing the Eiger's north wall was extraordinary. Harold Macmillan, then the prime minister, sent me a telegram: 'Warm congratulations on your courageous and skilful climb.' My mother's golf club in Barnet wrote to her offering their congratulations, which didn't do me any harm either. My father Charles, having been out of touch for years, was suddenly reminded of my existence. He had remarried and I now discovered the existence of three half-sisters, Alison, Rosemary and Liz, and a half brother, Gerald. When I went down to Bristol to talk about the Eiger they came along and I took them to the Avon Gorge so they could scramble around; I found that I liked the idea of having some siblings. I also began a new chapter with my father; I never felt any filial connection to him, but as an adult I enjoyed his company.

The newspaper coverage was the largest for any climb I ever did, including Everest in 1975. Every national newspaper ran a banner headline. I'd agreed to a deal with the *Daily Express*: 'Bonington who beat the killer peak starts his own story.' But I was naïve. The *Express* whisked us off to a hotel in the country the moment we got back to Britain to secure the exclusive. What I hadn't properly understood was to what scale they would syndicate the material. Although I'd been rewarded, the amount the newspaper made from that syndication dwarfed my end of the deal; Don thought I'd become a cynical manipulator of the press, writing to tell me so in a rather bitter letter, but in fact the opposite was true. What it did give me was a foot in the door.

Opportunities arose spontaneously to give lectures or write articles. More importantly it brought me to the attention of Livia Gollancz, then running her father Victor's publishing firm. Livia offered me an advance on a book about my climbing life so far and would prove an indispensable support on my first steps as a writer. At that point, I'd written a handful of articles for climbing journals. I had a more natural feel for photography and thanks to where I'd been – the Frêney pillar, Nuptse, the Eiger – there was a demand for my images. I was less experienced as a lecturer, despite my years in the army. My first climbing lecture had been a ruse to escape my regiment for a few days after a young Cambridge undergraduate called Nick Estcourt invited me to speak. We would become close friends.

The boost in my income from newspaper rights and the sudden rush of lectures meant I could take Wendy with me to Patagonia. Our relationship was not yet a year old; we'd only married a few months before and the prospect of being apart was intolerable. Barrie Page, the leader of the expedition, was bringing his wife Elaine and three-year-old son, Martin, so it didn't seem unreasonable that Wendy should join us. Before we left, the team gave an interview to the *Daily Express*, teeing up some despatches I'd agreed to send from the mountain. 'My wife's going as far as Trinidad,' Don Whillans told the feature writer Nancy Banks-Smith, 'and that's near enough for me.' The notion of having women along appalled Don, and I'm sure he wasn't the only one. 'Women are out of place in a base camp. They fuss. They expect attention.' For Wendy, as Banks-Smith noted, 'Patagonia is the wind in her hair and riding the half-broken horses of the nearest ranch.'

The expedition's objective was a magnificent series of three granite towers in the Torres del Paine national park, *paine* meaning blue in the local Tehuelche language. The first tourist to see them was Lady Florence Caroline Dixie, sister of Lord Francis Douglas, who perished descending the Matterhorn. She described them in

1880 as Cleopatra's Needles, but that doesn't really do justice to their scale. The southernmost is generally regarded as the highest but it was the central tower that seemed to us the plum. An Italian team had climbed the north tower in 1958.

Barrie had been deputy-leader of the first British expedition to the range two years before, together with Derek Walker, friends from Bristol University's mountaineering club. It had been a survey rather than a climbing trip, but the expedition's leader, Peter Henry, had tragically drowned after the little boat he was in capsized. Barry was effervescent, fast-talking and often difficult to pin down; Derek was more easy-going and modest, but had in fact done the bulk of the organization, including a sterling job on the food. Vic Bray had also been part of the 1961 expedition and was planning a film of our adventures.

Don Whillans had recommended me but we both felt we needed more climbers: John Streetly, who I knew from Nuptse, and Ian Clough, who postponed his teacher training for another year. I felt apprehensive about how Don and I would manage the differences between us. He'd told Derek all about it, how he'd told me to 'come back to earth and stop fucking around in the stratosphere'. For my part I felt his attitude unfair, based more on the notion that I'd somehow betrayed him going to the Eiger with Ian. It was no more than he would have done; the year before he'd set off for the Frêney pillar without us, while Ian and I were on a training climb. It was only bad weather that delayed him.

'I respect him and I like him,' I wrote in my expedition diary, 'but we are too far apart, too different to ever achieve any kind of intimacy. I think a lot of the trouble was from my own immaturity. I have never been at ease with Don – the nearest I get to it, I suppose, is on a climb, in really hard circumstances, when survival is the main problem. Then we are brought close together.'

The expedition to the Torres del Paine would be no exception. We embarked at Liverpool towards the end of October bound for Valparaiso, at the height of the Cuban missile crisis; I remember Derek wondering if he'd ever see his new wife Hilary again.

Arriving in Santiago in mid November, as Barrie completed permit formalities with the Chilean authorities, we learned an Italian expedition was on its way, intent on the same objective. We would have to get our skates on.

Those first days on the wide-open grasslands of Patagonia were a delight, rattling along rough dirt tracks from Punta Arenas in two beat-up trucks, Wendy alongside me, the sky filled with a huge fleet of Zeppelin-shaped clouds driven in from the Pacific by the Roaring Forties. At the last checkpoint two *carabineros* in neat grey uniforms, pistols at their side, waved us down and quizzed Barrie in Spanish. He produced our papers, but the conversation quickly became heated.

'Why won't the buggers let us through?' Don asked, as we gathered round in concern. 'We've got permission to climb the tower, haven't we?'

'Of course we have,' Barrie said, although, as it turned out, it was more of a general permission to go into the Paine massif; he'd talked about climbing Paine but didn't have it in black and white. Luckily for us, the police post was by an estancia and its English manager emerged to talk us through, but had to watch bemused as we carried on the argument with Barrie. Don smelled a rat, feared the 'Eye-ties' might use it to their advantage. And it was true there was something of the salesman about Barrie; he could be breezily vague over arrangements, and not just when it came to permits.

It was a joy to be back on the road in the cold fresh air of morning, flamingos lifting off a small lake as the trucks bumped past. We pulled up a small hill and there, across the rolling green waves of the pampas, some twenty miles away, was the slender blade of granite we had come to climb. I felt as though Wendy and I had escaped from a narrow constriction, the small bedsit in Hampstead, the nine-to-five of a sales rep, and stepped into a new and bigger life.

Our base camp was near another estancia nestling below the mountains. It reminded me of a Scottish hill farm, a small stone-built house blending into the landscape. That night, the owner, a heavy man of Slavic origin called Juan Radíc, invited us to feast on a spitted lamb. Juan was a businessman softened by the city; his brother Pedro ran the farm day to day and was everything one imagined a gaucho to be: tall, lean and hard, with a face battered by the winds and tinged with melancholy. We were initiated into the Patagonian practice of squirting wine down our throats from the wine sack. Pedro sprinkled a few mysterious drops over each of our heads and then the feast began.

Next morning, nursing monstrous hangovers, we set out for the Central Tower of Paine. The tower was hidden from base camp by the rounded bulk of Paine Chico, and we sweated round its shoulder in a fug of boozy sweat and flies, stopping for frequent rests. Beyond lay a long valley to the east of the mountain. From this angle the mountain looked impregnable. Our approach lay to the west of the peak but we would need an intermediary camp to bring supplies and equipment round before we could start climbing. Vic and I drew the short straws and were left behind to ferry loads.

So far the weather had been perfect, as it had been, we were told, for the previous fortnight. 'That could be the whole season's good weather gone,' Don grumbled, a little sourly. On the other hand, he had been here before and I hadn't; it is hard to conceive how bad the weather in Patagonia can be until you experience it. The weather held for a further three days, long enough for Don and Barrie to reach the col between the North and Central Towers.

'It'll go all right,' Don told us. 'There's a crack line practically all the way up, with only one gap on a slab at about quarter-height.'

That was on 4 December. It seemed inevitable that it was my turn to be out in front when the weather broke. The route to the west face of the towers climbed through dense scrub and then through a chaotic mess of boulders to the lateral moraine of a glacier. From there, the Central and North Towers rose up like Norman keeps on their earthworks: imposing and impregnable. The first snowflakes fell as we picked our way up the scree below. The sharply defined col acted as a funnel concentrating all the fury of the winds howling across the Patagonian ice cap.

Despite the gale, we sorted the gear and I started climbing but I was buffeted by the wind and my hands went numb. Having climbed the initial step I banged in a peg and abseiled off. We'd climbed the first twelve feet of the tower and having staked our claim, turned and fled down the scree. There was no point staying at the high camp, eating our way through food we had to carry up, so we collapsed the tent to save it from the gale and hiked down to the valley.

For the next few weeks we lived in a state of indecision, snatched opportunities and grumbling resentments. The uncertain Patagonian weather seemed almost designed to exploit my habit for internal debate. I frequently felt I was in the wrong place at the wrong time, unable to exploit the short windows of good weather. I wrote in my diary: 'Having taken a decision, I have the terrible habit of reviewing it and re-reviewing it – often deciding that I had taken the wrong decision after all . . . The thing I must realize, and then practise, is that a positive decision, once taken and then pursued, is more right than dithering . . .'

Easier said than done. It was agonizing to wake up under the tower in a raging storm, hike back to the valley and then watch as climbers there prepared to go up because the weather seemed to be clearing. Coming down from the mountain one day I bumped into Wendy unexpectedly. We were delighted to see each other and all thoughts of climbing flew from my head. Later that night, in Wendy's arms, gorged with lovemaking, the anxiety crept back over me. The sky was clear and studded with stars; I should be back up there, taking my turn in the lead. Whole weeks passed in this state of confused anxiety that we weren't making progress.

Looking back, I understand the conflicting pressures I faced on the Paine expedition, driven I suppose by a mixture of ambition and anxiety to make my new life work. I fretted over my dispatches for the *Daily Express*. On the Eiger they'd used a journalist to write up interviews, but this had sensationalized the story, which as a climber made me cringe. This time I wanted to be in control. Of course, the sub-editors sprinkled sensation over my copy like salt, and the resulting concoction irritated my companions.

Another source of tension was the presence of Wendy and Elaine, with little Martin, at base camp. Elaine had put her foot down about coming and Barrie had left the team with the impression that she, Martin and Wendy would be staying at a nearby estancia. Wendy imagined she would spend her weeks riding horses across the pampas. However, Barrie hadn't worked the plan out. Quite reasonably, their hosts had soon had enough of catering for two women and a small child, so the trio moved to Pedro's on the understanding that Wendy and Elaine would do the cooking. But the brothers didn't much like having a small child tearing round or Barrie and me dropping by to spend the night, so the women ended up in base camp. This did not please the team. The women were banned from the mess tent, as though it was a London club. Martin, poor little fellow, became an object of resentment. Wendy was shocked at the level of chauvinism. I found myself torn between my overbearing ambition and wandering through the pampas hand in hand with my new wife.

The arrival of the Italians changed everything. These were hard men from the Dolomites, their undoubted star being Armando Aste, who was none too pleased to discover that the South Patagonia Survey Expedition was in reality a climbing team on what he regarded as his route. Barrie's solution was to chat them up, ply them with wine and be reasonable. Our ropes were already on the tower and possession was most of the law.

Don knew better. 'If you haven't got proper permission for us to climb the tower, Barrie, they might well have us moved off altogether.'

The obvious solution, I suggested, was to move up the hill out of reach of the police, re-siting the top camp in the trees below the scree slope.

'I think that's still too low,' Don said. 'What we could do with is some kind of hut just below the tower. You could keep a pair in it the whole time and nip out when the weather got fine.'

Thus was born the first Whillans box, a prefabricated and near-bombproof box tent with a sturdy wooden frame looted from Juan's wine store and covered with heavy tarpaulin. It weighed 200 pounds but between all of us it was portable. On the wooden door we scrawled the inscription: HOTEL BRITANNICO – MEMBERS ONLY. That night, talking in broken French to one of the Italians, I discovered, as Don predicted, they had no intention of backing off the Central Tower. It was what they had come to climb. The race was on. The opposition judged us disorganized, even shambolic, betrayed by the vast pile of empty beer bottles outside our mess tent. Yet the presence of an invading force had united us.

On New Year's Day, despite the hangovers, seven of us set off for the mountain carrying the prefab as surreptitiously as possible. Once constructed, the hut allowed us to forge ahead. When the winds raged, the Italians would scuttle down while two of us waited out the bad weather. Dropping down to the valley for provisions, Barrie and I hid among the trees, like a couple of partisans, as the Italians moved up to their camp. I quite enjoyed the subterfuge. I don't think the Italians had much idea of the progress we were making.

Our newfound sense of unity extended to Don and me. Our relationship, so badly strained after the Eiger, was patched over, at least for now. One night at base camp, during a good session of drinking, I went out to relieve myself. I realized Don was out there, doing the same. The sky was clear and the same thought was in our heads: would someone beat us to the summit? I wrote in my diary: 'We looked at each other. He said: "I don't think we've miscalculated." I think the old bugger is as keen as I am to get to the top first. I replied. "You know Whillans, we haven't climbed together yet. We had best get together." Don said: "Aye, I'm thinking that – we'll go and do the next spell."'

Having tiptoed past the Italians so as not to wake them, we arrived back at the col to discover a huge mound of their equipment. It looked much newer and certainly better than ours. I joked that we could toss it over the other side.

'No need,' said Don. 'Well beat them by fair means.'

In 1963, our ropes were made of hemp, far weaker and more vulnerable to wear than nylon. It didn't bear thinking about what the wind was doing to them. We had no clamps, like Jumars, or other aids to climb the rope; in those days we simply pulled ourselves up hand over hand. There were no hard steel pegs, harnesses or expansion bolts. As Don pulled up on the long blank slab to our high point, the rope he was holding simply parted. Most people, me included, would have heeled back in surprise and fallen. Don had enough presence of mind and agility to keep his balance and then coolly tie the ends of the rope together. I think I was more shaken than he was.

From our high point, we surveyed the ground ahead. An open groove led to a square-cut roof and then soared out of sight round a corner. It looked like it would go. I felt the frustration of the last few weeks melt away. The rock was warm and rough; it felt satisfying, even pleasurable, touching it. Even after more than fifty years, the memory of that pitch leaps from my mind, every bit as hard as *Cenotaph Corner* and every bit as good. We could hear vague shouts below. The Italians had been drawn to the mountain as we were by good weather, but emerged from their tents to see us high up the tower. We saw them point, then go into a huddle, then start packing rucksacks. All thoughts of an independent Italian route had clearly been abandoned. When they reached the foot of the tower, they started zooming up our ropes. We were too absorbed to care much. As long as we didn't steer into any dead ends they wouldn't catch us.

The angle eased and we picked up speed, neither speaking, in total harmony, racing the sun as it slipped towards the horizon.

'It doesn't look too bad from here,' Don said. I worried about the time; it was easier but there was a long way to go still. 'We'll just have to go a bit faster. We'll leave our bivy gear and travel light.'

Even though the climbing was easier, it was choked with ice; I marvelled at Don's ability to cover this awkward ground so quickly. We were still in a race, not with the Italians, but the setting sun.

There was a series of short towers and at the bottom of each I thought we'd arrived at the summit. Don went into the lead, crossed a short, steep wall, went round the corner and let out a whoop. I found him sitting on a block the size of a table; he stuck up a thumb for the camera and then we took in the view, the sun's red orb dropping behind the ice cap, the mountains around us grand and impregnable. The wind had died completely and we felt bathed in peace after weeks of struggle.

By the time we reached the rucksacks we had been on the go for fifteen hours. Tortured with thirst, we hunted through the sacks for the matches. No matches, no melted snow. Don didn't care about that: 'I'm dying for a bloody smoke.' We found them, and he settled back contentedly to wait for dawn. When it came, we started on the first of many abseils, my weary mind urging caution. We met the Italians stirring from their bivouac, Aste glowering at us, while big friendly Taldo shook our hands and offered his congratulations in broken English.

'It is good you getting to the top! It is your route.'

Derek was waiting at the col, waving a bottle of booze. He and Vic were on their way to the top of the North Tower. We had just one more abseil but the rope was horribly tangled and jammed in a crack below us. There was a length of hemp fixed handy, so Don tied it to a peg and slid carefully down this instead. As I followed, I tried to free the jammed climbing rope but under the added force the hemp line snapped.

I somersaulted backwards, thinking: 'I'll hit the snow at the bottom.' I did, but kept going, rolling over and over, hands clawing at the snow, until I came to a stop on the brink of a 500-foot drop. Panting with fear, as the adrenalin faded I became aware of an agonizing pain in my ankle. I was sure it was broken. The exhilaration of the climb was gone, replaced by the long, drawn-out agony of hobbling down to our makeshift hut. I bashed out a report of our success for the *Daily Express* and handed it to John Streetly to take down, and then slumped back exhausted and in excruciating pain.

'You'd better do the cooking, Chris,' Don said. 'I'm no good at it.'

Once he'd had his spaghetti, he was off, suggesting I stayed where I was until the swelling went down. Derek and Ian came back from their ascent of the North Tower, so at least I wasn't on my own that night. Next morning, hobbling in pain, it took me four times as long to reach the camp in the woods. The other two were long gone, back to the wine and roast mutton at base camp. But Vic Bray was there. 'I've got to get a bit more film up here,' he said, offering to go down next day with me. I was deeply grateful for his company as I hobbled down to base camp.

Wendy and I got a lift to Punta Arenas where, at the hospital, an X-ray showed a hairline fracture, and my leg was plastered for a week. We spent it in bed, me in a fit of petulant frustration, playing Scrabble, which Wendy invariably won. I have always been an appalling loser, and the board went flying out of our first-floor window after one loss too many. The rest of the boys were probably on top of the South Tower by now. When the plaster came off, I calmed down. We booked a flight north to Puerto Montt and spent three weeks wandering through Chile's Lake District, catching steamers and local buses, cooking over wood fires, skinny-dipping and drinking cheap local wine. From Bariloche we travelled to San Martin de los Andes and went riding through the scrubby hills, Wendy for once the expert and me the bumbling beginner. The trials of the expedition were left far behind.

We arrived back in Britain that spring of 1963 in the curious position of having nowhere to live and the freedom to pick anywhere. I was freelance, but wasn't sure in what. Our possessions amounted to a few clothes, plenty of books, Wendy's paints and her guitar, and my climbing gear. I had spent all the money I'd made from the Eiger, but with the advance from Gollancz I bought a brand new minivan. My immediate task was obvious: write the book. Yet I kept putting it off, frightened at the scale of the task. I found myself veering off into easier, more distracting alternatives, of which there was no shortage.

Staying in London wasn't an option. We had no money and anyway, Wendy wanted to be deep in the countryside. Wales was somewhere I loved, and I thought idly of studying at Bangor University, but we settled on the Lakes. Each of its valleys, spreading like spokes from the central core of hills, had its own special character, the farms blending into the landscape, the scale more human and less stark. We felt at home there almost immediately and I realized that there was a whole new climbing world for me to explore.

Finding somewhere to live was a challenge, our romantic notions of a charming little cottage for a pound a week being fanciful even in 1963. The barman at the Royal Oak in Ambleside told me he had spent the previous winter in a room over a garage at nearby Loughrigg Farm. 'It's pretty rough,' he said, 'but at least it's a roof over your heads.' The barman's name was Mick Burke, one of a beatnik group who had quit their jobs to go climbing instead, in Mick's case giving up life as an insurance clerk in his native Wigan. We rushed round to ask the farmer to see if it was still available.

'It's a bit rough, you know,' he warned us.

Neither of them was joking. It was a fair-sized room lit by a couple of windows, but the walls were brown with dirt and the floor covered in rotting linoleum, the furniture most likely pulled from a dump with the nearest tap in the yard. As for the toilet, it was unspeakable: an earth closet at the back of the pigsty. On the other hand we could look across woodland to the still waters of Loughrigg Tarn and beyond to the open fell of Langdale Pikes.

We spent three months at Loughrigg, but it was a temporary arrangement that became more so when we discovered Wendy was pregnant. Wendy didn't want a child at this stage; she wanted more freedom, to develop her life as an artist and see something of the world. She embarked on a regime of hot baths and vigorous exercise. I had more mixed emotions: when viewed logically, the prospect of fatherhood was appalling but after a couple of drinks, a deep-rooted desire to procreate took hold of me.

Our pressing need for suitable accommodation was met through the intervention of the Lakeland artist William Heaton Cooper and his wife. We came home one day to an invitation from them to go round for tea and there met another artist, Fenwick Patterson, who knew of a furnished house called Woodland Hall Lodge, part of Woodland Hall farm, in the quiet and enigmatic country between Broughton-in-Furness and Coniston. The front rooms faced the endearing hump of Blow Knot Fell, a place to fall in love with. Woodland was a backwater, hidden from tourists, largely still is, a place that stands back from the bigger hills but looks across at them, the northern horizon dominated by the Old Man of Coniston. The owner Beeny Dickson, almost birdlike but with apparently limitless energy and curiosity, had planned to rent it as a holiday let but on the promise of a year's lease offered us the place for three pounds a week. We'd been paying five for our room in London.

With our new home sorted, I could focus on my next project. That summer we drove the van to Zermatt to meet Hamish MacInnes. After the Eiger, I'd had an idea for a film about the face, but in the way of these things, the plan had been kicked around and condensed to a smaller venture for the BBC about the north face of the Matterhorn. By the time we arrived Hamish had set us up nicely with the tourist board, which offered us subsidized lodging and free lift passes. What he couldn't organize was the weather. For week after week, we patiently waited for conditions to come good while Hamish filmed cows and goats and anything else that looked remotely interesting. We soloed the Hörnli with the crowds of guided tourists, but the summer was a bust as far as climbing went.

Yet that summer was the start of my real interest in photography, a subject that also obsessed Hamish. Inspired by his example, I sank our entire savings into a second-hand medium-format Hasselblad that could not have been more unsuitable for climbing. It was bulky, heavy and even the lens was worth a hundred quid. Yet for the rest of that summer in Zermatt, I wandered around the hillsides above the village taking chocolate-box images of mountains framed by trees or reflected in little lakes. In the process, I became more visually aware.

Coming home from the Alps had always been an anticlimax for me; the summer was over and there wasn't much to look forward to at home. This year was different. From our initial uncertainty about parenthood, we were both now excited at the prospect and also at returning to our little house in Woodland. Wendy was six months pregnant, and putting my hand on her bump to feel the baby was like a promise of the future. On the other hand, I also felt very vulnerable. Returning home meant writing my book, but the advance was now spent and we were flat broke. 'My finances are terrifying,' I wrote to my mother. 'A £100 overdraft and £100 unpaid bills: though lecture money is coming in now, it will be some time before we are out of the murky.' Through the autumn and winter I made the long journey south to give lectures on the Eiger. In those early years, an average lecture earned me ten pounds: a good gig earned twenty. I also had regular work for the Royal Navy in Plymouth lecturing to young sailors for a pound a go, although they would book me to do five of those a day. Over the winter I cleared our overdraft, giving us breathing space to have adventures in the summer.

Not surprisingly, it was often lonely and depressing, leveraging what appeared to be my only asset: an ascent of the north face of the Eiger, which is what people seemed most interested in. I would spend several days, even weeks away from home, sometimes sleeping in the van, in a different place each night. The joy and excitement I experienced as I neared home and caught sight of the familiar landmarks was my compensation. I developed a deep love of the Lakes in this period, and some strong friendships too, often with others who had chosen a less conventional way of life, like the writer Tony Greenbank, fighting like me to make the freelance life work, and my old friend Mike Thompson. Martin Boysen was another regular climbing partner. Many of my best new rock climbs were done in those years as I got to know the crags of Lakeland. They offered an escape from anxieties about my future.

At the end of 1963, Wendy went into labour. Our first child, a son, was born in the early hours of New Year's Eve. I had wanted to be with her for the birth: by the early 1960s that wasn't unusual in London. Not so in a Cumbrian cottage hospital. 'No one's ever asked for anything like that,' said the matron frostily. 'We haven't got the facilities, and anyway you've got to think of the feelings of the midwife.' The gynaecologist was more sympathetic – 'My dear chap!' – but no less inflexible: 'We just haven't got the facilities.' He concluded: 'I think it's best to let the wife get on with it on her own.'

When her contractions started, I was shooed out, and then sat in the waiting room for hours while Wendy went through a protracted labour, mostly on her own. Towards the end I could hear her crying out in pain but couldn't go near. I became so convinced she was dying I went down on my knees and started praying, somewhat hypocritically for a confirmed agnostic. When I finally got to see her, Wendy was pale and exhausted but wonderfully tranquil while the baby, freshly washed, seemed almost preternaturally ugly. We called him Conrad. I wrote to my mother: 'Were you at all disappointed not getting a girl or is the excitement of getting a grandchild sufficient?'

Life went on pretty much as before. We still got around a lot and in many ways our situation was idyllic. Wendy would come with me to some of my lectures and when the season was over I had long periods at home, skirmishing with my book. I sent the first two chapters to Livia Gollancz in early 1964, way behind schedule, but she sent back an encouraging note and said she was happy to wait if I could keep up the standard. Wendy learned to drive and then developed an interest in folk singing. She already played classical guitar and had a pure, haunting voice that was full of emotion, rather like Joan Baez. She'd drive over from Woodland to the Lamp Lighter in Keswick, a folk club run by my old climbing partner Paul Ross, where she soon developed a following.

Yet if our domestic lives were happy, my future still seemed cloudy. That first summer of parenthood, the year I turned thirty,

I spent weeks in the Alps, trying to recapture the glories of 1961 and 1962, without much success. Lacking a regular Alpine climbing partner, I took up an offer from Tom Patey to join him in Chamonix that summer. He was climbing with Joe Brown, and they had with them a third, a much younger and less experienced man called Robin Ford, for whom they wanted a partner. Sometimes these chance pairings work well, but not this time: we were just too different in terms of age and experience.

Tom was already a great friend, one of the outstanding Scottish mountaineers of the post-war period, having climbed two stunning peaks in the Karakoram, Rakaposhi and Mustagh Tower, the latter with Joe and my London friend Ian McNaught-Davis in 1956. Yet it was more his zest for life that endeared me to him. You could always guarantee that a holiday, even a short weekend, with Tom would turn into a magical mystery tour of pubs, people and mountains. He kept black books full of photographs and diagrams detailing prospective new routes, and the day rarely ended without an impromptu ceilidh and a host of interesting new friends.

He and Joe made a formidable partnership, as I wrote in my diary that summer: 'Climbing with Tom and Joe has certainly bumped my ego and complacency. They are so much more effective than I am at the moment, though I think I shall build up, as I normally do.' Yet Tom's approach to the big mountains was very different to mine. Alpinism for him was a light-hearted holiday, something to fit in around a fun night out playing his accordion in a bar somewhere. (It was around this time he wrote his very funny song 'Onward Christian Bonington'.) Tom relied on extraordinary speed in the mountains to get himself up and down, never too concerned if it was particularly hard or not. That summer we did do a couple of interesting new routes but nothing on the scale I wanted.

In early September, still without much to show for the summer, I travelled to Grindelwald to do an interview about the Eiger for the BBC. I'd hoped to be talking about my climb two years before, but the producer wanted something newer and persuaded me to talk about the next big thing on the face: the Eiger Direct. Several leading alpinists, including me, were contemplating this challenge: a line that went straight up the face taking its hardest challenges full on. It had been one of my targets that summer. But the most likely candidate was a charismatic American ex-air force pilot called John Harlin.

Describing the equipment and tactics required for such an immense challenge, I felt suddenly cheapened, doubting my own integrity. I didn't have the resources to mount a challenge, nor even the right climbing partner. The cold reality was that my ambitions were little more than pipe dreams. I'd spent the last two years in a kind of limbo, not moving forward. Now I was describing how someone else might achieve something I badly wanted for myself. I sloped back to Chamonix in a state of depression, unable to focus on climbing. All I wanted was to be home with Wendy and Conrad, reabsorbed into the security of our new family and our Lakeland retreat.

Chapter Seven

Eiger Direct

John Harlin was a year younger than me, with a reputation for extreme commitment and obsessive ambition. I met him in the summer of 1965, at his home in the Swiss mountain town of Leysin, introduced by Tom Patey. We had driven over with Wendy and Conrad to find Rusty Baillie, a Rhodesian climber who had made the second British ascent of the Matterhorn's north face, with Dougal Haston. Rusty and I met soon after when I arrived in Zermatt to work with Hamish MacInnes on our Matterhorn film. He seemed like the sort of man for a direct route on the Eiger.

At the time, I regarded John as a competitor rather than an ally. The idea of a direct line on the Eiger had been linked with his name from the start. He had climbed the original route shortly before Ian Clough and me, making the first American ascent, and his thoughts immediately turned to the challenge. John had camped under the face in the summer of 1963, but the weather was terrible that season. He had, however, got to know two Italians, Roberto Sorgato and Ignazio Piussi, my rival on the Frêney pillar, and they became the nucleus for another abortive attempt in the winter of 1964. John tried again that summer with French alpinists René Desmaison, whom we had also met on the Frêney pillar, and André Bertrand. They were stormed off from the top of the Second Icefield. The profile of this 'last' great problem was rising fast.

The Eiger was the natural stage for someone like John; he

revelled in its public profile. He was known, with some cynicism, as the 'Blond God' thanks to his Tarzan-like physique, rugged looks and shock of hair, but he had a mixed reputation. Sorgato considered him 'arrogant and presumptuous', and while he was undoubtedly an athlete, 'he didn't really have the habits, practice and understanding of mountains that every good mountaineer should have'. He inspired students at the school he worked at in Leysin, but others found him overbearing, even controlling. The American Larry Ware, introduced to climbing by Harlin, said: 'He was very selfish. But most ambitious and successful people are.' I'm sure people said the same about me.

When John opened the door, I understood his nickname: the thick biceps and thatch of blond hair. He ushered us into a spacious, minimally furnished living room whose walls were hung with brooding abstract paintings, which I later learned were his own work. John saw himself as very much the Renaissance man, a sort of warrior-poet-climber. He had served with the United States Air Force, but after spending a year sleeping near his fighter-bomber, armed with nuclear weapons, he told his commanding officer he was no longer prepared to drop his bombs on his designated target: the historic city of Prague.

My reservations quickly fell away. I found him outgoing, frank and immensely enthusiastic and we swiftly went from rivals to teammates, with Rusty of course. John invited us to camp in the small quarry behind his house; there was a freshwater tap, we could take occasional baths inside the house. 'Conrad certainly laps it up,' I wrote to my mother. 'He's outside all day and is getting a good tan.' Up the road was the Club Vagabond, the now legendary social centre for the English-speaking community and thousands of travellers and climbers who moved through Leysin with the seasons. The prospect of the Eiger Direct gave me a renewed sense of purpose, bringing to an end the mood of drift, even despair, that had settled over me the previous winter.

Back from the Alps that autumn, my worries still circled. My mother had acted as a sounding board for my writing; I'd sent her early chapters and paid attention to her suggestions. Now I was writing to her with a sense of desperation. Getting back into the book was 'hell', I wrote to her, underlining the word several times. A month later I wrote: 'Book goes slow and hard: God knows what Gollancz will do.' My mother was also at a turning point in her life, leaving advertising to take up a teaching career. I found myself telling her: 'I have just about decided to go to teacher training college next year.'

The start of 1965 was perhaps the hardest time. Gathering for Hogmanay in Scotland I felt disconnected from the excitement of my friends. The book was only half finished but a year over deadline and I'd just finished another long lecture tour talking about past glories with no real vision of where future ones might be found. Albert Smith, the first professional mountaineer, climbed Mont Blanc in 1851 and spent the rest of his life talking about it until he collapsed from exhaustion. I didn't want the same fate. Wendy, who wasn't prone to the same black moods, tried to persuade me not to take things so seriously; we were living life on our own terms, even if it wasn't what my mother judged to be the safe option.

The party on New Year's Eve was just north of Glasgow at the home of Mary Stewart, a friend of Tom's who shared his rare ability to make things happen. An American vet who had arrived for post-graduate studies and fallen in love with the hills, her weather-beaten face shone with warmth and kindness. She lived in bohemian chaos with her five children, dogs and numberless other animals and I remember her in old Levi's and bare feet, a frontierswoman with a mane of copper hair. She became a great friend to both of us.

That night I found myself watching John Cleare, a climbing friend and professional photographer, dancing with his striking blonde girlfriend; he seemed the very symbol of the success and self-confidence eluding me. Here was a man with a real skill and a career that was going somewhere. It never occurred to me that this shell of self-confidence might conceal the same doubts and fears I was experiencing but the grind of the last few weeks had made me lose perspective. Before midnight I had retreated to bed, Wendy following me up, upset, tearful, confused about the darkness of my mood.

We woke to bright sunshine and a hard frost; no depression could survive that stimulus. Piling into the car we drove north, leaving Conrad for the first time in the care of others, meeting up with Tom and sharing in another of his madcap forty-eight hours that ended with a gang of us narrowly escaping disaster having lost our way while following Tom down in the dark from Creag Meaghaidh. Wendy and Maggie Boysen, waiting in the valley for us to return, found themselves becoming increasingly anxious as the hours passed. It was undoubtedly an irresponsible way to start the year. Yet somehow those two days marked a turning point. I had been naïve to imagine that my new life as a writer, photographer and lecturer would happen quickly and easily; the necessary skills had to be learned, a head of steam built up. Becoming a good climber had taken time and commitment; the same was true of my new job.

I didn't have a phone at Woodland Hall Lodge, so anyone who wanted me had to send a telegram asking me to call them. I would then drive half a mile to the nearest phone box. Almost as soon as we got home from Scotland a telegram arrived asking me to call a television producer called Brian Kelly. Brian, known as 'Ned', would go on to work for the BBC's Natural History Unit, working with David Attenborough on landmark series like *Life on Earth*, as well as coming to Everest with us in 1975. I was immensely excited: there had already been a few climbing television films made and I'd found myself envying those who were asked to participate. The mainstream media was finally discovering climbing and the potential for a freelance communicator like me was vast.

When I called Ned, he explained he wanted to make a documentary of one of my climbs in the Avon Gorge, close to Brunel's famous suspension bridge. I didn't do a huge number of new routes in Britain, but Avon was one place where I did make a contribution.

This was during my time at Sandhurst, Avon being the best climbing centre within easy range. The biggest challenge was the Main Wall, Avon's most dramatic and frightening cliff, unclimbed until we came along. After several weekends making tentative attempts to get off the ground, I'd finally committed myself to a loose and very steep wall. We named it *Macavity*, after T. S. Eliot's cat, which 'breaks the law of gravity' and is never caught for his crimes.

Despite my fondness for Avon, it didn't seem a good location to me. The cliff, being an old quarry, didn't have the architectural appeal of other crags. I thought instead of Cheddar Gorge winding down to its village in the Mendips. Full of tourists in summer, the best time to climb was midweek in winter. I arranged a reconnaissance with Tony Greenbank, phoning John Cleare to come down from London to take some pictures, while we looked for a line that would make for a spectacular route. We didn't have trouble finding one. A light sprinkling of snow dusted the ground, turning the gorge into a stark, monochrome study. The three of us stood nervously under the tallest part of the cliff, some 400 feet high, and wreathed in ivy. At its right-hand end was a prominent groove that had already been climbed to the halfway mark before escaping right. This was called *Sceptre*. The true challenge went straight up into a steep crack before moving left under an overhang and then up another groove and crack to the top.

'It's bloody steep,' John said. 'Do you think you're on good form?'

'Bloody sure I'm not,' I told him. It was January, I hadn't rock climbed since the autumn and the ledges were covered in snow. Next day, under Ned's watchful eye, we made a brave attempt. I was amazed to climb the first difficult section free but when I moved left towards an overhanging prow I could feel the fear rising in my chest. There was a crack on its nearside, and I banged in a peg underneath it, using this to swing across and feel round to the far side, where I discovered the crack continued.

'There's a crack going right round; it's detached from the rock,' I shouted to John, slowly freezing on his stance.

'Looks pretty solid to me,' he shouted back. With dazzling clarity, I had a vision of myself falling through space with a ton of rock in my hands. Reluctant to commit and with only half an hour of light left, we retreated to fight another day, convinced the route would go. For the next few days, too busy to climb, we lived in fear that climbing wunderkind Pete Crew, rumoured to be interested in 'our' route, would snatch it before we could return. Meeting again under the steep wall, we couldn't see any evidence our route had been done in our absence but could only be sure once we were on it.

There seemed little point repeating the pitches we'd already climbed, so we abseiled to the small stance just before the large detached flake, which we dubbed the Shield. Feeling fresh and with the whole day ahead of me, it didn't seem so imposing. Tony had taken over belaying duties; his charm, as a second, was his enthusiastic flattery. Any leader would feel his ego swelling with Tony calling out encouragement. As he followed me round the Shield he said: 'Great, man, great. You must be feeling terrific about leading that.'

Flushed with pride, I contemplated the big groove above me, craning my neck to see two overhangs, one at thirty feet, the other at sixty. I couldn't believe it would go free, but it did. Wafting up on the hot air of Tony's praise, I found myself looking straight down between my outstretched legs to the ground 300 feet below, where a group of tourists stood slack-jawed watching our progress. The overhangs went more easily than I dared hope and we were soon on the top. We called the route *Coronation Street*, since the film we later made of it was for ITV, and its neighbour was *Sceptre*. It has proved immensely popular, no longer of the highest standard but still imposing. Perhaps the highest accolade was Joe Brown doing it twice.

Buoyed by my film fee, I could look forward to a more productive season in the Alps. The book was finally finished and I had the next instalment of my advance as well. Then Tom Patey called to say he'd been invited to the École Nationale in Chamonix as part

Maximilian, my grandfather, in the Andeman islands. (Chris Bonington Picture Library)

My father Charles on walkabout in Australia. (John Harvey)

Tensions between Nan, on whose knee I'm sitting, and my mum in our garden in Hampstead. (Chris Bonington Picture Library)

Me and Mum in happy times. (Chris Bonington Picture Library)

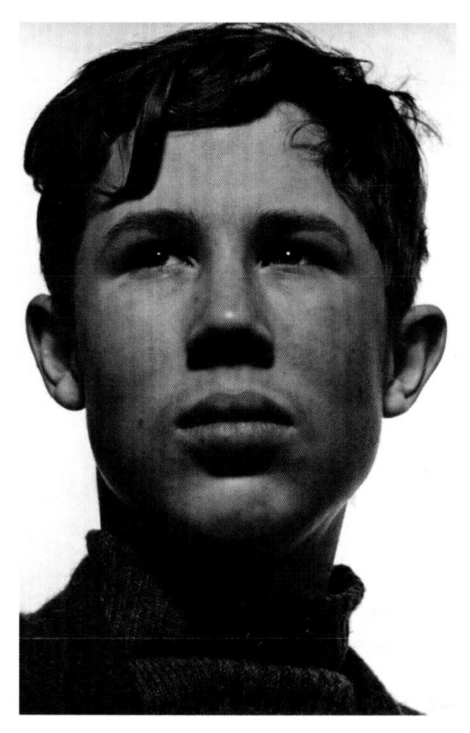

Me at sixteen, when I discovered climbing. (Chris Bonington Picture Library)

My first climb at Harrison's Rocks near Tunbridge Wells. (Henry Rogers)

Junior under officer at Sandhurst – inspection at company drill competition. I'm twenty years old, standing at the front, on the far left of the photograph. (Chris Bonington Picture Library)

)ur wedding day at the register office
ı Hampstead, May 1962. (Chris Bonington
cture Library)

Setting off for the North Wall of the Eiger, early summer 1962, with Don Whillans. (Chris Bonington Picture Library)

Our first home in the Lake District, May 1963 – a single room above a garage, gas light, camping stove for cooking, a cold tap in the farmyard and an earth closet as a loo. (Chris Bonington)

New routing on The Medlar, Raven Crag, Thirlmere, in 1963. (Chris Bonington)

Me with Conrad in spring 1964. (Chris Bonington)

The family: Me, Wendy, Daniel (Joe) and Rupert with our Staffie, Bessie. (Chris Bonington Picture Library)

First British ascent of the south-west Pillar of the Pet Dru, first bivouac – Paul Ross in foreground, Hamis MacInnes, semi-conscious with fractured skull, in the background. (Chris Bonington)

Tom Patey testing the strength of my climbing helmet with an ice hammer. (Chris Bonington)

Don Whillans and myself on bivouac on the Central Pillar of Frêney. (Chris Bonington)

Me and Don on the summit of Mont Blanc after climbing the Central Pillar of Frêney, eating sandwiches supplied by a journalist who had flown in by helicopter. (Chris Bonington)

North face of the Eiger in winter, with the moon on the left in the evening.

(Chris Bonington)

Summiting the North Wall of the Eiger on my first British ascent.

(Chris Bonington)

The Towers of Paine in south Patagonia, Vic Bray and myself recceing and planning the route. (Wendy Bonington)

Me climbing on the Central Tower of Paine. (Chris Bonington)

First descent of the upper reaches of the Blue Nile, from Lake Tana in Ethiopia to the Sudanese frontier, Captain John Blashford-Snell, leader of this army expedition, in command. I was the *Daily Telegraph* journalist and photographer. (Chris Bonington)

Early stages of Annapurna South Face 1970, with base camp just established. Left to right: Don Whillans in the one-piece windproof suit and the Whillans Box, both of which he had designed. One of our sherpas in the background and Mick Burke on the right. (Chris Bonington)

Ian Clough load-carrying on the fixed ropes on the ice ridge above camp 4 on Annapurna. Annapurna 2 is seen in the background (Chris Bonington)

Ian Clough emerging from the Whillans Box at camp 5, from which we supported Whillans and Haston in appalling weather, in our bid for the summit. (Chris Bonington)

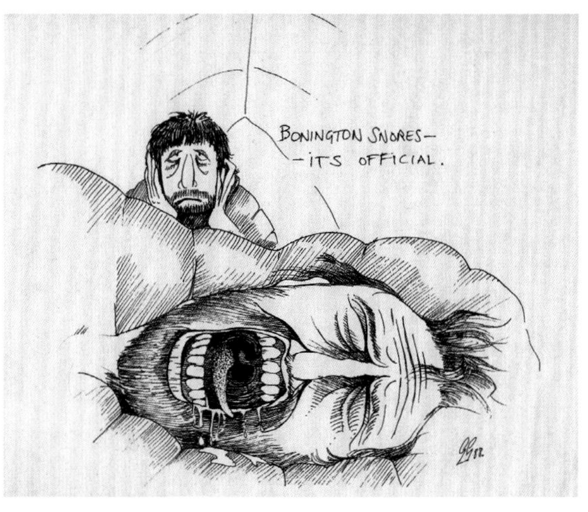

No caption required! (GG)

Me, Doug Scott, Dougal Haston and Martin Boysen examining the elegant spire of Changabang.

(Doug Scott)

The south-west face of Everest.
(Keiichi Yamada)

Everest 1972. Barney Rosedale, expedition doctor, on the radio at camp in the Western Cwm where he sat it out with an effective medical post for most of the expedition in extremely cold conditions. (Chris Bonington)

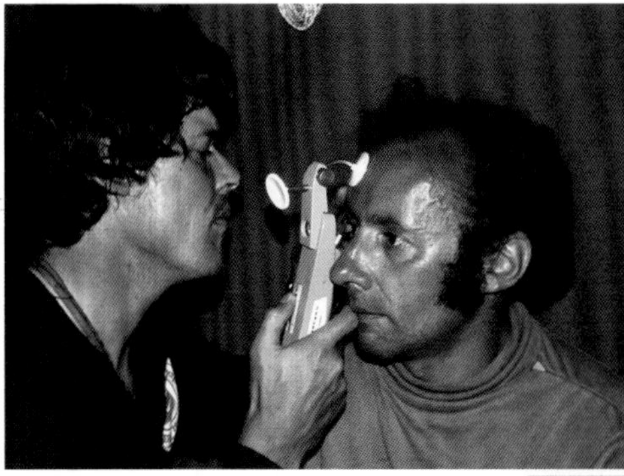

Everest 1975. Charlie Clarke, expedition doctor, also carried out a high-altitude research project. (Chris Bonington)

Dougal Haston climbing the Hillary Step on the successful summit bid on Everest in 1975. (Doug Scott)

of an international climbing meet, all expenses paid. Joe couldn't come, so would I take his place? The cuisine at the École lived up to its reputation; the meet itself was a cross between Noah's Ark, with the climbers two by two, and the Tower of Babel. We tried a new route on the remote south side of Mont Blanc, and completed one on the Aiguille du Midi. We also climbed with the great Lionel Terray in the Vercors, just a few weeks before his tragic death there. Then, after a final sumptuous feast with the very best champagne, we left for Leysin and our encounter with John Harlin.

There was plenty to occupy us as we waited for the right conditions on the Eiger. Rusty and I went to Courmayeur for another attempt on the Brouillard pillar, the route I'd tried with Tom on the south face of Mont Blanc. On our first try we failed to bring enough pitons. On the second we failed to bring our bag of food, each thinking the other had it, but stuck to our plan and came within fifty feet of the top before bad weather forced us to retreat; carrying on over the top of Mont Blanc would have been suicide. We spent a miserable night on a sloping ledge, high on the face, bolts of lightning and violent cracks of thunder shaking the peak.

Wendy and Rusty's girlfriend Pat were relieved to see us when we finally got back to Leysin, several days overdue. Pat was now pregnant with their first child and the two were planning to marry soon. There was a ceremony at the local church where I acted as best man but their honeymoon was interrupted by the return of good weather; Rusty and I, this time with John Harlin and the Scottish climber Brian Robertson, went back to Courmayeur to complete the pillar on Mont Blanc. I learned a lot climbing with John; he was not technically the most proficient, but I liked the steady rhythm of his movement and the confidence of his decisions.

Our difficulty was financing the Eiger. John Cleare had been in Leysin that summer and talked it over with Chris Brasher at the BBC. Chris was not just a famous Olympian, he was also a committed climber, the man behind many of the outside broadcasts that introduced the public to climbing in that era. Yet he was sceptical. The logistics were awkward, the outcome too uncertain.

My contribution was to contact John Anstey, editor of *Weekend Telegraph*, one of the new weekend magazine supplements. John wanted adventure stories as part of the magazine's staple, along-side serious pieces from Vietnam or Northern Ireland. The *Daily Telegraph* had supported the great explorers of the nineteenth century, and they could now do the same, but in colour.

It's hard to conceive of how much money was washing around Fleet Street in those days; the *Weekend Telegraph* didn't have a budget, it just spent what it needed. I'd done a small piece for John to go with an image from the Alps and feeling I had my foot in the door, approached him for backing. John Anstey offered the expedition £1,500, around £20,000 in today's money, sharing the cost with the *Sunday Telegraph*. He also agreed to leave the deal in place when we postponed the attempt until the New Year.

In late September, we drove home, not to Woodland Hall Lodge, but to a new home at Kirkland, below Ennerdale in the western Lakes. We wanted somewhere unfurnished we could make our own, even if it was still rented. The owner hadn't really wanted a family, but we moved into Bank End Cottage just before shooting began for *Coronation Street*. At first we cooked on a camping stove and slept on the floor, but over the months we picked up furniture at sales or inherited pieces from friends and family. Conrad was now eighteen months old and emerging as a rare character, both adventurous and sensitive to others. 'He has a passionate curiosity,' I wrote to my mother, 'and is in every drawer. Every day I lose more of my most precious possessions, but he's great fun.'

Conrad's wonder at the discoveries we made around our new home added to my own: on a wild and windy day I wrapped him up warm in his papoose and walked up Murton Fell as clouds scudded across the sea to break on the hills around us. Ennerdale's water was torn with flecks of white as the wind roared into our faces. Warming ourselves in front of the coal fire, sipping tea, Conrad's cheeks pink from the cold, his eyes glittered with excitement. Wendy was happy too, her singing career picking up momentum and her guitar playing getting better and better.

Restored to this contented equilibrium, I began to reflect on the wisdom of John's plans for the Eiger. It felt like I'd been enchanted, given up my own judgement in favour of a fantastical scheme. I hadn't climbed in the Alps in winter and had lots of questions. John had talked breezily about a ten-day spell of good weather in January, but forecasting wasn't remotely as good then as it is now. What if you got halfway up the face and the weather broke? It's hard for a young climber now to appreciate how poor our clothing was compared to modern high-performance fabrics, which function well when wet. Death could come quickly, and it paid to be cautious. Rusty had withdrawn, uncertain how seriously to take John's plans. I knew John had approached others, like Don Whillans, and been rebuffed.

Then, in November, a journalist called Peter Gillman rang us on our new phone. Not long graduated from Oxford, Peter had been working for *Weekend Telegraph* since that July; he had done some climbing and was an avid hill walker and so was a natural fit for the Eiger story. He wanted to know if he could come and talk to me about it. Hanging up the phone all my doubts surfaced and, more importantly, I told Wendy about them. Ordinarily she accepted any climbing project I might cook up, but if I told her I wasn't confident then she was, quite reasonably, less stoical. Looking back, I can see that I faced a classic dilemma for the professional adventurer, balancing the integrity of what I wanted to do as a mountaineer with the demands of a newspaper editor. It was so easy to tip the balance too far in the direction of your paymaster. Better to offer them your dreams on your terms, and let them decide whether to accept. I had built up a good climbing relationship with John Harlin on the Brouillard pillar; his narcissism was less appealing and in the absence of a concrete plan positively dangerous. I could hardly talk to Peter Gillman with all this in my head, so I cancelled the interview and wrote to John pulling out of the climb.

Almost immediately I wondered what I'd done. Here was the next big thing in world alpinism and I had just stepped back from it, a potential disaster for someone whose only tangible asset was his climbing ability. Was I past it? Was I going soft? Then I got a letter from John Anstey asking if I would photograph the climb for the magazine. The magazine's photo editor Alex Low would be there at the start, but John wanted shots from the mountain, especially the summit. Suddenly, everything changed. This was the chance I had been waiting for, the opportunity to exploit my mountaineering skills in something creative. John arranged for me to fly out to Switzerland as soon as Harlin started.

Other opportunities now presented themselves. Chris Brasher, who had masterminded the BBC's adventurous outside broadcasts, had seen the film of *Coronation Street* and wanted me involved in the next one, not only for the film, but in finding the right location. We agreed to meet on Anglesey in early February, but my van, prematurely aged from the lecture circuit, broke down on the way. By the time we tracked down the BBC team, they had moved on to the Pen y Gwryd Hotel. We'd hardly been introduced when I was called to the phone. John Harlin was about to start. By the following evening I was in Kleine Scheidegg, below the Eiger.

I doubted very much if the team had left; the sky had a light scum of high grey cloud and the forecast was poor. I found John in the team's lair, an attic of the hotel's outbuildings, offered at a discount by our host, Fritz von Almen. John was cooler towards me than he had been in the summer, unsurprisingly given my loyalties were now split. I was the middleman, the conduit for the *Telegraph*. With John was Layton Kor, a big, slightly awkward cowboy, six foot tall and a master aid climber, completely attuned to the latest techniques in Yosemite. Layton was also a rather innocent soul, lured to Switzerland after seeing one of John's lectures in the States, surprised that not everyone in Europe spoke English. He proved his worth on the Eiger with the hardest rock leads.

John's other teammate was Dougal Haston, who, unbeknown to me, had featured in an earlier version of the enterprise. They had fallen out but then settled their differences when I resigned. Dougal and I had met but barely knew each other. He cut a striking figure, always elegantly turned out: Dougal knew the impact of a neckerchief. Yet the cast of his features precluded accusations of pretension. He watched you with hooded eyes, his long face enigmatic and serious, a mixture of high asceticism and lupine menace. Many found him arrogant, and he was, although I suspect it was more that he knew what he wanted and generally did it. The previous spring, driving drunk and without a full licence late one night in Glencoe, he had run down and killed a young student called James Orr and served a short prison sentence in Glasgow's Barlinnie jail.

The accident was not a subject Dougal spoke about but it undoubtedly changed his life for the better; he was much more focused afterwards. I'm not sure anyone ever got to know him, not fully. He was too opaque, too controlled. Yet over the course of the Eiger Direct we became friends and I learned how to handle him. He could be wholly indolent if he felt there was nothing to his advantage by making an effort, but once he fixed on something, nothing would stop him. At heart, he was an intellectual, a philosophy student who saw the world in those terms, an interesting contrast to Layton, who worked as a bricklayer.

The forecast had worsened as I arrived in Switzerland, but I was happy enough, in the pay of the *Weekend Telegraph*, with a comfortable hotel room and some of the best skiing in Europe on my doorstep. Yet my misgivings returned. There was a gulf between John's grand pronouncements and the practical planning and execution required for a climb like this. John had collected an impressive amount of food and equipment but it seemed a lot to carry up the face, especially as he was still contemplating a continuous push. Getting this lot up the first lower-angled part of the wall would be exhausting and take time. To get round this, John proposed to use the train to ferry gear to the tunnel window and cache it there. It made me wonder: if you were prepared to do that, why not start from the window yourself, or else fix some ropes?

The weather remained poor, days drifted into weeks. We did some practice climbs and drank in the hotel bar. We photographed

John posing on the ski slopes until, trying to balance on one leg, he caught an edge and dislocated his shoulder. The team retreated to Leysin to lick their wounds, while I held the fort. A couple of mornings later, having breakfast, one of the waiters called over to me that someone had started up the face. A glance through the hotel's powerful binoculars confirmed it. John had mentioned there was a large German team preparing an attempt but we didn't take it too seriously. Who needed such a large team? Where would they all sleep? As it turned out, they were more prepared and experienced than we knew.

I called John, but he seemed rather non-committal, telling me to keep an eye on them while the team returned. I skied over to the face, wondering what kind of reception I might get. Coming close enough to use my camera, I found out. They started throwing snowballs at me. They had their own media deals too. It was clear what their approach was. They were fixing ropes, essentially sieging the face, allowing them to stay on the face and be resupplied as necessary. They seemed systematic and effective. That night I reported back to John all I had seen. The situation was clear enough: a race was underway.

Next day Layton and Dougal set out for the face, following the line of German ropes, even using them at times, to the rock band, where Layton set to work, applying his immense skill to the difficult aid climbing required. On the ground Layton seemed awkward and rather gangly. Hanging from the face, he was attuned and entirely at home. Even so, the climb was desperately hard and he spent the whole afternoon making thirty feet of progress. That night the weather broke and the pair were engulfed in powder avalanches inside their bivouac tent. The inside became fetid and thick with condensation, soaking their clothes so at dawn they fled down to the valley. The Eiger was winning.

So too were the Germans. They realized the logical approach was to dig a snow cave under the rock band. This would offer much more comfort and security. It could be blowing a gale outside, but inside you would barely know it. Clearly, we were going to have to adapt our tactics to something similar but that meant a bigger team, at least at the start. Once we got higher, the climbers could cut loose from their umbilical cord and go for the top. I could support them while they were low on the face and get better pictures for the *Weekend Telegraph.*

And so, eight days after the storm, Layton, Dougal and I set out for the face. Dougal belayed Layton on our line, which was more direct but harder, while I dug a snow cave. After a few minutes, I realized it would take an eternity with an ice axe and since the Germans had dug theirs with a shovel, I might be able to borrow it. We had already reached agreement over the fixed ropes; they had fixed the first 1,500 feet but we'd done the next 500, which were more difficult. For now our routes diverged, but that didn't mean we had to be enemies. I emerged from my tiny burrow and climbed across to their sizeable palace. I heard the purr of a petrol stove and smelt the delicious aroma of fresh coffee.

'Guten Tag,' I said, poking my head in the entrance. There was only one of them inside, lying in a sleeping bag on a foam mat. 'Do you think I could borrow your shovel?'

'I don't know,' he said. 'Why didn't you bring one up yourselves?' I didn't know it at the time, but this was Peter Haag, co-leader of the Germans, who had a rather impish sense of humour. We went back and forth for a while, him claiming he needed authority, me making speeches about the fellowship of mountaineers, and I stomped back to our miserable little hole and started digging furiously with my ice axe. After five minutes, I heard a little cough behind me and there behind me was Peter Haag, with a wicked grin on his face, offering the shovel.

'Come and have some coffee and cognac when you're done,' he said. His co-leader, Jörg Lehne, was not so happy-go-lucky, but as the weeks passed and the Eiger took its toll, both groups came to respect each other.

That afternoon I watched as Layton made fast progress on what was obviously desperate ground. I was impressed. At no stage did he feel the need to drill a bolt, something the Germans did several times on their easier line. I took some pictures and then got back to work on the cave. As the afternoon wore on the weather grew worse and snow began to fall. Almost immediately the spindrift avalanches started; the climbers retreated but as Dougal abseiled under the weight of falling snow, his rope jammed and he was left upside down, stuck a hundred feet above the cave. Alerted by their cries, I put my head out.

'I think I'll have to cut myself free,' Dougal announced, very matter-of-fact. 'Can you get a knife?' I had to borrow one of those off the Germans as well.

The state of our ropes was a constant worry. Over the next few weeks we made slow progress up the face, constantly battling the weather, and all the while our seven-millimetre fixed lines were rubbing against the rock. John had taught us how to use the new Jumar clamps the summer before in Leysin, but it felt alarming as the ropes sagged under our weight. Where they crossed an edge they were prone to fraying. At least the ropes meant we could bale out when things got bad, back to the hotel with its crowd of excited journalists and gawping tourists. It wasn't a wilderness experience, but I quite liked the juxtaposition and revelled in my new job. When Dougal's girlfriend Joy, who had been taking my exposed film to Zürich, crashed our hire car for the second time, I persuaded Wendy to come out to take her place, leaving Conrad with friends. Her presence made the tension of those weeks bearable, even though we saw little of each other. Each time I came down she had to head off with the photos.

My participation in the climb oscillated between total involvement and observer status, and it wasn't always a happy arrangement. There was a tense moment in the snow cave at the top of the Flat Iron when I excused myself from going back into the night, down the ropes, to fetch the stove. I was the photographer, it wasn't my responsibility, but after Dougal disappeared into the dark, I felt John's gaze, and my own shame. I didn't feel like an observer.

In mid March I went back on the face with Layton to tackle the central pillar that led up to the White Spider and the upper face.

John was sick and Dougal needed rest. This was a critical section of the climb; the other two felt confident we had picked the best line but Layton had to climb a fiendishly awkward rock pitch to reach a steep ice gully. As we arrived at the top of the fixed ropes, Jörg called across to me.

'The bottom of the pillar looks very difficult. I don't think it's possible.'

He needn't have worried. Layton was in his element, choosing the right piton, hammering it in, stepping up, doing everything exactly, like a master craftsman. That style of climbing takes time but I don't think any of us, German or British, could have managed as he did. Yet when it came to the ice pitch above, he faltered. Layton was a genius on rock, but had only limited ice experience. It took him ages to place an ice screw and he kept getting tangled in his crampons. If he fell, I doubted the screw would hold and my belay didn't look too secure. Time was passing and it would be dark before he got up.

'Do you want me to have a go?' I hadn't intended to lead anything on the route; I was just the photographer helping out. Yet here I was, crossing the line.

'Okay, this just isn't my scene.'

The pitch was steep, as steep as any ice I'd ever climbed before. I reached the top of a little gully and I paused to take stock. The angle was about seventy degrees, and with 1960s ice axes that meant patiently cutting handholds as well as steps. The ice was also punctuated with rocks, a sure sign it was in reality a thin white skin on the rock below. I had to work gently, precisely, because if that skin came away I would be riding a toboggan all the way to the meadows 5,000 feet below.

The higher I got, the thinner the ice became, until it was an inch thick and lifted away from the smooth rock beneath. The only protection was that distant ice screw Layton had placed. I might as well have been climbing solo. Finally I reached a gangway of white snow that was thicker and more reliable. I could have kicked up this in my crampons but my nerves were exhausted so I patiently cut steps a little further until I could reach a stance and bang in a peg. A great bubbling wave of joy ran through me. We had climbed the crux of the pillar; the way to the White Spider was open.

The Germans on the other hand ground to a halt. That evening, just above the Flat Iron, I passed the German snow cave. Jörg Lehne was sitting in the entrance looking discouraged. Their line had proved a dead end, as we suspected it would. He asked if they could use our ropes; there was another way, he said, but it would take time. I doubted this other way existed, but I was happy enough. Next morning, as we were preparing to go up, Jörg appeared at our cave, anxious to share an idea.

'We should like to see this competition end. Would it not be a good idea if today Karl climbed with Layton?'

Given how things unfolded, I've often wondered if I accepted his suggestion too readily. It made sense to me. We all now respected, even liked each other. The notion of separate routes had always been a little daft. Besides, I wanted to get back to taking pictures. And so I agreed, on the proviso that so did John. It wasn't my place to offer any guarantees. At our next radio call I put the idea to him. In a way, I manoeuvred him into it. Had I continued with Layton and dropped a rope for the Germans, there would have been no question that we had helped them. But I was tired of the politics. I was absorbed in the creative excitement I felt for the job at hand, getting a pictorial record of the final climb to the summit.

So Layton went back up with Karl Golikow, among the strongest of the Germans. I climbed up their ropes for photographs and then abseiled down the face and skied back to Kleine Scheidegg. Two days later, on 22 March, having conferred on the weather and anxious that the Germans were suddenly racing for the top, Dougal and John set out from the snow hole at Death Bivouac to reach the White Spider. Dougal made it but, as Peter Gillman watched through the telescope at Kleine Scheidegg, he saw a figure dressed in red fall through his field of vision, the body stretched out and turning. As the shock of what he had seen spread, Fritz von Almen took his place at the telescope and scanned the face for clues. Could it just have been a rucksack that fell? The only way to find out was to go up there and look.

Layton and I skied in silence, dreading what we might find. I came to some gear scattered in the snow, the contents of a rucksack and felt a wave of relief I knew wasn't justified. Above us I saw something else in the snow. It was John, lying spreadeagled on his back, arms outstretched, his features undamaged, even after his 5,000-foot fall. It would have made an incredible photograph, but I wasn't remotely tempted. There was a strange, terrible beauty to the juxtaposition between this broken man and the vast, gloomy face behind him. I forced myself to check for a heartbeat, pointless really, and then we sat in the snow and cried.

Chapter Eight

Life and Loss

Three days after John's death, I was at the summit of the Eiger to watch Jörg Lehne and Günther Strobel emerge from the white maelstrom of the north face. They had been without water for at least two days, let alone sleep or food, battling a savage storm. Somewhere below me, Dougal was fighting for his life, with two more of the German team, Sigi Hupfauer and Roland Votteler, the latter nursing a badly injured shoulder.

None of them had ice axes, expecting the final section to the summit to be fixed with ropes, but there was a gap of 200 feet. Dougal's crampons were loose, his hands frozen but with a short ice dagger he was able to follow the steps Jörg had cut. With the next rope dangling off to one side, he bashed in his ice dagger as far as he could, no more than an inch, and using tension from their climbing rope edged his way across, hoping his crampons stayed fastened to his feet. 'There was no real point in worrying because it was out of my hands,' he wrote after the climb. 'Three lives on an inch of metal.'

For the previous two nights I'd been sleeping in snow caves just below the summit on the west flank of the Eiger with Mick Burke, whom we had hired as my assistant. A French helicopter pilot had flown us to the mountain, inviting us to jump out onto a thirty-degree slope. We had expected the climbers to be on the summit next morning, and so to lighten the helicopter's load, had dumped food, gas and equipment we thought unnecessary. When the terrible conditions slowed them down, we had to retreat from the summit and dig a second snow cave. It was a confused, chaotic situation, with messages from the mountain relayed through Peter Gillman back at Kleine Scheidegg.

When Lehne and Strobel finally did emerge, and posed on the summit, I discovered my camera had frozen. So had my second, hanging inside my jacket round my neck. I led the two Germans down to our snow hole where I had a spare wrapped in my down jacket for protection and got a picture of Lehne kneeling in the deep snow, his face and beard encrusted with ice, a tangle of hardware around his neck. Then I climbed back to the summit in time to snap Dougal coming up the fixed rope to the top. They weren't the greatest shots; they couldn't be given the conditions, but I was mightily relieved. There was a lot riding on them. My shots from the face itself had persuaded John Anstey to offer me another plum commission: climbing a remote volcano in the Andes of Ecuador. I didn't want him changing his mind.

That night, eleven us of crammed into the snow hole. The atmosphere was thick with cigarette smoke and someone passed round a flask of schnapps. We laughed and joked in relief, as much for our survival as the success of the climb. Dougal had suffered terribly over the last few days, but I sensed that in some strange way he had enjoyed it. I took his boots off and massaged his feet, which were cold but not frostbitten. His hands were in a mess though, covered in black blisters. In the morning we carried on down the west flank back to Kleine Scheidegg and the waiting media.

Back in the hotel, pulling off our boots, Mick was grumbling that his feet were soaked and his boots were rubbish. I felt a smug glow of self-admiration. 'Mine are bone dry. My feet haven't been cold once, during the whole business. You should throw those away and get a pair of these.' Then I peeled off my socks to reveal five black toes. I had been frostbitten without even realizing it. Mick and I collapsed on the bed in hysterics at my comedown.

I spent the next three nights in a hospital at Innsbruck, hugging a tearful Wendy goodbye as she raced home to be with Conrad.

The Eiger Direct came in for criticism, mostly for the use of fixed ropes. I doubt very much it could have been done at that time any other way. By the time it was climbed in Alpine style, equipment had improved dramatically. In 1966, setting out up the Eiger's north wall in winter for a continuous ascent of a route that hard would have been unjustifiable. There was also a feeling of hubris and nemesis surrounding John's death, but it could easily have been Dougal or one of the Germans who was hanging from that rope when it broke. My own experiences in those two months were powerful lessons for the future.

Six weeks later I was sitting on a mule in the jungles of Ecuador, rain trickling down my neck, the trail beneath me a brown morass. The contrast with the bitter winds on top of the Eiger could not have been greater. With me was a charming Old Etonian called Sebastian Snow, looking considerably more dishevelled than the first time I had met him, over lunch at Quaglino's. Mountaineers tend to be a self-deprecating bunch, not given to showing off on first meeting – one of the reasons John Harlin provoked such mixed reactions. Sebastian on the other hand revelled in making outrageous statements, simply to watch their effect on others. Nowadays, professional adventurers are the Ed Stafford or Bear Grylls type, attuned to developing their brand. Sebastian was one of the old-style gentleman amateurs.

Sangay was Sebastian's idea and John Anstey couldn't resist the idea of spectacular images of an erupting volcano. Sebastian had a passion for South America, if not always a competence, especially the Amazon region. Wandering in the Andes he had conceived the idea of following the Amazon all the way down to the sea. What made the adventure so endearing was Sebastian's total lack of planning. He just went, and saw what happened. Looking at him now, sitting on his mule, his spectacles misted up and a trickle of water running off his nose past his slightly pendulous lower lip, it was hard to credit, but he proved a doughty adventurer. 'The tougher things get,' I wrote to my mother, 'the better he is. In London, he presents a rather brittle shell of snobbishness and affectation that he sheds out here.'

What impressed me most was his ability to organize an expedition during a marathon sequence of cocktails and dinner parties. All necessary permits, supplies and other paraphernalia materialized as though from thin air in the course of this socializing. Happily, the first secretary at the embassy was also an Old Etonian and couldn't do enough for us. Sebastian even succeeded in enlisting the help of the local climbing star, Jorge Larrea Rueda, who worked in a bank and had climbed Chimborazo. He had also climbed Sangay, having become involved in the rescue of two Americans. Without Jorge, I doubt either of us would have got within a hundred miles of our objective.

It was now the end of May, and my life had been moving at top speed for several months. Once I was done in Ecuador, I had committed to joining an expedition, led by Dennis Gray, to the beautiful peak of Alpamayo, but the thought of getting back to Bank End Cottage and Wendy and Conrad meant I was having second thoughts. 'I've done little for you these last months,' I wrote to Wendy. 'We have lived at such an impossible bloody rate, but love, you are the most important thing in my life. I'm going to have to be careful to adjust my working life so that it doesn't damage us, doesn't wound our love, without which nothing would be worth anything.'

Sangay had been climbed several times before, but always from the west, just three days from the road-head over grassy hills. I wanted more of an adventure and a first ascent, and to experience the rainforest, so proposed to climb it from the east, from the small town of Macas in the Amazon basin. There was an airstrip in the frontier town of Macas, but that would have deprived me of the sight of Sebastian still dressed in his suit and old-school tie squashed on the bus between me and a splendidly fat Indian lady nursing a small pig. That night we stayed in a hosteleria run by an enigmatic German: 'Martin Bormann, without a shadow of a doubt,' Sebastian assured me.

It took three days riding mules through intense rain to reach Macas. Thirty-five miles away, from a bluff high above the Upano river, Sangay appeared to the north, unreal in its symmetry, as though from a Hokusai print, framed against a copper sky with a gentle plume of smoke drifting from its summit. That was the last time we saw it for a week. Our guide Don Albino confidently predicted it would take three days to reach the volcano up the Jivaro river, a tributary of the Upano. Yet after three days of torrential rain we were less than halfway through the sepulchral gloom of the rainforest.

On the fourth day I developed a fever. Unable to control my shivering, I retired to my sleeping bag, relieved on waking to find that it had gone. Yet that morning our porters said they would go no further. Don Albino, plainly terrified, said he would continue. Sebastian, who revelled in melodrama and had a touch of the masochist about him, watched enthralled. I was sour and bad-tempered, anxious we wouldn't even reach the volcano and my second assignment would end in disaster. Jorge, patient, phlegmatic Jorge, just got on with things, persuading the porters to try doing the cooking.

That night we camped on the crest of a vegetated ridge. It was much colder and everything was soaked. Lighting a fire was almost impossible. In the morning Don Albino was even more miserable, saying that the porters had mutinied. 'If we stay here any longer we shall all die.' Jorge, with promises of bonuses, persuaded them to stay put while we pressed on. The vegetation changed to a form of giant weed of huge umbrella-like leaves on fleshy stalks. I felt like a pygmy in a science fiction film, half expecting a sixty-foot spider to come round the corner.

That night we escaped to the uplands and as dusk fell, our efforts were rewarded. The clouds unrolled and Sangay appeared before us, squat and foreshortened. There was a dull, heavy rumble and a great mushroom of ochre-brown smoke welled up from near the summit, somehow more menacing than lava. Then we settled down for a miserable night, crammed in a leaky two-man tent. Sebastian, the eternal stoic, lay still and silent in the middle of a puddle. Behind us the jungle stretched in an unbroken carpet of green to the horizon. It was only thirty-five miles to Macas, but it had taken over a week to get this far. For the last three days we had been cutting our way through the jungle from the Rio Volcan. We had two days' food. If on the way back we missed that narrow path we were done for. We were on our own, and the responsibility was mine.

Next day we waded through chest-high grass, leaving a trail of marker wands, and camped beneath a ridge of lava. I guessed we were at 10,000 feet, still another 7,000 to the top: a long day even on easy ground. Worse, there was no water and we only had the bottle we carried. Restless with worry, I stuck my head out of the tent at midnight. The sky was velvety black and studded with stars.

'Come on Sebastian, wake up; it's a perfect night.' He groaned, and rolled over, but I got the Primus going and boiled the last of the water for coffee. It was today or never. I told Sebastian to follow as quickly as he could and marched out into the night. The angle was easy, but the slope was covered with lava pebbles, which skidded underfoot. I was fixed on the summit, plodding remorselessly towards the top. Higher up, the lava changed almost imperceptibly to ice and I sat down to wait for the others. An hour passed and cloud engulfed the mountain, the pressure between my ears building like that of the volcano beneath me, until I was in a towering rage and stormed back down for 2,000 feet until I found Sebastian. He had forgotten the rope and only realized his mistake an hour into the ascent.

'Frightfully sorry, Chris, all my fault,' he said.

Back at the ice, I fished out my crampons and saw Jorge doing the same. Sebastian was trying to put his on back to front.

'I really am most frightfully sorry, never worn these things before,' he said, as I strapped them to his feet. Uncoiling the rope, I tied a loop in the middle and dropped that over Sebastian's head. Jorge tied into the other end and with Sebastian between us we continued. 'Terribly sorry, Chris,' Sebastian said behind me. 'My glasses are steamed up. Can't see a thing.' I told him to follow the rope. At that point we crossed a gaping crevasse on a narrow ice bridge, fringed above with a portcullis of icicles, Sebastian tapping his ice axe in front of him like a blind man.

Lava bombs started flying out of the clouds above, filling me with fear. It felt like the whole mountain could blow. The mist was now blended with sulphurous smoke and the chill wind was interspersed with gusts of warm fumes that caught the back of our throats. At my feet were small fissures in the ground, green and yellow, with smoke rising from them. 'Follow me,' gasped Sebastian. 'We must plant the Union Jack on the summit.' We didn't have a Union Jack, but Jorge and I followed anyway, in time to watch Sebastian collapse from the fumes. We picked him up and carried him down the slope until he recovered and we all rushed back down to camp.

Escaping Sangay proved an epic journey, made worse by knowing I didn't have worthwhile pictures. My whole future rested on persuading Sebastian to go back and help me get them. He was sceptical at first, but I reminded him that we could go in from the west next time: much quicker. 'My dear Christian,' he said, 'all I ask is a single hot bath in Quito and I'll go to the ends of the earth to help you get your pictures.' We spent a week there getting more food and money and whooping it up in the Intercontinental. There were letters from Wendy, full of love and her own adventures in the Lake District. She was looking forward to a trip to Scotland, staying with Mary Stewart and performing her first professional gig.

Sebastian and I climbed Sangay for a second time but while I got better pictures I still wasn't satisfied. What I really wanted was liquid lava spraying in the air with fiery brightness. Sebastian, ever loyal, agreed to a third ascent, but as we were sorting out our gear for the morning, a Kichwa man arrived carrying a message for me. The moment I saw him I knew something was terribly wrong. I dreaded opening it, fearing something had happened to Wendy, and felt a moment of relief that it wasn't her. Then the reality of the message struck me: it was Conrad. He had died in an accident. I collapsed onto the ground and wept while our indigenous porters stood in sympathetic silence. Sebastian gripped my shoulder, offering all the strength he could.

I had to pull myself together, get home as fast as I could to be with Wendy. The tragedy had happened a week earlier and the fact that I learned of it so soon was thanks entirely to an old climbing friend from the Nuptse expedition, Simon Clark. He was now working in Ecuador and we had met in Quito. He had seen the accident reported in *The Times*, and while he knew no more than the embassy about my whereabouts, he made enquiries and drove out himself to send the Kichwa messenger. I still feel a tremendous sense of gratitude to him. He had left a Land Rover and a driver to bring me to Quito.

We walked through the dusk and as darkness fell I looked back to see Sangay as a dark conical silhouette against a star-studded sky, a flaming red snake of lava coiling down its slopes. Even in my grief, knowing I would never see Conrad again, I was aware of the intense beauty in front of me. Then I turned and walked through the darkness, drugged with fatigue, repeating to myself the awful fact that I would never touch my son again. There were horses waiting for us at the last outpost and we reached the road at dawn. Our local porters shook my hand, their leader, a fine, grizzled old man crying as he raised his in farewell. We drove past Cotopaxi, snow-capped and pink in the morning sun and on to Quito where friends of Simon offered me refuge until I could catch a flight home.

At Heathrow, Wendy pushed past the barrier when she saw me and we just clung together, oblivious to the world around us in the totality of our shared grief and love for each other. I discovered Conrad had been playing outside Mary's house. There had been a sudden downpour, turning the small stream at the end of her field into a torrent. Conrad, ever independent and adventurous, had strayed from the others and fallen into the swollen waters. Wendy had found him and suffered a solitary hell while she waited for me to come home. She had wonderful support from family and friends but neither of us felt whole without the other. Together we found strength.

A letter I wrote to my mother's sister Thea captures some of what I felt at that time: 'It is still difficult to believe that it has happened. In the house, where we still have his scribbles on the wall, it is difficult not to imagine him next door; that he will come running in, that it never happened. We want another child as soon as possible. We shall never replace Conrad; you can't replace a part of yourself.' I was moved by how many people had been touched by Conrad's presence. Don Whillans, for example, was one of those most upset. I felt a tremendous sense of pride in him, that despite being so young he had given so much to people.

'I think the only thing that has carried us through this,' I wrote to my mother not long after getting home, 'is our love for each other: it brought home to me the knowledge that if anything happened to Wendy, I don't think I should want to go on living. And then this brought home my own responsibility to her, the dangers I have risked.' Wendy, perhaps inevitably, felt a sense of guilt that she had been singing when Conrad died and blamed herself. I found myself fighting a constant battle to change her mind; no one could have been a better mother. 'Her wounds are slowly healing,' I wrote to my mother, weeks after the tragedy, 'but it is going to take a long, long time.'

The truth is you never get over it; you just learn to go on. Every time I saw a young boy in the back of a car or hand in hand with his parents, I could see Conrad and the longing for him brought on tears. I tried to visualize light at the end of a long tunnel, but at first it seemed impossibly long. It was a blessing that Wendy became pregnant so quickly. I wrote to Mum in September with the good news, telling her 'it will have a tremendous difference to both of us'. The latter stages of the pregnancy weren't easy; the babe was judged to be in the breech position. Joe, christened Daniel, was born by Caesarean section at Whitehaven Hospital in April 1967.

(His mother and I continued calling him Daniel, but hereafter I've called him as he's known now.)

The months of Wendy's pregnancy were intensely busy. Livia Gollancz published my book that summer. I had always lacked self-confidence in my writing, telling Mum the autumn before that working on the book had left me disheartened. 'God knows what I am going to call the damned thing.' The title we finally settled on was a succinct appraisal of my life so far: *I Chose to Climb.* Although Mike Thompson, in his witty way, suggested it was more accurately: 'I chose not to sell margarine.' Like many first-time authors, anticipating a wave of media attention, the silence that followed publication was a little dispiriting, but favourable reviews began to come in. The book was deemed a success.

That autumn was packed with lectures to escape the grief of Conrad's death and boost our finances. 'At the moment,' I told Mum, 'I'm going to have one, sometimes two lectures a day for a solid three months – I'm going to be limp at the end of it.' Before starting, I got a quixotic invitation from Tom Patey to climb the Old Man of Hoy, 'the finest rock pinnacle in the British Isles', as he termed it, far to the north in the Orkneys. The invitation was Tom's way of getting us out of our immediate environment; it was typically compassionate, and typical also that he would tease me for my reaction when I realized just how tall and slender the tower was. It was like a vast wobbly needle, 450 feet high, with a grassy summit no bigger than a billiard table.

'Looks bloody loose to me,' I said from the top of the cliff opposite. 'That sandstone will just crumble away as you climb it.'

'Och, no,' he said. 'Where's your spirit of adventure? Those are no words from Bonington of the Eiger.'

Rusty Baillie, who had arrived on the island before us with his wife Pat and their young baby, was a little more practical. 'That crack should go. Just the right size for bongs.' These were wide pitons, probably unfamiliar to many British climbers now.

On our first exploration, the following morning, Tom set off up a rickety staircase of ledges climbing solo, as was his habit on easy ground, before pulling off a shelf-sized block that had looked perfectly solid. He scuttled back to sea level, and we did another circumambulation of the tower's base, looking for weaknesses. On the seaward side the rock was sheer and featureless; a series of pendulous folds of sandstone, like rocky double chins, overhung the crashing sea. The route on the landward side still looked the most promising.

Tom returned to the fray, this time with a rope, climbing the loose staircase to a platform eighty feet up perched on the edge of the tower. To the right, on the overhanging landward face, was a steep crack that probed through a series of overhangs to more broken ground. Climb this, and the route was in the bag. Rusty climbed up to the platform and then, draped with all sorts of ironmongery, lowered his weight onto his arms and climbed across into the crack. The sound of a hammer driving home a piton rang out above the crashing of the waves. Tom settled down to wait in the sun, smoking endless cigarettes or burrowing through his rucksack for something to eat, more or less ignoring the rope. I was on the steep slope opposite, festooned with cameras, watching the action from afar.

Rusty, ape-like with his long, muscled arms, spreadeagled in the crack, inched his way up deep in shadow. The crack was overhanging and coated in fine grit that acted like ball bearings. He had to scrape all this loose material away before making any progress. When the angle eased off and Rusty tried to climb free, his fingers slipped off a powdery hold and he was almost spat out of the crack. He slithered down to his top piton and gratefully abseiled off. It took another six hours the following day to finish this one pitch and as he finally hammered in his belay I scrambled down to the base of the tower.

'You don't need a rope,' Tom shouted over the crash of the sea. 'This is a piece of duff.' Yet I was very frightened. The climbing was easy, but I had done nothing on rock since the Eiger Direct that spring. The holds were loose and the atmosphere immense. As my head drew level with a flat ledge, I came eye to eye with an indignant fulmar chick, a little bundle of down with a yellow beak, which vomited a gob of foul slime into my face. I reeled back and almost fell, cursing loudly, but rather admiring the furious little bird.

Tom was keen I should take the pitons out of the next pitch, not being in the least bit a fan of aid climbing. I pointed to the cameras round my neck. 'Wish I could, but remember I've got to get the pictures. I'll Jumar up just above you.' The shot I got of him, cigarette clamped between his lips, tangled up in ropes and *étriers*, became something of a classic, but Tom never cared for that ponderous style of climbing; it took two hours of him hammering and grunting with effort to reach Rusty by which time it was getting dark again. The Old Man was turning into a longer siege than the Eiger.

We could have bivouacked, but Tom couldn't see the point of missing an evening's whisky and song, and the promise of a warm bed, so we abseiled off again. Next morning we climbed back up the ropes and in short order were stood below the final pitch, a splendid, square-cut corner. 'This pitch is mine,' I said, in my best tank commander's voice. It was covered in big holds and we were soon at the summit, where we built a cairn and lit a small bonfire. It had been a delightful, light-hearted adventure at the worst of times.

Less than a year later we came back, part of a huge outside broadcast the BBC put on over the Whitsun weekend. Tom and I spent the days beforehand climbing a sea stack on Handa, another carefree adventure. Gazing across the wind-whipped sea, I shrank with dread at the prospect of this immense happening; I was once again the small boy dreading the children's party, shy and a little scared at the public exposure, but knowing too it would be fun. And the Old Man of Hoy broadcast was tremendous fun. The BBC gambled a great deal, drafting in a platoon of Scots Guards, a landing craft, tonnes of equipment and a range of vertiginous camera platforms masterminded by John Cleare and Hamish MacInnes.

There were three climbing teams: Tom and me on the original route, Joe Brown and Ian McNaught-Davis on a new route on the south face and two modern hard men, Dougal Haston and Pete Crew climbing the overhanging south-east arête. Joe had already repeated our line, taking an hour where Rusty had needed eight, and doing it free, without hanging on all those pitons. 'It's not too difficult,' he said, trying to reassure me, but the fact Joe had found it easy didn't mean much. I had no illusions about our respective ability as rock climbers and so I practised the long crack pitch the day before the broadcast. You can overdo spontaneity. At least I knew the pitch went free. Attacking with confidence, to my amazement I reached the top in half an hour.

The broadcast was a bit of circus, but it had some good climbing and was hugely popular with the public, perhaps the most significant mainstream view of our sport since the 1953 Everest success. The scale of the Old Man was just right, big and steep enough to seem imposing, small enough not to dwarf the climbers. There were crises and dramas, radios failing, Tom swinging into space and climbing up the rope, Mac's off-the-cuff wit, always ready to fill any gaps in the action, and Joe's laconic asides. The showstopper would feature a climber abseiling the entire height of the tower, all 450 feet, in one go. I was the last to reach the top, where Joe greeted me with a broad grin. 'We've decided you should have the honour.' I wondered aloud what would happen if the rope got jammed; after a couple of hundred feet my usual abseiling device would be so hot it would burn through the rope.

'Simple,' said Joe. 'Don't stop.'

Hamish offered me some Heath Robinson affair with an asbestos clamp. In the end, with minutes to go before the abseil was broadcast, I went on strike.

'I'm bloody well not going to do it.' In the end, Joe came up with a neat solution that allowed me to descend the Old Man in complete safety, still clipped to the abseil rope, waxing lyrical into my microphone about the spectacular surroundings. Two days later, all the gear had been stripped from the tower and the climbers went their separate ways.

We had at last got some cash in the bank from the book and my photojournalist assignments and decided to buy our first house. Bank End Cottage had so many reminders of the joy we had shared with Conrad and work was taking me away from home more often. The long drive round the Lake District hills was increasingly irksome, so we chose Cockermouth in north-west Cumbria and in the early summer of 1967, not long after Joe was born, bought an Edwardian semi-detached house with a nice garden. Wendy was singing again and with a friend called Muriel Graves started a club, part of the great 1960s folk revival. She was becoming fulfilled and happy but I was increasingly restless. Looking back, the strength of her network of friends from Moor Row and Cleator Moor, a network that did so much to help her through our tragedy, was something with which I had little in common. I am ashamed to say there was even a touch of jealousy on my part. My friends tended to be from outside the Lakes, with horizons wider than those I experienced in Cumbria.

Work often took me away. The February before Joe was born I was on Baffin Island to cover the changing lives of the modern Inuit. The days were short and the sun never rose more than a few degrees above the southern horizon. Temperatures dropped as low as –40°C. Sebastian Snow was once again slated to write the story, but he struggled in the cold and almost immediately suffered frostbite on his nose. His natural stoicism got him through in the Andes, but he was floored by the cold; I remember helping him into his sleeping bag one night and discovering his feet were frozen solid. He flew home and I was promoted to writer as well as photographer.

Motorized skidoos were already squeezing out the dog teams and there were only a handful left among the few Inuit who still went hunting for seal and caribou in the traditional way. I joined them on one of their hunting trips, travelling for ten days, building igloos each night to sleep in. After we failed to find caribou, we went down to the floe edge to shoot seal. There's no question that my climbing experience proved invaluable in situations like this; I was able to handle risk and fatigue and still come back with publishable images. By now I was working with a combination of Leicas and Nikons, and had them winterized to deal with the cold. Even so, it was a trial to keep the film stock from snapping when I rewound it at the end of the reel.

I had a similar experience later that year when I went to the Hunza valley, Pakistan, with the novelist Nicholas Monsarrat. He was due to write about the extraordinary longevity of the people there. Monsarrat was then in his late fifties, still selling 20,000 copies of his most famous book, *The Cruel Sea*, every year. We flew to Gilgit but the jeep journey to Hunza tested Monsarrat's patience. Two-thirds of the way, we discovered the rough track had been wiped out and we'd have to walk the last twenty-five miles. After a grim night in a local guesthouse with just a hard-boiled egg and a rubbery chapati for dinner, Nicholas disappeared back to Gilgit, muttering about a publisher's deadline, and I was left to carry on alone to research the lives of the people of Hunza.

I think I must have been away from home more at this time than I was in the later big expedition years. Another story for the *Telegraph* on outdoor education took me to John Ridgeway's adventure school in the Northern Highlands and the Alps. That summer I was commissioned by *Drive* magazine to do a rock climb on each of the 'Three Peaks' in 24 hours, *Centurion* on Ben Nevis, *Central Buttress* on Scafell and *White Slab* on Cloggy, racing between them in my battered Cortina. It was Mike Thompson's idea and he came along as co-driver. On top of all that were the autumn lecture tours and more television work. I seemed consumed with restlessness while Wendy was ever more rooted in the Lakes. The early days at Woodland seemed a long time ago now; I felt isolated, both from climbers and other journalists, and decided we should move to London. Wendy, with her strong network of friends to see her through my absences, was happy where she was, but reluctantly agreed.

By the end of a desultory weekend house-hunting, I had lost my enthusiasm for living in London. We couldn't remotely afford the sort of place we wanted. On the way home we broke our journey at Alderley Edge, south of Manchester, to stay with Nick Estcourt, an old climbing friend, and his wife Carolyn. We had a relaxed, convivial supper with them, slept on the living-room floor and went for a walk in the morning. I saw a compromise: settle somewhere south of Manchester, where I already had climbing friends and with Snowdonia, the Peak District and the Lakes within easy reach. It was handy for lectures and not too far from London.

With a major assignment for the *Daily Telegraph* looming, covering an expedition planning to make the first descent of the Blue Nile, we snatched at an ugly yellow-brick Edwardian semi in Bowdon. The move was undoubtedly tough on Wendy. Suburban Cheshire was an alien environment far from the open country she loved. She was suddenly separated from the close friends who had offered such strong support. I was happier, surrounded by climbing mates, like Nick and Carolyn Estcourt, who moved into Bowdon Vale, just below the main village. Dave and Lynn Potts were another couple in a growing network of friends who coalesced in the area, moving onto the same street as us. Our kids went to the same primary schools; we climbed together every Tuesday and at weekends. I felt back in the mainstream again, reconnected to my passion for climbing and my career. It was that passion that drove me to achieve, but how lucky I was to have Wendy's deep and selfless love.

PART THREE

Peak Years

Chapter Nine

Annapurna South Face

Don Whillans was seated outside a cave under a boulder, smiling like a benevolent gnome.

'You're looking a bit slimmer than when I saw you last,' I said. 'How did it go?'

'Not too bad.'

'Did you see the face?'

'Aye.'

'What does it look like?'

'Steep. But after I'd looked at it for a few hours it seemed to lie back a bit. It's going to be difficult but I think it will go all right.'

I felt an immense pressure lift from my chest. So much was riding on those first few words. Behind us, down the valley, was a vast train of porters and equipment. Ahead of us was one of the greatest challenges in the Himalaya: the south face of Annapurna. Three miles wide and a mile and a half high, a wall of white snow and golden granite that steepens at 7,000 metres at a near-vertical rock band. We had spent two years poring over photographs, talking, speculating and plotting. Would it be possible? The expedition was a new direction for me, the first time I'd led a team to the Himalaya, my baptism of fire. Had I overreached? What if the route was unjustifiably dangerous? Don had gone ahead of the main party with my old army friend Mike Thompson to assess the difficulties and find a site for base camp.

'I looked at it for about four hours,' Don said. 'A big avalanche came down on the left but our line looks fairly safe.' I trusted Don's judgement. I never climbed with anyone else with the same feel for big mountains. It was a mixture of intuition, profound common sense and the ability to interpret the features of a mountain and the complexities of climbing them. I had almost dreaded hearing Don's verdict. Now it was in, I could relax.

In the autumn of 1968 I came home from the Blue Nile expedition. My latest experience of someone else's adventure had left me determined to paddle my own canoe. Captain John Blashford-Snell's military team had a period quality about it, as though drawn from a Rider Haggard novel. We were frequently thrown out of our rubber boats and I almost drowned in a huge stopper wave. Nobody had told any of us what to do and there were crocodiles all over the place. While carrying our rafts round some cataracts, a fellow crewmember and SAS corporal called Ian Macleod was swept away and drowned while crossing a swollen tributary.

If that wasn't bad enough, local tribesmen living near the banks of the river attacked us on two occasions. The second attack was at night and only the vigilance of our sentry saved us from being massacred. We dashed down to the boats to protect them, fired off a few rounds and escaped down the river in the pitch dark. Afterwards, I realized that I was a voyeur, with no control, observing an enterprise that could have got me killed.

That October, Nick and I decided, come what may, we would go on an expedition in the spring of 1970. Included in our little group was Martin Boysen, living nearby in Altrincham. Martin and I had been climbing together for years, from the days when he was a prodigy at Harrison's Rocks, outside Tunbridge Wells. His father was German and his mother English, and his earliest memories were of Lancaster bombers dropping bombs on Aachen near his home village. Martin was passionate about the natural world, as well as being one of the most gifted rock climbers Britain has ever seen. His long limbs seemed gangly on the ground, but once poised on a stretch of rock he would drift up effortlessly, like a hugely intelligent sloth, assured and methodical. Martin had recently attempted Cerro Torre in Patagonia with a team that included Dougal Haston, who we immediately pencilled in as a fourth member without yet telling him. We knew he'd come.

Nick, compared to Martin, was not a natural climber. Wiry and strong, and very competitive, he had forced his way to a high standard of climbing. His background was more typical of pre-war climbers. Educated at Eastbourne College and Cambridge, he had been president of the university's climbing club. His father had introduced him to the Alps as a schoolboy and consequently he had a broad range of experience. He'd climbed in Greenland, but this was his only experience outside Europe. He and his wife Carolyn, like Martin and Maggie Boysen, were part of our close network of friends.

We had a team, but no objective. In 1968, following a series of conflicts in the Himalaya, the mountains were off limits. You could reach the Hindu Kush of Afghanistan but that didn't appeal, so we looked instead at the mountains of Alaska. Then, in early 1969, Nepal reopened a limited number of peaks. We immediately forgot about Alaska. Where the idea of the south face of Annapurna came from is a little hazy. Martin had heard Dennis Gray mention it as being like the north face of the Grandes Jorasses, only three times the height. I remembered a photo of the face Jimmy Roberts, my expedition leader on Annapurna II, had shown me. He had seen it while trying Macchapuchhre in 1957. I phoned two of the members living in Britain.

David Cox, a fellow in modern history at Oxford, was vague but not dismissive. He promised to send us a photograph. Roger Chorley, later a distinguished chairman of the National Trust, was incredulous. 'Going for the south face of Annapurna? It's swept by avalanches the whole time.' Then I got a letter from Jimmy himself suggesting our idea wasn't so crazy after all: 'The south face of Annapurna is an exciting prospect – more difficult than Everest, although the approach problems are easier.' When David's photograph arrived, Martin and Nick came round and I projected the

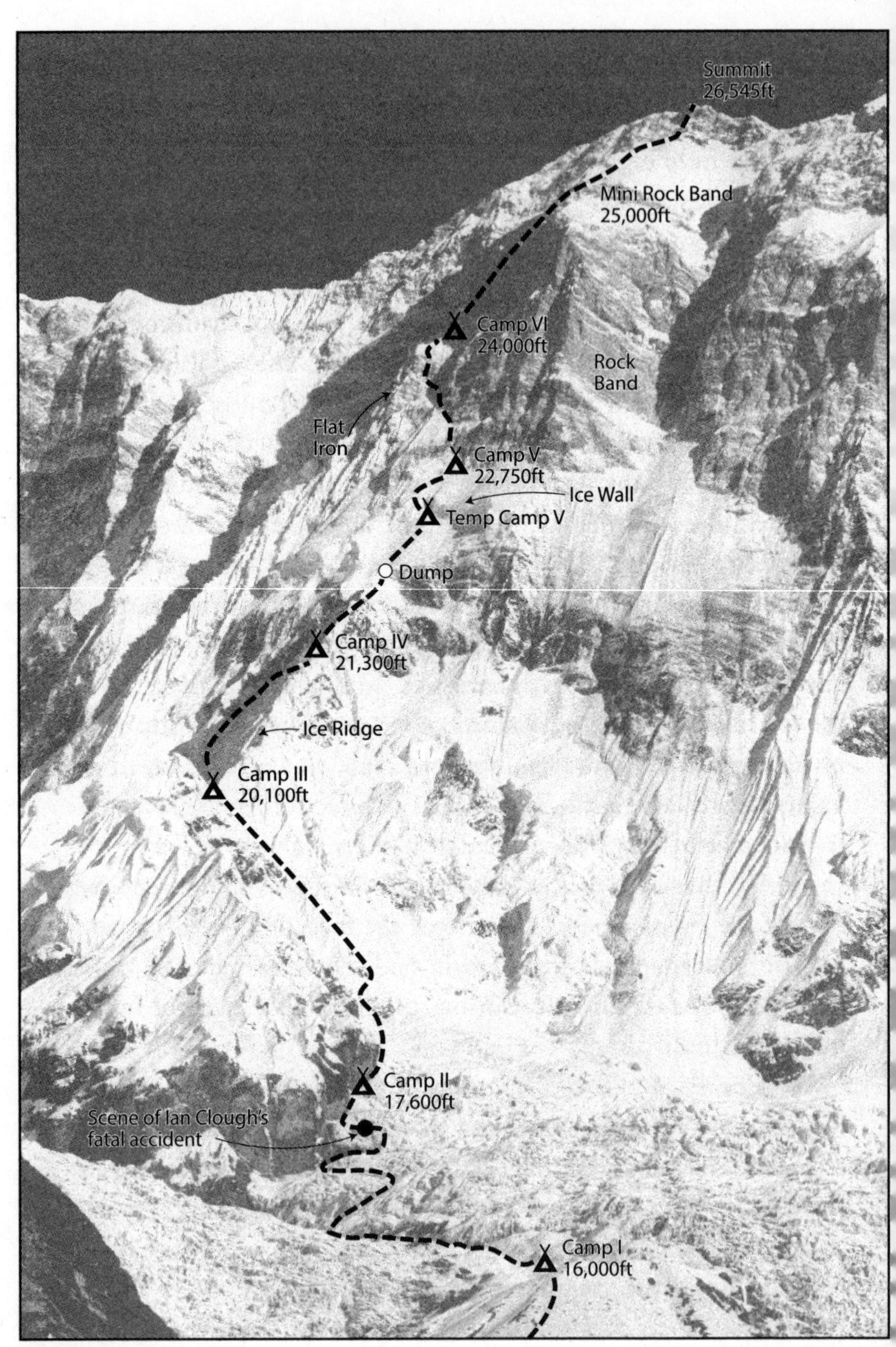

Annapurna's south face, 1970.

image onto the wall of our living room. We sat there gazing at it, slack-jawed.

'There's a line all right,' Martin said, 'but it's bloody big.'

He was right on both counts. From the glacier we traced a hard, uncompromising route on the left of the face all the way to the top, starting with a squat snow ridge like the buttress of a Gothic cathedral, leaning against the steeper upper face. Immediately above was an elegant ice arête; even at this distance you could tell it was knife-edge. This ended at a long snow slope leading to a band of ice cliffs.

'I wonder how stable they are,' Nick said, then traced his finger through them to the rock band. 'That must be at least a thousand feet.'

What would hard rock climbing be like at more than 23,000 feet? Nothing like it had been done before. Above that, it didn't seem far to the top but we weren't fooled: the picture was foreshortened. I dug out some shots taken from Annapurna II that showed the top of Annapurna's south face. We could look across at the top of Annapurna's rock band. It was another 3,000 feet from its top to the summit, with a rocky crest to finish.

The scale of this route was mind-blowing. The north face of the Eiger was not quite 6,000 feet high, much the biggest challenge among the classic faces of the Alps. Annapurna's south face was almost twice that and at altitude. Yet I felt confident we had a good chance with the right team. Almost by default, I became leader, although I didn't think of myself as one. I'd approached Mike Ward to see if he was interested, but wisely he turned us down. It was as much a desire to make the expedition happen that prompted me to make decisions; the others were happy enough to go along with that. It was only as I learned my role that I discovered I enjoyed it, and was good at it.

One thing was clear: we were going to need a bigger team. I preferred a small, compact group but the scale of this adventure was unprecedented. Blitzkrieg wouldn't work; it could only be a siege. We settled on a group of eight. Choosing the other members was crucial. Shortly before we left, a reporter asked me about discipline: what I would do if someone turned round and told me to get lost? The short answer was 'nothing'. I would already have failed if things got so bad. Climbing leadership was nothing like the army. Discipline came from below not above. If I had to make an unpopular decision it would be accepted only if the others respected my judgement and team spirit was strong. That meant knowing each other.

Two old friends immediately sprang to mind, both from my Eiger days. Ian Clough was now running a small climbing school from his cottage in Glen Coe, which he shared with his wife Nikki and their young daughter. I had known Mick Burke from our early days in the Lake District; he had since made the first British ascent of *The Nose* on El Capitan in Yosemite Valley. On the Eiger Direct, suffering in snow holes with almost no food, we had come to know each other better and my respect for Mick deepened. He was argumentative, but never sulked.

My third choice was the most obvious and most problematic. Don Whillans and I had done great climbs together like the Central Tower of Paine. I thought I could handle the differences in personality, even though he might chafe at the notion of me as leader. The biggest problem was his physical condition. In the last few years he had let himself go, developing a beer-belly through long sessions in the pub. I wanted Don because of his Himalayan experience. He had been three times before the region closed in 1964 and performed brilliantly. But that was five years ago: could he still function on a high mountain?

I suggested we drove to Scotland to do a climb together, without telling him about Annapurna. But when I got to his house at around closing time he was still in the pub. He finally rolled in at two-thirty in the morning, having sunk eleven pints. I drove north in a state of icy fury all the way to Loch Linnhe. That day we walked up to the Great Gully of Ardgour with Tom Patey to try a first winter ascent. Don lagged behind, nursing his hangover, happy to follow our lead, until we arrived at the final pitch, an evil, ice-lined chimney just too wide to bridge comfortably. It was at this point, to our surprise, that Don took charge.

'I think I'll have a try at this,' he said. 'It's about my turn to go out in front.'

What followed was a masterclass. Not bothering to place any runners, Don danced up the pitch, almost doing the splits on the wide bridging. Both Tom and I had a struggle when it came to our turn. I made up my mind to invite him. When we got down to Ian Clough's cottage, I showed him David Cox's photo. He pondered for a while and then said: 'It'll be hard, but it should go all right. I'll come.' Given Don's experience, I promptly made him deputy leader.

So far, the team all knew each other but now money played a hand. My new agent George Greenfield suggested I recruit an American: 'It would make my job a lot easier in the States.' Various names presented themselves, but Don and Dougal both spoke warmly of Tom Frost, one of that extraordinary group exploring Yosemite's big walls. A Stanford engineering graduate, Tom had climbed Kangtega, a difficult peak in the Everest region and put up new routes in the Andes. I had doubts when I discovered he was a Mormon, a faith that forbids not just drinking, gambling and smoking, popular activities with many of the team, but also bad language and tea. As things turned out, he proved not only a popular Mormon, but a tolerant one too.

We had our eight climbers but needed some trustworthy workers lower down the mountain to keep supplies flowing. I approached Mike Thompson, my old friend from Sandhurst. The army had tried hard to hang onto Mike but, with characteristic style, he finessed their objection by standing for Parliament. Thus liberated, he studied anthropology, earning a doctorate and delving into complex ideas about society and the environment. Good fun and equable, he didn't have the same experience as the lead climbers but would offer incredible support organizing the expedition's food.

I was lucky with our doctor. Dave Lambert was a registrar in Newcastle, who heard about the expedition and offered his services. He had climbed in the Alps and impressed me with his enthusiasm and energy. He was even prepared to pay his way. I invited him on the spot. That just left someone to manage base camp. I needed someone used to logistics that could manage Nepali staff, so I asked Charles Wylie, a serving army officer who had been to Everest in 1953. He suggested Kelvin Kent, a captain in the Gurkha Signals stationed in Hong Kong. He was a wireless expert and spoke Nepali fluently.

Our expedition gained stature almost in spite of ourselves. This was partly down to George, a superbly connected figure on the literary scene, whose clients included John le Carré. George also looked after Enid Blyton, and following her death in 1968 was managing her literary estate. He had a double first from Cambridge and served with distinction in North Africa and Italy during the war, though he never mentioned either. He had also collected a small posse of notable adventurers like Sir Francis Chichester, Wally Herbert and Robin Knox-Johnston.

George's great wisdom was to listen, find out what made you tick and act accordingly. He also had plenty of experience raising the finance for expeditions, having negotiated deals for the Commonwealth Trans-Antarctic Expedition in the late 1950s. He now brought all his experience and exceptional contacts to the problem of financing Annapurna, arranging a meeting with the banker Pat Pirie-Gordon, a power behind the scenes in the expedition world. Thanks to him, we got the full support of the Mount Everest Foundation (MEF).

I'd always felt under suspicion from the establishment, having earned disapproval for the newspaper headlines and lecturing I'd done after the Eiger. Now I was drawn under its wing, with a committee appointed to look after us that read like a who's who of mountaineering, with Lord Hunt as one of our patrons. George put together a deal with various newspapers, publishers and television companies. We took an outstanding film crew with us to base camp, which ultimately produced an excellent documentary. But payments were related to height gained. Bringing the MEF on board meant the whole thing was underwritten and I could relax a bit.

That spring I was preoccupied with my family. Not long after moving into our new house, Joe, just eighteen months old, suffered an acute attack of gastroenteritis. Not having signed up with a local doctor, we got a number out of the phone book. The doctor told us not to worry and suggested something from the chemist. Joe continued to get weaker and twenty-four hours later we were both out of our minds with worry. It felt almost unreal that something could be so wrong with our second son. He was slipping into a coma when the doctor finally arrived; he immediately called an ambulance. Joe was rushed to Wythenshawe Hospital and we spent another agonizing night at his bedside before we were told he would be fine.

His recovery was an immense relief and we settled into a happy spring. Wendy was pregnant again, giving birth to Rupert in July 1969, at the same hospital where we'd watched over Joe a few months before. This time the birth was easier and it was wonderful to be there to see his little head emerge and then hold him in my arms. A few months later Rupert developed a stomach condition that caused him intense pain. The poor little soul just screamed and no amount of patting or burping helped though I did seem to ease him into sleep with the way I held him. The doctors told us it would cure itself, and it did. We got a cat, Tinker, a big tabby, and a dog, Bessie. The family was growing. I also hired a secretary, Joan Lister, to help me plan the Annapurna expedition. Joan was the first of several, all of whom became close friends with Wendy and very much part of the family.

Don had agreed to organize equipment for Annapurna but on the phone one day, he said: 'Eh, this expedition organizing is 'ard work.' The penny dropped. He had so far only contemplated this hard work and not done any, so I took over while Don concentrated on design. He worked on a new version of his box tent to use on the face and worked on a harness, the first webbing harness ever. It worked superbly and soon became a bestseller.

I would get up at six, work until late afternoon, jump in my car and drive up to eighty miles to give a lecture, coming back the same night to do it all again next day. I had never worked harder in my life but was enjoying myself. After years of other people's stories, I was writing my own, no longer a spectator but fully engaged. The responsibility was intimidating, but at the same time I felt elated. By mid January 1970 we had gathered everything together in a furniture store near Don's house in Rawtenstall: 15,000 feet of rope, hundreds of pitons, buckets, plates, soap, tin-openers – everything. Now you can equip and supply a similar expedition in Kathmandu, but in 1970 it all came with you.

Getting our kit to base camp was the crux of the enterprise. We'd thought about sending it in trucks, but that would require several of us to drive them; none of us had the time. We would send it by boat to Mumbai. Two days before our ship sailed, the agent rang to say it was in dry dock with engine trouble. After a day of nervous tension, he called back. The *State of Kerala* was leaving next day from London. We dashed down with our cargo just in time. In late February Don and Dave Lambert flew to Mumbai to meet it. Soon after, a cable arrived from Don saying the *State of Kerala* was still in Cape Town, delayed with engine trouble, and wouldn't arrive in Mumbai for a fortnight. We wouldn't be able to start the approach until early April. I plunged immediately into despair. The entire expedition seemed doomed before it had started.

I did what I would have done in the army: wrote an appreciation of the situation so I could formulate a plan. I would send an advance party ahead of the main expedition to scope the route on the face and site base camp. Don was already in India so it made sense that he should lead it. There was no point in him waiting in Mumbai. In a happy coincidence an army team, under the leadership of Major Bruce Niven, with Henry Day as climbing leader, was planning to climb Annapurna from the north, the route of the first ascent in 1950. They agreed to lend us some food. I also airfreighted a small amount of extra equipment to tide us over. Needing a good man to shepherd the gear off the boat, when it finally arrived, I asked Ian Clough if he would go. He was endlessly patient, unselfish and tactful – the ideal man for the job. Then I left London in a flurry of snow on board an Air India 707 bound for Mumbai.

Don, by now in Kathmandu, was predictably sceptical when he heard I was on my way. 'The only useful strings 'e could pull would be a bloody great big one attached to the ship.' But delivering the gear as fast as possible was essential. When I got to Mumbai I discovered the boat had been delayed a further five days. I met with officials and watched my agent, a tubby man called Freddie Buhariwala whose charm masked a shrewd mind. I knew he'd see us right and so went on to Nepal, staring at Annapurna's huge white shape through the window of the Fokker Friendship as it approached Kathmandu. When I'd flown in ten years before, the airport was a grassy strip. Now there was smooth tarmac and a terminal building. Inside it, Kelvin Kent and Mike Thompson were waiting for me.

I had never met Kelvin before. His job was already important, but the delay had made it critical. He was quite short, lean and sharp-faced, but bubbling with nervous energy and warmth. He plunged into details about the latest developments while guiding me through customs, solving bureaucratic problems with the same enthusiasm the rest of us reserved for mountains. He'd been down to the border at Nautanwa to prepare for Ian's arrival and dashed up the approach trek to order food and fuel. In Kathmandu he had charmed a typist at the British embassy into working as the expedition's unofficial secretary. 'If you wear an open shirt,' Kelvin warned me, 'you might be mistaken for one of the hippies. You've got to look the part if you want results.' He whisked me through a sequence of meetings with officials, me playing the gracious, properly attired figurehead. Then we would leap on bicycles and pedal off to the next meeting, dodging cars and buffalo.

Next morning, Mike and Don went on ahead to begin their reconnaissance. I felt a little envious but had to stay behind to meet the rest of the team. That night I was taken out to dinner by the owner of a famous travel company. He quizzed me on my approach to leadership. 'I wish I was a bit more self-confident,' I wrote to Wendy. 'You know, the big leader type. I feel anything but at the moment. I hope I can make a good job of this.'

The team arrived looking more like a rock group than a climbing expedition, their shirts very much open. Ian Clough had flown south from Delhi to meet the *State of Kerala*, now due any day. Kelvin was a blur of activity. Finally it seemed we were making progress. Despite all the setbacks, we left Pokhara just one day behind schedule, largely thanks to Kelvin and Henry Day's army expedition. The walk to base camp was short, but late spring snow had sent avalanches into the upper reaches of the Modi Khola, an awkward and sometimes dangerous proposition for our porters. They took off the shoes we gave them to walk through it barefoot.

Even before Ian and Kelvin arrived, we began work on the route. Don and Dougal, teaming up from the start, threaded their way across the glacier to a rocky feature, called a rognon, that split the glacier. Here we placed camp one, at around 16,000 feet. Camp two went in 1,200 feet higher, tucked under the shelter of a cliff. On 7 April, Don and Dougal pushed the route up a gully to a col beneath the delicate ice ridge we had spotted in our photograph. Bad weather shut us down for a few days, but on 11 April, Martin and Nick put up one of Don's box tents on the col on a wide flat area free from avalanche risk. After all the uncertainty of the last few weeks, we were safely established at the start of the hard climbing.

Tom Frost and I teamed up for the first part. The more time I spent with him, the more I liked him. He reminded me, as I told Wendy, of a character from a John Steinbeck novel, full of quiet dignity. At night, he read his Bible while I read novels full of violence and lust. On our third morning trying to force the route straight up the ice ridge, Dougal arrived, shouting up from below: 'I think there's a good route round here, Chris, which will bypass the whole of the ridge.' He was right. We'd made a mistake and wasted time.

As we descended, I couldn't help snapping at Tom, but instantly regretted it. My temper came from insecurity that the team wouldn't listen to me after such a basic error.

Back at base camp, we watched Don and Dougal crawling up the ice ridge, tiny insects on a gigantic white elephant. Yet they were making progress, and in two more days camp four was established, dug into the crest of the ridge like an eagle's perch, the tent door looking out into a yawning gulf. Above, the crest of the ridge was barred by a series of white towers like gigantic ice creams. It was Nick Estcourt and Martin Boysen's task to surmount these and open the route to the rock band. Martin solved this puzzle, sneaking past the first tower through a sort of tunnel in the ice and then using all his genius on what was undoubtedly the hardest ice climbing yet done at altitude.

Despite their great efforts, in three weeks we'd climbed only 1,500 feet. We still had weeks in hand, depending on when the monsoon broke, but the route was fraying nerves and wearing us down. For every day a climber got to spend pushing the route, another dozen were spent ferrying supplies. There were grumblings of discontent during our radio calls, not surprisingly in a team full of ambitious climbing stars.

On 3 May, Dougal and I emerged from the top of the ice ridge, after five weeks of effort. Above us lay a thousand feet of easier ground ending at huge ice cliffs. Just beyond these lay the rock band. Don came up to join Dougal and I went down for a rest, suffering from a nagging cough that I put down to altitude. It got worse at base camp and Dave Lambert diagnosed pleurisy.

'What's that?'

'Inflammation of the walls of the chest. I can put you on a course of penicillin.'

'How long before I can get back up?'

'Four or five days – at least.'

It sounded like a life sentence. Ian had also retreated, suffering pains down his left side, more muscular than anything sinister. Mike collapsed between camps, suddenly incapable of breathing, simply through over-exertion. Nick kept plugging away, carrying loads every other day on the huge stretch between camps four and five. Martin was going superbly well, making five carries between camp four and five in seven days. 'I need a rest,' he wrote in his diary, 'mentally as well as physically. God, it gets you down. Still, it won't go on forever; in a few days we should take over from Mick and Tom.'

Above them, Mick Burke and Tom Frost were fighting their way through the rock band, Mick at his irrepressible best, scrapping for every foot gained on fiercely technical ground, brushing ice and snow from holds – thinking his way up each pitch. Tom, patiently paying out the rope, recorded the rhythm of each day's weather, the few threads of cloud in the early morning quickly swelling until they blotted out the lower face. That tide of cloud was an ominous reminder the monsoon was on its way. All of us at base camp were fretting at the pace of progress. From down below, it seemed the route Tom and Mick had chosen was making things harder.

Nick and Martin were due to take over, but their heroic efforts to keep Mick and Tom supplied had left them exhausted. Dougal and Don were impatient to be back in the lead and I felt they had a better feel for the route than any other pair. Things came to a head during a radio call two days later. Discussion ranged back and forth between the different camps. I wanted Don and Dougal to spend a day carrying supplies. Dougal argued forcefully they should go straight up to the front of the route. I began thinking aloud, trimming my plan as I listened to the arguments. Mick wanted to stay in the lead. Nick was at camp four and knew the logistical situation. The camp had become a bottleneck. 'There is too much of a job here,' he argued. We needed to get supplies moving faster. So I confirmed that Don and Dougal should spend a day on the big carry between camps four and five and then move to the front.

I should have ended the discussion there, but Dougal told us Don wanted to say something. 'I don't know what Mick thinks he's playing at . . . unless they get their finger out . . . they should make way for somebody else to try. He's had a week and progress seems very poor.' The others were furious, especially Mick and Tom, who had been making good progress in the last few days. The radio waves hummed with frustration and anger: 'Cut it out,' I said. 'Let's not have an argument here. Everyone's trying their bloody guts out to do this climb, and I think we can sort this out without any of this kind of argument.'

The plan was agreed and we went off air, but the row had fractured the group. Up at camp five, Mick resolved to show Don and fix all the rope they had left – 800 feet – the following day. He was as good as his word. With Tom in support, Mick found a line to the top of the flat iron, fighting his way up a rocky groove, clearing the ice as he went. At the top, having run out 200 feet of rope from where Tom was belaying, the wall steepened. In overcoming this final barrier, at the limits of his strength, Mick made the team's eventual success possible.

I was on my way back up to support Don and Dougal when Mick and Tom passed me on their way down to base camp. 'Don't think we've come down out of spite,' Mick said, 'we just couldn't have gone on any longer.' Tom didn't hold back. 'I think you've destroyed the spirit of the expedition by pushing Don and Dougal in front out of turn; it was a real stab in the back for Nick and Martin.' We talked for a while, quietly and amicably. Privately I was appalled. Of all the team, I respected Tom's selflessness and judgement the most. I explained my logic; that we had to snatch the chance before it was taken from us by the monsoon. I'm not sure I changed his mind but we strengthened our friendship.

The final days of the expedition were a war of attrition. Don and Dougal spent nine days at or above camp six, perched on top of the flat iron at 24,000 feet, climbing to the top of the rock band. The rest of us tried to keep the flow of supplies going. Martin got sick and had to go down, having flogged himself to the point of exhaustion for the benefit of others. I moved into camp five with Nick. It was a grim, inhospitable place. Powder avalanches poured off the rock band onto it whenever it snowed. There wasn't the energy to keep things tidy, so the tent became a sordid mess. Most of us took sleeping tablets but I'd be awake from two, dozing, and then firing up the stove at five, making sure to fill the pan with snow from the right-hand side of the tent and not the left, where we relieved ourselves in the night.

Ferrying loads to camp six was brutal work, dragging myself across hand over hand where the rope ran sideways. I felt like a senile Tarzan attempting a comeback. On the way down from my first carry, I sorted out the ropes to making the job easier, so absorbed I barely noticed it was almost dark. The box tent looked very homely; Nick was busy making a stew, a little worried I wasn't back yet. As I snuggled into my sleeping bag later, we were both full of optimism. We discussed the tension caused by Don and Dougal moving through; he didn't share Mick and Tom's anger. 'The trouble is, Chris, you tend to think things out aloud. That's why you often appear to change your mind and seem over-impulsive.'

Next morning, Nick realized he'd reached the end of his strength and disappeared down the ropes to base camp. I did another carry, leaving behind the tent to bring more rope. Yet when I reached Don and Dougal they told me they were near the top of the rock band and ready to place camp seven.

'Have you got the tent?' Dougal asked.

I had to confess I had left it behind but promised to bring it next day. 'I could move up myself and help you establish camp seven.'

'In that case, why not move up with us and come to the top?' Dougal said. I was immensely touched by the warmth of his suggestion and as I abseiled back down felt a thrill at the possibility.

I had expected Ian to be at camp five when I got back that night but the tent was silent. Bad weather lower down had forced him back. I dosed myself with sleeping pills and slept fitfully. In the morning, I put my personal gear on top of the tent and food Don and Dougal needed but could barely lift my rucksack. Raging with frustration, I had to accept the summit was beyond me. Then, ashamed at my weakness, I shouted at the tent walls: 'Get a grip of yourself, you bloody idiot.' Halfway up the ropes, feeling stronger, I cursed myself for not bringing my sleeping bag but in retrospect instinct had stopped me. I simply wasn't strong enough and anyway, we didn't have enough food for three.

That night, Ian was waiting for me in camp five when I got home from my vertical commute. Cheered by his arrival, and with a brew in my hand, I began to plan the final climb to the summit. The following day Don and Dougal would establish camp seven, while Ian and I carried to six. They would go to the summit the following day. Ian and I would follow a day later. Mick and Tom would try the day after that. It was a great plan, but in the morning the sky was laced with high cloud, a sure sign of bad weather. During the night I'd suffered with diarrhoea, dragging myself out of the tent in temperatures of –30°C. Once we got going, I had to stop and relieve myself, dropping my trousers, which instantly filled with powder snow. The weather deteriorated, savage winds driving across the face and hammering against us as we fought our way up.

When we reached camp six, Ian was shivering, his hands numb with cold. We piled into the tent and tried to defrost them over the stove. Five minutes later, Don and Dougal arrived, beaten back by the wind. Their clothes were encased in ice and Don sported a magnificent icy moustache. It was too late to go down, so the four of us, squashed in a two-man tent, waited for dawn. I'd had a hundred bivouacs in the mountains, but that night was among the very worst. Next morning the weather was no better, and with camp five now occupied, Ian and I retreated to camp four. It snowed solidly for the next two days and I fretted that within sight of success the monsoon had arrived.

We spent 27 May in a state of deep gloom. Don and Dougal had said on the radio that morning they would try to establish camp seven that morning but it seemed unlikely given the continuing bad weather. At five o'clock, I switched the radio on for a routine call.

'Dougal, this is camp four. Did you manage to get out today?'

'Aye, we've just climbed Annapurna.'

It was stunning news. They had climbed the fixed ropes to where they ended and then carried on unroped, plodding up steep snow to the top of the ridge. They found a spot on the plateau to put up the tent, but it was just before the final steep wall, and since they were now so close to the summit there didn't seem much point. Dougal left it on a platform in its bag. Don then wove an elegant line up a series of little ice pitches and scattered rock moves. Dougal was struggling to keep his right crampon attached to his boot, and so was a little behind Don when he disappeared over the top on the final short section to the summit; he just had time to get out his little movie camera and shoot some footage. There was no celebration, just a kind of numbness. Elation would come later. It was for both of them I think the greatest moment in their climbing careers.

The relief and excitement in camps up and down the mountain was palpable. All the effort and suffering had been worth it. The question now was what next? Tom and Mick were still set on trying for the summit and it seemed only fair to let them try. But that night I barely slept, half excited at our success, half anxious about what I should do about Tom and Mick. In the morning I told Dougal to take camp six down but Tom persuaded me again. 'We won't be slowing your evacuation at all.' He sounded so reasonable I relented. He and Mick would carry on and those of us at camp four would go down to camp three. Mike was waiting for us there, his tent immaculate as ever, and at around midday Don and Dougal arrived.

'You want to get everyone off the mountain as quickly as possible,' Don warned me. 'It's falling apart. The whole place feels hostile somehow.' I felt the same.

Mick and Tom tried for the summit next day but Mick turned back with frozen feet. Tom carried on alone. Reaching the top of the difficulties and seeing how far it was to the summit, he paused in indecision, praying and taking pictures before finally turning for home. Now that they were on their way down, I decided to head down myself, leaving Mike, Dave Lambert and Ian to wait for them. I noticed an avalanche had wiped away Don and Dougal's steps from that morning over an area spanning 300 yards. The mountain really was falling apart.

Back at base camp I experienced relief rather than elation. Taking my crampons off for the last time, relaxing in a warm sleeping bag in our communal tent, these were great pleasures, yet I was ill at ease. In the morning I set up my desk outside and began tapping away at the typewriter, bashing out a report.

I remember Martin saying, 'Relax Chris, it's all over. Nothing can happen now.'

I looked up from the typewriter. 'I don't think I'll be really happy until everyone is down.' Then I started tapping away again. Kelvin was on the radio broadcasting our success when Mike rushed into base camp, throwing his ice axe into the ground like a javelin.

'Ian's been killed, for fuck's sake,' he shouted. 'Ian's been killed.'

Just above camp one, with Ian just a little ahead of Mike, an ice cliff had collapsed, engulfing them both. Mike was sure he was going to die but when the cloud of ice dust cleared, he was only lightly buried in small blocks of ice. Ian had caught the full blast. Mike and Dave found him at the bottom of the debris, his body emerging from the jumble of blocks. He'd been killed instantly.

We decided to bury him at base camp. Nick and I set off to meet our small band of Sherpas who were helping Dave bring Ian down. It was terribly difficult to believe that the inanimate bundle tied in a tarpaulin, strapped to a ladder, had only half an hour or so before been a breathing, active person: my friend. Ian had been the kindest and most selfless partner I ever had. He had faced so much in bringing the equipment up from Mumbai alone, but he kept his frustrations about the expedition from me. I would only read about them later, in his letters to Nikki.

His grave was a hundred feet above base camp, below a slab of rock where he had spent so many hours teaching ropework to the film crew and our Sherpas. I gave a short tribute and Tom said a prayer. The Sherpas placed a wooden cross at the head of the grave and decked it with wreaths of purple flowers. It was a simple ceremony, but had beauty and dignity.

Our tents had already been pulled down and loads packed. Our porters had arrived from Pokhara to bring us home. All we had to do now was turn downhill into the gaping jaws of the Modi Khola. Don, always ready with a pithy assessment, put it well. 'If you knew at the beginning that you were going to lose someone you wouldn't go. You go with the idea that you might.' Even now, after so many years since that spring in Nepal, I can offer no justification for the risks.

Chapter Ten

No Success Like Failure

Nick Estcourt saw them first as he peered through the camera's telephoto lens at the upper reaches of the south-west face of Everest. There was someone at the top of the gully. We crowded round impatiently to see for ourselves. It was 24 September 1975, more than five years since our success on Annapurna, five years since Ian had been crushed under the terrible weight of that collapsing ice cliff. That morning, at around nine o'clock, we had first seen Dougal Haston and Doug Scott at the bottom of the gully that led to the south summit. As they entered the gully they disappeared from view and as the day dragged on, we would take it in turns to scan its upper slopes, searching for the two black dots crawling towards their goal. By mid afternoon we were starting to think we had somehow missed them. Perhaps they had crossed to the other side of the summit ridge and were already at the top.

Then, at around four o'clock, as Nick took his turn at the camera, he shouted suddenly with excitement. At first we assumed whoever it was would be coming down but then it became clear the figure was still moving up, going for the top. Dougal and Doug would likely reach the summit that day, but had no chance of making it back to our top camp that evening. Crawling into my sleeping bag that night, I barely slept: excited they had most likely succeeded but anxious for their safety. No one had bivouacked so high on Everest before. I will never forget the feeling of undiluted joy next morning when we saw two tiny figures crawling back across the snowfield to camp six. When Doug signed off on the radio, I couldn't help crying with happiness. Dougal's throat was so parched and sore he could barely speak.

There was no chance yet to relax. Not only were Dougal and Doug still high on the mountain, a second summit party of four was on its way up to camp six, with two Sherpas in support carrying oxygen for their attempt next day. There was little I could do but wait and hope nothing went wrong. My last two big expeditions had ended, right at the last, in tragedy. I prayed this one would finish only in triumph. It felt like the culmination not just of an expedition but also a phase of my life. Nothing would be quite the same after it was over. The last few years had been the most intense of my life and Everest had never been far from my thoughts. I even dreamed about it. But my obsession had also stretched the woman I loved close to her breaking point. 'I felt,' Wendy said of that time, 'as though I was in a little cockleshell boat being tossed around in the wake of the great liner that was Chris, ploughing remorselessly through life.'

On Annapurna I had found my métier. In planning and putting together the south face expedition, I discovered something I was good at. There was a creative pleasure in it; it was like the games of strategy I'd played as a boy, but with a vast physical dimension and a high degree of risk. Thanks to the hard work and sacrifice of the team, we had stuck it out and succeeded. We had done something that was in the league of Everest's first ascent, or that of Kangchenjunga in 1955. Being part of that had been immensely satisfying. I still felt the old insecurity, my unusual childhood coming back to haunt me, but earning the respect of my peers made me happier about myself and the direction I was taking. After Annapurna, the obvious question was what would I do next? The equally obvious answer was the south-west face of Everest.

The idea had been planted years before while planning the direct route on the Eiger in the summer of 1965. John Harlin was always full of schemes, some fantastical, others visionary. He told Dougal and myself about his idea for an international team to climb the south-west face of Everest; I thought back to reaching the summit of Nuptse, with its grandstand view of the face and how at the time I'd barely considered it. I was intrigued. Our route on Nuptse, from 1961, was probably the hardest face yet climbed in the Himalaya. Everest's south-west face was much higher than Nuptse and split at two-thirds height by a vast band of rock barring the route to the summit. Solving this would be the key. After the Eiger, and John's death, both Dougal and I spent wearisome hours in hyperbaric oxygen chambers at the Royal London Hospital to treat the effects of the frostbite we'd suffered. To pass the time, we discussed future challenges. At that stage, I had no inclination and not enough experience to lead a Himalayan expedition. So we talked in loose terms to the doctor overseeing our treatment, Mike Ward, who had been on Everest in 1953 and had the right credentials to put something big together. Then politics intervened and the Himalaya closed; our ideas were put to one side.

In April 1969, as I was thinking about Annapurna, Jimmy Roberts, leader of our Annapurna II climb, wrote to me from Kathmandu. He wanted advice about equipment for an attempt he was co-leading, with the Swiss-American Norman Dyhrenfurth, on Everest's south-west face. Norman, born in Germany, had led the American team that succeeded on the west ridge in 1963. I wrote back with the information he needed and to ask if I could join. Jimmy promptly made me climbing leader. A few weeks later, I met Norman at Heathrow. He had immense charisma, looking like a movie star, appropriately enough since he had run the film school at UCLA. But he was also deeply sincere, even idealistic. He wanted climbing to move beyond narrow national self-interest. Norman, with his media experience and financial acumen, was the ideal front man; Jimmy, with his military understanding of logistics and his affection for the Sherpa people, was the perfect expedition organizer. They had worked together before, and it seemed like a good project. After that, Annapurna took over my life and I put the expedition to one side.

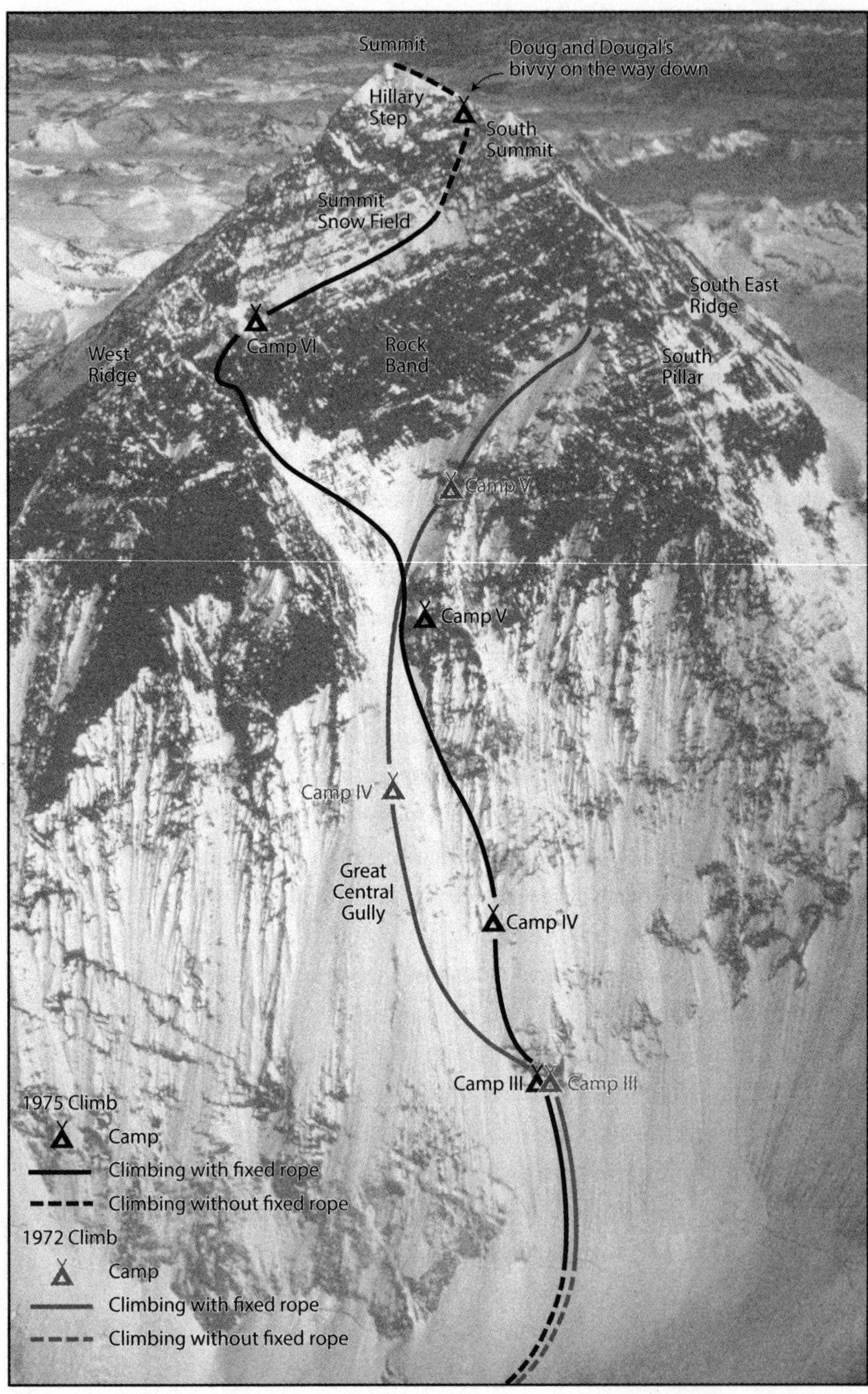

The south-west face of Everest.

I wasn't even sure the expedition would go ahead. While we were on Annapurna, a vast Japanese team had been trying the face and there was every chance of them succeeding. There were thirty-nine Japanese members, including a media team of nine, and seventy-seven Sherpas, twenty-six of whom would carry to high altitude. They had done a reconnaissance the previous autumn that had established a route as far as the rock band. Naomi Uemura, Japan's star climber, had spent the winter in the Sherpa village of Khumjung to stay acclimatized and manage the huge amount of equipment being gathered. They had sturdy aluminium frames to use as ledges on the face and plenty of oxygen.

Their mistake was over-complication. The face wouldn't be the expedition's only objective. The Japanese planned to climb the normal route as well. And while Saburo Matsukata was the nominal leader, he was seventy and didn't leave base camp: not the best place to lead an expedition. The climbing leader was Hiromi Ohtsuka, and he found himself torn between competing groups. It was too tempting to focus on getting the first Japanese to the top of Everest than pour resources into a speculative attempt. One of the south-east ridge climbers, 28-year-old Kiyoshi Narita, suffered a fatal heart attack. The Japanese did reach the summit and Naomi Uemura was one of the successful pair. But they stalled on the face, without doing any better than the reconnaissance party had in the autumn.

The main problem was that in autumn snow lay deeper on the mountain. In spring, the face was blacker, requiring more rock climbing on insecure ground, like padding up a roof of loose tiles. When falling rocks struck two climbers, Ohtsuka used the threat as an opportunity to call a halt and focus solely on the ridge. In his expedition report Ohtsuka warned those trying again not to make their party too unwieldy. They should make a plan and stick to it. It was good advice that went unheeded.

When I got back to Kathmandu after Annapurna, I went to see Jimmy to explain I was resigning from his expedition for the following spring. The team had grown and was now truly international, with all sorts of stars from all sorts of countries. It would also have two objectives: the west ridge direct and the south-west face. Having experienced quite enough problems organizing people I knew well who all shared the same language and the same ambition, how would I cope with such a disparate group who very likely wanted different things? I suggested Jimmy take Don Whillans instead of me, having already recommended Dougal.

While I ploughed through the aftermath of Annapurna, I began to rethink my decision to pull out of the Everest team, plagued with self-doubt and acute depression. I would rage about my choices, driving Wendy to tears. How could I turn down Everest? A large part of my sense of self, let alone my career, was devoted to climbing. When Jimmy visited me that August to talk further about equipment, I couldn't resist asking him if I could come back on board; Jimmy and Norman kindly agreed. Yet the same problems bedevilled the expedition as before and once again I resigned, a sequence of changes of mind that left me feeling quite ashamed.

I wasn't easy to live with in the months before the expedition left, in February 1971. That spring I was in Sicily, working again for the *Daily Telegraph* magazine about an eruption of Mount Etna. Wendy and I were also touring the Lake District, looking for a bolthole. She had never really settled in Bowdon. The suburbs left her feeling rootless and she missed the wilder country of the Lakes. Sean Williams, a friend from Hale who had moved to the Lake District, tipped us off about a cottage he had seen, above the village of Caldbeck. Badger Hill, named for a nearby sett, seemed the perfect weekend place to reconnect to the world we'd known when we first married. The cottage and its surroundings would become central to our lives together.

I couldn't help feeling relieved when I got the news that the international expedition had failed. It had been full of talented climbers and properly organized, but just as I feared, the expedition proved hard to manage, even acrimonious, with divisions in the team about its ultimate ambition. The Indian expedition member Harsh Bahuguna had died in agonizing circumstances, left behind in worsening weather on the west ridge. Yet Dougal and Don had acquitted themselves well. They had tried a different line to the Japanese, trying to turn the rock band on its right rather than the left and in reaching over 8,300 metres, had gone higher on the face than anyone else.

The important thing, as far as I was concerned, was that the face was still unclimbed. I put in an application with the Nepali authorities for the next available slot, presumably years in advance, and then focused on putting together an expedition to the Trango Tower in Pakistan. Then, quite unexpectedly, I was offered another invitation to Everest, this time from the Austrian expedition leader Karl Herrligkoffer. Chilly in manner, with a bristling moustache and swept back white hair, Herrligkoffer's motivation was always hard to fathom. Although not himself a climber, he had led several notable expeditions, including the first ascent of Nanga Parbat and the first ascent of the same mountain's gigantic Rupal face, when Reinhold Messner came to prominence. It's fair to say these successes were despite Herrligkoffer's leadership rather than because of it. He had survived some legendary feuds, and was at the time fighting Messner in the courts: a tough man. Herrligkoffer had permission for the spring of 1972 and had already asked Don and Dougal, but there was a place for me too. I had contacts with media and sponsors; Herrligkoffer needed money. Knowing Herrligkoffer's reputation, I would rather have gone to Pakistan. We had a great team of friends, including Joe Brown, Martin Boysen and Hamish MacInnes, so I stalled.

In November, Herrligkoffer and I met for the first time, improbably during filming for an episode of the television show *This Is Your Life* that featured Don Whillans. (They had contrived the scenario where an unwitting Don emerged from a tent in the studio to be greeted by host Eamonn Andrews holding a microphone. Don spoiled it rather by asking: 'What the fuck are you doing here?') It soon became clear that Herrligkoffer had made little progress with funds or organization – and the expedition was only a matter of a few months away. Even more disturbing was his apparent lack of curiosity about mountaineering in general. Only his own expeditions held any interest for him. In December I flew to Munich with George Greenfield and met Herrligkoffer at his apartment, beautifully furnished with statues and friezes collected on his travels. There was no sense of shared endeavour, no excitement: just a straight negotiation of media rights that allowed us to do deals with newspapers and television companies. But as we began to talk to the media about rights in Britain, it became clear that back in Germany Herrligkoffer was trying to generate enough funding to cut us out altogether.

In January 1972, I was climbing in the Alps with Dougal. We were trying the north face of the Aiguille d'Argentière but got caught in a storm two-thirds of the way up. We passed the time discussing the expedition to Everest. Both of us had deep misgivings. Dougal had already experienced one divided team and didn't want to repeat the experience. I knew Herrligkoffer hadn't organized oxygen or a team of Sherpas and I felt there was little chance of success. We both decided to pull out.

As consolation, we agreed to try a new route on the north face of the Grandes Jorasses, up the steep wall to the right of the Walker Spur. As on the Eiger, we fixed ropes up the face and thanks to the generosity of our friend Bev Clark could even charter a light aircraft to fly us and our supplies to the head of the Leschaux glacier. Being more of a conformist than Dougal, I worried a little what others might say about this. Dougal didn't care much about ethics and almost nothing about what others thought. The weather was bad, time was short and we should just get on with it. We thought we had the route in the bag with a just short distance to go when the weather broke. After three nights bivouacking in a narrow ice slot below the final headwall, we ran out of time and slid down our fixed ropes. Flying home, I found myself once again plagued with doubts and regret about Everest.

Don stayed on board. He knew as well as I did what Herrligkoffer was like. But he desperately wanted the chance to climb Everest, especially by the south-west face. It often seemed to me that Don's interest in climbing was not for the activity itself. His rock climbing in Britain had almost ceased in the 1960s. What he wanted were ambitious projects: strong, direct lines to the top of big objectives. In that sense, Everest was perfect for him. Securing his future was part of it; he liked the idea of crowning his career in this way. But it was deeper-rooted than that. The challenge spoke to him. So to replace me, he asked Hamish MacInnes to come, and called Doug Scott, fresh from success on El Capitan's Salathé Wall. Son of a Nottingham policeman, Doug was physically powerful, a former PE teacher with a passion for rugby. Rather than work his way through the obvious classics in the Alps, he had preferred exploration, leading expeditions to the Tibesti in Chad and the Hindu Kush, as well as putting up new routes on Baffin Island in the Arctic. All that strength and zeal would do very well on the upper slopes of Everest. Don now had a strong British nucleus but even so, Herrligkoffer – 'Sterlingscoffer' as Don called him – proved too a big hurdle. He had taken one look at Doug, with his long hair and round spectacles, and wanted nothing to do with him. Don was adamant: one out, all out and so Doug had stayed.

When they got to base camp, it transpired that Herrligkoffer, who kept things like equipment lists close to his chest, had failed to provide the Sherpas with enough warm clothing and had to fly back to Germany to get more. At least that kept him out of the picture for a while. Even when he was gone there was little trust on the mountain: progress stalled despite good weather. The British climbers finally withdrew to base camp and a desperate summit bid from the Germans ended below Don and Dougal's high point from the year before.

While Herrligkoffer was still on the mountain, I had a bit of luck that also presented me with a problem. Having put in an application for Everest in 1971, I had expected to have to wait until the late 1970s for a chance. I knew of several expeditions in the queue ahead of me. Then, soon after I quit Herrligkoffer's team, news reached me from Kathmandu. An Italian expedition led by Count Guido Monzino, a wealthy businessman and amateur climber, had the permits for the next two climbing seasons, post-monsoon 1972 and spring 1973. Now there were rumours he might pull out. Getting the 1973 permit would be ideal, but my sources warned me that Spanish emissaries, with a letter from Prince Carlos himself, had arrived in Nepal. They also thought the Canadians were sniffing around too. When I told Dougal, spending the winter skiing near his home in Leysin, he thought my politicking hilarious.

In April word came that Monzino had given up his 1972 permit, but was still thinking about the following year. I could either take the chance presented to me, or hang on and hope Monzino didn't take up his slot in the better climbing season the following spring. It wasn't an easy decision. I had mixed information about climbing the 8,000-metre peaks after the monsoon, none of which had yet been climbed in the autumn. In late September and early October the weather is more stable but colder. But as the weeks pass and winter approaches, the jet stream lowers in altitude, sweeping the tops with savage intensity, ripping tents apart and making movement almost impossible. Go too early and you face the monsoon snows and increased avalanche risk. Too late and you face the horrors of winter. That makes for a narrow window for such a big challenge. The Japanese had enjoyed unusually good conditions in the autumn of 1969 but I had also been in touch with an Argentinian team that had tried the South Col route in the autumn of 1971. Their leader, *Coronel* H. Cativa Tolosa, reported winds of 100 miles an hour and temperatures of –38°C. He also told me he thought the south-west face was more sheltered.

Deciding that I should take the chance, I developed the idea of a small team, just four climbers, attempting the south-east ridge. I found the whole idea of a lightweight expedition on the highest peaks increasingly appealing. There would be no jockeying for position, no tedious logistics, just a pure climbing experience. It was also the only way you could climb Everest without bottled oxygen, one of the great challenges left on the mountain. That challenge was still in the future, but my low-key plan was met with approval from a British climbing scene becoming rather jaded with large-scale sieges. Dougal was obviously part of the team, as was Nick Estcourt and Mick Burke. I also asked Mike Thompson along for support and added a doctor, Peter Steele. Then, as we began to develop our plans for the autumn, news came through that Herrligkoffer's attempt had failed.

My mind was in turmoil for ten days. So much about climbing Everest with a small team appealed to me. I would need to raise an extra £60,000 and gather far more equipment and supplies to try the face. Yet the appeal of a hard, unclimbed route was too great to ignore. In mid June I announced the change in objective: we'd be going to the south-west face. That left just eight weeks in which to prepare for departure in mid August. If Annapurna had been hard work, this was even more challenging. I was trying to finish my new book, *The Next Horizon*, while that horizon was racing towards me faster than I could face it. I would get up at 3.30 a.m., write until late morning, and then switch to the expedition, often working straight through until 9 p.m. or later. No wonder Wendy found life so hard, with a husband so completely absorbed. But the prospect of Everest galvanized me, blew away the anxiety and depression I'd been feeling. When my secretary Joan Lister's husband had moved for work, she had recommended her friend Betty Prentice as a replacement. Betty helped us through some very tough times during the 1972 Everest expedition; when we eventually moved back to the Lakes she switched to being my lecture agent, a role she filled superbly for many years.

My first problem was to find more climbers, in some ways the easiest task since there were a lot of good ones available. There had been eight lead climbers on Annapurna but this seemed too many for Everest. On the south-west face, difficulties started at 27,000 feet, higher than the summit of Annapurna. We already had a team of six, with four lead climbers. I now proposed to add two more lead climbers and two more in support. We had hired a few Sherpas for Annapurna but they didn't have the skills or experience to do the hard carries, especially between camps four and five. On Everest it would be different and so I settled on hiring forty, relying on Jimmy Roberts to pick the best men available. I also asked him to come with us as deputy leader and was mightily relieved when he couldn't resist. Most of the Sherpas would be bringing loads through the icefall to camp two beneath the face, but seven would carry to the higher camps at the foot of the rock band.

For the climbing team, the first two obvious choices were Doug Scott and Hamish MacInnes, who had both performed well that spring. But there was no place for Don Whillans. Hamish and Doug tried to persuade me otherwise, but other members of the team, particularly Mick, Dougal and Nick, understood my decision. Don's abrasive style had caused tension on Annapurna and he'd written critically of me when we got home. He had more experience of the south-west face than almost anyone, but our differences were just too great. Ten years before in the Alps, Don had been the senior partner; I deferred to his genius. Not now. 'The other feller,' Don told the *Daily Mail*, unable to use my name, 'will be up there playing his British Army captain bit. It doesn't wash with me.' I didn't mind climbers speaking their mind or being critical. Mick Burke had a similar background to Don, had the same sparky, sharp sense of humour. You could never tell Mick anything without him arguing about it. He shot from the hip. Yet there was no malice in it and having blown up, all his rage would dissipate. Don would brood. I understood his bitterness, regretted that our friendship was for many years effectively broken, but I never regretted the decision.

With so little time to prepare, there were huge hurdles to overcome. Looking back, I still can't believe we actually managed it. A further recruit to the climbing team was a friend of Dougal's and mine called Dave Bathgate. Bringing in Graham Tiso as a support climber, which Dougal encouraged, was another smart choice; he was running a small shop in Edinburgh, the perfect choice to manage the equipment. I also persuaded Kelvin Kent to delay taking up a new post at Sandhurst to work his magic again. Mike Thompson and Peter Steele were forced to withdraw, for perfectly understandable reasons, but we were lucky in their replacements.

Barney Rosedale had a very English, public school background, a modest but steady mountaineer, lean, intense, but with a lovely sense of humour. He had worked in Nepal as a doctor and was a driving force behind the Britain Nepal Medical Trust. Mick's wife Beth was a nurse, and he asked if she could come along, since he'd been away filming a great deal and they missed each other. She spent the expedition working at base camp, freeing Barney to move up to advance base, making a huge contribution in the process.

Money was ferociously tight and I made no secret of the fact. The *Daily Mirror* ran the headline 'Everest on the cheap'. Annapurna had been easy in that regard, having the backing of the Mount Everest Foundation. This time we needed to stitch the finances together ourselves, relying on George Greenfield to work his magic. Shortly before leaving for Nepal, we needed to have a meeting about the ethics of taking money from Rothmans, the cigarette brand. The lure of Everest is such that we were all on the VC-10 in mid August, on our way to Kathmandu.

Walking towards base camp I confessed to Wendy that I was struggling to cope with the stress. 'The responsibility weighs more heavily than it did on Annapurna and I'm tired. On top of that I've gone and caught one of my colds.' The two months of frenzied preparations had taken their toll. 'I'm sorry to be negative but I can only let everything out to you. I've got to keep a very stiff upper lip here.' Despite the pressure she was under, Wendy could always lift my spirits. Her letters were full of news about life at home and what the boys were up to. I would read them over and over again. Now she wrote back to me: 'The *Daily Mail* came to interview me for the usual "little wifey" bit and got talking to Joe. "And why is your Daddy climbing Everest?" "To earn some money."' The pressures of the media were something Wendy always dreaded. 'The realities of the expedition are beginning to hit me,' she wrote a few weeks into the expedition. 'Mostly brought to a head by un-put-offable newspapermen who keep on ringing up and asking all the usual twaddle now you are nearing the summit push – and all this sort of thing just gets me all tensed up, and I hate it. *The Sun* "newspaper" just asked me how we would celebrate your homecoming and I'm afraid I couldn't help saying: "in bed".'

In retrospect, it's hardly surprising that our 1972 expedition failed. Anxious about the risk of monsoon avalanches, and with so little time to get everything in place, we'd left for the mountain too late, by at least a month. We were also short of climbers, both in the lead and in support. We'd managed to rope in two extra bodies, an Australian friend of Doug's called Tony Tighe, who happened to be in Nepal and gave valuable assistance to Jimmy at base camp. The other was Ken Wilson, influential editor of *Mountain* magazine, whom I'd invited in a moment of madness and hadn't expected to show up. 'I hope he isn't going to be a thorn in my side,' I wrote to Wendy. Given our shortage of bodies, I put him in charge of camp one, where he spent a week on his own during bad weather, suffering the unusual experience of having no one with whom he could share his opinions. In the end, he proved a great practical help and certainly livened up conversation at base camp.

We had got about halfway up the face by mid October when the first of the post-monsoon winds hit us. I was at our highest camp, camp four, three box tents clinging to a little bluff in the middle of the huge couloir leading to the rock band. Up until that point, the expedition had worked more or less like clockwork. Dougal and Hamish had established camp five a couple of days before and I was hoping to stock it next day with a group of four Sherpas. But that night the wind struck out of a clear, star-studded sky, thumping into the upper face with the same noise a train makes entering tunnel. It roared down the face, smashing into the tents, bending poles and making any progress impossible. I was pinned down at camp four for a week, loath to abandon our toehold on the face. Yet the wind was, as I wrote in my diary, 'mind-destroying, physically destroying, soul-destroying'. I was overcome with lethargy, questioning my desire to lead from so high on the mountain.

Then a massive storm came in, driving us off the face and dumping three metres of snow. I lay in my tent at camp two playing chess with Barney Rosedale and listening to Bach. Most of our tents on the face were destroyed. Even so, we held on, Doug Scott and Mick Burke rebuilding camp four, where in an amazing stroke of luck the tents had filled with spindrift that had set like concrete, protecting them from further damage. I had got to know Doug much better during the previous weeks, writing to Wendy how the more time I'd spent with him, the more I liked him and the more his physical strength impressed me. Like Dougal, he was immensely strong at altitude; unlike Dougal, he was emotionally open. I often wondered what Dougal was thinking. Doug would leave you in no doubt, as I soon discovered. In trying to avoid some of the tensions on Annapurna, I had assigned climbers specific tasks. Hamish and Dougal were, I felt, the strongest pair on the team, so I gave them the summit push. Doug and Mick got the rock band. Yet now, having expended so much energy sorting out the ruined camps, they both needed to come down for a rest. I decided to move Hamish and Dougal up the mountain to tackle the rock band and regain some momentum.

When Doug got down to the Western Cwm that night he seemed to accept my plan, although he asked a number of searching questions. No one had ever told him when he should or shouldn't climb; having led his own expeditions he was not used to someone else setting the agenda. Next morning he arrived at the tent I was sharing with Barney. Having slept on my decision, he wanted to talk.

'I've been looking forward to the rock band for two and a half months and have got it firmly fixed in my mind that I'm going to do it. I don't see why we shouldn't; I don't see that anything's changed. We could go straight up tomorrow.' Having just come all the way down the face because they were tired, that didn't make sense to me, and I said so. 'You've been planning this all along,' he countered. 'In some ways you're no better than Herrligkoffer in the way you manipulate people.' After going back and forth for a while I finally lost my temper and told Doug that if that's how he felt he could start heading for Kathmandu. Through all this Barney remained a benign presence and with a broad smile began pouring balm on the situation. Doug and I temporized and the crisis passed: we came out of it stronger.

As so often happens, the situation on the mountain made our disagreement irrelevant. Nick and Dave Bathgate made a heroic effort pushing the route close to the site of camp six, but we were now in mid November, it was too cold and we didn't have enough oxygen and other supplies high on the mountain. Several of the team were back at base camp, more or less injured and out of the expedition. 'We're close to the top,' I told Wendy, 'but have a mass of problems: oxygen sets packing up in the cold, stones falling, running out of rope and the inevitable personality problems. We're also running out of time.' I went up with Ang Phurba to establish camp six, finishing off the work Nick and Dave had almost completed, shocked at how cold it was at night, even inside two sleeping bags. Then I made a carry, shouldering forty pounds of rope and oxygen up to our high point, the site of camp six, despite my own set malfunctioning, quietly proud of myself for sticking it out.

Staring across at the summit of Lhotse from 8,300 metres, I had never been so high and felt I had never seen anywhere so bleak or cold. I glanced up, hoping to see the snowy line of weakness Dougal had described in 1971, the key to our route. All I could see was an open corner of bare rock that would have been hard at sea level. On my way down to camp five, I paused to look across at the left-hand fork of the main couloir, where the Japanese had tried in 1970. That looked far more appealing. I found Dougal and Hamish at camp five, with Doug and Mick in support, readying for a final throw of the dice. I was almost done in, just wanted to be home with my love under the duvet, but there was no room for me there. Hamish handed me a cup of hot soup and I felt sufficiently revived to continue down to camp four.

Next day, when Dougal saw that grim, blank corner he knew we were done. Back in the Western Cwm, I wrote to Wendy on 16 November: 'You'll know by now we haven't got up, but it doesn't matter much, because I just want to get home to you and in addition it's been a bloody good expedition.' But now, just as on Annapurna, there was a tragic sting in the tail. Tony Tighe, desperate to see the Western Cwm for himself after so many weeks at base camp, had asked me if he could go up to camp two before the expedition left. It seemed churlish to refuse such a cheerful selfless worker, even though he wasn't officially allowed. Coming down from the face, Doug met Tony as he came slowly up the icefall, smiling happily as they talked. But as we sat drinking tea in base camp, Kelvin took a radio call. A section of the icefall had collapsed. One of the Sherpas, Ang Tande, had been left hanging from a fixed rope seventy feet in the air when the cliff he was standing on disappeared from under his feet. A section of trail below had been wiped out. Tony was missing. We searched for him that evening and again the following morning but it was clear what had happened. Tony was buried under hundreds of tons of ice.

It felt cruelly random. The Sherpas had made so many carries through the icefall without incident. The day before I had spent twenty minutes standing under the same cliff. But on his only trip to camp two, Tony had been caught. I had met him in Leysin, a friendly face when staying with Dougal, but on an expedition you depend on others to a degree that is impossible to explain. All of us felt his death keenly and turned for home with a mix of emotions: sorrow at Tony's death, disappointment at our own failure but also a sense of unity and friendship, of an adventure shared. I didn't know then if I would ever come back to Everest, but I now understood the true nature of the challenge we had set ourselves.

Chapter Eleven

The Hard Way

Home from Everest, Wendy and I drew closer. The memory of those bitter nights at high altitude, the stress and worry of a big expedition were fresh enough to make me welcome the warmth and domesticity of family life. The months of my absence, with two young sons aged five and three, had also driven Wendy to her limit. As our attempt had pushed towards winter, doubts about our fate and then news of Tony's death had taken their toll on her morale. The final straw was a female journalist with television crew appearing in our little front garden just as Wendy was taking Joe to school. She always struggled with the more intrusive elements of the media; close to breaking point, she turned on her heel and fled back inside. The journalist pursued Wendy up the garden and literally stuck a foot in the door when she tried to close it. Wendy collapsed in tears, close to breaking point.

What kept her sane through my long absence in 1972 was a mixture of meditation and weekends at Badger Hill, the little cottage in the Lake District we'd bought the year before. It nestled at the foot of High Pike, a rounded hill forming the north-eastern bastion of the Lake District's Northern Fells, just to the south of Caldbeck, a deeply traditional Cumbrian village. The huntsman John Peel is buried in the churchyard. A winding lane leads up onto the open fell-side where two farmhouses crouch to one side and on the far edge, part-hidden by a young ash and overgrown hawthorn, stands a low slate-roofed cottage. Its secluded garden, knee-high in unkempt grass when we first saw it, is still a haven. There was a warmth and serenity about the place.

Neither of us much enjoyed living in the suburbs. Bowdon, with its big Edwardian houses, had a rather melancholy feel. While there was open country within walking distance, the rivers were polluted and you were never free from the noise of traffic. I would often say grandly that you should never become too attached to a house: it didn't really matter where you lived. Perhaps that came from the sudden changes of address I experienced as a boy. But while I had the promise of the next adventure just round the corner, Wendy had no such escape. She felt trapped somewhere she didn't belong, removed from the network of friends she had spent years building. It's only now, with the hindsight of fifty years, that I have come to realize how obsessed I was with my passion for climbing and my own career – and how lucky I was with Wendy's unselfish love.

We were at Badger Hill that Easter after Everest. Working in the garden, I thought about packing up that evening and the tedious drive south. My heart sank. It felt like such an anticlimax. Before I had time to think about it, an idea popped out of my mouth.

'You know, love, there's no reason why we shouldn't live up here, is there?'

Wendy hadn't allowed herself to imagine us living back in the Lakes full-time. But she was delighted. At first we considered finding somewhere bigger but the atmosphere at Badger Hill had soaked into our bones. With a little bit of imagination we could extend the cottage sympathetically. We would spend the rest of our lives together nestled on the side of our hill: so much for not caring where I lived.

Even though I didn't have a big expedition on the horizon, I was full of plans. That summer Nick Estcourt and I climbed in Kishtwar, at the invitation of Narendra 'Bull' Kumar. Located in Jammu and Kashmir, Kishtwar, like other parts of the Indian Himalaya, was closed to foreigners so it was a golden opportunity. Our objective was a peak called Brammah and we drew on information provided by exploratory expeditions led by a young doctor, Charlie Clarke. Among the Indian contingent was an army colonel called Balwant Sandhu; both would become close friends. Nick had been a great friend on the big expeditions I'd organized and I'd come to rely on him. He was always prepared to do the awkward jobs that no one else would do or else would do badly. Brammah was far more relaxed, more like an Alpine holiday, and we snatched the summit on our second attempt in a spell of bad weather.

The following year I had another invitation to a remote Indian peak, this time to the Garhwal, close to the western Nepali border. Changabang is a beautiful tooth of white granite almost 7,000 metres high that I had come across as a boy in the writings of W. H. Murray. Tom Longstaff, another great explorer from before the Great War, called it the 'most superbly beautiful mountain I had ever seen'. The region it lies in is just as beautiful, with Alpine pastures and fir trees that remained remote for much of the twentieth century. Eric Shipton and Bill Tilman had explored nearby Nanda Devi from the west, unlocking a route via the Rishi Gorge to the beautiful flower-filled sanctuary at its foot. Travelling as co-leader of a joint Indian and British expedition, I now had the chance to follow in their footsteps.

Arriving in Delhi, I met my Indian co-leader, Balwant Sandhu, who commanded a battalion of paratroopers. First impressions were of a caricature pre-war British Army officer, a tall and dignified man with a keenly intelligent face and rather hooded eyes. In fact, Balwant, known to everyone as Balu, was a free spirit, liberal and highly cultured, one of five farmer's sons from outside Lahore. He was obsessed with mountains and became a great servant of Indian mountaineering. Balu wanted Indian alpinists to learn more about technical climbing and lightweight expeditions.

Balwant introduced me to his team, including Tashi Chewang Sherpa, who had got to know Tom Frost when Tom and Tashi had been involved in a secret CIA operation to place a listening device on a ridgeline of Nanda Devi. Tashi had carried its small atomic-energy power pack, called a 'SNAP' generator. ('Very heavy but it kept me warm and went bleep-bleep,' he told us.) I introduced the Indians to the other British climbers: Dougal Haston, Doug Scott and Martin Boysen. Travelling with us was Alan Hankinson, who had been on Annapurna as the man from ITN. He normally did the obituaries, appearing alongside Reginald Bosanquet when someone notable died. ('Yes, my dears,' he told us. 'You're all on file.') 'Hank' would be collating our stories for an expedition book.

I felt much happier and certainly more relaxed as part of a small team than on a big expedition – and we had a great deal to discuss. In the autumn of 1973, a Japanese team had made another attempt on the south-west face of Everest. As before, they also had a team trying via the South Col. Their attempt on the face failed in roughly the same place that we had, but they did succeed in reaching the summit on the normal route. For the first time, Everest had been climbed after the monsoon. Then, that December, I heard a Canadian expedition with permission to climb during the post-monsoon in 1975 had withdrawn. I wasn't immediately sure whether I could face another Everest expedition but the idea of a lightweight ascent hadn't gone away. After a few days, I put in my application. When I arrived at the Officers' Club in Delhi, there was a telegram for me. I had my permit.

Walking up the Rishi gorge and exploring the Rahmani glacier, looking for a route up Changabang, the conversation turned to Everest. Travelling with such a small group reminded me of what fun it was. I was still attracted to the idea of a small group trying the standard route without all the heavy logistics. On top of that, raising money for the 1972 attempt had been a nerve-racking experience. I wasn't sure I wanted to go through that again. Doug and Dougal, on the other hand, were keen to solve the riddle of the rock band. 'You couldn't just walk past the south-west face,' Dougal said. 'Anything else would seem second best.' I knew he was right, but said that if we were going back, then it would only happen if I could find a single sponsor.

Our expedition to Changabang proved a great success. We

thought of attempting the west face, the route eventually climbed by Pete Boardman and Joe Tasker, but it looked too hard for our mixed party and anyway, the mountain was unclimbed. It made sense to find the easiest way up. So we found a route over the Shipton Col and relocated to the Changabang glacier, below the peak's south face, part of the inner sanctum of the Nanda Devi Sanctuary. Bad weather kept us tent-bound for three days but the skies cleared just as we were running out of food. We left our high camp at two in the morning and reached the summit after a fourteen-hour push.

Dougal and Doug, the advanced guard, were sitting in the snow when I arrived at the top. The view from the ridge, bathed in evening light, was stunning, the Tibetan plateau stretching endlessly to the northern horizon. 'We've decided that this is the summit,' Dougal said with his usual pragmatism. I looked across at the other summit, a hundred yards away. I was sure it was higher. 'We can't claim this,' I told him.

Dougal looked exasperated. 'Bloody hell, I'll go and do it myself.' Martin and I agreed to go down with the two Indians, Balwant and Tashi, while Doug and Dougal carried on. They had caught us up before we'd descended a quarter of the way.

Back in England, Wendy was happier and more relaxed than I had ever known her to be after one of my long absences, despite spending seven weeks in a caravan with the boys while Badger Hill was being refurbished. The weather had been perfect and she couldn't have been closer to the quiet beauty of our environment. Joe and Rupert were settling in well at their new school. The house was still not finished, but it didn't really matter. We both could now let ourselves gently take root in our quiet corner of the Lakes.

Our first houseguest was Pertemba, one of the strongest Sherpas supporting our Everest climb two years before. It was a delight having him to stay and getting to know him better. Now in his mid-twenties, Pertemba had been one of the first Sherpas to benefit from an education at the school in Khumjung that Ed Hillary had built. Taking the chances offered them with both hands, the younger Sherpas employed in mountaineering were starting to take much more control of their working lives. I took Pertemba climbing on the Lake District crags and he played patiently with Joe and Rupert, even helping me lay out a new lawn. When he came to leave, I knew we had the foundation for an enduring friendship. I also knew he would be a powerful force in our attempt on Everest.

Funding the expedition had been the issue that made me hesitate most in trying again. Yet it proved almost childishly easy. George Greenfield knew I might be going back to Everest, but only as a small team at a cost of around £12,000. He flinched when I told him we now needed around £100,000, but he had powerful friends, one of whom, Alan Tritton, was a director of Barclays. Alan had sat on the organizing committees of several notable expeditions over the years, including that of Sir Vivian Fuchs across Antarctica. George suggested I meet him. A week later, I was ushered into his Pall Mall office and I showed him my plans. He was friendly but non-committal and I went home to the caravan to write an article on Changabang to help pay off the last expedition.

Then I got the news that Barclays were going to back us. It seemed a miracle. I will always be grateful to Alan Tritton for putting forward our case, and to the chairman Anthony Tuke for making the decision. Tuke had a reputation for going with his gut instinct, supporting my theory that when large companies support such enterprises it's because the project caught the imagination of someone very senior. The commercial justification usually comes later. Tuke's general managers had recently turned down his wish to back a cricket tournament and the story goes they didn't dare turn him down again.

Despite their confidence in the expedition, I suspect Barclays were shaken by the voices of dissent questioning the wisdom of supporting such a quixotic project during a time of economic hardship. This was 1974, the year of the three-day week and stagflation, so the notion that a major bank was paying for a group of hairy mountaineers to go on holiday was intolerable to some. There were letters in the press from disgruntled customers and the Labour politician John Lee threatened to ask a question in Parliament. Closer to home, Ken Wilson, from his pulpit in *Mountain* magazine, asked about the wisdom of spending that much money on an expedition with so little chance of success.

In fact, Barclays hadn't given us the money: they had, from their advertising budget, underwritten loans to the expedition, to be recouped from sales of the expedition book, lectures and television rights. As it turned out, Barclays got their money back, although of course they weren't to know that and I might have got my sums wrong. Their support was a key factor in the expedition's success. Whether the expenditure was justified is impossible to judge. All I can say is that over the years thousands of people have told me that following the expedition, through the papers or on television, or else reading our accounts, has brought them a lot of pleasure and perhaps a little inspiration as well.

First on the agenda was finding a secretary. I knew very few people locally, so I put an advert in the *Cumberland News*. By great coincidence, Louise Wilson had known my mother, having worked at the same advertising agency, but had then applied to be secretary to Lester Davis, head of Ullswater Outward Bound School to be closer to the outdoors. There she met her husband Gerald, the chief instructor. Since then she'd been a secretary at BBC Radio Cumbria. She was incisive and efficient, yet also had a twinkle in her eye. She warned me that she could be bossy: I hired her immediately, without even asking for references. She stayed for twenty-five years and she and Gerry became dear friends to all of us.

I've been immensely lucky over the years with my back-up team. Margaret Trinder took over from Louise in 2000, though she had worked part-time a year or so earlier than that, so knew the job. She was a wonderful PA: very thorough, unflappable with a great telephone manner and a quiet sense of humour, finally retiring in December 2015 well into her seventies and handing over to Jude Beveridge. Frances Daltrey took over my picture library, which Wendy had started to get in order in 1988. She has done an

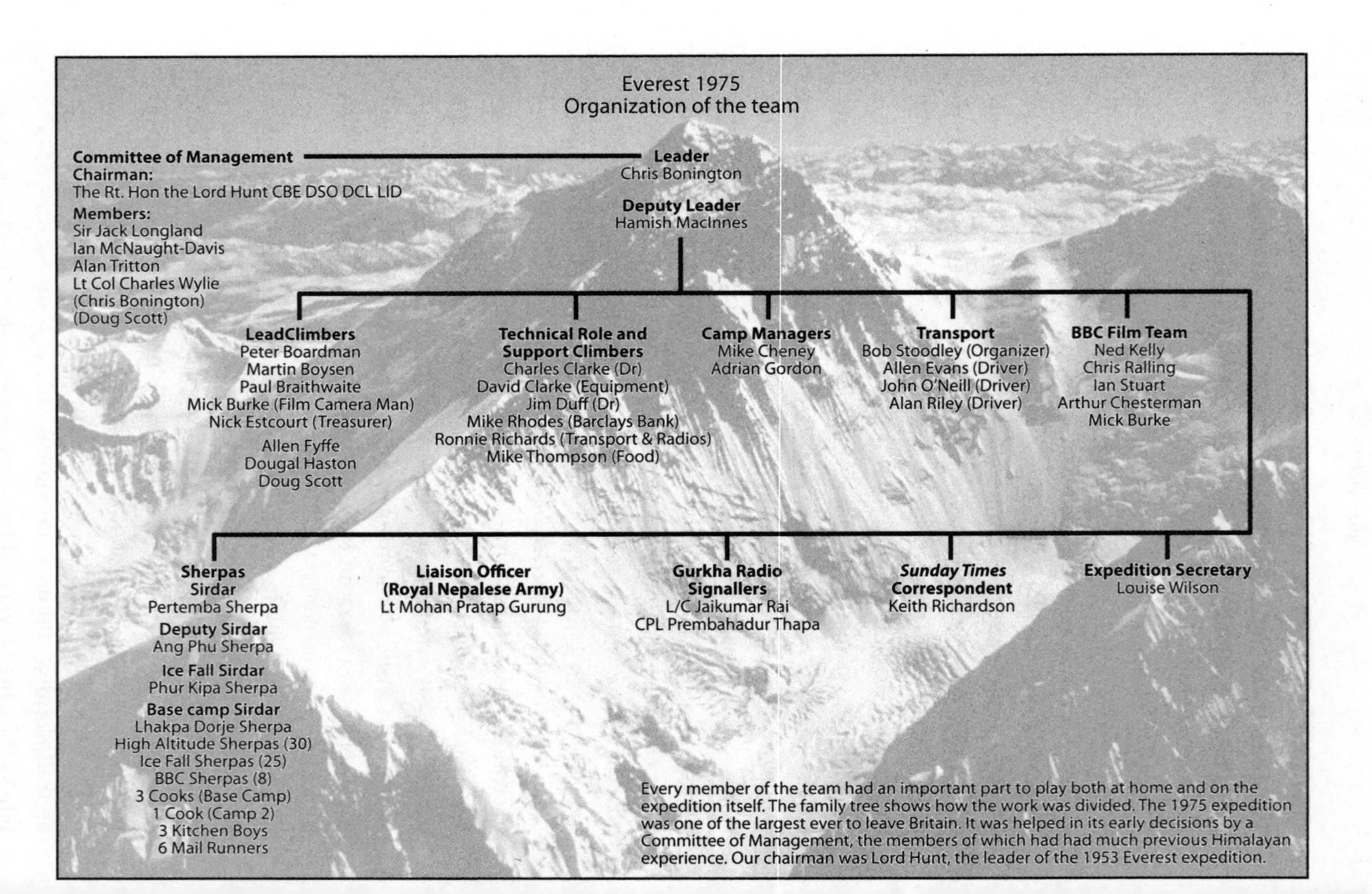
Everest 1975
Organization of the team
Committee of Management
Chairman:
The Rt. Hon the Lord Hunt CBE DSO DCL LID
Members:
Sir Jack Longland
Ian McNaught-Davis
Alan Tritton
Lt Col Charles Wylie
(Chris Bonington)
(Doug Scott)
Leader
Chris Bonington
Deputy Leader
Hamish MacInnes
LeadClimbers
Peter Boardman
Martin Boysen
Paul Braithwaite
Mick Burke (Film Camera Man)
Nick Estcourt (Treasurer)
Allen Fyffe
Dougal Haston
Doug Scott
Technical Role and Support Climbers
Charles Clarke (Dr)
David Clarke (Equipment)
Jim Duff (Dr)
Mike Rhodes (Barclays Bank)
Ronnie Richards (Transport & Radios)
Mike Thompson (Food)
Camp Managers
Mike Cheney
Adrian Gordon
Transport
Bob Stoodley (Organizer)
Allen Evans (Driver)
John O'Neill (Driver)
Alan Riley (Driver)
BBC Film Team
Ned Kelly
Chris Ralling
Ian Stuart
Arthur Chesterman
Mick Burke
Sherpas
Sirdar
Pertemba Sherpa
Deputy Sirdar
Ang Phu Sherpa
Ice Fall Sirdar
Phur Kipa Sherpa
Base camp Sirdar
Lhakpa Dorje Sherpa
High Altitude Sherpas (30)
Ice Fall Sherpas (25)
BBC Sherpas (8)
3 Cooks (Base Camp)
1 Cook (Camp 2)
3 Kitchen Boys
6 Mail Runners
Liaison Officer
(Royal Nepalese Army)
Lt Mohan Pratap Gurung
Gurkha Radio Signallers
L/C Jaikumar Rai
CPL Prembahadur Thapa
Sunday Times Correspondent
Keith Richardson
Expedition Secretary
Louise Wilson
Every member of the team had an important part to play both at home and on the expedition itself. The family tree shows how the work was divided. The 1975 expedition was one of the largest ever to leave Britain. It was helped in its early decisions by a Committee of Management, the members of which had had much previous Himalayan experience. Our chairman was Lord Hunt, the leader of the 1953 Everest expedition.

amazing job organizing slides and taking us into the digital age. They all became very much part of the family.

Having the money from Barclays in place so quickly gave me a year to plan the expedition, compared to the eight weeks of the 1972 attempt. I could afford not to cut corners. More importantly, we had hard-won experience of the route itself and what it would take to climb it. I narrowed my focus on three main problems: time, or rather the lack of it, before winter set in; getting enough supplies to the high camps and, perhaps most importantly of all, our choice of route. The Japanese expedition of 1973 had arrived at base camp on 25 August, the date in 1972 our team had left Kathmandu to start the trek. We had arrived at base camp on 8 September, a fortnight later. The advantage the Japanese had enjoyed seemed to outweigh the risks. As for logistics, the answer was more support climbers and Sherpas. In 1972 there were times when we had needed to delay our progress in order to build up supplies at a lower camp. We'd had six lead climbers and five in support. In 1975, after juggling numbers, I came up with a figure of eight of each, totalling sixteen. Still not convinced, I later added two more.

When it came to the route, the argument was all about where to cross the rock band. The 1969 Japanese reconnaissance and the 1970 attempt had focused on the left-hand side, aiming for the deep-cut gully I had looked at on my way down in 1972. In the spring season, this had been much more awkward, with the threat of falling rocks. The four subsequent expeditions had moved to the rock band's right-hand end. From there, as Don Whillans had seen, it was possible to make a long traverse rightwards to join the south-east ridge or climb the snowy gully Dougal had spotted in the spring of 1971. Yet we discovered in 1972 this gully was stripped of snow post-monsoon. Doug and I agreed that trying to the right was a blind alley; we should try instead to climb the deep-set gully on the left. Even better, we could climb it from camp five, speeding up our progress and boosting morale. For the first time, thanks to Ian McNaught-Davis and his company Comshare, I had access to a computer to run through the logistical permutations; it appeared that establishing more than six camps would be beyond us.

We already had a core of experienced high-altitude climbers who knew each other well. Dougal was the likely arrowhead of the expedition, having been twice to the south-west face. Doug seemed a good partner for him. Martin Boysen was a natural choice, perhaps not as single-minded as the first two, but he had that strong drive to do great things, despite the laid-back manner. Nick Estcourt and Graham Tiso had been down to come on the lightweight Everest attempt I had originally conceived but Graham wouldn't come for the south-west face. I understood his decision. In 1972 he had carried the burden of organizing equipment and carried loads to camp five in support of the lead climbers. The lightweight attempt had offered him a chance of the summit. Dave Bathgate, who had worked so hard to push the route out to camp six in 1972, also withdrew, with plans for a small expedition to a lower peak.

Hamish MacInnes, among my oldest friends, agreed to come as deputy leader. If Don was a genius at equipment design, Hamish was the ultimate engineer. As well as overseeing our oxygen equipment, he created a new series of box tents to withstand the savage storms that had wrecked our camps in 1972. I think at first Hamish doubted our chances but the lure of Everest proved too much, and as he got deeper into his work, his pessimism dissipated. The same was true for Mick Burke: 'I mean, just think how ropey you'd feel if someone got to the top this time and you weren't mixed up in it?' Mick's position was complicated: having trained as a cameraman he was now working for the BBC. Did he want to go as a filmmaker who climbed, or a full member of the team but carrying a camera? He chose to be a climber and in the years since I have often wondered about that decision.

One of the remaining two places went to a friend of Doug's, Paul Braithwaite, known universally as Tut and one of the leading alpinists of his generation. A former art student, Tut had dropped out to go climbing, working as a painter and decorator to pay the bills. Tall and willowy, he was a naturally talented rock climber, with plenty of hard first ascents, but had also recently climbed at altitude in the Pamirs. We soon became good friends and over the years I have developed a great respect for his judgement. The other new boy was Peter Boardman, at only twenty-three something of a stripling for an Everest expedition. Despite his years, Pete already had a highly successful expedition to the Hindu Kush under his belt, climbing the north face of Koh-i-Mondi, a peak that's almost 7,000 metres high. I was immediately struck by his maturity and obvious strength.

There were other key roles to fill. Jimmy Roberts was struggling with a bad hip and was happy for me to ask his deputy Mike Cheney if he would fill the role of our man in Nepal. I'd known Mike for years. A former Gurkha, he had retired to take up tea-planting in India only to be diagnosed with terminal cancer. He was given two months to live, and so, resolving to get the most from life, drove to Nepal in his Land Rover in defiance of his doctors. Like Francis Chichester, he defied his diagnosis and, finding himself still alive, got a job working for Jimmy. Mike, a fluent Nepali speaker, would manage base camp and recommended another Gurkha, Adrian Gordon, to manage camp two in the Western Cwm.

Replacing Graham Tiso was another priority. Thankfully, I recalled that an old friend of mine, Dave Clarke, had written to me just before the 1972 attempt offering his services as an unpaid Sherpa. Dave was a civil engineer I'd known since the early 1960s; we'd climbed together in the Lakes and shared adventures in the Alps. Having worked at a quarry in the Lakes for a few years, he'd left his profession to open a climbing shop in Leeds. He seemed the ideal person to take on Graham's role but it was a huge job, equipping not just the eighteen climbers of various kinds, but thirty-eight high-altitude porters, thirty icefall porters, four BBC crew, a *Sunday Times* journalist and various base camp personnel.

Finding more support climbers was a challenge. It meant asking strong mountaineers to make an intense effort with no chance of going to the top. Happily, Mike Thompson couldn't resist and agreed to the mammoth task of organizing twelve weeks' food for a hundred people. Doug suggested Ronnie Richards, a climber he had met in the Pamirs who lived in Keswick near me, a suggestion endorsed by Graham Tiso. When Graham also said: 'You must have Allen Fyffe,' I agreed, somewhat impulsively, creating for myself a small problem, since Allen was very much a lead climber, being among the best ice specialists in Scotland. Barclays also had their own man along, an easy-going, enthusiastic young rock climber called Mike Rhodes.

Barney Rosedale, our doctor in 1972, now had a practice in Marlborough and a second child on the way. To fill his place, I invited Charlie Clarke, a very different character from Barney. At first I thought him almost too smooth, a registrar neurologist at Barts with boyish good looks and an elegant house in Islington. So much for appearances: Charlie proved himself on Everest with his steady strength of character and professional judgement. At the suggestion of Sir Jack Longland, one of our committee members, I also brought along a second doctor, asking Jim Duff, with a strong recommendation from both Doug and Mick, already working in Nepal.

Working backwards from our start date in late August, we needed to arrive in Nepal in late July. Mike Cheney warned us that to be safe, we should get all the equipment and supplies to Kathmandu in early May, before the monsoon. I opted for the overland route, finding support from my friend Bob Stoodley, who ran a garage group in Manchester. Through him we hired two sixteen-ton trucks at nominal rent. With Ronnie's help, he plotted his way through all the problems of documentation.

In early April, at a chilly warehouse in Leeds, a dedicated team of volunteer scouts helped us sort forty tonnes of equipment and supplies for the mountain into weather-proof sixty-pound loads, the maximum a porter could carry to base camp, and packed them into standard-sized boxes. My long-suffering secretary Louise spent an entire night typing out the manifest and on 9 April the two lorries rolled out of the warehouse on their way to Nepal with Bob, Ronnie and two professional drivers on board. They reached Kathmandu in twenty-four days, having driven 7,000 miles. The loads were flown to Lukla and carried to Kunde, the Sherpa village above Namche Bazaar, to be stored in a barn.

With so much done in advance, I found myself in a much stronger state of mind when we arrived in Kathmandu, partly because I knew Wendy was better placed to cope with my absence. A week into the expedition, and walking towards Everest, I wrote to Louise: 'So far so good – Mike Cheney has done a wonderful job of the organization out here and our Sherpa cook is ace ... It's all much more relaxing than last time. This is good, for when the going gets rough, as it surely will, I think I shall have the reserves to cope.'

Things immediately got rougher. I came down with my usual early-expedition flu and then got a letter from Wendy quoting excerpts from Keith Richardson's first dispatch for the *Sunday Times*. It made awkward reading. According to Keith, some of the team felt we were 'over-organized' and our logistical planning would crumble under the pressures of the mountain. 'If [Bonington's] team fails it will be a long time before British climbers organize on this scale again.' He wondered whether the team was too experienced and if the youngsters, Tut and Pete, might 'waltz up and embarrass the old sweats'. Finally, he asked why Mick Burke got the best girls, a distressing thing for Beth to read, waiting at home for news of her husband. Wendy wrote: 'God knows how one can give a bloke a crash course in tact and sensitivity ... Beth is so vulnerable at the moment, she was really taken aback and *very* upset. It gives a poor bloody impression of the expedition that has cost so much – George [Greenfield] is very unhappy about it all.'

Keith was a forthright Yorkshireman and his blunt refusal to show anyone his articles rather alienated the team. I found myself caught in the middle, but events overtook the problem. Keith failed to acclimatize well and Charlie Clarke became increasingly anxious about him as he struggled to breathe while sitting down in the medical tent to bash out his articles. ('My skin was turning blue . . .' was the pull-quote from his last article.) An examination of his eyes, a new diagnostic procedure in those days, revealed retinal haemorrhages. Keith's expedition was over.

Managing a large group of highly individualistic climbers was undoubtedly a challenge, one I sometimes failed to meet. Doug told a BBC team that there was a hierarchical element to the expedition, of 'them, the leaders, the foremen, bosses, and us'. A decision I took to split the team didn't help. This was simply a method of keeping the trekking party to a manageable size, particularly at meal times. 'Perhaps unwisely,' Mike Thompson wrote, '[Chris] labelled these the A team and the B team.' A lot was read into how the climbers were split: was the summit team with me planning the final assault? Or, as Mike described, were the two groups divided between 'chaps' and 'lads'?

The truth was a little more mundane; mostly I had with me those who were in charge of different aspects of the approach to base camp: Mike Cheney, our Sherpa co-ordinator and base camp manager; Pertemba, the expedition *sirdar*; Dave Clarke, our equipment organizer. On the other hand, I did try to split up good friends on the approach so that all the climbers could get to know each other. And I was thinking ahead of different pairings. Dougal and Nick were superb climbers who in theory could make a strong summit pair but their temperaments weren't complementary. 'Tut,' as I told my diary, 'is a very easy-going kind of person, I think he'd get on well with Nick; they've climbed together before.' I fretted about whether Hamish still had ambitions for the summit and what Dougal thought about that. Doug's drive and strength were immense but his personality was equally strong. Dougal, I thought, wouldn't be worried about that. 'By getting the team as big as this,' I told my diary, 'I have given myself the reserves I felt that I needed, but at the same time this means that those reserves will be sitting around at times and that I can have idle hands . . . this is something I'm going to have to try to watch the whole time.'

I relied heavily on Wendy's letters, which were full of support and love without ever glossing over news from home that might worry me. 'The big double bed has felt very empty as I've got into it each night – but twice in the early hours a small Rupert-sized body has been sidling in saying he's had bad dreams or was scared – I suppose it might well be a bit of a subconscious reaction to your disappearance.' She was a great support in practical ways too, managing the reels of film arriving back from Nepal, and acting as a liaison for the wives and girlfriends of the team.

More than a week after reaching base camp, I could record in my diary that 'so far we're up to schedule and the thing seems to be running well. And when it's running well, it's very satisfying and when things start going wrong it can be very nerve-racking indeed.' I was delighted with Adrian Gordon, who had taken on managing camp two. He was incredibly steady and intelligent. Mike Cheney, whose health was always fragile after his struggle with cancer, was a tough old bird, highly intelligent and full of compassion. Pertemba made sure that the inevitable problems with his team of Sherpas didn't get out of hand.

On 13 September, two days before we'd even arrived at base camp in 1972, Dougal reached the site of camp five, our jumping-off point for the rock band. I had come to rely on his shrewd mountain judgement, and the tents were located in a sheltered spot on the right of the main gully, just before the traverse left to the crux of the route, the deep-set gully. A few days later I moved up to camp five and stayed there for eight days, sharing with Doug the job of pushing the route up to the rock band. Leading from the front had its advantages but there were problems too: Ronnie Richards, a qualified electrical engineer, looked on in amusement as I shook a malfunctioning radio set, yelling into the mouthpiece, before taking it off me and patiently restoring it to full working order.

While Tut and Nick moved up to tackle the rock band, Mick and I followed behind with loads of rope for them to fix. It proved one of the crucial days of the expedition. The route was like a

Scottish gully in winter, curving up between sheer walls of black rock, spindrift cascading down the walls. Tut was in the lead, his first obstacle a huge chockstone smothered in snow. It would have been easy at sea level, but at 8,300 metres it was a desperate, lung-bursting fight. Above, the gully steepened, and Tut was perched on a narrow rocky gangway when his oxygen ran out. Tearing at his mask, on the verge of falling, a warm trickle flowing down his trouser leg, he clawed his way to a resting spot and took a belay a hundred feet above Nick. Had he fallen, he would most likely have died.

Tut had stopped where the gully widened slightly and a fork led off to the right beneath a leaning yellow wall of rock. Nick had also now run out of oxygen and Mick and I were too befuddled to offer him ours. Instead, he gasped his way up the ramp, constantly thrown out of balance, using every inch of skill and experience to fight his way up, goggles misting up, panting helplessly. He brushed snow off a rocky lump with his fingers and hung on, refusing to give up, even though we feared watching from below that he might fall. For Nick, this was his summit and he wasn't going to admit defeat. Between them, Tut and Nick solved the crux of the route.

Dougal and Doug were at camp five when we got back, ready to establish the top camp above the rock band. I now had decisions to make and I announced a rest day before the final push. That night and the following morning I pondered the expedition's future. I had decided Doug and Dougal, obviously my most talented pair, should make the first summit bid but hadn't told them in case they weren't going well. Originally, I'd planned on just two attempts, but thanks to good weather, our strong team and excellent logistics, we were now in a position for two teams of four to try after Dougal and Doug. They weren't getting it on a plate. The day after moving up to camp six, I asked them to fix a line of rope across the snowfield towards the South Summit to safeguard their return and give subsequent bids a greater chance of success. The day after that would be their chance.

It was now that my team selection proved most difficult: I had too many lead climbers anxious for a chance at the summit. Nick and Tut certainly deserved their chance, but they were still recovering from the rock band, so I put them in the third summit team with Ang Phurba. It was important that there was at least one Sherpa on each team, to reward their immense effort, leaving four places for the other lead climbers. Mick Burke was with me at camp five and had earned his chance. Allen Fyffe hadn't acclimatized well. Hamish had inhaled a lot of powder snow in an avalanche, and I felt he wasn't capable. That left Pete Boardman and Martin Boysen, and I announced on the radio at the two o'clock radio call that these two would join Mick Burke and Pertemba on the next team. I would take the fourth spot on the third team, with Tut, Nick and Ang Phurba. I switched off the radio and spent the afternoon dozing, resting for the next day's effort.

When I finished the routine afternoon call, Pertemba took the radio and issued instructions to his Sherpa team. Instead of signing off, he told me Charlie wanted to talk, but later and privately. In his reassuring bedside voice, Charlie suggested that from my slurred speech and sometimes muddled sentences it was likely I had spent too long at altitude and should reconsider my position on the third summit team. Then he put Hamish on. My old friend's clipped Scottish voice crackled through the receiver: 'I've decided to go home, Chris.' I was shocked but understood his decision. Leaving him out of the summit teams had been a blow. Hamish had done so much for the expedition, keeping the team safe through the icefall and with his strong box tents on the face. I didn't think Charlie was right that I was becoming muddled; I'd just done some of the most complex logistical planning of my life. But it would be another seven days before the third summit bid, and that was too long. I could do more for the expedition at advance base, so I decided to give up my place to Ronnie Richards. I also spoke to Mick who was facing the same problem, but he said he was fine and determined to stay to film their ascent.

The following morning, on 22 September, eight of us set out for camp six, Doug and Dougal going ahead, the rest of us – Ang

Phurba, dressed only in ski pants and sweater, just behind the lead pair, Mick, myself, Pertemba, Mike Thompson and Tenzing – carrying the equipment and oxygen they would need for the summit. It was a great effort from Mike, far in excess of what he had expected of himself. For me too, there was a great feeling of fulfilment. I had played my part and now it was up to Dougal and Doug. Back in camp two on 24 September, trying to follow their progress through the telescope, there was nothing more I could do. We last saw them late in the evening on the little col between the south and main summits, still going up. Lying awake with worry in my tent, I kept the radio on through the night and felt huge when, at nine next morning, it finally burst into life and Doug reported their success. They had survived the highest bivouac in history, sheltering in a snow cave, and were somehow unscathed. Very few climbers would have endured what they had.

The joy was short-lived. The second summit team reached camp six that day and set off the following morning for the summit. Martin turned back with malfunctioning oxygen equipment but Pertemba and Pete Boardman reached the summit at one o'clock. They assumed Mick had returned to camp six with Martin so were amazed to meet him just above the Hillary Step as they descended. Mick even tried to persuade them to come back to the top so he could film them. They agreed instead that Pete and Pertemba would wait at the south summit. I'm sure Mick made it to the top, but by four-thirty he still hadn't returned. A storm was brewing, growing stronger by the minute. Daylight would soon begin to fade. Pete and Pertemba were dangerously exposed. If they had waited any longer they would most likely have perished. It seems likely that Mick stepped through a cornice on his way down from the top.

The storm raged through the whole of next day and while I clung to the remote chance that Mick – cocky, funny, exasperating Mick – might return, in my heart I knew he was dead. Another expedition had ended with tragedy right at the end. There was now no justification for a third attempt. Despite our grief, despite wondering if I should have been firmer with him, knowing how hard he had pushed himself, I couldn't deny the real satisfaction the whole team felt at our success. Even our most ardent supporters had given us only a fifty-fifty chance. Mick himself would have revelled in it. Any division in the expedition, what Mike Thompson had called the 'underground and overground', had long since disappeared. The most complex, demanding but rewarding organizational challenge I would ever face was over.

Chapter Twelve

The Ogre

The great gorge of the Indus slowly unwound beneath the noisy helicopter and Islamabad appeared below. I heard the pilot's voice through my headphones.

'Where are you staying? Might as well get you as close as I can.'

'At the British embassy.'

'I can't land there. The closest I can get is the golf course.'

We landed on the eighteenth green. A small knot of golfers waited respectfully, braced against the downwash from the rotor blades, no doubt expecting to see a smartly dressed Pakistani general emerge. What they got was a skeletal British mountaineer, dressed in filthy red long johns, heavily bearded, unkempt and with his arm in a sling. The helicopter took off and I walked to the clubhouse. People actually shrank away as I approached the desk, where I asked to make a call. Within half an hour, a friend from the embassy had arrived to pick me up.

Mountains are really just vast lumps of ice-covered rock, and it seems foolish to ascribe them personalities. But the Ogre had felt to me a malign presence. In the story that had just unfolded, the mountain had been the villain, toying with us, a malevolent power playing cat and mouse. He had enjoyed his fun and then, having battered and mauled us, had let us go. I was the last to escape, marooned in a remote Balti village, on my own for almost a week.

Yet we had all been left with wounds, psychological as well as physical; they would take a long time to heal.

My life unquestionably changed after the south-west face of Everest, as it did for all of us to a lesser or greater extent. For a while, we became public property. Many people asked me what I would do next. Some assumed that at the age of forty-one I would now retire. I suppose I could have followed a path into public service similar to that taken by John Hunt. I certainly appeared to be becoming more of an establishment figure, for want of a better term. I was honoured with a CBE, made vice-president of the British Mountaineering Council, was appointed to the Sports Council and asked to do an increasing amount of charitable work. Yet Everest was not the end, it was simply the end of a chapter. It had been a demanding but ultimately rewarding logistical challenge, the most complex I'd faced. In mountaineering terms, it marked the high-water mark of siege-style expeditions. After 1975, although many climbers carried on using fixed ropes and oxygen, interest among leading climbers shifted to doing these challenges without that support. Reinhold Messner picked up a newspaper in Salzburg reporting our success and knew what the next great challenge would be: Everest without oxygen.

My love of mountaineering was, if anything, greater than ever, and I had no intention of hanging up my boots. So if the lecture tours were now more hectic, and I found myself flying out to exotic parts of the world to speak at business conferences, my lifestyle didn't really change. I enjoyed the freedom of being a freelance writer and photographer and loved our home. Climbing itself remained for me a relaxing if physically exacting recreation. What I really wanted was to go back to the mountains with a smaller, more tight-knit group, without the heavy responsibility that command of a large expedition imposes. And so, when Doug Scott called me in the summer of 1976 asking if I wanted to join his team for an attempt on Baintha Brakk – nicknamed the Ogre – in the Karakoram I accepted without hesitation. It would be a magnificent contrast to Everest: a small team, no responsibilities, more like an

Alpine holiday than an expedition. I'd never climbed in Pakistan before and couldn't wait.

'I've asked Tut, Dougal, Mo and Clive,' Doug said. 'I'll send you some pictures. Tut and I are going for the big rock nose but Clive prefers a route to the left. If you want to come you can decide which route you want.'

The photos arrived a couple of days later. The Ogre was no shapely summit of soaring ridges meeting at an airy summit. It looks like an ogre, solid, chunky, a complex of granite buttresses and walls, threaded with icy gullies and ice slopes, leading to a three-headed crown towering above the Baintha Brakk glacier, more than 7,200 metres above sea level. Doug had marked his line up a pillar of rock that looked like El Capitan, but which only went a third of the way up the peak to a band of snow ledges that wrapped around the Ogre's waist like a cummerbund. Doug's route then went up a ridge of serried walls to the left or western summit.

I didn't fancy it at all. The mountain seemed big and hard enough by its easiest route. This appeared to be a wall to the left of Doug's buttress, stringing together a series of snow and rock arêtes, before traversing the cummerbund across Doug's line to reach a big snow slope that comprised the Ogre's south face. That led to its three heads; the one in the middle seemed highest. Dougal felt the same way, preferring the most reasonable line up what appeared to be an extremely difficult mountain. Doug had proposed we'd climb as three pairs and while Dougal and I didn't say so specifically, I think both of us took it for granted we would be joining forces.

In January 1977 I drove to Chamonix for some winter climbing with Dougal and to talk about the summer. I gave a lift to Mo Anthoine, also on the Ogre team and one of the great characters of British climbing, immortalized in the book *Feeding the Rat* by the writer and critic Al Alvarez. Al I knew from poker sessions in Hampstead, back in the 1960s; those were high-stakes games, nerve-racking and totally addictive. Al and his scriptwriter mates had a lot more money than I did; the night before I set out for the

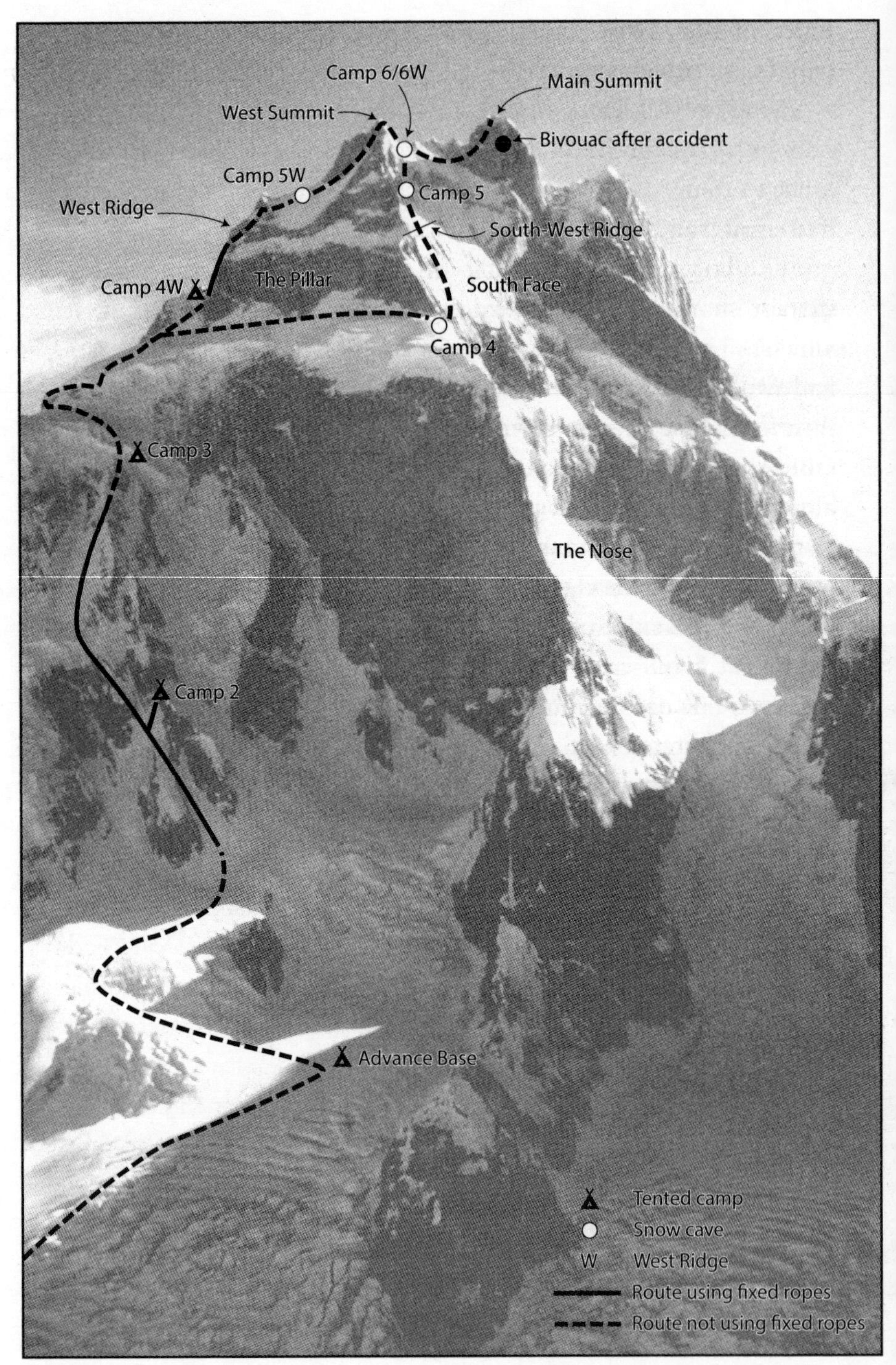

The Ogre, 1977.

Eiger in 1962, I lost about a hundred pounds, the money for our trip, but hung on until five in the morning until I'd won it back.

I had known Mo for years too, mostly bumping into him in the pub. He was exuberant and extrovert, with a near-obsessive reluctance to compromise his wild sense of freedom. He and Joe Brown had started an equipment business together, but never allowed it to grow so large that it interfered with expeditions. Among his many extraordinary adventures was the first ascent of Trango Tower, which he had climbed with Martin Boysen the previous summer. Mo had a vulgar, Rabelaisian wit that easily tipped over into biting satire. As a former public school army officer with a national profile and a CBE, I was, perhaps inevitably, something of a target. Yet we rubbed along pretty well and I was looking forward to climbing with him.

The weather was bad when we arrived in Chamonix, and Dougal persuaded me to stay there and ski while he put the finishing touches to the novel he'd been writing. George Greenfield was waiting for the manuscript in London. Mo and I, with Bill Barker, had a riotous few days charging down the slopes, all self-taught with appalling technique but quite bold. When I called Dougal again on the Sunday, he said that he was almost done and would come over in a couple of days, even though the weather was still poor. The next evening, we were drinking in Le Chamoniard when the proprietor, Titi Tresamini, called me over. There was a phone call from England. It was Wendy and she was crying.

'Have you heard about Dougal?'

While skiing the north-east face of La Riondaz that day, near his home in Leysin, Dougal had been caught in an avalanche. He was dead. Wendy had been trying to find me, anxious that I might have been caught in the avalanche too and that my body had yet to be found. She hadn't known I was still in Chamonix. I experienced the familiar wave of shock and grief, except it was more acute this time, coming as it did so unexpectedly. Dougal had survived plenty of near-misses in the high mountains, so to die in a skiing accident so close to home seemed oddly cruel. We drank through the night and grew maudlin, as you do in such circumstances.

I felt Dougal's loss acutely, both as a good friend and a like-minded climbing partner. We didn't speak much, even when we were sharing a tent. He kept his counsel in a way Don did not and consequently avoided conflict; as an expedition leader I valued his support. I don't think I ever got really close to him, in the way I did to Nick Estcourt, but then I'm not sure anyone did. There was something profoundly unknowable about him. George Greenfield's last glimpse of Dougal somehow captures that enigmatic quality. George described hearing from him on the Friday before his death: the novel was finished. On the following Tuesday, the day after Dougal's death, a package arrived at George's office containing the manuscript. The protagonist is an expert skier who runs a climbing school in Leysin, likes to get his kicks triggering avalanches and skiing down ahead of them. That's not what happened in Dougal's case: that was just plain bad luck. But, as he sat reading, George sensed that Dougal, 'indolent as a purring cat, almost seemed to be slumped in the armchair across from my desk'.

Quite apart from my sense of loss, I no longer had a climbing partner for the Ogre that summer. Luckily I didn't have to think too hard: Nick was the obvious choice. Doug was quick to take advantage of Nick's conscientious organizational ability, handing him the job of getting together all the food. Tut, who had recently opened a climbing shop, sorted out the equipment we needed. Clive Rowland was driving it all to Pakistan in Mo's van and would meet us in Islamabad. I had practically nothing to do, a delight after the last few years.

We were fortunate to be staying with Caroline Weaver, a secretary at the embassy whom Mo had befriended the previous year on his way to Trango Tower. Our days were spent alternating between the well-stocked bar and swimming pool at the British Club and the hot and dusty bazaar in Rawalpindi buying sacks of rice, flour and dal to feed our porters. In those days, the Karakoram Highway didn't go all the way through the mountains and the only way to our jumping-off point was via a notoriously unreliable flight to Skardu. People could get stuck for weeks waiting for a flight, but we were delayed only for a day. As the Fokker Friendship lifted above the foothills that ring Islamabad, snow peaks appeared above the cloud and Doug and I raced to the windows, ignoring the plaintive cry from our liaison officer, Captain Aleem, that photography was forbidden.

All of it was new to me, the ruined fortress overlooking Skardu, the brightly painted trucks smothered in chrome, the melodious singing of the porters as they helped paddle our ferry across the Indus, water sparkling in the sunlight of early morning with the arid desert valley beyond. I enjoyed my non-role, just absorbing the sights and sounds around me. I thought it prudent to keep quiet when Doug and Mo decided to press on, leaving the selection of porters to Captain Aleem. I didn't see the need for hurry, but it wasn't my call. 'Doug's system,' I wrote in my diary, 'is not to direct anything, to let it all happen. In theory this is good.' As it happened we were delayed and so did have a hand in choosing the porters after all. I tried to conceal my satisfaction. As half a dozen police towered over the gathered crowd, wielding their *lathis*, Mo strode down the ranks picking out those that looked the strongest.

Haji Medi was the headman of Askole, a small, plump man with shrewd eyes dressed in homespun and a woollen cap. His hands were soft and clean: he owned much of the land and sold surplus flour for a handsome profit to passing expeditions. The houses were flat-roofed, single-storeyed boxes of stone rendered in mud, each with store-rooms, byres and living quarters opening onto a tiny courtyard. On the roofs were piles of firewood, chillis and apricots drying in the sun, and a small penthouse where the owners could sleep in the heat of summer. It was fascinating comparing it to what I'd seen in Hunza a decade before.

The person I knew least on the expedition was Clive Rowland, an old friend of Doug's who had been with him to Baffin Island and an earlier trip up the Biafo glacier in 1975. Clive, like Mo, had a caustic wit and I quickly concluded that he took a dim view of me, either because of my background or because of my reputation as the big expedition leader. I'm not sure he was happy I had filled

Dougal's place with Nick. By chance, I found myself walking up the Biafo glacier with Clive and Captain Aleem and overshot the campsite. We spent that night huddled under a wet boulder but this rather dispiriting experience brought us together a little.

I was more taken aback by the fury our disappearance provoked in Doug and Nick, who had gone all the way back to the last campsite to look for us.

'Why the hell didn't you get back to our campsite really early? Surely you realized we'd be worried?'

We defended ourselves, a little huffily, because we knew we were in the wrong. But I was touched by Doug's concern. He could be aggressive in argument but underneath it there was a big heart. That night I was happy to sleep out under the stars in a sleeping bag made from a new kind of fabric I'd never heard of before called Gore-Tex, which promised to keep the rain off but somehow allow condensation to escape. It was little more than ten years since the Eiger Direct, but equipment was changing out of all recognition.

Next day we reached base camp on the Baintha Brakk glacier. Scrambling across broken rocks, we climbed a high bank of moraine and found ourselves on the brink of a gentle haven, a hollow carpeted with grass and flowers, holding a small lake and dotted with boulders. A few tents were already clustered round one of these; we knew there would be another British expedition trying the neighbouring peak of Latok I. It was like being at the campsite in Chamonix. That evening Paul Nunn and Tony Riley wandered over to chat and Nick picked up a conversation with Paul that he'd been having a fortnight before in a Peak District pub. That night we talked long into the night, gossiping about the climbing scene back home, listening to Mo's outrageous stories, with the peaks flanking the Ogre silhouetted against the star-washed sky.

That level of harmony proved hard to maintain. The idea of three teams of two sharing the mountain, of having common cause but different agendas, inevitably led to frustration. We kept six of the best porters to ferry loads to an advance base camp, and then set to work on our various projects. Doug and Tut were headed for the dramatic and difficult nose; while Clive and Mo waited for their wives to arrive at base camp, the two of them joined Nick and me in climbing the shared portion of our respective routes, fixing ropes on a broken wall of granite buttresses and snow gullies that outflanked the nose. This broken wall led ultimately to the col beneath the west ridge.

We placed a camp halfway to the col on the crest of a little rock spur, safe from avalanche. It was a magnificent eyrie. Our two teams shared the task of fixing rope above it but we acted independently when it came to food and the pace we set. Mo and Clive were altogether more relaxed in their approach, without the sense of urgency Nick and I shared. We thought we should get on with it, while the weather was good, get established on the col and then go for the summit Alpine-style. Mo and Clive, who were sticking to the west ridge, wanted to take their time, and when their wives arrived they headed down to base camp. Things became more complicated when Tut was struck on the thigh trying to dodge a football-sized rock approaching the bottom of their route. He was out of action, at least for a while, so Doug was without a partner. The chances of them climbing their route had largely disappeared.

Pushing the route towards the col in late June, Nick and I saw three figures climbing up towards our camp on the face. We assumed it was Doug with the others and so were a little nonplussed when we got back to camp to find they only had brought up a few cans of gas, a few pegs and three ropes. If they were serious about committing to the mountain, they would have carried more. So we decided we'd commit to reaching the top of the col on our own. Next day, as we came down in the afternoon, we found Mo and Clive in residence, having put up a second tent. Our resentment soon melted away; it hadn't been Doug we'd seen, it was Jackie Anthoine. Clive and Mo agreed to go up the following day and try to reach the col. They came back having pushed the ropes to within a few metres of the crest. Nick and I now decided to make our push for the summit. We reckoned we had around a week's worth of food and fuel, just enough for the round trip.

When we left next morning, shouldering loads of twenty kilos, Clive and Mo were still in their bags with the tent door zipped shut. They were too far behind in their load-carrying to come with us: they didn't have enough food. But they were vague about their plans, adding that Doug may well want to join them later if Tut didn't recover. The fixed ropes, 500 metres or so, ended at a fragile snow arête. There hadn't been enough rope to bother fixing this, so we climbed its crest with dizzying drops on either side, glad to reach the bottom of the next rope. This final stretch ended below a big curling cornice. I dumped my sack and led off round the corner, climbing a runnel of bulletproof ice with a covering of soft snow that led to the broad, gently rising plateau of the col.

All the tension of the morning ebbed away: we had overcome the wall, were on our own and committed to the climb. I slipped back down the ropes and picked up a cache of food while Nick prepared the campsite. When I got back, exhausted from hefting twenty-five kilos back up the ropes and across the exposed ice ridge, I was relieved to hear the purr of the stove inside the tent. That night we both slept well, Nick too exhausted from the day to be bothered by my snoring. The alarm went at two, but without saying anything we dozed for an hour before I started breakfast. We were out of the tent at five, climbing in frozen shadow through a maze of crevasses onto the top of the col.

The mountain was still in shadow when we reached the slope leading to the 'cummerbund'; we planned to traverse this to the south-west ridge and then onto the south face. It proved nervy going, more soft snow on iron-hard ice, but Nick, out in front, suddenly let out a whoop. By chance he'd found a fixed rope left in place by an unsuccessful Japanese team. He tugged it cautiously and then followed it to the top of the slope where he found two coils of unused rope. It was clearly their high point. To our right, the cummerbund stretched off to the right under a sheer wall of granite and although it was only half past ten, we opted to return to camp and explore it the following morning.

Next day, we were both anxious, overpowered perhaps by the

scale of the mountain and our own isolation. Nick shouted up he thought I had drifted too high and was on the wrong route.

'Can't you trust me to pick the best line? Just bloody well shut up and leave me to get on with it.' My short temper betrayed the fact I was worried he was right. We soon made up, but the traverse was much longer than we anticipated and more insecure too. Finally we could look round the corner at the south face: a band of granite slabs separated us from the steep snowfield that led towards the Ogre's summits. Back at the col, we were shaken to discover we only had four cans of gas left, barely enough for three days. Looking down the mountain we could see the others were on their way back up but we were loath to go down and get some more. We wanted to stay out in front and remain independent, even if that meant pushing closer to the edge. I persuaded Nick we should leave the tent behind and dig a snow hole. He didn't like the idea, but when we left next morning neither of us picked it up: our sacks were heavy enough as it was.

We were back at the end of the traverse in just an hour and a half and decided to fix our two ropes across the slabs in preparation for the morning. Nick climbed delicately up hard ice and then tiptoed up the granite slabs on his crampon points, banging in a peg and tying off our first rope. I followed and looked nervously at the next fifteen metres of smooth slabby granite that led to the snow and ice of the south face. It resembled the Etive Slabs in Scotland. What if I fell? Any injury would be desperately serious in our current position. I reached a hairline crack, tapped in a knife-blade peg and tensioned off that, brushing snow from the rock to find something to stand on. The pitch took an hour and a half of total concentration until I reached a solid crack where I could place a good peg. Beyond that was good ice where I could place a screw and tie off the rope. We had found the key to the south face.

That afternoon we dug a snow hole, burrowing into a prow of snow that seemed to hold enough material, gasping for breath as we worked at over 6,500 metres. In three hours we had a secure shelter and settled in for the night, but when the alarm went and I handed Nick a mug of tea, he could hardly stay awake, exhausted from the week we'd spent above advance base. A day's rest meant a day's less gas, and when Nick collapsed back into unconsciousness, I fretted in my diary about whether he would be fit enough to go on. He woke later that morning refreshed, writing in his diary that 'the problem was probably accumulated lack of sleep aggravated by Chris's snoring and thrashing about – how does Wendy stand it?'

By the afternoon I felt rather ashamed at my lack of patience but I was no less determined, even when I saw a dark bank of cloud approaching us next morning. I lashed out at Nick for needing a rest, and then instantly apologized. It was wholly unjust. We agreed to at least try, since we only had one more can of gas, but by the time we'd climbed the ropes we'd fixed the day before, the wind was lashing spindrift around and ragged clouds were forming around the Latok massif. The climbing was horribly precarious, half a metre of snow on hard ice, but I was totally committed. Nick was convinced I was leading him to his doom. Yet he kept climbing, overcoming the most frightening pitch of the route while I sheltered from the spindrift below.

We spent that night in a scrape in the snow, with some shelter above our heads. 'Had a brew,' Nick wrote, 'felt miserable and Chris snored all night. I sat and watched the swirling mist and wondered what it was going to be like to freeze to death.' At first light the weather was still threatening but we stayed put for a bit, and then it cleared a little, luring us on. Doubt only crept into my mind when we arrived at the bottom of the summit tower. It had seemed little more than a knobble of snow-veined rock from advance base. I assumed there would be a gully or ramp to take us to the top. But from where we now stood it appeared massive and invulnerable. We had eight rock pegs, one gas cylinder and a day's food.

'We'll never make it,' I told Nick. 'We haven't enough stuff. How about going for the west summit?'

That looked a lot easier so we veered towards the crest of the ridge that linked the two peaks. When we reached it, the cloud disappeared as if by magic and we peered down the shadowy north face of the Ogre in bright sunshine. Range upon range of peaks stretched away to the north. We were surrounded by the most dramatic mountain views in the world. My spirits soared.

'You know, we could still have a go at the main summit.'

Nick almost exploded.

'For pity's sake, Chris, can't you keep to a decision for ten minutes?' The reasons we had backed off the main summit still held and I knew he was right. Later he wrote in his diary that if I'd had my way I would have spent the rest of my days up there. Looking back, after forty years, I'm now astonished at the level of my commitment. We dug out a snow hole for the night and then lazed in the sun. The following dawn was perfect and although Nick had developed a dreadfully sore throat and was coughing blood, it wasn't too long before we were at the top. The view was simply magnificent, with the whole of the Biafo glacier stretched out at our feet. Yet the main summit 200 metres away and only fifty or so higher seemed to mock me. We had done the sensible thing but I couldn't escape a sense of anticlimax.

We were back at the snow cave on the cummerbund at six that evening, a long diagonal abseil taking us across the awkward granite slabs. But where were the others? There was no sign of them until we rounded a corner on the traverse back to the col and saw two tents on the plateau with four figures around them. What had been the delay? The obvious explanation was an accident – but to whom? As we approached, Mo was bent over a stove, Doug and Tut were packing rucksacks and Clive was taking down a tent. They were clearly on the move but barely reacted as we approached: our dash for the summit had not gone down well.

'Don Morrison's dead,' Doug said, flatly. Don, we learned, had stepped through a snow bridge and disappeared into a crevasse. It was so deep Paul Nunn and Tony Riley hadn't been able to reach him. I hadn't known Don, and exhausted from ten days on the mountain felt blank. I also sensed hostility from the others and their relief when we told them we'd only been to the west summit. I felt an odd mixture of guilt that we had gone for the top and disappointment that we had failed. The others weren't interested in repeating our line; they were pressing on up the west ridge and were about to establish a camp beneath a steep rock pillar barring access to the west summit. From there, they would try for the top. I looked at their pile of food and gas.

'Is that all you've got?'

'Yeah, should be enough,' Mo said. I told them I didn't think it was, and explained how long it had taken us and how hard the final summit tower would be. They were in danger of making the same mistake we had. My motivation wasn't altogether altruistic. If I could persuade them back to base camp for more supplies then Nick and I would have time to rest and come back with them. Nick, suffering from his dreadful sore throat, was already two weeks overdue for work. In convincing the others, I had committed him to even longer away without really thinking about it. 'Chris at his most cunning,' was how Mo put it.

Base camp was an oasis of green. You could smell the grass, lie in it – grasp it with your hands. The fear and doubt of the harsh world of rock and glaring snow we had just stepped out of had ceased to exist. Paul and Tony were packing, having built a small memorial cairn to Don. Doug and the others talked long into the night, but I sloped off to bed, suddenly exhausted. In the morning, I realized how tired I was, barely able to get up for meals. I scribbled a brief note to Wendy, telling her our plans. Doug, Mo and Clive left next day for the mountain. The plan was I should follow with Nick and Tut the day after to recover equipment Doug and Tut had left behind at the base of the nose. Then we would follow them. But when we got back to advance base with the gear, both Tut and Nick had decided enough was enough. Tut's leg was still bothering him and Nick's throat needed time.

I wonder now at the decision I made to go up alone and find the others. Had Nick and I been on our own, we would have already gone home happy with what we'd accomplished. Now I was hell-bent on my second new route on a 7,000-metre peak in two weeks. What drove me was a combination of feeling that we had failed and the very human, but rather childish, fear of being excluded from a successful party. At three in the morning, as I set off for the mountain, my resolve wasn't quite so strong. It was a warm night and the snow was still soft. The fear of stepping through a snow bridge, just as Don Morrison had done, preyed on my nerves. Every time the crust gave way, I felt a stab of terror. Even when I reached the wall and the security of the fixed ropes, I discovered the surface snow had melted off to reveal the hard ice beneath. Each step had to be worked for, kicking in my crampons. By the time I reached the single lonely tent on the plateau I was too tired to cook. I made myself a cup of tea and collapsed into sleep.

Climbing up the fixed ropes next morning I could see the others, three tiny figures at work on the sunlit granite pillar high above my head. I was going painfully slowly and knew I needed rest. The others wouldn't be in any mood to wait for me, but perhaps we'd have bad weather? I was also worried about my reception. Clive in particular had made it clear what he thought of our dash to the summit with some well-chosen epithets back at base camp. But they seemed happy to see me and enthused about the quality of the climbing. It wasn't just ego drawing me back, but the whole exciting enterprise of that final summit block.

I slept that night under the stars in my Gore-Tex bivouac sack, since the tent was too small for all of us, and next day, while Clive and Mo returned to complete the pillar, Doug and I dropped down to the plateau for more food. I was worried at how easily Doug pulled away from me on the climb back up: how would I cope if we went for the top? That evening a bank of high cloud moved in and the others agreed to wait a day. I was off the hook.

The following morning dawned fine and we packed up our gear for the summit. Climbing the ropes, I was impressed with the steepness of the pillar and the ingenious, serpentine route the others had found up it, first on the left, then the right and into an ice gully. We had to strip the ropes off this section to carry on climbing once we reached the top of the pillar, cutting off our umbilical cord back to camp. The ground above was time-consuming, even with Doug on bullish form, and we bivouacked that night short of the west summit. When we reached it next morning there was barely time to savour the moment of my return. Doug surged into the lead and the rope was pulling at my waist for me to follow. That afternoon we expanded the little balcony Nick and I had dug into a commodious snow hole.

Next day, Doug was no less forceful. We moved together across a steep snow slope skirting the rocky crest of the ridge and then one at a time when it steepened towards the tower. The summit rocks now soared above our heads and Doug led the first pitch up a series of icy grooves. I was breathless by the time I reached him.

'You might as well keep the lead, while I get my breath back,' I said.

He pushed on straightaway, running out the rope and tying it off so I could Jumar while he scouted the route ahead. He was out of sight when I arrived, so I coiled the rope and followed his steps down a little and round a corner to find myself on a col beneath the final tower. An open groove capped with an overhang seemed the likeliest way. Doug was already festooned with pegs and nuts and had uncoiled the other rope.

'I think it's about time I did some leading,' I said.

'Not here, youth,' Doug replied. 'It's going to be hard technical climbing up that. It's getting late already.'

Doug's drive overwhelmed me. In surrendering one lead, I seemed to have surrendered any initiative. I was too tired to argue. Perhaps he was right. Doug grabbed the end of the rope, threw down the coils and tied on, but in doing so left an almighty tangle that I then had to unpick. When I followed the pitch I realized I could have climbed it; why had I let myself be steamrollered? The pitch above on the other hand looked desperate: a thin crack up a steep wall. I didn't volunteer to lead that one. I started retrieving the rope but it jammed and we lost another half-hour while I went down to free it. Then I sat in the sun and belayed Doug, watching Clive and Mo climbing up to the crest of the ridge.

'The crack's blind,' Doug called down, 'let me down.' I lowered him twelve metres on the rope. 'Hold me there. I think I might be able to pendulum to that crack on the right.'

Then Doug began running back and forth across the wall, gathering enough momentum to reach the crack with an outstretched skyhook and then get his fingers jammed. He tried to get a foothold but his big clumsy mountain boots slipped and he was swinging again. Next time, he managed to hang on, and get his boot jammed in the crack. It would have been strenuous at sea level: at 7,000 metres it was incredible. My resentment evaporated in wonder at what Doug had accomplished. By the time I joined him, raving about the quality of the route, the sun was low on the horizon. Mo and Clive had decided to return to the snow cave.

I climbed a snow crest to the final summit block of brown granite, scouting round it for a weakness I could climb and finding a scoop that seemed to lead to easier snow and then the top. Hammering in a peg, I found I couldn't muscle my way up.

'You'd better come and have a try,' I shouted to Doug.

Standing on my shoulders, he heaved himself up and immediately took a belay. Without a shoulder it was desperate, and I landed at Doug's feet like a stranded fish, gasping my lungs out, but he was quickly gone, running the rope out up a snow gully even though I was the one who still had his crampons on. His energy was like that of an erupting volcano, unstoppable, sweeping everything aside. He disappeared from view and there was a shout. Doug was up. When I reached him, there was little time for jubilation. The mountains were silhouetted against the purple of the gathering dusk and we had no bivouac gear or warm clothing but we had climbed the Ogre. Now all we had to do was get back down.

Chapter Thirteen

K2: End of an Era

It's a sound I will never forget: a moan turning to a penetrating scream, rising out of the darkness below me. Then, just as suddenly, it was quiet again. I tugged at the ropes and found they were still tight, a sure sign Doug was still attached to them. A moment ago I had been staring around at the mountains, the fierce black teeth of the Latok group, the powerful triangle of Muztagh Tower. To the south-west the sun's afterglow lingered on the bulk of Nanga Parbat. I was content, the frustrations of earlier gone in the satisfaction of the summit. Then came that scream.

Doug had led off on the first abseil, straight down from the summit block, then tensioning across some wet slabs to a couple of pegs I'd placed earlier to make the next abseil easier. Yet in the night air, dampness on the rock had become smears of ice and Doug's boots skated off it. He swung in a sickening arc, turning and spinning, his legs raised just in time as he smashed into the opposing wall, fracturing both just above the ankle. Had he struck his head or body, the damage would have been far worse. Ignorant of all this, I tugged again on the rope. Was he unconscious? I wondered how I would reach him, how I could abseil down with his weight on the rope. Then he called out.

'I've broken my bloody legs.'

I felt a flood of relief.

'Can you get your weight off the rope?'

'I'll try.'

Doug managed to get himself onto a ledge and the rope went slack, allowing me to abseil down. I felt full of anxiety but knew I had to sound positive.

'What ho, mate!' Perhaps that wasn't quite the right tone.

It was now nearly pitch dark and we didn't have torches. A few metres below I could see a snow ledge that looked wide enough for a bivouac.

'We'll just work at getting you down,' I told Doug, still trying to sound cheerful. 'Don't worry, you're a long way from being dead.' The idea hadn't even crossed Doug's mind.

Once on the snow ledge, having pulled through the ropes, he tried to stand, but there was the distinct sound of bone scraping on bone and he howled with pain, dropping to his knees. Then he crawled over and started helping me to dig a ledge. We had no food or drink, no extra clothing, and we passed the night as best we could, tucking our stockinged feet into each other's crotches, doing the best I could not to cause Doug pain while massaging his toes. All I could think of was the prospect of reaching the snow cave and drinking something. I nodded off briefly and then realized Doug was massaging my toes, which I took as a hint. Because of his injuries, the risk of frostbite was much greater. Slowly dawn came around and we prepared to escape, getting Doug's boots back on as carefully as possible. Then we started abseiling down the summit block, four rope lengths in all.

At the bottom I set off to alert the others, meeting them just before the cave. They had seen Doug fall the night before and were on their way to help. While I collapsed inside, they found Doug already a third of the way along the tracks I'd made. He wasn't waiting around. Clive picked up his sack and Mo dug great buckets in the snow for Doug to crawl across. Two hours later we were all reunited in the cave, optimistic that Doug could cope. He hadn't suffered compound fractures, so while we didn't have painkillers, as long as he stayed off his feet he was reasonably pain free. For the rest of the day we drank and ate our fill, played cards and laughed at Mo's jokes, confident we would be off the mountain in two days.

Next morning, I woke to darkness. It must still be early, I thought, checking my watch. It was six o'clock. It should have been broad daylight. I looked across to the entrance where Mo was lying: his bag was covered in spindrift. The entrance itself was blocked with fresh snow. We had discounted the bank of cloud coming in the evening before, but the weather had broken. Clive and I burrowed our way out into the teeth of a screaming wind and while I held the rope he waded thigh deep towards the west summit. There was no sense in pushing it; we retreated to the sanctuary of the cave. Even though the last of the food was gone, there was no sense of despondency. We had more supplies at the camp below.

Yet next morning the storm was still raging and we had no option but to move. Doug needed all his strength to crawl through the deep snow, hauling himself up on his jumar. It took him four hours to reach the west summit, teeth bared against the wind. I shivered behind him, recovering and coiling the ropes as Mo and Clive led the way. Following Doug as he abseiled down the other side was nerve-racking. I had to down-climb after him, coiling the ropes as I went with visibility almost zero and no one to catch me if I fell. That night we crammed into the tiny snow hole Mo and I had dug on the ascent, everything covered in melting spindrift.

Everything was wet. It was my ninth day on the mountain; for the others it was two days more. Exhausted, emaciated and hungry, we felt the cold bitterly and still had the pillar to descend. Mo went first; Clive and I put Doug between us. We could do little for him, other than carry his gear. He went carefully, steadily, never complaining and at last we reached the top of the pillar. Mo had already set the ropes and vanished down them. Clive and I watched Doug abseil into the swirling mist. There was a shout, and the rope went slack. Clive followed and I waited once again. Then it was my turn. I slid down efficiently, could see Clive off to one side, knew we were close to the fixed ropes and then – I was falling, plummeting headfirst. Had the anchor failed? I felt a stab of panic; this was it. Then – a jarring thump against my chest and I stopped.

Looking down, I saw that one of the two ropes still ran through my karabiner. I realized instantly what had happened. The ropes were uneven in length and I had gone off the shorter end. Doug had gone off both, but had by chance grabbed the fixed rope we'd left across the gully, stopping him from falling thousands of feet to the glacier. As he fell, he'd pulled one end through. Clive had seen this, tying off the longer end to a granite spike. That is what had stopped me.

There was no time to contemplate near-misses. The storm had built to a crescendo, spindrift poured down the spur above us, blinding us. It seemed incredible that we might die now after so much effort, but at last we reached the tents, which Mo was busy clearing of snow. Inside their sanctuary, sipping sweet tea Mo had made for me, I explored my injuries, realizing I was more badly injured than I first thought. The pain in my chest was terrible; my left wrist was swollen and numb. I lay in a semi-stupor for the rest of the day trying not to move, trying not to cough, hugging my ribs to relieve the agony.

Next morning the weather was no better. I escaped the tent to relieve myself and understood immediately how weak I'd become. I was coughing up a bubbly froth and fretted I was developing pulmonary oedema. If I didn't lose height soon I could easily die, and I was now in the tent on my own, with the other three sharing the larger tunnel tent. I shuffled over to talk to them about my fears but I didn't get much sympathy and as Mo pointed out, we couldn't see to cross the plateau below us. We had no choice but to stay put and wait for clear weather. 'We're going to make a fortune out of this with the book,' I told them, only half joking, but the very idea got a frosty response.

When night turned to day and I saw sunlight on the tent wall, I felt a surge of relief. The wind was still strong but we could see; we could escape our trap. The following evening, stopping every few yards to revel in the sun, I reached base camp. It was 20 July. All the tents were gone; Nick and the porters had left that morning to report us lost. Mo was already on his way to intercept him. Clive was still shepherding Doug off the mountain somewhere above me. Our cook shelter was still up, full of pots and pans and a store of food.

I lay in the long grass nibbling biscuits and drinking soup, my first food in five days, and before I knew it, I was asleep. I woke with a start. It was dark. The others were nowhere to be seen. Feeling both anxious and guilty, I pulled on my boots and headed back up the trail with my headlamp. Finally, in the distance, I saw a pool of light. It was Clive. Just behind, on his hands and knees, Doug was crawling across the broken rocks of the moraine. A few days later he was flown by helicopter from the Biafo glacier. The others would leave me in Askole, expecting the helicopter to return for me that day. It did come but not for another week. The original aircraft had crash-landed in Skardu. I passed the time going quietly mad on my own in the village. I was immensely grateful to Nick for waiting in Islamabad, despite being terribly overdue, until he was sure I was on my way.

When I made it home to Badger Hill I could barely do anything for the whole of August. My ribs ached and my broken wrist was still partly paralysed. The froth from my lungs had not been pulmonary oedema, but was from a bout of pneumonia, a consequence of my injuries. I had lost more than ten kilos in weight. As a consequence I couldn't walk more than a few hundred metres without stopping to rest. I turned forty-three that month, but felt more than the age I am now. For a while just being reunited with Wendy and the boys was enough but time was passing and I had an expedition to plan.

Even before Doug's invitation to the Ogre, I had been looking for another big long-term challenge and had put in an application for K2. At that time, in 1976, the mountain had only had one ascent, twenty-two years before, by a large and talented Italian expedition led by Ardito Desio. They had climbed the south-east ridge, known as the Abruzzi Spur. Since then there had been attempts on other routes: Jim Whitaker's American team had tried the north-west ridge in 1975 but barely made any ground. In fact the whole western aspect of K2 looked tough, steeper than the south-west face of Everest. I wanted to tackle a new route, but do it with a small expedition and so was drawn to the north-east ridge, almost climbed by a Polish team in 1976. The route was more on snow and ice, and seemed more amenable for a small team, rock climbing being more time-consuming.

I had put together a small team, asking six of the Everest expedition, but Dougal's death had reduced that number to Doug, Nick, Tut, Pete Boardman and our doctor Jim Duff. We met at the Clachaig Inn in Glencoe in February 1977, a few months before the Ogre, to talk through our plans for the following year. As on Everest, I came under pressure to switch objectives. On Everest it had been Doug and Dougal applying the pressure; this time it was Pete Boardman, fresh from his success on Changabang's stunning west face. He argued a strong case for trying a route on K2's west face, with strong support, inevitably, from Doug. That fired my own imagination and I agreed, on the understanding that we increased the size of the team to eight and used fixed rope. We settled on the west ridge, so far wholly untouched. Throughout the Ogre expedition, my eyes often strayed over to the distant pyramid of K2.

Naïvely, given my experience with Everest, I thought companies would be falling over themselves to support us. No Briton had climbed the world's second-highest mountain, it's a tougher and more beautiful peak than Everest and we were a proven combination. Yet raising funds proved a mountain in itself. Luckily my agent George Greenfield discovered funds in an unlikely place. At a cocktail party, he had a chance meeting with the wife of the managing director of the London Rubber Company, whose brand name Durex is still very familiar. They were looking for new markets, including, as I learned once we arrived in Islamabad, in Pakistan. They were prepared to back us with a third of our budget of £60,000.

As part of our commitment, each of the team was required to

visit one of the London Rubber Company's factories. Mine was in the East End. I can still visualize the long baths of liquid latex, with hundreds of large phalluses going round and round on a long spindle, dipping into them. On either side were seated women whose job was to peel off the contraceptives as they set. I felt like the Queen, asking polite but meaningless questions.

'How do you maintain quality control?' I was shown another phallus onto which a worker placed randomly selected sheaths before blasting compressed air into it.

Securing backing allowed me to increase the size of the team, but in the process I became estranged from one of my oldest friends. There were two more slots to fill and one obvious contender was Martin Boysen. That summer, while we were nearby on the Ogre, he had made a superb first ascent of Nameless Tower, part of the Trango group. He had more or less assumed he would be coming to K2, but I wasn't alone in wondering if Martin was right for the objective. I felt I owed it to him to explain in person, but it didn't soften the blow, may in fact have made it worse. The decision led to an immediate severing of our relationship, something I deeply regretted. It would take decades and Wendy's final illness to bring us together again.

The two climbers brought in to boost our effort were Tony Riley, who had been on Latok that summer and was a film-maker, useful for our media commitments, and Joe Tasker, Pete's partner on Changabang. Joe struggled with the formality of our expedition meetings, but this formality ensured everyone had a say and decisions were acted upon. Joe had a shrewd, inquisitive intelligence, honed during his time at a seminary training to be a priest. When it came to signing the expedition contract, he baulked at a clause agreeing that team-members should obey the leader at all times. This wasn't an idea anyone took seriously; the contract was something George had drawn up for someone else many years before. But Joe did question it and I found myself bristling at his challenge, judging Joe a barrack-room lawyer, the classic reaction for any bureaucrat who has a system he feels is working comfortably.

The whole notion of leadership, mine in particular, came under scrutiny on K2. I had a persona for dealing with the public side of expedition leadership, the media and sponsors, and this is the side of me Joe came to know first. Pete too saw me as a rather remote figure, but that changed on K2 when we climbed and worked together and my natural enthusiasm for climbing took over. But my public persona left me open to a certain amount of mockery from my peers, and I could be oversensitive about that. Mike Thompson wrote a lauded satire of the Everest expedition for *Mountain* magazine called 'Out With the Boys Again'. ('One needs a leader who changes his mind a lot and has difficulty in remembering one day to the next what he has decided. We were very fortunate to have such a leader.')

Mike's ribbing hurt me more than it should have done, but it did feel unfair, coming from one of my oldest friends. The team on K2 had fun opening a book on whether they could persuade me to change my mind about something I had already decided. Yet the counter-argument, that I should have been less open, wouldn't have gone down well among the individualistic anarchists who comprised the average British expedition. Debates were raging within mountaineering about the tactics used to climb big mountains. Should we try K2 in full siege style, with fixed ropes to the top; Alpine-style, where you carried everything you needed on your back; or a combination of the two, going lightweight for the summit from a top fixed camp? How much, if any, oxygen should we use? Ken Wilson at *Mountain* magazine, who had criticized the Everest team for being too big, now decided our K2 expedition was too small. Given that our route on K2 would be harder than Everest and almost as long, he had a point.

The idea of not taking any oxygen at all was a personal worry. I had few illusions about my own high-altitude performance and doubted I could reach the summit of K2 without it. On Everest I had mostly sublimated my own ambitions, but I didn't want to do so again. My health also remained an issue. Just before Christmas I noticed a big septic pustule on the side of my chest where I'd broken my ribs. The consultant told me it was osteomyelitis, a bone infection resulting from my injury. I was put under anaesthetic, and he scraped out the pustule, down to the bone. But only weeks later the pustule returned. I was in the middle of a lecture tour but I had the pustule scraped out again, I was stitched up and packed off to my next lecture with an aching side.

The surgery put back my training for K2. Before Everest in 1975 I thought a brisk walk up High Pike behind the house was enough but now I was running. It was my indefatigable secretary Louise who got me started. A quick lunchtime run became a regular feature, slowly expanding into a round of five miles, up to the summit of High Pike, with 400 metres of ascent. I started going further afield, across to Carrock Fell, whose summit is girdled with the remains of an iron-age fort, and south-west to Knott, with its sprawl of grassy ridges. This intimate exploration of my own home ground gave me a deeper sympathy for it.

By the start of May, I felt I had built up my fitness. The expedition gear was on its way, supervised by Tony Riley. I flew out to Pakistan early with Pete Boardman to get some of the administration done and to shop for local food. They were a happy few days; I spent more time with Pete than I had on the whole of the Everest expedition. He was very much the writer, appearing sensitive and laid-back, but underneath was both mentally and physically tough. Pete was an ox at altitude. In a way, he was rather like Dougal, hard to know at a deeper level but once on the mountain totally committed. Pete had even considered writing a biography of Dougal.

When the team arrived there were the usual receptions. The London Rubber Company introduced us to a host of Pakistani dignitaries as part of their charm offensive to open a condom factory in Karachi. The night before we left for Skardu, there was also an all-night party at Caroline Weaver's, our friend from the embassy. Next morning, like an overworked sheepdog, I chased my hungover flock onto the aircraft. Doug took charge of selecting the porters, since he had the experience and recognized some familiar faces. We needed a small army of them, around 300, to reach base camp.

Unlike the Ogre, we not only had a cook, called Sher Khan, but a high-altitude porter too. Like Sher Khan, Quamajan was a Hunza, the ethnic group I had written about ten years before for the *Weekend Telegraph*. They are in many ways the Sherpa of the Karakoram. Like many Hunzas, Quamajan had ginger hair and European features, very different from the Baltis living near the Baltoro. He also spoke excellent English and became very much part of the team.

Our liaison officer, Captain Shafiq, was a short, well-built man, also affable but with a sensitive regard for his own place in the world. At Paiju, a delightful glade of trees in which to spend a rest day before the Baltoro glacier, he got into a tremendous argument with one of the porters, sitting in the entrance of his tent, sheltering from the rain. A crowd gathered round, entertained by the exchange, until Shafiq suddenly leapt to his feet and began hurling stones at them. As I got up to intervene, he chased one of the porters with a rock in his hand and in a moment had the man on the ground. Several of us rushed over to disarm him before he could smash the porter's brains out.

'He insulted me,' Shafiq shouted. 'He assaulted me. I'm going to put him in prison.'

It seemed to me it was Shafiq who had done all the assaulting, but eventually we had calmed everyone down and found out the cause of the trouble. The porters were unhappy with the equipment we had given them and wanted payment in advance. With Nick's help, we negotiated our way through it and order was restored. The extraordinary thing is we had £20,000 in cash in a metal trunk with no special security, a fortune to us let alone the porters.

Next morning it was still raining, and we delayed setting out along the Baltoro glacier, that great rocky highway to the heart of the Karakoram. The rocky spires flanking it were wreathed in mist and even the fresh snow had a dismal grey quality. From the top of the first moraine, we gazed over an apparently endless ocean of rocks piled like waves, stretching thirty miles up the glacier to Concordia. It was, as Joe Tasker described, the hardest thing you could do without it actually being climbing. Two days brought us to Urdokas, the last grassy campsite with its awe-inspiring views of serried granite peaks, including the slender finger of Nameless Tower. Here we rested for a day. The weather continued to be poor with two inches of fresh snow and I wondered what it would be like higher up. I sent Doug and Joe ahead with eight porters to scout the route to base camp.

The Baltoro has some of the most exciting mountain scenery anywhere. At the far end is Gasherbrum IV, a wedge of ice-veined granite that is among the hardest peaks in the world, still with only a handful of ascents. To our right was Masherbrum, fierce and inhospitable and bristling with ice towers. A day out from Urdokas we saw the Muztagh Tower, bulging and steep. I had friends who had climbed on all these peaks: it was like walking through a gallery. That evening we reached Concordia, the porters weary and cold huddling under their tarpaulins. Some were still missing at dusk, straggling in after dark.

Luck was with us. It dawned fine, the freshly fallen snow glistening in the sun. K2, vast and white against the richly blue sky, towered over the end of the Baltoro glacier, framed by the amorphous bulk of Broad Peak and the fairy towers of the Savoia group. The glory of the day warmed the porters' limbs and spirits and they were anxious to start, crossing a wide snow basin at the confluence of the Savoia glacier to the west and the Godwin Austen to the east. From the Savoia glacier, the west ridge rose like the corner of a gigantic pyramid, a vast complex of snowfields and rock walls, gullies and runnels. It would take careful route finding. It looked so much harder than the south-west face of Everest but seemed safer and feasible.

K2 threw up very different leadership challenges to Everest, which had been a huge, structured operation, with the team distributed in camps and me issuing instructions via radio. My job had been to keep things heading in the right direction. On K2, there were far fewer of us. I always understood that my authority as leader depended on the team's respect but all of us were strong characters who wanted our opinions heard. Doug in particular was straining at the leash, wanting to get on with the route, even though we had yet to establish base camp. I found that my role had changed: I was still the figurehead, but on the mountain I was more of a co-ordinator, trying to find a conciliatory path to the best solution. If sometimes I resisted attempts at commandeering the expedition, I did this to maintain consensus and freedom of discussion.

A week after reaching base camp, I was with Joe, pushing the route up from the high point Doug and Pete had reached the day before. Tut was at base, feeling weak from a chest infection. Tony Riley was also unwell and Jim Duff was keeping an eye on them both. Nick was there too, paying off the last of the porters. Released from my duties, I felt invigorated and enthused by the prospect of climbing. 'Chris was becoming a different person now that he was on the mountain,' Joe wrote afterwards. 'He seemed to relax from his assertive role once free of his paperwork.' I was also getting to know Joe better, and appreciated his company. He could be argumentative, with the annoying habit of often being right, but beneath the prickly exterior he was incredibly warm-hearted and thoughtful about his companions.

We climbed a narrow, snowy gully and onto a rock rib that led directly up to the ridge. Its profile was broken with steep rocky towers and it was impossible to say how long it would take to weave our way around these. Joe was initially in favour of climbing up to the ridge, but I argued we should climb beneath the ridge, across a broad snow slope. The first part was a little steep, but then the angle dropped back, and we were able to carry on without bothering to fix any rope, since it was little more than a walk. Having traversed 600 feet we reached a cleft in the slope, twenty feet below some rocks. It seemed a safely sheltered spot for camp two. Above, the ground steepened and the real climbing started. The camp would be a launch pad for the real difficulties. Pete and Doug caught us up and dumped their loads of tent and rope and we all returned to camp one.

Nick had come up during the day with his familiar energy and abrasive good humour. Pete, eight years younger than Nick, and sixteen younger than me, reflected in his diary on our differences. 'Nick is the one most in danger of being put-upon on this trip because he becomes adaptable and unassuming (whilst still his usual funny argumentative noisy self). Chris is very enthusiastic, big boyish, single-minded and I find I have a lot more time for him on a trip like this.' I was happy to have a rest the following day and continue acclimatizing, but that meant agreeing who would move up to occupy camp two and with it pole position for leading the next section. Pete was keen, so Doug said to him: 'Well, shall you and I go up tomorrow?'

I felt myself bristling slightly that Doug was taking control but Nick intervened, suggesting we draw matchsticks. Pete and Joe drew the short ones. 'Changabang rules,' Nick said. Doug was obviously disappointed, and reminded them rather clumsily of their responsibility. 'You could waste days if you make a mistake.' That evening, before we turned in, Doug asked if I minded him switching tents. 'I was awake for at least three hours last night, what with your breathing and snoring and thrashing about.' Nick said he was used to my snores and moved in with me, vacating the tent he was sharing with Quamajan so Doug could move in. It was a petty matter, but at altitude such things irritate out of all proportion.

Joe and Pete moved up to camp two, but for the next two days foul weather and heavy snow confined us to our tents. Pessimism settled over the expedition during our regular radio calls; time dragged and we all felt headachy as snow built up on the tents, turning the air inside stale. The third day dawned clear but windy, and we emerged blinking into the sunlight, determined to carry supplies up to camp two, but heavy new snow made the going hard and we turned back early. Pete and Joe also emerged and we could see them above working on the route, running out six hundred feet or so of fixed rope. We were starting to make progress.

That night I was overwhelmed with a cold that blocked my nostrils. My head felt like a swollen melon. I kept Nick up as well, but he still left that morning with Doug and Quamajan to make sure Pete and Joe had enough supplies to keep going. I lay in the tent snuffling, but feeling a bit brighter with the sun shining. Then I heard a shout, and emerged to find Jim Duff at the head of a group of porters. I dropped down to give him a hand, carrying his rucksack up the last stretch, feeling much stronger. Then I made the Balti porters some tea and listened to the news from base camp. Tut had decided to return home and had intended leaving without saying anything. I wasn't surprised, but felt a little sorry that he hadn't felt able to mention it. I understood his decision, and although it would leave us short-handed, it was entirely up to him.

We sat in the sunshine, talking about Tut and the expedition's prospects, perched among some of the most magnificent peaks in the world, relaxed and happy, when I heard the muffled thump of an avalanche starting. A huge cloud of snow billowed down the icefall lying between where we sat and the main mass of K2. Instinctively I dived for my camera and started taking photographs.

'For God's sake,' Jim shouted, 'the lads could be in that.'

'They can't, I'm sure they can't. That's just broken away from the icefall. They'll be above it.' But I stopped taking pictures.

The cloud dispersed and the mountains appeared as changeless as they ever had. It was as still as it had been before the avalanche. I tried to pretend there was nothing to worry about, and continued digging out a platform for another tent. Jim said he'd heard someone shout, which seemed unlikely to me, but when he suggested I turn on the radio I did so. We listened to static for a few minutes, and then heard Doug's voice.

'Hello, is anyone on the air?'

'This is Chris. Are you all right?'

'Nick's copped it. The whole bloody slope went and he was in the middle of it. Didn't have a hope.'

'Roger. Can you get back down? Over.' Keep a tight grip. Hold back emotion. Get them back, find out what's happened.

'Yes, we're on our way back now.'

I switched off the set and crouched in the snow, too stunned to process the news. Nick, my closest friend, was gone. Then a terrible pain welled up, mixed with a powerful sense of guilt. I had chosen the route. I was the one who had been convinced it was safe. A figure appeared, half running and half tumbling down the slope. It was Doug. He slumped beside the tent, face in his hands. We sat next to each other and wept.

Pete, a thousand feet above the snowfield, had looked down from where he was climbing to see two figures, one further towards the middle of the slope, engulfed as a slab of snow 500 feet wide detached from the mountain. Doug had been closer to the safety of camp two, trailing a five-millimetre rope to fix the gap Joe and I had left a few days before. Nick was behind him, but hadn't bothered to clip in. Quamajan was some distance back with the reel of rope, feeding it out. Doug had watched the slope break into huge floes, jostling with each other, breaking into smaller chunks that flowed downhill faster and faster; Nick was in the middle of it, struggling to stay on the surface until he was swept away. Doug had been dragged off his feet by the rope as the avalanche sucked it down, sending him head over heels towards the rushing torrent, but was then suddenly released. The rope had broken.

'I'd written myself off there,' he told me.

That night, reunited with Pete and Joe at camp one, we avoided the subject of the accident, just told stories about Nick, his outrageous behaviour, wild weekends climbing in the Llanberis Pass, as though we could summon him back. I half expected to see his gap-toothed grin appear at the tent door, unable to accept the reality of what had happened. Pete and I lay awake in the tent I'd shared with Nick the night before, sometimes speaking, mostly just lying there in the dark. Joe, alone in his tent, came over to ours, wanting solidarity. In the morning it was snowing again, the sparkling mountain of yesterday shrouded from view. We retreated to base camp, stopping on the way to search the avalanche cone for any sign of Nick. It seemed wholly unchanged from when we had come up, yet high above, a giant sickle scar showed where the slab of snow had broken off.

As soon as we got back we convened in the mess tent to discuss what to do next. So far, only we knew the truth. To Carolyn and their children Matthew, Tom and Martha, Nick was still alive. I spoke first, and explained that I wanted to go on with the climb, not as a way of justifying Nick's death, nothing could do that, but simply because this was part of what we had undertaken. I put it to the vote. Doug had no doubts at all. He wanted to end the expedition and could see no point in going on. He pointed out the agony all our wives would go through if we stayed. I knew that he had experienced the avalanche in a way none of us had. Jim agreed with Doug, Tut was already planning to leave and then, to my surprise, Joe said he also couldn't see much point in going on.

'Only Chris, with me, wants to go on,' Pete wrote in his diary. 'Nick would certainly have gone on, would have been consistent . . .' Tony quietly said that he had come to make a film and would stay to finish it. But without the others there was no decision to be made. So we turned to the business of breaking the news to Carolyn and the rest of his family before the story got into the papers. As leader, I had a duty to the expedition to get it back from the mountains in good order and after the vote I actually felt relieved, sensing that the majority had been right. With Nick being my closest friend, I felt a stronger responsibility to his loved ones and so Doug and I left next morning with Quamajan to race back to Islamabad and call Wendy.

I had already lost too many friends to climbing. As Mike Thompson observed, the attrition rate among our friends was like being prematurely old. Yet this death hit me hardest of all. Nick was not only a great mountaineer; he had been loyal and supportive, not just to me but the whole concept of what we were doing. Most of all, I missed him as a friend, someone I was glad to see, whom I could drop in on and go climbing with whenever I felt like it, someone who was argumentative but never cruel and always great fun.

Other things ended on K2. It was the last big siege-style expedition I led; they had probably had their day anyway. It was also obvious that Doug and I had fundamental differences in our approach to expeditions. He liked a spontaneous style, coming to decisions as the moment dictated, without structures or plans. Often, however, he would end up being the decision-maker simply by his immense force of character. I was happier with a plan, and one that everyone had discussed and agreed on. Temperamentally, I could see we'd reached the end of the line. After we left base camp, Pete noticed how the mood cleared with the 'sparring partners' out of the way. 'If Joe and I have problems,' he wrote, 'they're nothing on Chris and Doug's.' By then, the two of us were racing down the Baltoro glacier, desperate to be home, and with little thought for the future.

Chapter Fourteen

New Horizons

Two nights after I got back to Britain, the old wound in my ribs erupted with infection and burst. It was as though my body had suppressed the poison until I could complete my journey and talk to Carolyn, sharing her grief and reliving those last few days on K2. A week later a section of my lower rib was removed, leaving a gaping cavity that was left open to heal from the inside, making sure no more pockets of infection remained. At least it was a bone I could do without.

Returning to Badger Hill was an immense consolation, the familiar Northern Fells and our close family unit. Wendy's new passion was pottery and she began building a kiln in the garden. We also had a shared interest in orienteering; I'd done a story on it for the *Weekend Telegraph* and introduced Wendy. We joined a local club and would go off to races together, and though we usually ended up on different courses, afterwards we could come home and compare notes about the trials and tribulations of the day. But it was our shared values and pace of life that brought us close. Wendy managed to combine being both kind and gentle with an inner core of strength, supporting me in practical ways too, helping with book design and picture editing, and helping me write. I needed that strength now, mourning Nick; many others relied on her wisdom and support over the years in facing the cost that climbing exacted.

The boys were growing up fast, on the cusp between primary and secondary school. Wendy hadn't wanted them to go to the village school, where the only teacher was a woman, judging they needed a male influence since I was away so much. So they went to a larger primary in Dalston and I became good friends with the head teacher, Harry Barrow, doing the round of the Northern Fells together, twenty miles and 7,000 feet of ascent in ten hours. Inevitably I wanted to share my love of climbing with the boys. Joe had no fear of heights and thoroughly enjoyed it. I took him up the classic route *Little Chamonix* on Shepherd's Crag in Borrowdale when he was ten, not so difficult but with an awkward step that is intimidating for a second and a spectacular top pitch. Joe coped with aplomb.

I remember too a day on Gillercombe, also in Borrowdale. We took along Bodie, short for Boadicea, our crossbreed who combined sheepdog, Alsatian, a bit of lurcher and goodness knows what else. She was a nimble climber and I often left her at the bottom of a crag. While I climbed, Bodie would go round the side and meet me at the top. But on Gillercombe that day, Bodie decided to traverse across the crag along heathery ledges to where I was belaying Joe up the cliff. I couldn't get both of them up the route, and I only had a couple of slings around my neck, so I tied the dog to Joe with the slings and took a diagonal line up across the heather and broken rocks to get us off the crag. If Joe had slipped, or for that matter Bodie, they would both have taken a massive pendulum but Joe kept very cool and we all escaped without further incident.

Rupert, on the other hand, inherited his mother's head for heights, but was from the start very athletic, winning junior fell races and playing for the local football team. Wendy and I, at least when I was around, would take him to all the fixtures and cheer from the touchline. Saturday morning swimming lessons in Penrith were a regular fixture for all of us but it was in skiing that we could share the most. We had our first skiing holiday together in the spring of 1979 in Verbier. It was a delight to watch the boys catch up with my own level and then outstrip me.

Also around that time, we drove up to the north-west Highlands for a summer camping holiday, spent a couple of miserable wet nights on a crowded camping and caravan site before escaping to stay with Wendy's folk-singing friends Dave and Claire Goulder at Rosehall in central Sutherland. They had bought a plot of land and built a timber A-frame on it. Next door there was another empty plot of one and a half acres of felled woodland with a magnificent Scots pine on a little knoll in the middle. On impulse, we bought it and from then on spent all our Easter holidays and some Hogmanays camped on it. We never got round to building a house, since we stayed with our friends if the weather was terrible and even when camping could use their bathroom and dry our clothes. We were often invited over for supper.

We had some wonderful family adventures, putting the boys in an inflatable boat and watching them float down the lower River Cassley into the tidal Kyle of Sutherland, which flows down to Bonar Bridge. We followed them in the car, but most of the time Joe and Rupert were out of sight, hidden by the bog and rushes that flanked the river. As we got to know people locally, there were kayaking trips in the sea lochs of the west coast, paddling alongside seals. I devised escape and evasion games around the wooded banks of the Cassley and before the fishing season you could swim in the many deep pools alongside the salmon returning up the river to spawn.

The boys' school careers were more mixed. Joe didn't settle at St Michael's and so he moved to a new, progressive but certainly not permissive school in Carlisle. They took children from the start of secondary to O level but had just opened a primary class run by Hilary Spencer. There was an immediate impact on Joe's behaviour: he became interested, attentive and did well. Sadly the school didn't have the numbers to survive, and so Joe moved to the comprehensive school in Wigton, which had a good reputation. Unfortunately, he was badly bullied; having a famous father didn't help. This was an era when I was appearing in television advertisements for hot, beefy Bovril. ('There's nothing like it.') Even one of the teachers called Joe 'the Bovril boy', an incredibly insensitive thing to say to a boy uncertain about his place in the world. We could see he was struggling, and so Joe moved to St Bees, a boarding school on the west coast of Cumbria, Mike Thompson's old *alma mater*. It was here he acquired the nickname of Joe, rather than Daniel, as he was christened. Joe's strategy for popularity at St Bees was to be spectacularly naughty, and he was eventually defenestrated just before his O levels, although allowed back to sit them. Wendy guided him through, tutoring him patiently through his revision, and he passed five.

Rupert settled down happily at St Michael's, made plenty of friends, worked hard and moved on with his mates to the comprehensive next door, Caldew School. Rupert also faced some initial bullying, once again because of his father. He was small for his age, but picked out the largest of his tormentors and went for him, fists flying. Rupert was never bullied again. I think at a later stage, during Rupert's teenage years, our relationship became quite tenuous. He developed a broad Cumbrian accent and would take off at the weekends with his friends, wandering the fells and dossing in a disused shooting cabin. Sometimes he would tell us on a Friday morning he was staying at a friend's house on the Solway Plain and then skip school, slipping out to the nearby River Caldew, where he'd camp for the weekend, catching the school bus home on a Monday evening. Both the boys found my absences difficult, especially in the emotional aftermath of a fatal accident, when Wendy was supporting the wife or girlfriend of a dead companion.

After Nick's death on K2, I found myself at something of a crossroads. My next expedition was to have been to Kangtega, a lower but still difficult peak not far from Everest, but I had planned on climbing it with Nick. I had also expected to be writing a book about the K2 expedition, but its brevity and sudden collapse made that a non-starter. My agent George Greenfield had already suggested I write a broader book on the whole subject of adventure and I took on his idea, almost as therapy. It took me out of my own narrow climbing world to look at a wide cross-section of those making major innovative steps into the unknown: the first men on the Moon, the first to row the Atlantic, cross deserts, explore the Poles and so forth.

In the late 1970s, my self-imposed rules meant the book *Quest for Adventure* was almost exclusively male. That wouldn't be the case now; the rock climber Lynn Hill for example, in making the first free ascent of *The Nose* of El Capitan in 1995, set a standard for all climbers. But there was one area even then where women seemed already on an equal footing. There is a long tradition of great women travellers like Hester Stanhope, Gertrude Bell – also a highly able alpinist – and Freya Stark. One great modern-day traveller came to stay with us at Badger Hill. Christina Dodwell had been wandering across Africa using horses, camels and dugout canoes. I took her climbing one afternoon and despite the crag being turned into a skating rink during an unexpected downpour, she worked her way up it with great aplomb.

My research for *Quest for Adventure* broadened my outlook and brought me new friends across the globe. For two years I was immersed in interviewing my subjects, flying round the world to meet them. It was intriguing to puzzle out the similarities and differences in people with such widely different backgrounds but the common factors were a taste for risk and a passionate curiosity. The one who impressed me most was Geoff Yeadon, the cave diver. I could not contemplate swimming and wriggling down passages far beneath the earth's surface, barely able to see in the muddy water, knowing that if anything went wrong with his equipment drowning was inevitable. Geoff's ventures into the cave system of Keld Head beneath the gentle limestone country of the Yorkshire Dales came closer to true exploration than any other form of adventure on the surface, where the remotest spots can be reached by aircraft or scanned from satellites.

Geoff was as alarmed by the prospect of rock climbing as I was by cave diving, but one adventure I did share, in a modest way, was joining Robin Knox-Johnston off the coast of Scotland, sailing with his family from Oban to Skye in *Suhaili*, the boat he had sailed single-handed non-stop to win the Golden Globe race. The deal was I should show him climbing in return. Mildly seasick, I clutched the tiller under his watchful instruction as we approached Loch Scavaig in a choppy sea, and then it was my turn, as I led him up the Dubh ridge in the Cuillin, several hundred metres of rough, delightful gabbro and a moderate grade.

I learned a great deal in those few days at sea about sailing and sailors and felt we had at least something in common. A few weeks later, at NASA's manned spacecraft centre, I didn't feel the same about the astronauts I met. It wasn't just their total dependency on technology, which was undoubtedly impressive, but the way they had been selected and then trained, almost programmed, to fulfil a role. Yet a few days later I met Neil Armstrong, then chairman of an engineering firm near Lebanon, in his home state of Ohio. When he began talking about his work as a test pilot flying the X15 rocket plane that reached speeds five times the speed of sound, I could see that he was taking himself to his own personal limits in a very similar way to a rock climber.

I found my own love of climbing was undiminished after meeting so many adventurers from different disciplines. And the research gave me lots of opportunities to squeeze in a route. I sent Wendy a postcard from Alassio on the Ligurian coast that read: 'Research work is really tough. I'm off to see Reinhold Messner today and hope to get a climb in.' I used the excuse of a lecture tour on the west coast of the United States to visit Yosemite and climb among the City of Rocks in northern California. But I wasn't planning an expedition for the first time in a decade. Then an opportunity arose that I just couldn't ignore: the chance to climb in China.

Expeditions to China are now routine, although at times still difficult in terms of permission, especially in Tibet. But in the late 1970s, following Richard Nixon's overtures to Chairman

Mao and Deng Xiaoping's economic reforms, it was only just becoming possible to go there, and still required some serious diplomatic support. The idea of mounting an expedition there came from Michael Ward, who had not only been doctor on the 1953 Everest ascent but had been one of the prime forces behind the 1951 reconnaissance that opened the route to the Western Cwm. It had been Mike who treated Dougal and me for frostbite after our Eiger experiences in 1966. Before Cambridge he had gone to Marlborough, where his housemaster had been the 1930s Everester Edwin Kempson; later he climbed with the great but troubled rock climber Menlove Edwards. Mike, still saturnine and handsome in his mid-fifties, was chairman of the Mount Everest Foundation, established after 1953 to support exploratory mountaineering. In that capacity he invited me to go to Beijing in early 1980 to negotiate with the authorities.

We were offered eight peaks and chose the only one still unclimbed: Mount Kongur in western Xinjiang. The combination of its height, 7,719 metres, and the fact so little was known about it made it particularly attractive. The other thing we learned was that climbing in China would be extremely expensive. In this regard, we were very fortunate, on our way home via Hong Kong, to get a promise of sponsorship from the famous trading house Jardine Matheson. So little was known about the Kongur region that a reconnaissance seemed essential and so Mike, myself and the young mountaineer Al Rouse set out that summer for a closer look.

It was a rare and rather wonderful trip, a little adventure in mountain exploration with none of the concentration of vision that accompanies the attempt of a single mountain. As the three of us travelled through Xinjiang we were welcomed into the yurts of Kirghiz tribesmen leading the same nomadic life they always had, travelling with their herds of sheep and goats from one desert pasture to the next. They were now members of a collective rather than a tribe, with a chairman rather than a chief, but it appeared family life was much as it had always been. They were a jolly, friendly people, with the natural hospitality and courtesy of all nomads. We were offered bowls of delicious yoghurt drink accompanied by a plate of cake-like bread whenever we visited one of their camps.

Our small team covered a broad age range, with Michael in his mid-fifties, me in my mid-forties and Al in his late twenties. Al was a Cambridge maths graduate and played chess to a high standard but his commitment to climbing had stopped him from following a conventional career path. Like me, he was making a living from a combination of writing, lecturing and working with equipment manufacturers. Al was a great talker. It came in a bubbling, promiscuous flow of climbing plans, schemes and stories. At times I would switch off and let the torrent flow past me unheard. There was no competition between us. Mike had started climbing just before the war, I had started just after and Al was a product of the 1970s, all long hair and flower power. He couldn't quite get over the fact I was the same age as his mother. The odd thing was I didn't feel there was a vast difference in our ages; I enjoyed his company and conversation and found his approach to the mountains was broadly the same.

At Kashgar we visited the now-battered residence of Eric Shipton, who had served as consul during the early years of the war, and wandered through the bazaar. Most people had seen hardly any Europeans and we attracted crowds of curious onlookers wherever we went. The drive to Kongur had all the excitement of any first visit to a new mountain area, but from the Karakol Lakes our objective seemed to offer few technical difficulties. Kongur's massif looked like a huge whale stranded on the high and arid Pamir plateau. But our liaision officer Liu Dayi knew better: he had climbed Kongur's sister peak, Kongur Tiube, and assured us Kongur would be a tough challenge. The summit itself was like a Kirghiz conical hat, peering from behind the rounded shoulder of an intermediate summit.

The three of us packed food and tents for a week and strode off across the desert, delighted by small clumps of dwarf iris and primula hiding among the rocks. It was a wonderfully relaxed trek that took us to a snow-clad col with a steep drop on the far side, leading to a glacier that flowed from the southern flank of Kongur. The route to the summit mass was still obscured so we decided to climb the mountain to the south to get a better view and bag an unclimbed peak in the process. Mike stayed at the col to rest, while Al and I set out in the cold of morning, crampons biting into smooth, hard ice: real climbing at last. Little more than 20,000 feet, we called it Sarakyaguqi after the nearest Kirghiz settlement. To the east we could see a myriad of unclimbed peaks, to the south a tiny but conspicuous pyramid that somehow dominated everything around it. What it was we had no idea.

We returned to camp full of ideas for the next few weeks, but Al, while running down some easy moraine in sheer exuberance, stepped awkwardly and fell, twisting his ankle badly. He still hobbled about, as cheerful as ever, and contributed as much as he could as Mike and I completed the reconnaissance. It formed a sound basis for the attempt itself the following year when the main expedition established base camp on a grassy alp at the side of the Koksel glacier. Although there were ten of us on the team, only four were climbers: Al and I were joined by Pete Boardman and Joe Tasker. Four more were scientists using us as their guinea pigs: Mike, our doctor from Everest in 1975, Charlie Clarke, and two highly regarded high-altitude specialists, Jim Milledge and Edward Williams, who was also a pioneer in nuclear medicine. Added to this high-powered group were the film-maker Jim Curran and David Wilson, then political adviser to the governor of Hong Kong, and later governor himself. His fluent language skills were a great advantage, along with the immense diplomatic clout he brought with him.

Al's garrulous sense of fun gave a rather skewed view of the challenge we faced. At a press conference beforehand, when asked what would happen if there were any unforeseen difficulties, he replied: 'We'll have to get the rope out.' This rather demoted the climbing challenge Kongur presented in the eyes of the British climbing world. Don Whillans wondered if it was some kind of new dance. ('Aye-aye-aye-aye Kongur!') But then, as we arrived at base camp and the summit first appeared through high scudding clouds, Pete turned to Al with an incredulous expression and said: 'I thought you said it was going to be a walk? It looks bloody big and serious to me.' We were rather on a hiding to nothing: if we got to the top then it was a foregone conclusion, if we didn't then we'd failed on a high-altitude walk.

My role as deputy leader was quite demanding, especially when Mike Ward and Jim Milledge disappeared to Shanghai to give a lecture. I was caught between sticking with the climbing team and looking after the distinguished crew of trekkers we had brought with us as guests of Jardine Matheson. Included in their number was David Newbigging, at the time the company's *taipan*, one of the most important commercial positions in Hong Kong. Another trekker was Jim Boswell, who had turned the family firm into an agri-business empire, had huge land holdings in California and was then serving on the board of General Electric. They were a fascinating group. They were also a lot keener on running than my fellow mountaineers, especially Joe, who wasn't going to waste energy jogging. Pete had been busy before leaving working on a book and was equally reluctant to expend effort. I was childishly happy that I was holding my own in the fitness stakes.

I found myself stretched with all my various responsibilities: as well as marshalling our forces for Kongur I was also busy securing permission for an attempt from Tibet on Everest's north-east ridge the following year. Al and David Wilson were a great help when we got to Kashgar, sorting out equipment. I rather envied Joe and Pete who could just kick back and watch the world go by. Perhaps that was the most sensible course to take, because a few days after we set up base camp on a grassy alp beside the Koksel glacier I found myself becoming desperately ill, as ill as I'd ever felt in my life. Several team members had suffered from a flu bug, but my susceptibility to respiratory infections seemed more pronounced than usual, perhaps because of my rib injury. Charlie Clarke diagnosed lobar pneumonia, not telling me just how serious the infection could be. He put me on antibiotics and gave me a couple of Valium to help me sleep. Next morning I felt extremely weak but well enough to potter around base camp photographing the scientists while the others went on a training climb. The weather remained unsettled and as a result I missed almost nothing.

It was fascinating to compare the two groups at base camp, the scientists and the climbers. Jim Milledge put on some Dvorak and Al was almost beside himself with glee. 'Good God,' he said, 'we really are in a pre-war expedition environment, people talking about the Weisshorn and the Dent Blanche and playing classical music.' Personally, I felt happy in both groups, but given my physical condition I was pleased to have so many leading high-altitude doctors around me. What worried me was the notion that my lungs could be damaged for next year. I was already thinking about Everest.

Although my title was 'climbing leader', my role was to chair the discussion whenever we needed to make a decision, just as most other small climbing expeditions work. You need a leader to apply for grants and sponsorship, but leadership is collective. Our debates often pitted Al against Joe and Pete, who were very much a pair after Changabang. I think Al was used to being listened to among his usual group of friends, and didn't like being steamrollered. Equally, Pete wanted unity on the choice of route. We had already established an advance base on the Koksel glacier and from there we decided to try the south ridge, the steeper but shorter of the two routes we could access. This rose from the Koksel col at around 6,000 metres to a subsidiary top we called Junction Peak. From there we could access the summit ridge of Kongur itself. It took us all day from the col to reach the crest but I was reassured to find I could keep up with the others, despite my recent bout of pneumonia.

I was sharing a tent with Joe. He didn't talk much, and neither did I, but we got on well as partners. He was content to swap his meal duties for a little more trail breaking, especially towards the end of the day when I was tiring, and we soon developed an understanding. I began to appreciate that underneath quite a hard protective shell Joe had a warm, sympathetic heart. Al talked non-stop and hadn't brought a book whereas Pete, as a writer and literature graduate, was always reading. Yet Pete was also the most forceful of us; with that big barrel chest of his and his strong legs he had a great reservoir of stamina. I think at times Joe was quite pleased for me to argue caution since it saved him from appearing uncertain in front of Pete.

From our position on the south ridge we got our first close look at the summit pyramid; we could now appreciate more fully just how formidable and committing it was. Despite our reconnaissance the year before, we had clearly underestimated the scale of our objective. Our anxiety wasn't helped by the weather, which was worse than anticipated with only two or three days of clear skies before the next storm rolled in. We lay in our tents, listening to the flap and rattle of the nylon that only emphasized our vulnerability; Pete and Al even packed up their gear in the night for a fast exit should theirs collapse. Having crossed Junction Peak next day through driving clouds of spindrift, we were keen to get out of the wind altogether, digging a snow cave at the bottom of a knife-edge ridge that led to the bottom of the summit pyramid. It took us four hours but at least we now had a secure and relatively comfortable base in which we could all fit and plan our next move together.

The wind continued to scream across the ridge next day but Pete was all for the summit. We settled for a reconnaissance to the end of the knife-edge ridge and spotted a couloir on the north side of the summit pyramid that looked promising. But we were running short of food and it would clearly take another two days to reach the top so in the snow cave next morning I counselled retreat. Pete was still pushing for the top but after an hour of discussion the forces of caution won and we retreated to base camp along the west ridge. It was a good choice. Next day the weather broke; we would have been beaten by the weather and forced to wait out the storm without provisions.

After four days relaxing at base camp, we returned to the snow cave at the foot of the knife-edge ridge. We planned to cross this and then dig another snow cave, but the snow was shallow and we soon hit hard ice. There was little room for anything but two narrow slots, effectively snow coffins in which each pair squeezed nose to tail. The roofs were only centimetres thick; we could see light permeating them and there was barely room to sit up. By the time we'd finished scraping them out, bad weather had rolled in and we were trapped for three days and four nights.

There was nothing to do. No books and little conversation. The days were punctuated by random events: I managed to drop beef stroganoff all over Joe's sleeping bag; Pete put his foot through my coffin, prompting a Bonington outburst; we dug and refashioned our shelters. The world almost ceased to exist. I lay in my sleeping bag, staring at whorls in the roof of my cave, dreaming of lavish fried breakfasts, of home and Wendy, of the climb ahead, until everything blurred into a kaleidoscope of hallucination. We had almost run out of food but no one thought of quitting.

Then, on the evening of the third day, the altimeter showed the air pressure rising, and next morning, when I poked my hand through the roof of my cave, I could see through the swirl of spin-drift blowing across the ridge that the sky was blue. Still being in shade, it was still bitterly cold and the north side of the summit pyramid proved as steep and inhospitable as the north face of the Matterhorn. So much for Kongur being a pushover. Pete led the first pitch and as Al led the next, Pete pulled off his mitten and discovered his fingers were tinged with frostbite. It was a relief, when it came to my turn, to reach the warmth of the sun. We still had a long way to go, but we were now on the ridge and could move together more quickly. Joe was in front when he spotted the summit and let out a yell.

The views were incredible: nothing to the north, east and west was as high as we were and to the south K2, our nearest rival, was sunk in cloud. The distinctive pyramid Al and I had seen the year before was still clear, prompting Pete's interest. The only doubt in my mind was Kongur's east summit about half a mile away. Could it be higher? That evening it took us two or three hours to dig a snow hole just below the top; during the night my doubts percolated. Next morning I persuaded the others to come with me to the other summit where we discovered, predictably, that it wasn't higher.

We had now been climbing for eight days and the shortage of food was taking its toll. Kongur had been one of the most committing routes of my life; I had never taken such liberties before. Descending the ridge and then rappelling down the north face of Kongur, I could sense we were all approaching the limit. On the last abseil to the base of the pyramid, Pete's rope flicked a football-sized rock off and we watched aghast as it hit him on the helmet, knocking him out. He slid down the ropes and was only stopped from flying off their ends when his mittened fingers jammed in his abseiling device. At least the pain brought him round.

Success and tragedy are divided so narrowly. Descending the west ridge I felt on the brink of collapse yet somehow still had something left. We spotted two figures about a thousand feet up the ridge and speculated whether they had food and drink – all of us were almost mad with thirst and hunger. As we drew closer we saw it was Jim Curran and Mike Ward. Jim told me later that Mike had almost burst into tears when he saw us; after nine days they had almost given up hope we'd ever come back.

The aftermath of Kongur was difficult. It had been Al who had applied to the Chinese Mountaineering Association to climb the north-east ridge of Everest the following year, a rerun of the Kongur trip but without the medical research team. Because of my links with Jardine Matheson and my role as climbing leader on Kongur, it made sense for me to lead Everest too, but I was now under pressure from Pete and, to a lesser extent, Joe to drop Al from the team. There was no escaping the fact that Pete had been frequently irritated with Al's constant chatter. For his part, Al sensed something was wrong but being good-natured couldn't really fathom it. If Al had been as strong as Pete on Kongur, then perhaps it wouldn't have mattered so much, but the simple truth was that Al didn't have the same level of stamina at high altitude.

As leader, it was my responsibility to drive down to Sheffield and tell Al that in the interests of team harmony he'd been dropped from the expedition. It was, I know, desperately upsetting for Al and I felt most uncomfortable about the whole situation. Happily, Al and I managed to maintain our friendship and we climbed together again, and under rather ironic circumstances. The vision of the unknown, shapely pyramid we'd seen from the summit of Kongur had stayed with us. Pete had taken a bearing and figured out it couldn't be K2. When he got back to Europe he worked out that it was a peak called Karun Koh, 7,350 metres high and almost on the frontier between Pakistan and China. There were no photographs: not even Eric Shipton had been anywhere near it. Pete and I agreed to explore and try to climb it in 1983, after we got back from Everest.

When Pete died on Everest in 1982, I had no stomach for Karun Koh and I postponed the expedition. Then the lure of that unknown pyramid began to reassert itself, especially when two Austrians had a go in the summer of 1983. Since Al and I had first seen the mountain on our reconnaissance in 1980, I asked him if he'd join me. It's a tribute to his forgiving nature that he accepted. We could only climb in that area of Hunza as part of a joint team with Pakistanis, and we met our two climbing partners in Islamabad in May 1984. Ikram Ahmed Khan was a major in signals and, it soon became apparent, a good organizer. Maqsood Ahmed was in his early twenties and a real mountain enthusiast; he ran a woodcarving business and had done a climbing course in Chamonix. Neither had deep climbing experience but they were immensely keen.

Robert Schauer, who had explored the peak the year before, was a friend and he had sent us photographs. His climbing partner had got sick and he wasn't able to try the peak, luckily for us, because his pictures made Karun Koh seem straightforward. Yet as we got closer, the harder the climb appeared to be. The key to the route was the west ridge, but its lower part was blocked with crumbly, blank pinnacles of rock. We thought we could bypass these on steep snow slopes to the side, but through the binoculars we saw the telltale gleam of ice. It was no place for comparative beginners. Ikram and Maqsood took it well and after wishing us the best of luck, Al and I started up the ice. It wasn't difficult, but it was nerve-racking and after several pitches of this, at a slight levelling just below one of the rock towers, we looked at each other.

'There must be a better way up this bloody mountain,' I suggested.

'I'd been thinking along those lines,' Al replied.

Down we went, and spent the rest of the day sweltering in our little mountain tent. Our Pakistani friends were a bit bemused by our retreat but were happy to join us in exploring the south and eastern aspects of the mountain, looking for a better route. We didn't find one. The east ridge soared up in a knife-edge rippling with cornices, broken by the occasional rock step, beautiful to look at, but a pig to climb. We walked round to the col overlooking the northern flank of the mountain but that was no better. Yet despite the frustration, I was thoroughly enjoying myself. I still seemed capable of long days in the mountains.

'The old war horse has stamina even if the joints are creaking,' I wrote to Wendy. I'd suffered a skiing accident that winter and the bruising on my back was giving me trouble. 'Oh my love, I do love the mountains, love feeling part of them, walking through them, climbing them, looking at them. Al is proving excellent company. I let the chat flow over me but he comes out with a lot of good ideas and we work well as a team.'

Having examined the mountain from almost every angle, we decided the west ridge was the best option after all. Then a storm set in, and while we welcomed it at first, needing a rest, it continued for the next ten days. We were joined by another team, again Austrian and good company, and having run out of time we left the mountain for them to climb. There was a slight stab of regret that we hadn't grabbed the first ascent, but the five weeks I shared with Al were great fun, without stress or serious disagreement. It was a great sadness, and a great loss to British mountaineering, when he perished coming down from the first British ascent of K2 in 1986, trapped high on the mountain in bad weather, gradually weakening until he was unable to move.

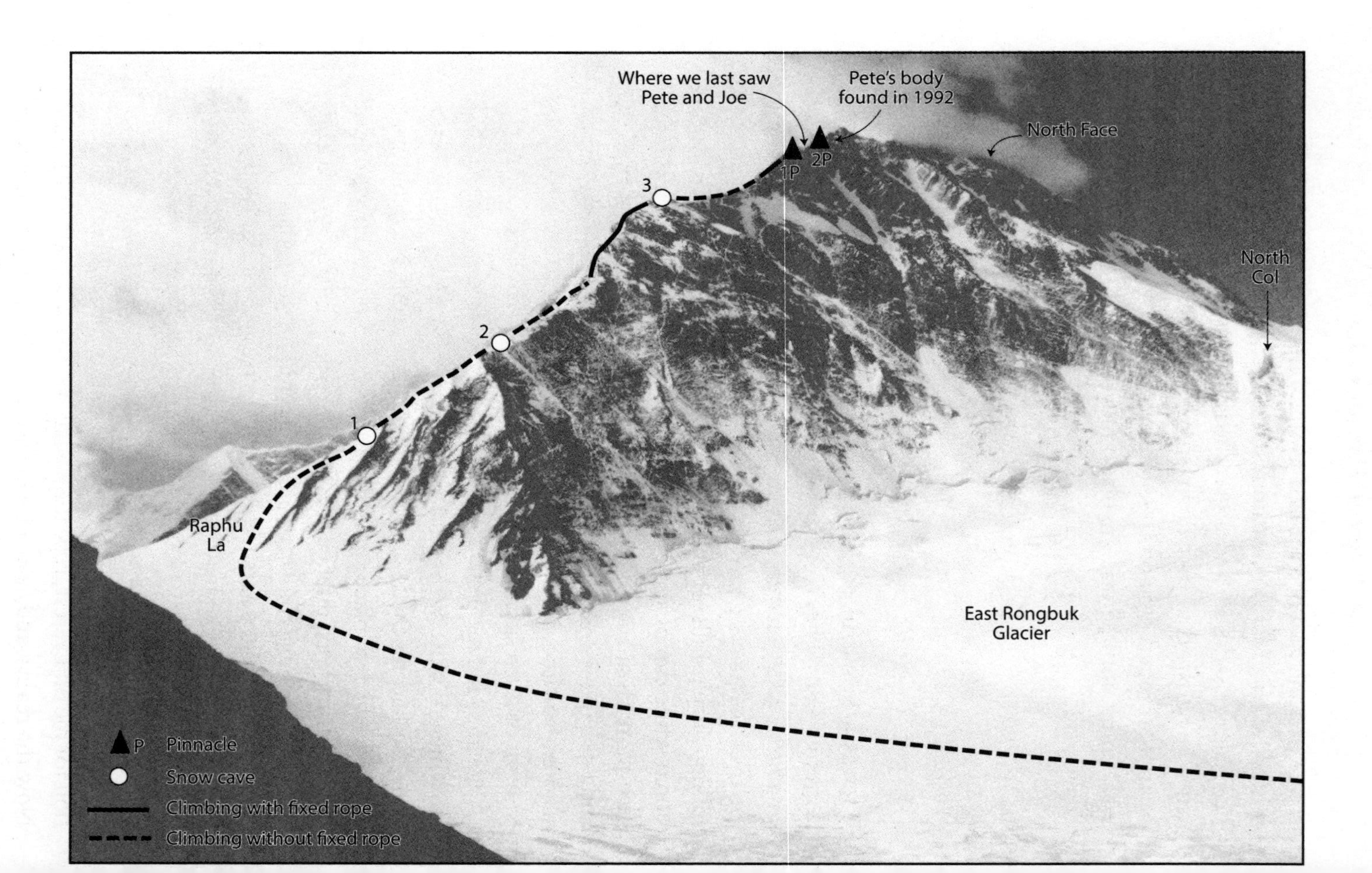
Where we last saw
Pete and Joe
Pete's body
found in 1992
North Face
1P
2P
3
2
1
North
Col
Raphu
La
East Rongbuk
Glacier
P Pinnacle
Snow cave
Climbing with fixed rope
Climbing without fixed rope

Chapter Fifteen

Dream's End

It was a beautiful day, cold and clear, and I had time to gaze around me. The North Col was far below, the summit of Changtse, 7,543 metres, seemed almost level with us and we could see over the peaks guarding Everest to the north and east, to the rolling purple hills of the Tibetan plateau, broken by the occasional white cap of some distant snow peak. It was the view I had seen more than twenty years before from the summit of Nuptse, and now, in my forty-eighth year, I was conscious that my days at such high altitudes were numbered. I was painfully aware that the summit of Everest was another 1,400 metres above us.

Just ahead of me, Pete Boardman was making slow progress. All movement is slow at that altitude. Front-pointing up on his crampons, he had reached some rocks and was probing around for a crack in which to place a piton and secure the rope. Above his head was a feature we'd dubbed the 'first buttress', the first significantly difficult climbing challenge on the unclimbed north-east ridge of Everest. The ridge soars like a flying buttress from the Raphu La, the col at its base, to its junction with the north buttress that runs up from the North Col, the route taken by the pre-war Everest expeditions of the 1920s and 1930s.

The dream was to climb it with a small team, a recurring ambition for me on Everest, repeating what we had achieved on Kongur. Now the reality and scale of what we had taken on was beginning to weigh heavily. We had started out in early March full of optimism, myself, Pete, Joe Tasker and Dick Renshaw, brought in to replace Al Rouse. Dick had been just a name to me, someone Joe had often mentioned; they had done some of their best climbing together. In the past few weeks I had come to like and respect him. Dick, neat and compact with dark, Celtic looks, had a quiet love of the mountains, was always ready to help others and yet also immensely determined. Charlie Clarke and Adrian Gordon, who had both been with us on Everest in 1975, came in a support role but we didn't envisage them going above advance base. Adrian's quiet support and Charlie's warm good humour gave us a welcome escape from the pressures of the climb.

Although we were only four in number, we never planned to do the entire climb Alpine-style, carrying everything we needed and climbing in a single push without fixed ropes. The route was too long and before the junction with the north buttress was a series of three serrated pinnacles, like the spikes on the back of a dinosaur, at around 8,200 metres. They would take a long time to overcome. We therefore decided to make several forays onto the ridge to gain a jumping-off point at around 8,000 metres, from where we could make a continuous push for the summit carrying bivouac gear.

I knew at the back of my mind that this was a tall order for a man of my age. A couple of days before, I'd been struggling to keep pace with Pete as he led up the ridge below us. I'd told him that while I would do all I could to support him and the others on the climb, I was moving too slowly. He'd told me to shut up, that it was a long campaign and there was time to recover. Now, following Pete's lead, I felt a renewed vigour. Although I was no quicker than Pete, I found the climbing enthralling. From below we had seen that a gully split the buttress barring the way, but it had looked steep. Once in it, it didn't seem quite so bad, although still around sixty degrees, with bulges that were considerably steeper. The fascination of breaking new ground and the fear of falling banished my fatigue. It took me an hour to climb fifty metres, and while it must have seemed like an age to Pete, to me it felt like a few minutes.

I was now halfway up the gully and could see a ledge with some thin cracks off to one side. Would they take a peg? I hammered in a knifeblade and Pete climbed up the rope, leading the rest of the gully to a boulder at the top of the first buttress. We crouched in its lee, nibbling chocolate.

'You know, that's the first time we've actually been on a rope together,' I told him.

'Not quite,' Pete said. 'Don't you remember?' He reminded me that I had summoned him to the Lakes before the 1975 expedition to give him the once-over and we'd climbed at White Ghyll. I'd forgotten. On K2, Joe and I had got off to a bad start, becoming mutually suspicious. But on Kongur we had climbed together and come to a good understanding. At heart, he was thoughtful and generous. Pete and Joe, after so many adventures together, particularly on Changabang and then their ascent of Kangchenjunga with Doug Scott, often bickered with each other, like an old married couple. There was a strong element of competition in their relationship, and this was growing stronger as they expanded their ambitions and talents, particularly into writing. Mountaineering partnerships are vulnerable to the pressures of fame and changing fortunes. Pete was tremendously strong and mentally tough, despite his gentle exterior. Joe, it seemed to me, often kept going on willpower alone.

Back at our snow cave, the second we'd dug on the ridge, I could see Joe and Dick had been busy. Digging into the snow bank, we'd soon hit rock. Making a space habitable for four people had been a major effort. Now they had made it weather-tight, cutting snow blocks to protect the entrance and sealing it with a sleeping mat to stop spindrift blowing in. They had seen us coming down and had a brew ready. It would be their turn in the lead next day, so I could look forward to lazing in the morning. I sensed my energy was limited and needed guarding. It was after noon when we followed Dick and Joe out of the door. It was a much hazier and warmer day than the day before, with almost no wind, just mist drifting across the ridge, softening its outline. It was possible to rest without becoming chilled to the bone and Pete was able to doze as he waited for me to climb up the first buttress.

When he started again, he quickly caught the others, while I dragged along behind, having added the gear we'd stashed the night before to my rucksack. Dick and Joe were at work on the second buttress, climbing a gangway that cut through it that was little more than scrambling over loose rock. At the top, they anchored a rope to make descent safer, and continued for a short distance, but then it started snowing heavily. The view ahead diminished and then disappeared. Pete was keen to push on, as always, but Joe pointed out they couldn't see where they were going. By the time I reached the top of the second buttress, they were already on their way down and soon disappeared from view. I could have been alone on Striding Edge in a Lakeland blizzard. There was no frame of reference, except my leaden limbs and creeping exhaustion.

The mood was subdued in the snow cave that night. On the way down Pete had narrowly avoided disaster. Preparing to abseil from the anchor he'd placed the day before, he'd grabbed the rope to move into position and the peg had come straight out. If he'd had all his weight on it, most likely he would have disappeared down the gully to his death. Having been on the go for five days, even Pete recognized we could use a rest but was frustrated we hadn't yet got a close look at the pinnacles.

For my own part, I was eager to get back. We had seen from high above Charlie and Adrian returning to advance base and heard on the radio they had brought letters for us. This was welcome news. The last time we'd gone down for a rest I'd been bitterly disappointed to discover nothing had arrived from home. It was a painful reminder of how much I relied on Wendy's emotional support and I withdrew to my tent to sulk, like Achilles. The climb, I told her, was 'grinding hard work. I'm frightened and I don't mind admitting it.' Of course, I felt all the more remorse when we got back to advance base and found not one but three letters from Wendy.

At home, she wrote, the cuckoos had returned and the larks were singing over High Pike. She was back in the garden, rearranging things with Rupert's help. 'We haven't had any letters through from you yet so obviously communication is going to be a bit slow,' she wrote. 'Thinking of you a lot – our "pearl" wedding anniversary this weekend – thinking back to that rainy happy weekend in Wales thirty years ago – I just love you more and more.' I sensed from her letters that she was finding my absence hard. When I reached base camp next day, I wrote her a long letter with news of the climb but also my own doubts. 'I think things have been too hectic, too rushed and crowded this last year – I also feel drained. I just want to do my best by the lads – not particularly get to the top – but help them to do so.'

After the privations of the ridge, life at base camp was luxurious. Charlie and Adrian pampered us with fantastic meals. Pete was bent over his diary, reflecting on our prospects. 'This mountain is so big, our project so vast, so long, that all our energies are consumed by it and have to be directed towards it. Even Chris has little left over for other things. Life inexorably becomes blinkered ... Yet we are a great compact little team, hardly a cross word ever between us. In a way, we all respect, sort of love each other, for we know that when the crunch comes each of us will do the right thing.'

As Pete sat writing, Dick worked on the swan he was carving from a block of mahogany he had brought with him. Dick and Joe had been a strong partnership in the early 1970s, climbing many hard classics in the Alps, but then in 1975, while climbing Dunagiri, a near neighbour of Changabang, together, Dick had suffered bad frostbite. Joe and Pete had then developed their partnership. In the past few weeks, however, I had come to like and respect Joe. Softly spoken and always ready to help others, he had a deep connection with nature that informed his development as a sculptor, a calling he still follows to this day. His need to push himself to the limit in the mountains had nothing to do with anyone else.

The days at base camp slipped away agreeably. We had a picnic at the site of the old British base camp, recalling George Bernard

Shaw's image of those expeditions as being 'like a picnic in Connemara surprised by a snowstorm'. Our Chinese staff found picnics incomprehensible and frivolous, but lying in the sun with the tape deck rolling, nibbling Stilton and salami, swilling red wine, it was easy to forget the presence of Everest towering above us. Charlie stood nearby, flying a kite with all the exuberance of a small boy. The weather was becoming kinder; the ice on the pool near base camp was cracking and melting and at midday it was possible to wander round base camp in a T-shirt.

Returning to the mountain was brutal. The wind howled across the Raphu La as we climbed up from base camp, sweeping fresh snow from the ridge and giving us perfect conditions underfoot for our crampons. But it was so strong that in the worst gusts we had to stop and crouch, clinging to our ice axes. I seemed to have retained no benefit from our prolonged rest. Pete wrote: 'Chris walks very slowly, resting it seems at every step, and eventually not far from the bergschrund the others overtake us. "Does Chris always go so slow?" whispers Adrian.' Pete kept his views to himself, but privately I think he knew that the summit was beyond me. On bad days, I felt the same.

I felt stronger once we were up on the ridge. Dick, with his quiet self-discipline, urged us to get organized and we sorted out food for the next five days. Pete was still agitated about who would be teamed with him, and what his role would be, 'but not so much that I dare risk saying anything and being misunderstood. So I trust that Providence will guide us.' We drew lots to settle the plan and Providence rewarded him. He and Dick would go up to the shoulder above the buttresses to the foot of the pinnacles, the crux of the north-east ridge where all our hopes and fears now rested. Here they would dig a snow hole, the jumping-off point for the pinnacles and the ridge to the summit beyond. 'Well, I'm glad, anyway,' Joe said. 'At least it will give me another night sleeping at a lower altitude.'

I found my energy levels were mercurial; in the morning I was first off but Pete predictably caught me at the top of the first buttress, and then Joe. On the shoulder, where I dumped my load, Pete was digging a snow cave where a spur from the Kangshung face met the ridge. I could see his boots sticking out of the hole. Afternoon cloud had rolled in, filling the eastern valley and spilling over the ridge, like breakers, to be shredded by the tearing wind. Our tracks were now completely covered with driven snow. When I finally reached the second snow cave, Joe was in his sleeping bag and the stove was purring gently, melting snow for a brew. I slumped onto my mat, overwhelmed with exhaustion, frustration and despair at my own weakness. Joe just waved away my apologies and handed me a drink. He promised I would feel better in the morning.

With so much space, I slept well and was first out in the morning but Joe soon caught me and above the second buttress pulled away. I was reduced to setting a target of ten paces, then resting, but it was all I could do to squeeze out the eighth step, then the ninth, before slumping against the snow, panting for breath. I could see I was nearing the crest of the ridge and beyond it lay the snow cave. Then I saw a figure below me and was suddenly confused. Dick and Pete were at the cave; Joe had already passed me. Who was this? But it was Joe, after all. He had come down to find me, an extraordinarily generous act given the circumstances. He had missed me and was now climbing back up.

We plodded together up those last few metres to the top of the shoulder, and the view suddenly opened out: Kangchenjunga, the world's third-highest peak on the horizon, Makalu towering above the Kangshung glacier, huge ice cliffs bristling up Lhotse, the great snowy sweep of the Kangshung face and the summit itself, so distant and unattainable. The jagged teeth of the pinnacles loomed above us, piled one on top of the other, barring our way to the easier upper reaches. What a strange mixture of suffering, apprehension, elation and friendship this experience had brought us.

The prospect of exploring the pinnacles gave me a new lease of energy next morning, despite climbing towards 8,000 metres. Dick dropped down to collect some spare rope while the three of us continued, prospecting the route. This was now the highest I had been without bottled oxygen. Yet even though the weariness I'd experienced the day before had left me, I couldn't keep up with Pete. It took him two hours to the base of the first pinnacle, while Joe and I arrived forty-five minutes later. We flipped a coin to see who would belay him, and I won. There was no question about who was leading; Pete had already uncoiled the rope and tied in. I sat crouched on a rock while he bridged precariously up a smooth slate groove.

When the rope ran out I tied on another. If he fell now nothing would stop him and he would probably pull me off too. Then I heard the sound of a peg being hammered in and I followed him, but Pete was already gone when I reached the peg, trailing a rope behind him. Afternoon cloud was bubbling up but Pete was remorseless, determined to reach the ridge above the first pinnacle. I stamped and shivered behind him, silently urging him to turn back.

Next day it was Dick and Joe's turn, while Pete and I carried loads. I felt exhausted, and dumped mine early at the foot of the pinnacles but Pete had already caught up with the others. At least I could have a meal ready when they returned. Back at the cave, I had hardly started melting snow when Dick appeared. With typical understatement, he explained he had led his pitch and was setting up a belay when a strange numbness spread down his left arm and leg. At first he thought it was the cold, but then his left cheek and the left side of his tongue became numb. He could bite it without sensation. He was also worried about frostbite in his nose.

'Does it look funny?'

'It's a bit purple. Let me feel.' It was warm to the touch, not remotely frostbitten.

Dick's condition didn't register as profoundly as it should. Both he and Pete thought we should press on a bit further, making sure we had crossed the pinnacles before going down for a rest. Next morning, however, we agreed we should descend immediately. The route down was slow and insecure and at one point Dick's crampon came off. I tried to help him, but he lost his balance, grabbed me and we both somersaulted down the slope, scrabbling to stop ourselves. Our nerves were shredded. When Adrian and Charlie came up to film our return, Charlie thought we crept in like old men.

On the way back to base camp, Charlie told me he thought Dick had suffered a stroke and would have to go lower immediately and probably home. I too was coming to a decision. Even planning the expedition, I knew that because of my age and performance at altitude it was unlikely I would reach the summit without oxygen. Now I was faced with the reality that I couldn't keep up. The others tried to reassure me and I became suddenly emotional.

'You've no bloody idea how much I've been pushing myself.' I was almost tearful. 'I've never pushed myself so hard, never felt so out of control. I'm sorry. I know my own limits and I've reached them.'

Joe and Pete remained committed, and so I suggested that while Charlie took Dick to Chengdu, Adrian and I would climb to the North Col, offering them a line of retreat. I felt optimistic about their chances, at least of crossing the pinnacles. Pete was superbly strong. Joe had some worrying physical symptoms, blood in his stools, but his throat was crusty with blood from the thin air, which could have been the source. He remained as determined as ever. On 12 May, Joe turned thirty-four, and we celebrated with champagne. Next morning we returned to advance base and after a day's rest Pete and Joe set out in the late morning to return to the mountain. We all tried to underplay the moment they walked out of camp.

'See you in a few days.'

'We'll call you tonight at six.'

Two days later, I was scanning the mountain through the telescope, starting at the site of the third snow cave and tracking right, becoming anxious when I didn't spot them and then – there they were, already on the first pinnacle, moving beyond the high point of the last attempt. Then progress stalled. They missed a scheduled radio call at three o'clock. We tried again at six and then every half an hour after that. At nine that evening, with the sun long gone behind Everest, we saw them for the last time. One figure was silhouetted against the fading light on the small col immediately below the second pinnacle. The other was moving to join him. They had been on the go for fourteen hours and still had to dig a platform for their tent.

There was no sign of them next day. Adrian and I set out for the North Col, reaching it the following morning. We watched the ridge for three days and then returned to advance base, where Charlie was waiting, after seeing Dick safely on his way. My first impulse was to climb after them but I couldn't go alone and the others lacked the experience. I think we knew they were dead, but I wanted to try every last option. So when Charlie suggested we look at the ridge from its far side I agreed. A week later we were looking up at the vast white expanse of Everest's east face and I knew all hope was gone. As we left, cloud was beginning to form below the summit, drawn slowly across the mountain like gossamer, concealing details but leaving the shape of the mountain just discernible. I fantasized we'd made a silly mistake and they would be waiting for us at base camp, chiding us for panicking. Of course, that's all it was: fantasy. Ten years later, a Kazakh climber called Vladimir Suviga, part of a Kazakh-Japanese team on the north-east ridge, sent me a picture of Pete, lying in the snow as though asleep, just above the second pinnacle. A mass of rope was visible, disappearing into the snow beneath him. I feel sure Joe was at the other end of it. I feel equally sure that if Joe had been sick, Pete would not have left him.

Charlie, perhaps more realistic than me, had been chipping out a memorial stone. We placed it on a plinth above our base camp, with the memorials of others, and turned for home. Once again, I went ahead to bring bad news, the wives and girlfriends of the team now anxious at the long silence from the mountain. Once again, it was Wendy, with Louise, who took on the dreadful task of breaking the news. I was shattered by the deaths of Pete and Joe, not just as friends and climbing partners but also because of their creative abilities, as writers and film-makers. Seeing the impact on their loved ones, I understood very well what my death would mean to Wendy, but even in my worst grief I knew I wouldn't stop climbing. But I did make one promise: I would never go back to Everest.

That promise to Wendy required me to break a commitment. Three years before, while working on *Quest for Adventure* in early 1979, I'd had a phone call from a hugely successful Norwegian businessman called Arne Naess, nephew of the famous philosopher, ecologist and mountaineer of the same name. He was, he told me, organizing an expedition to Nepal and wanted my advice. I was happy to help, but suggested he come in the afternoon, after I'd finished writing for the day.

'That's fine. Have you got an airport near you?' I suggested Newcastle, sixty miles away. He said he would check and call back. An hour late, the phone rang again. 'You've an airfield near Carlisle. I'm chartering a plane. I'll be with you at two o'clock on Monday.'

I was impressed.

Arne arrived with a side of smoked salmon he'd caught in Iceland and two bottles of Burgundy of the very best vintage. Slightly built, with a mop of receding hair that framed an irregular but expressive face, he had an intense, boyish enthusiasm. Arne had made several fortunes when I first knew him, in shipping and oil. Later he moved into data and property. A keen climber in his youth, business had dominated his life, but now he wanted to make time for some thwarted ambitions. He had booked Everest for the spring of 1985 to lead the first Norwegian expedition. He wanted my advice on equipment and the general planning of an expedition – and to run logistics on the mountain.

After the tragedy on Everest and my promise to Wendy, I told him I couldn't contemplate going back but would offer whatever support I could. In the following months he played me like a fly-fisherman would a trout, teasing me with questions about equipment or planning, quietly mentioning his offer still stood. As 1983 wore on, and I had successes in India and then Antarctica, all my enthusiasm returned. Here was a chance of reaching the highest point on earth being handed to me on a platter: Sherpas, oxygen, the easiest route and the added bonus of indulging my passion for organization. How could I resist? How could I tell Wendy?

In the end I didn't have to. Walking into the office one day she overheard me conspiring on the phone with Arne. She was, inevitably, deeply upset but in her heart she wasn't surprised. I think she understood I had unfinished business. The boys were less forgiving: 'But you *promised*. You can't go back. What about Mum?' Yet once she accepted it, Wendy gave me total support and concentrated on getting me fit for the climb. She had been a vegetarian for several years, and I'm sure her close attention to my diet made me more resilient on this climb to my regular respiratory ailments. Meanwhile, I liaised with the full-time expedition organizer, a young journalist and climber called Stein Aasheim, whom Arne was paying to manage things while he concentrated on his businesses.

In February 1985 I flew to Oslo to meet the rest of the team. Originally there had been twelve, but two of the very best, Hans Christian Doseth and Finn Dæhli, had been killed descending from the first ascent of the Great Trango Tower in Pakistan. Stein had been on the mountain with them, but descended earlier when they ran short of food. It had been a bitter blow to him personally and to the Everest group, which had lost its best climbers. The deaths shocked Norwegians and cast a shadow over Arne's enterprise. I felt a little apprehensive about how I would get on, but was relieved to discover all of them spoke excellent English.

Waiting at Kathmandu's affably chaotic airport was my old friend Pertemba, not looking a day older than he had on the southwest face. I had recommended him as *sirdar* to Arne but Pertemba had promised his wife he wouldn't be going through the Icefall, the great fear among Sherpas, so we hired a climbing *sirdar* too. Pertemba would run operations from base camp. For the first time I flew to Lukla, a very different experience from my first trek a quarter of a century before when we climbed Nuptse. The village had mushroomed and the men now wore Western clothes. The great tourist boom that has transformed the Everest region was fully underway.

Namche had been a little village in 1961. Now there were hotels, some of them worthy of the title, the most lavish belonging to Pasang Kami, my *sirdar* on the 1970 Annapurna expedition. Fine-boned with horn-rimmed spectacles perched on his nose, he had always been more a shrewd organizer than a climber. On the other side of the Dudh Kosi, I looked up Ang Phurba, with whom I had shared the memorable final days of the 1972 Everest expedition. He was sitting on his porch, cradling a rosy-cheeked baby, his youngest child.

It was fascinating working with the Norwegians, a different experience from a British expedition. A little reserved, certainly self-restrained and disciplined, these Scandinavian qualities were best exemplified in the figure of Odd Eliassen. More than six feet tall and blond, Odd was among the most experienced in the team. He had pioneered new routes on the huge granite walls of his native Romsdal in the 1960s and gone to Everest as part of the ill-fated International Expedition of 1971. He was quite simply among the best expedition people I ever met, a wonderfully kind and generous man. A carpenter by trade, his practical skills were invaluable in making the repairs that are always necessary on a trip like this. If work were to be done, Odd would just get on and do it.

Coming down from a reconnaissance of the Icefall, I stopped off at the base camp of an American expedition trying the west ridge. Their climbing leader was Jim Bridwell, an old friend and one of the wilder pioneers from the great days of Yosemite climbing. I had last seen him on the east side of Everest, while looking for Pete and Joe. He looked as cheerfully debauched as ever, puffing on a Camel cigarette and full of gossip. His team were very different from the Norwegians: long-haired and quite macho, more extravagant in their claims and more individualistic. They were also good fun and we got to know them better over the coming weeks, playing poker for increasingly high stakes.

Pertemba's promise to stay out of the Icefall didn't last long. A week after we arrived at base camp, I was having breakfast in the Sherpa's kitchen tent when he came in dressed for the hill.

'I think I'll have a look at the Icefall today,' he said.

I certainly didn't mind. Apart from anything, the club of Everest climbers who had broken promises to their wives had just grown by one. I had sensed a growing frustration in Pertemba about his administrative role, struggling to get all our gear and supplies to base camp in the face of a yak shortage. Relations between the Sherpas and climbers had been generally good, but there had been some petty misunderstandings too.

Arne and our base camp manager Christian Larsson were used to doing business in a context of contracts being honoured to the letter. Business in Sherpa country was rather different. Pertemba had needed to pay a premium to get porters and yaks and there were petty disputes about ration allowances. The Sherpas had opted to be paid for rations so they could get their food locally, and make a little more on the margin. Of course, they couldn't resist the chocolate and other goodies the climbers were eating. This infuriated Arne, but it was an inevitable part of expedition life. Things came to a head over a sack of oranges flown up from Kathmandu in the helicopter sent to fly out our support trekkers, wealthy friends of Arne. When the Sherpas asked for a few, Arne put his foot down. It was the only time we came close to a row.

'What on earth are a few oranges compared to keeping them happy?'

In the end he backed down and the Sherpas immediately lost interest in the oranges. Most of them went bad. But from then on Arne relaxed and a good team spirit emerged. Thanks to the Norwegian's great sense of shared responsibility, the expedition moved smoothly ahead. The Sherpas Ang Rita and Sungdare, who eventually climbed Everest five times, fixed the route from camps three to four with Bjørn Myrer-Lund and me in support. Tall and thin, Bjørn's natural reticence masked a wry and very rich sense of humour. Arne urged us to catch up so the Norwegian press wouldn't say the Sherpas were doing everything, but the Sherpas were expert rope-fixers on this sort of ground. Bjørn and I were content to act as their porters, carrying spare rope. With camp four in place and well stocked, we went down to the little hamlet of Pheriche to soak up the extra oxygen and prepare for the summit. It was barely the middle of April, more than a month before the end of the season.

I was put in the second summit group, with Odd and Bjørn, behind the all-Norway team of Ralph Høibakk, Håvard Nesheim and Ola Einang. Ralph was the managing director of a big computer firm, and at forty-six was almost as old as me, but he was the only member of the team who could keep pace with the Sherpas. His group set out for the top at four in the morning, later than many climbers do now, with Ralph breaking trail for most of the way. He had reached the South Summit and considered pressing on, but they were a team, and so he waited. By the time the others caught him, the wind had risen to storm force and the Sherpas wanted to turn back. Now Odd and Bjørn had the chance of being the first Scandinavians on the summit.

With me at camp four was Pertemba. Just before leaving for our rest at Pheriche, he had come over to me and said quietly: 'You know Chris, I'd really like to go to the top with you.' It was something I had thought about, especially after his decision to go into the Icefall, but I hadn't wanted to influence him. His decision meant a great deal to me, because of our friendship over the years. He brushed aside my offer to cook and made us a delicious tsampa stew. I didn't sleep much that night. I doubt any of us did. Yet I was more excited than anxious. There was none of the stabbing fear I'd felt before the Eiger or the Central Tower of Paine so many years ago.

Drifting into sleep I soon woke to the purr of the stove. It wasn't yet midnight, but Pertemba was already heating water for our flasks. I dozed off and then he thrust a mug of tea into my hand. I wriggled out of my warm sleeping bag, fully dressed, crammed on my boots, zipped up my down jacket and then crawled out into the night like an overstuffed Michelin man. It was –30°C and very dark with ominous gusts of wind blowing around the tents. Each of us in his own world, we followed the pool of light from our headlamps, mine gradually falling behind as we crossed the South Col to the slopes of the south-east ridge. I felt exhausted, not just out of breath but listless, finding it hard to place one foot in front of the other. After ninety minutes the others stopped for a rest far ahead of me but were ready to move on again as I arrived. I slumped in the snow, almost overwhelmed with frustration.

'I'll never make it,' I muttered to myself.

Odd heard me. 'You'll do it, Chris. Have a good rest. I'll stay behind you.' It was typically generous of him. Odd had his own worries; his blood was making too much haemoglobin, making it dangerously sticky. Back at base camp, our doctor had drawn a pint off and replaced it with a saline transfusion. But here he was, quietly supporting me. As the ground underfoot turned to deeper snow and Pertemba's pace slowed, I was able to keep up.

Above us, the sky lightened and then the soaring peak of the South Summit was touched with gold as the sun cleared the mountains to the east. When we reached the ridge's crest, the sun's low-flung rays were lighting all the peaks around us, the Kangshung glacier still in shadow far below. I looked across to the north-east ridge, picking out the shoulder where we had dug our third snow cave and the pinnacles where we had last seen Joe and Pete. I changed my oxygen cylinder. It was now five o'clock and I noticed the summit of Lhotse was still above us. The crest of the ridge was harder than I had expected, but before long we were on the South Summit, buffeted by the gusting wind. We gathered at the cornice just below, where Doug and Dougal had bivouacked in 1975. I could look into the gully they had climbed as it dropped steeply down the south-west face.

The ridge ahead looked formidable, and Odd fretted about our oxygen supply. I had at times been using four litres per minute, more than the others, but at this stage was prepared to risk anything to get to the top. Summit fever had definitely gripped me.

'We go on,' Pertemba said decisively.

We'd been climbing unroped thus far, but Bjørn now tied a rope round his waist and took the lead. The climbing was more spectacular than difficult but the Hillary Step loomed above us, about twenty metres high. Bjørn wallowed up soft snow, getting an occasional foothold on the rock wall, and then fixed the rope round a bollard at the top. I was once again near the back, and struggled on the step, panting, breathless and apprehensive. Then I became aware of Doug Scott floating at my shoulder; I could see his long straggly hair and wire-rimmed glasses. He was quietly talking me up it and then, as I reached the end of the fixed rope, he vanished. The others had moved round a corner, and for a moment I had the mountain to myself, but they soon came into view, standing on what I took to be the summit.

Soon I was at the top myself, the world on all sides dropping away. I hugged Pertemba who crouched beside me. He had brought with him the T-shirt Pete Boardman had worn to the summit in 1975, hand-painted and presented to him by his local climbing club, the Mynydd. Hilary, Pete's widow, had given it to Pertemba when he had visited her in Switzerland. Now it was back on the summit in memory of his friend.

Odd and Bjørn raised the Norwegian flag and then photographed it and themselves. Now they came over and embraced me. There was time to look around. To the north, from west to east, lay the Tibetan plateau, that rolling ocean of brown hills. To the east was Kangchenjunga, first climbed in 1955 by Joe Brown and George Band, both friends. To the west I could see Shisha Pangma dominating the horizon, where Doug, with Alex McIntyre and Roger Baxter-Jones, had climbed a new route three years before. Below us, on the other side of the Western Cwm, was Nuptse, looking rather stunted, the very opposite of the view I had enjoyed twenty-four years earlier, when Everest had seemed so unattainable. We lingered for twenty minutes, but then I was first away, pausing just below the top to collect pebbles of shattered limestone as a keepsake. It was time to come down.

PART FOUR

Beyond Everest

Chapter Sixteen

Back to the Future

Friends have often remarked that climbing Everest changed me; that I was more at ease with myself afterwards, more fulfilled. I've sometime wondered about that. Walking back to Lukla, I certainly experienced profound contentment. Yet I hadn't broken any records. I was only the seventh Briton to reach the top and had taken full advantage of bottled oxygen. I did have the dubious honour of becoming the oldest man to have reached the top, but only by ten days, and Dick Bass soon took it from me. As George Greenfield observed, most people in Britain thought I'd done Everest several times over, and those that knew better didn't care. So why did it mean so much?

There had been little physical pleasure in it at the time: none of the elation of rock climbing on a sunny day where the air is rich with oxygen and your limbs don't feel as though they're filled with lead. On Everest there was no journey into the unknown. It had been all I could manage to follow the others to the top. For a quarter of a century I had been caught up in an immense force, call it ambition if you like, sometimes at great cost to others, especially Wendy. On my climb to the summit I could feel that intensity, along with my physical endurance, had weakened.

Yet it had also been a profoundly moving experience. There had been the awareness of the mountains slowly dropping away, the summit caught in the first golden glow of dawn, the north-east ridge with all its memories. That day on Everest wasn't merely about reaching the top, it was for me the focal point of a climbing life, a gathering of so many ambitions, dreams and memories that climaxed in that upwelling of joy and sorrow I experienced at the summit.

I cannot regard Himalayan climbing lightly: the catalogue of loss doesn't allow it. Four of the eight lead climbers on Annapurna's south face died in the mountains, all of them great friends. Of the four of us who climbed Kongur, I have been the only survivor for over thirty years, after Al Rouse died in 1986. Looking across from the summit of Everest to Kangchenjunga, of Doug Scott's team of four that climbed a new route in 1979, he was within four years the only survivor. Both his partners on the summit of Shisha Pangma in 1982 were killed in the mountains. I have absolutely no illusions about the broad streak of good luck that kept me alive. I can think of a dozen times when I should have died.

As I slowly descended to camp four from the summit, pausing frequently to rest, I noticed what looked like a tent in the middle of the slope and veered towards it without thinking. Then, as I came closer, I realized it was a woman sitting upright in the snow, sun-bleached hair blowing in the wind, teeth bared in a rictus grin. I guessed this was the body of Hannelore Schmatz, who died from exhaustion in October 1979 descending from the summit. I averted my gaze and hurried past, but then needed to slow again. My oxygen had run out, and the short gentle uphill walk back into camp, no more than fifty metres, took a quarter of an hour.

I never became inured to tragedy. If anything it got harder as the years passed. I dreaded the next accident because I understood the personal sadness, the void created in the lives of others, bearing bad news to the parents and the woman who loved that man. Their grief had an intensity that went so much further than the sorrow you experience at the loss of a friend. That is something I understood from my own grief at the loss of our son Conrad. Even now, when he would have been fifty-three, I still wonder what he would be doing.

I dozed through the afternoon at camp four, drinking endless cups of tea, and in the morning, surprisingly refreshed, caught up with

Odd and Bjørn at camp three. Arne and Stein were on their way up for their attempt and we hugged and laughed. When I came to the Icefall, I almost ran through it, to get through this danger area for the last time as quickly as possible. We celebrated at base camp but the weather turned and summit bids were put on hold. I couldn't help thinking of previous expeditions when there had been tragedies right at the end. I grew impatient, eager to be with Wendy but wanting to stay to support my friends.

In the end, the team's perseverance paid off. Not only Arne and Stein but Ralph and Håvard too made the summit. Ola, with his bushy Viking beard and ready laugh, had agonized over trying again, not wishing to use up our dwindling supplies when he didn't feel fully fit. Instead he went repeatedly to the Icefall, ensuring the route stayed open after ice cliff collapses. He didn't see why the Sherpas alone should face that risk. Of all of us, he would have been the least disappointed not to go to the summit. Ola had such a generous spirit and was just happy to be in the mountains, yet had given as much as anyone to the success of the expedition.

The rhododendron forests around the monastery at Tengpoche were still in bloom, seeming to me more lush and fragrant as I came down from the sterile world of high altitude. I joined Pertemba at the little nunnery just below, where we were entertained by his three aunts, all of them nuns. We drank homebrew and ate potato pancakes spiced with hot chillies, and I sat back as the flow of Sherpa conversation swept over me, basking in the warmth of their friendship. This time the fates had been kind to us. We were alive, all of us, and could celebrate wholeheartedly.

Wendy knew I was safe and could relax, but I longed to be back in England so I could hold her close once again. Her letters to base camp had been full of news and love; mine had lacked the tension or fear of the north-east ridge. Yet how could I claim to love her when my passion for climbing threatened her with a cruel and catastrophic loss? She had spent her birthday on her own, stricken with flu. Not for the first time, I marvelled at her rare combination of sensitivity, even vulnerability, and her extraordinary inner strength, which allowed her to cope with a long marriage lived in the shadow of constant danger. We clung to each other at Heathrow, while our two lads looked on, slightly embarrassed at their demonstrative parents.

Just as in 1975, after the south-west face, many people assumed that I would now gracefully retire from the Himalaya. I did for a short while join Wendy on the golf course. She discovered a passion for golf when she turned fifty, another new interest that gave her huge fulfilment. Gill and Dennis Clarke were golfers and great friends, and as the kids grew up, Wendy decided to give it a try. It suited her well: golf is contemplative, you work at your own pace, you need a great deal of patience and practice is essential. My golfing career was shorter. While Wendy practised, I couldn't be bothered, and she quickly started beating me. A few tantrums later we decided it would be better if I stuck to climbing.

Wendy was always a perfectionist. When we first met and she was earning her living illustrating children's books, she would spend hours perfecting each drawing. When the children arrived, she focused on their care since I was away for so much of the time. Now they were growing up, she could spend more time again on her own creative life and started going to Carlisle Art College to explore pottery. She always preferred building her pots from coils rather than throwing them on a wheel. I think it was the controlled quality of the process. Even in conversation, she was deliberate and thoughtful before expressing an opinion; I was the very reverse, all too often thinking aloud.

Wendy had always had problems with her back and she became intrigued when a friend told her about the Alexander Technique, a system of training to realign posture and alleviate muscular and psychological tension. Wendy went for a lesson and was so impressed she signed up for the three-year teacher training course, spending three years driving to Windermere two or three times a week in all weathers. Having qualified, she practised for twenty years in what had been our children's playroom downstairs at Badger Hill, in Cockermouth and at the practice of our friend Richard Lloyd, an osteopath. She had great empathy and never stopped learning, taking courses in neuro-linguistic programming and developmental behavioural modelling to make even better use of the Alexander Technique.

Had you asked me at twenty-five if I would still be climbing in the Himalaya in my fifties I would have laughed. Even after the summit of Everest, I no longer deluded myself that I would reach the point where I'd be happy to give up serious climbing. Before leaving Kathmandu for Everest, I had been given permission for a beautiful but obscure mountain in Tibet called Menlungtse, at just over 7,000 metres one of the technically harder challenges in the eastern Himalaya. Even so, I had to acknowledge that the passing years were starting to bite. I no longer had the recovery of a younger man, taking a week or more after a hard push at altitude, rather than a day or two. I had certainly been much slower than Odd or Bjørn. I had a few good years in me yet but now I had to switch from testing the limits of the possible to testing the limits of what was possible for me.

The way forward had always been there, but an expedition to India two years before, perhaps the happiest I ever experienced, brought it home to me. It started in the spring of 1980 as I was wandering along the bottom of Shepherd's Crag in Borrowdale. It was the first time I'd attended the Tuesday evening gatherings of the Carlisle Mountaineering Club. A different crag was chosen each week to act as a focus for people to meet and climb, then go for a pint afterwards. There's probably an app for that now. I hadn't seen anyone I knew, so I soloed a fairly straightforward route called *Ardus* that takes a comfortable, clean-cut groove. It was very familiar, so climbing it without a rope didn't trouble me. I was just trying to summon up the courage to do the same on a harder route when another climber came along, also without a partner. We tossed a coin for who should lead it.

That was how I met Jim Fotheringham. He was slightly taller than me, had bluff, friendly features, and once on the crag was sound and forceful. We did two climbs that evening and in the pub afterwards I learned more about his background. He had qualified as a dentist from Birmingham University, part of a strong little mountaineering community there, and already had wide experience in the Alps and further afield. Over the next three years we climbed together regularly around Lakeland; we operated at around the same standard, though he definitely had a bit more push, making bold leads with minimal protection.

While I was on Kongur, he had his first Himalayan experience, climbing a 6,000-metre peak in the Karakoram. While I was on Everest in 1982, he was in Alaska making a fast ascent of the Cassin route on Denali. In the immediate emotional aftermath of the tragedy on the north-east ridge, I hadn't the stomach to go to Karun Koh, not least because it had been Pete's trip as well. Yet by early 1983, my old restlessness was reasserting itself. Jim and I were holed up in the bunker-like hut at the foot of the north-east face of Ben Nevis, peering out at the rain that was hammering down and enjoying a leisurely breakfast of bacon and eggs. I told him about my invitation to a tourism conference organized by the Indian Mountaineering Foundation in Delhi that September. I had a free flight, and figured I could negotiate another one for Jim. It seemed too good an opportunity to miss.

Neither of us had much time to spare. I was writing *Everest: The Unclimbed Ridge*, which was due for publication at the end of September, while Jim had started a new job and was buying a house. We needed a fast trip to the nearest mountains, more a super-Alpine holiday than an expedition. I knew some fine new routes had been done among the granite peaks above the Gangotri glacier, part of the Garhwal region where some of India's holiest sites are found. The village of Gangotri was only a two-day bus ride from Delhi and the walk-in was much shorter than most Himalayan expeditions of that era. In the following weeks we both collected photographs. Doug Scott had been there two years earlier and done a fine new route up the north-east ridge of Shivling, a stunning twin-summited peak on the east side of the Gangotri glacier. The year before, Allen Fyffe, who had been with us on Everest in 1975, had put up a beautiful and hard climb on the west pillar of Bhagarathi III. There was sure to be a worthwhile objective for us up there.

That winter I did more climbs on Ben Nevis than I had in the past thirty. Most were snatched in lightning visits, driving up the evening before, sleeping in or by the car and returning the following evening to work again on the book. In this way I did the big classics on Ben Nevis: *Point Five* and *Zero Gully*, *Orion Face* and *Minus Two*. Ice-climbing equipment had changed out of all recognition during my climbing life, allowing a man in his late forties to climb routes that were desperate in his youth. Hamish MacInnes had played a prominent role in this. Armed with a pair of modern axes and rigid crampons, my passion for Scottish climbing knew no limits. This wasn't training for the Himalaya: it was an end in itself, climbing steep ice in swirling spindrift with a backdrop of rolling, snow-clad mountains whose tones and shades altered as the clouds raced across a low-angled sun.

That summer was a good one for rock climbing too. My zenith was probably in the late 1950s and early 1960s, when I was climbing the hardest routes of the time and putting up a few of my own, but I never lost touch with it. It's the simplest and most joyous pleasure the mountains can offer. Through the 1970s, standards had soared and I was preoccupied with climbing in the Himalaya, but I still tried to push my own standard, getting a little thrill when I broke new barriers. As the crags dried out I ticked off routes I had long coveted, like *The Lord of the Rings*, a complete girdle of the east buttress of Scafell, more than three hundred metres of superb climbing. I did *Saxon* too, a tenuous crack that cuts through the smooth wall of the upper part of central buttress. It must be among the most spectacular stretches of rock in Britain.

The following year I presented a five-part television series called *Lakeland Rock*, filmed for Border Television, which allowed me to trace the more recent development of rock climbing on my home patch. We featured routes from the previous five decades, charting the astonishing rises in standard and improvements in equipment by using the equipment available when the climb was first done and featuring the climber who did it. The 1970s pioneer Pete Livesey, leading me up his masterwork *Footless Crow*, teased me mercilessly, waving a ten-pound note over my head while I shouted for a tight rope. What the viewers couldn't see was Pete surreptitiously paying out more rope to ramp up my fear. It was a great tragedy when he died at the age of only fifty-four; often controversial and provocative, he was a great thinker about climbing and a funny writer too.

While making *Lakeland Rock* I climbed with Don Whillans for the last time. By then he was in poor shape, bloated with chips and beer; it was a sad experience. After not asking Don to come to Everest in 1972, we hadn't spoken much and remained on fairly bitter terms. My plan was to ask Joe and Don to climb one of the Lake District routes together: Dovedale Groove on Dove Crag, which they did originally with Don Cowan. Sadly, Joe pulled a ligament in his knee and couldn't perform so I filled in for him. We planned to use hawser-laid ropes and gym shoes and just slings for protection, as Joe and Don did on the first ascent in 1953.

The crew was based at Wasdale Head Hotel. The owner was an old friend of Don's and the night before filming they drank a bottle of Scotch. In the morning he was in no fit state to do anything so we had to take the day off while he dried out, which must have cost the producers thousands. A penitent Don spent the rest of the day on the wagon and in the morning was ready to go, flying up the difficult climbing with surprising aplomb. During the filming, we talked and arrived at some kind of understanding about the past, but I could feel Don's sadness at how he had let himself go. I was only a year younger and still climbing at my limit. Not long after I got back from Everest in 1985, Don died of a heart attack, undone by the fags and booze, aged just fifty-two.

Jim Fotheringham and I were building up as a team. We understood each other's style of climbing, our thought processes and weaknesses. There was an element of competition to get the best pitch but even this was muted, since we both tacitly acknowledged that he had the edge on me when it came to hard and particularly bold climbing. The age difference probably helped too. We had some great adventures in Scotland, driving up to Aviemore on Friday night to sleep on the shores of Loch Morlich. Then up early to walk over Cairngorm to the Shelterstone at the head of Glen Avon, one of the finest crags in the whole of Scotland, 300 metres of steep, dark granite. We climbed a route called *Steeple*, a mixture of slabs and overhangs, culminating in a clean, sheer corner. It had an Alpine scale, pitch after pitch of exhilarating climbing and we only saw three people all day, three tiny figures on the shores of the loch. We were in good shape for India.

I flew out to India ahead of Jim for the tourism conference, opened by Indira Gandhi, three days of speeches, exquisite Indian buffets and meetings with old friends. The organizers had asked the conference speakers to lead a series of treks and had produced a handsome brochure, unfortunately just days before the conference started. I had agreed to take a party to base camp above the Gangotri glacier, but only one Australian, a girl called Jean, signed up. Happily, some of my fellow delegates came along to swell the numbers. There were three Everesters, Barry Bishop, who had been to the summit with the first American expedition, the Pole Wanda Rutkiewicz, one of the best women mountaineers ever, and Laurie Skreslet, the first Canadian.

We also had with us Adams Carter, the hugely distinguished editor of the *American Alpine Journal*, the most authoritative compendium of mountaineering information in the world; John Cleare, whom I knew of old from climbs in the 1960s and the Old Man of Hoy; and Warwick Deacock, an old friend from army days who emigrated to Australia to found their first Outward Bound school. We all piled on board our bus garlanded with flowers from our hotel on Janpath with Ad Carter cutting a ribbon that had been stretched across the door by our hosts. Jean looked rather bemused.

North of Rishikesh, the road wound through the foothills of the Himalaya to the town of Uttarkashi, where the Nehru Institute of Mountaineering is located, then run by my old friend Balwant Sandhu. We hadn't seen each other since our adventure on Changabang, almost ten years before. He had hardly changed, his hair perhaps slightly more grizzled, and he was as warmly enthusiastic as ever. He had married a German called Helga and they had a six-year-old son. Balwant was as active as ever, and was coming later to the Garhwal with India's first expedition to include both women and men. He promised he would come via Gangotri to see us.

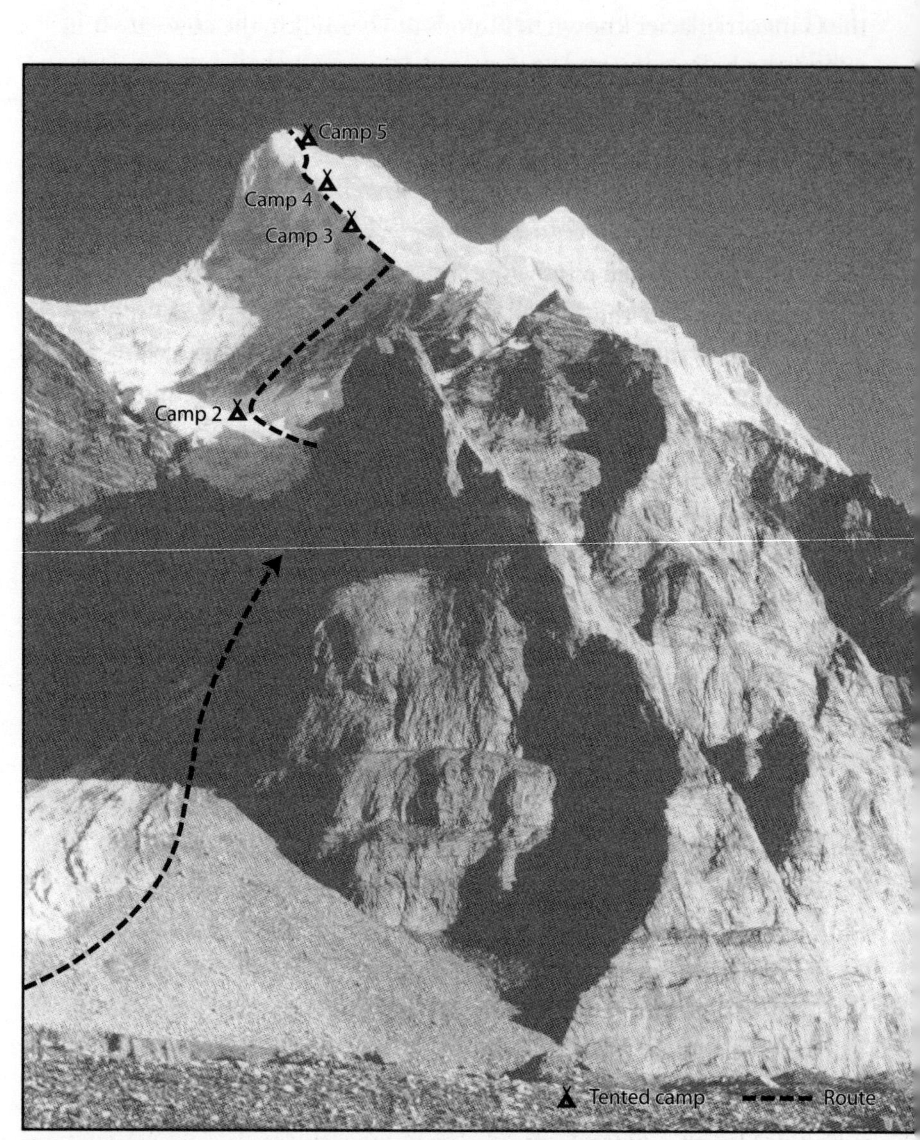

The west summit of Shivling, 1983. The lower part of the route where it's in shadow went up a wide snow gully threatened by a huge crumbling serac which we avoided by a gully behind the pinnacle. Here we obtained a safe bivvy platform (camp 1, hidden from view behind the pillar, unseen on the diagram), from which we were able to find a route up to camp 2.

The trek to Tapoban was just three short days, past the mouth of the Gangotri glacier known to Hindus at Gaumukh, the cow's mouth, one of the holiest sources of the Ganges, where pilgrims wash away the sins of a lifetime. The rock scenery was magnificent: great towers of weathered granite that in Europe would be a climbing hotspot but here were simply the foretaste of what was waiting up the valley. On our third morning we crossed the Gangotri glacier, smothered in rocky debris, and then climbed up the far side to the alp at Tapoban, as lovely a spot in the Himalaya as I had ever seen. Wild flowers nestled among the rocks, clear streams trickled among the boulders. Above our heads was the west flank of Shivling, Shiva's lingam, a magnificent phallus of granite and ice.

We were not alone at Tapoban. A Polish women's expedition was attempting the neighbouring peak of Meru North, but they were already climbing, their base camp occupied by one member who was sick, and their liaison officer Mala, a student from Calcutta. We invited them to dinner and sat around a fire under a full moon eating boeuf bourguignon and drinking wine. The grass was soft beneath our feet and the jagged mountains silhouetted against the starlit sky. Balwant arrived in time for dessert and we cracked open a bottle of whisky. It felt far too much fun to be a Himalayan expedition but we paid for it next morning with appalling hangovers.

We had settled on a mountain called Kedarnath Dome as our objective and we established a camp under its west face. I had never seen a peak in the Himalaya that looked so much like Yosemite. We stood underneath it, trying to find a way up it that wasn't too demanding for our schedule. There seemed a softer option to the left, with a glacier approach taking us high on the face. I climbed up onto a boulder to get a better view.

'There's no way I'm going on that,' I told Jim. 'It's just a bloody slog.' Jim suggested it was probably harder than it looked.

'But it looks so boring. How about the south-west summit of Shivling?' I said. 'It looks good and it's unclimbed.' We talked it through and Jim agreed. It was the evening of 12 September, Jim was due home in a week and we had just switched objectives to a difficult mountain we barely knew. I felt a confidence that had no basis in logic and that familiar tingle of anticipation. We cooked a huge meal, washed it down with the last of the wine and lay down under the stars with the alarm set for three o'clock.

Three days later we were bivouacked on the crest of a spur at the base of the rocky ridge that curved up to the south-west summit, scraping ice from the back of a crack to make a brew. I contemplated our isolated position. No one would be coming for us. No one knew where we were, although we had left a note with our stash of gear. The ground we had covered was convoluted and dangerous. To avoid an icefall spilling from the southern end of Shivling, we had climbed a dangerous gully. Halfway up, a boulder the size of a car rattled down it, bouncing from wall to wall. There was nowhere to hide and no reason to move: you couldn't predict where it was heading. It shot past two metres from me and after that, despite the altitude and my fifteen-kilo rucksack, blind panic drove me up until I ran with sweat.

Neither of us fancied retreating. We would have to climb out and go down the other side of the mountain. Snow conditions were bad, and the climbing often felt spooky; it was a relief to reach solid granite and start rock climbing. From time to time the weather built up, clouds boiling over Meru and Kedarnath, thunderheads to the west. That night was our fourth on the mountain. We built up our little eyrie with loose rocks so we could pitch the tent. Once inside, we listened to snow pattering on its skin. I imagine Jim was wondering, just as I was, what we would do if the weather worsened, but I felt strangely content, perched above the vast drop, listening to the purr of the stove, chatting amicably. It was as good and easy a partnership as any I've experienced in the mountains. Darkness fell. There was time for a last brew before sleep, so Jim opened the door to collect more ice. I heard a rattle as our only headlamp, propped in the entrance, disappeared into space, its beam shining erratically as it ricocheted off the slabs below.

'That'd give someone a shock, if there was anyone down there to see it,' Jim said cheerfully. I couldn't complain. I'd already dropped my torch. At least we now had an excuse to have a lie-in in the morning.

About an inch of snow fell in the night but the sky was clear and it soon burnt off. We'd fixed two rope lengths the night before and at the top of these I led a steep crack to the base of overhanging corner. It looked as though Jim had bagged the crux. He bridged out widely, got a runner to protect himself, swung out on the overhanging wall and let out a yell of joy. Continuing up, he disappeared from view so I watched the rope gradually work through my hands until it stopped and there was another shout. Moments later Jim reappeared, abseiling down to collect his rucksack, before Jumaring back up the rope. This way he could climb without the heavy weight of his rucksack.

The angle now relented but every ledge was piled with rubble, which threatened the man below. We weaved from side to side, but the higher we got the more insecure the rock became, with great flakes piled on top of each other. There was no point putting in runners; nothing was solid. Yet we were almost there. Pulling onto a huge block, I found myself on steep snow, just below the crest of the ridge. The summit seemed barely a rope length away. The snow, we agreed, would be frozen in the morning so we dug out a ledge for the tent, our fifth night on the mountain, with immense drops on either side. That evening we finished the last of the food.

'You know,' Jim said next morning, 'we're just about on top. We've climbed the route. Don't you think we should start getting down?'

'Don't you want a picture of yourself standing there on top? Where's your sense of glory?'

'I'm more interested in getting down in one piece.'

'It'll only be twenty minutes or so. You'll regret it.'

It was a bit more than that, but I have never been on another summit like it. There was barely room for one person to balance on its tip. I stood there waving my ice axes triumphantly, not at having conquered, but in joy, in the beauty of the peaks and sky, and the route we had climbed. The descent terrified me with, as it turned out, good reason. But climbing Shivling was a delight, an intense, fast-paced experience on a challenging and highly committing climb. It had felt Alpine, in character and style. We had changed our plans and reacted to circumstances, creating a sense of freedom and agency you never feel on a large expedition. It all added up to one of the best mountain experiences of my life.

After Everest, it was smaller-scale adventures like Shivling that offered me the best way to experience what I love most about mountaineering: exploration on unknown or little-known peaks with good friends. Menlungtse, the peak I'd been seeking permission for in 1985, was a good example. In 1987 I put together a small Anglo-Norwegian team comprising Jim Fotheringham, Odd Eliassen and Bjørn Myrer-Lund, friends from two of my happiest expeditions. We crossed the Nepali-Tibetan border on the Friendship Highway and drove to Dingri, where we hired yaks for the approach to base camp. It was exhilarating country, like stepping back through time. We made a strong attempt on the south-west buttress, but were caught in a vicious storm. Jim had a near miss from a lightning bolt and was rendered unconscious for a short while. The tents rattled violently all night and by morning that of the Norwegians had been torn to bits. There was no choice but retreat. While abseiling down, the snow stake I was leaning against pulled out, catapulting me down the slope. I heaved myself round and snatched at the ropes, successfully, as this book proves. We made two more attempts, reaching roughly the same point, but the weather was awful that season and we were driven back by storms.

While exploring the Menlungtse region, I had noticed a magnificent peak, a steep and almost perfect pyramid. Checking the map I discovered it was called Drangnag Ri and was 6,801 metres high. I filed it away in my memory as something I'd love to climb and when Arne Naess decided to organize an expedition to celebrate the tenth anniversary of our Everest climb, I suggested Drangnag Ri as an objective. All of us bar one returned to Nepal for the attempt and six of the Sherpas too. We didn't climb it in the best style, fixing

Collecting my CBE after the 1975 Everest expedition, with my mum.

(Chris Bonington Picture Library)

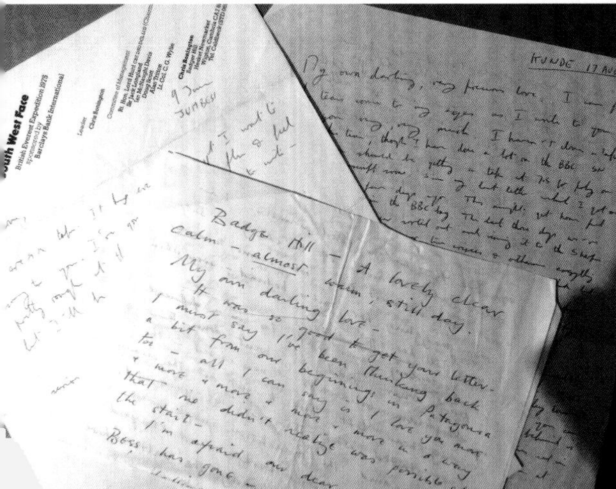

KUNDE 17 AU

My own darling, my precious love.

Badger Hill – A lovely clear calm – almost warm, still day.

My own darling love –

It was so good to get your letter.

I must say I've been thinking back a bit from our beginnings in Patagonia too – all I can say is, I love you more & more & more & more

that we didn't realize was possible at the start –

I'm afraid our dear Bess has gone

Letters between me and Wendy during the 1975 Everest expedition.

(Chris Bonington)

Our home of forty years, nestling under High Pike above the village of Caldbeck, in the Northern Fells of the Lake District.

(Chris Bonington)

Me at work in my office at home on the final proofs of *Everest the Hard Way* with Wendy and Judy, who helped with our pictures, working at the light box behind. (Chris Bonington)

On the summit of Everest in 1985, with Ang Lhakpa. (Chris Bonington)

Me and Pertemba after summiting Everest in 1985. (Chris Bonington)

Guards of Honour at a very special wedding. Left to right: Tony Howard, Doug Scott, Jane and Paul Braithwaite, Dave Clarke and a very hairy me. (Chris Bonington Picture Library)

'he Ogre team at advance base with the Ogre ehind. Left to right: Clive Rowland, myself, ʌick Estcourt, Doug Scott, Paul Braithwaite nd Mo Anthoine – a super-lightweight xpedition, no porters and we didn't even have cook or a doctor. (Chris Bonington)

Doug crawling down the Ogre, belayed by myself at the back, with Clive Rowland picking out the route for us. (Chris Bonington)

ack at base camp on the Ogre, after a ve-day descent without food and with ıree broken ribs, I'm being strapped up y Clive Rowland. (Chris Bonington)

K2 – arguably the most challenging and dangerous of all the 8,000-metre peaks. (Chris Bonington)

Nick Estcourt and myself on a wonderfully happy little expedition when we made the first ascent of Brammah in the Kishtwar Himalaya. (Chris Bonington)

British K2 Expedition 1978, showing the foreline of the avalanche that killed Nick Estcourt. (Peter Boardman)

Kongur 1981 – Al Rouse, Peter Boardman and Joe Tasker in our snow hole on the col between Junction Peak and the main summit. (Chris Bonington)

Jim Fotheringham at our fourth bivouac on Shivling; we both slept in this tent. (Chris Bonington)

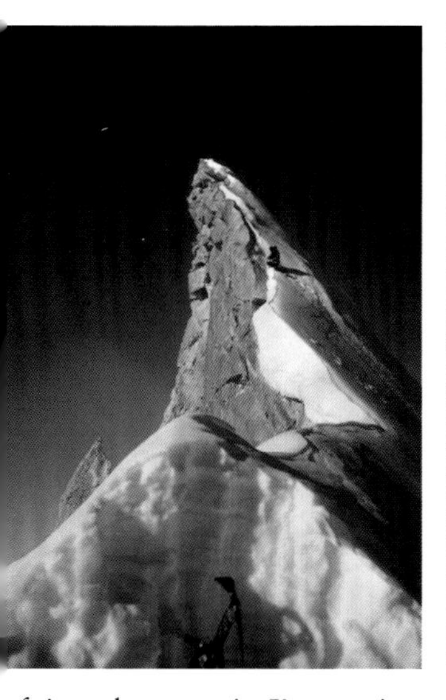

. fairytale summit: I'm out in
ont and Jim took this picture
·om our fifth bivouac on the
ımmit ridge of Shivling.
m Fotheringham)

Suhaili and our first iceberg on the way to the East coast of Greenland in 1991. (Robin Knox-Johnston)

Our Greenland crew in 1991. Left to right: me, Perry Crickmere, Robin Knox-Johnston at the helm, James Burdett, John Dunn and Jim Lowther. (Chris Bonington)

I'm giving Robin a quick masterclass in snow climbing. (Jim Lowther)

First ascent of the West face of Panchchuli II, which Graham Little and I climbed Alpine-style. (Graham Little)

Panchchuli V – Stephen Venables after a fall of 80 metres, when his abseil anchor came out on the way down from the successful ascent. (Victor Saunders)

Sepu Kangri, Tibet 1997 – into the internet age with satellite communications.
(Chris Bonington)

Kilimanjaro 1992 summit group after our successful family ascent by the rarely climbed Credner glacier. Me next to Joe, Gerald, my brother, on the far right and Rupert seated second from right, in front row, an friends. (Chris Bonington)

'he annual trip to Morocco – myself with 'ete Turnbull and Joe Brown. (Chris Bonington)

Fantastic climbing – me on first ascent of Cordon Rouge, Tafraout, Morocco. (Chris Bonington)

Me and Wendy in the later stages of her illness, by the shores of Bassenthwaite Lake. Her little red buggy gave us both freedom and real joy. (Chris Bonington)

Leo Houlding and myself on the top of the Old Man of Hoy in 2014 – Leo first climbed it at the age of eleven, the youngest to have done so and I, at eighty, was probably the oldest. (Chris Bonington)

After Wendy's funeral with my family on top of Cat Bells above Derwentwater. Back row, left to right: Ann, Rupert, myself, Joe and Jude. Front row, left to right: Edie, Will, Emily and Honor. (Chris Bonington)

I'm so lucky to have found love a second time with my new wife Loreto, enjoying the bluebells of Rannerdale in the Lake District. (Paul Ross)

Our lovely wedding at Our Lady of Victories Church, Kensington, April 2016. In front, our eight grandchildren (David Usill)

ropes to near the summit so everyone had a chance to reach the top, but I was pleased to lead some of the hardest ground, going better than I had for years, reading the ground, still attuned to the mountain environment, intensely elated. This, I reflected, was why I was still climbing in the Himalaya at sixty. And the expedition helped cement an enduring friendship, leading to regular reunions in the Lakes and Norway.

Sadly, in January 2004, Arne was killed in an abseiling accident in South Africa. We had only just started discussing where to go for our twentieth Everest anniversary. I flew to Norway a few weeks later for the funeral. Since Arne had first called me all those years ago, he'd met the singer Diana Ross at a resort in the Bahamas. They'd married in 1985, the year we climbed Everest, and had two boys together. Although they divorced in 1999, and Arne had a new relationship with Camilla Astrup, Diana was at his funeral in a wonderful wooden church in Oslo. During a trumpet voluntary of 'Amazing Grace', she couldn't help but sing along. As her voice filled the church, I found I was crying, along with the rest of the congregation.

Chapter Seventeen

Ice with Everything

I first met Robin Knox-Johnston in 1978 on a special Christmas charity edition of the television show *The Krypton Factor.* Filming took place soon after I returned from K2, when my damaged ribs flared up again. I eyed my opponents with cautious optimism, the two others being the polar adventurer Ranulph Fiennes and the balloonist Don Cameron. Fiennes, tall, lean and ex-SAS was a shoo-in for the assault course, but I reckoned on second place. A mountaineer should be able to outstrip a sailor and a balloonist. They just sat still and steered, didn't they? At the gun, Fiennes shot off into an early lead but I was shocked to see Knox-Johnston hard on his heels. No matter, my mountaineer's stamina would tell in the end, but all I saw of Robin after that was his back, and I trailed in a very poor third. Happily for me, my pride was restored in the cerebral part of the challenge and I came out the overall winner.

A year or so later we met again as part of my research for *Quest for Adventure*. He suggested that instead of just interviewing him we could gain direct experience of what the other was about and he invited me to Oban in July to join him and his wife Sue and daughter Sara for a short voyage through the Western Isles. Things didn't start tremendously well. I arrived late at the wrong part of the harbour, having scoured the shops for a map of the Cuillin, having left mine at home. Robin and Sue seemed wholly relaxed about my late arrival, and I brought my gear on board his thirty-two-foot ketch *Suhaili*, a name that means 'companion'.

Inspiration for *Suhaili* came from the Norwegian sailing life-boats of Colin Archer, who also designed the *Fram*. She was built from teak with the help of experienced dhow-builders in Mumbai, where Robin was second officer on a passenger ship that did the Basra run. He had given up his job to sail *Suhaili* home via Cape Town and, having written a few articles for the *Guardian* about the voyage, was introduced to George Greenfield at the dockside when he arrived back in London. George took Robin's idea of becoming the first person to sail solo non-stop around the world to the *Sunday Times*, who promptly turned his idea into a race, leaving George and Robin fuming. Happily, they got sponsorship elsewhere and crossed the finish line first. It was hard to imagine, chugging up the Sound of Mull, Robin sailing this small boat alone through the Roaring Forties, shaken awake when the boat capsized.

By the time we reached Loch Scavaig next day I was captivated by this style of sailing, watching the Highlands crawl past, having time to savour their changing character as we crawled round Muck and Eigg, as the jagged ramparts of the Cuillin loomed closer. That evening Robin rowed me ashore and I gave him his first taste of rock climbing on a little crag just above the bay. Robin wasn't a natural but he was quietly determined and not at all daunted by the prospect of a fall.

Next morning we set out for the main ridge, walking alongside Loch Coruisk then up the Dubh Ridge, a magnificent but easy climb, padding up rough gabbro. Things went well, but I had forgotten a vertical step, the Dubh Gap, required an abseil. I did at least have a rope and having dropped the ends, gave Robin a quick tutorial.

'You know, Chris, I think it would be much better if I did this the way I'm used to.' He rigged the ropes as a pulley around the karabiner and prepared to set off. 'This is how I go up and down the mast.' I didn't like the idea at all, but Robin was adamant. Down he went, as though sitting in a bosun's chair.

Cloud swallowed us up as we reached the ridge and I soon realized the large-scale map I'd bought in Oban was almost useless. I stumbled on, anxious not to admit my absent-mindedness. Luckily, two other climbers emerged from the mist, and I fished for details about our exact location, and having ascertained we were heading in the right direction, continued to the Thearlaich Dubh Gap, where Robin repeated his pulley trick. The rock climbing on the other side is pretty taxing, but Robin arrived at the top grinning, while admitting that shinning up the mast of *Suhaili* was more his usual line.

I was enjoying the swirling clouds on this wild mountain day, but couldn't deny the wind was now gusting hard round the pinnacles along the ridge crest. Robin seemed worried. As I came to understand so well, only two things kept him awake at night: an insecure anchorage and losing all power. *Suhaili*'s anchorage in Loch Scavaig was open to the south and he was afraid the anchor might drag. We decided to descend to the boat. Robin dropped me off at Tobermory and I went home to my book, but the memory of my few days with Robin stuck with me. I had liked him very much, and seeing the mountains from such a fresh angle was a revelation. The boat offered a sort of base camp. I even started talking about buying one. As with my plan of overwintering with the Inuit, Wendy dealt firmly with that idea, reminding me of my attitude to fixing engines and generally maintaining things. The experience of sailing and climbing remained a delightful one-off.

More than ten years later, Robin called out of the blue. Would I like to sail to Greenland and do a climb? It was the logical extension of what we'd done on Skye, but on a much grander scale. As an idea, it was impossible to resist, so I started researching an objective. It didn't take long to discover that Greenland's most challenging mountains are on the east coast, which was also the most difficult to reach by boat. I was also told we'd be mad to take *Suhaili* into its ice-locked fjords. Robin set to work studying the Admiralty Pilot, trying to work positively around its blunt warnings and find us a possible anchorage.

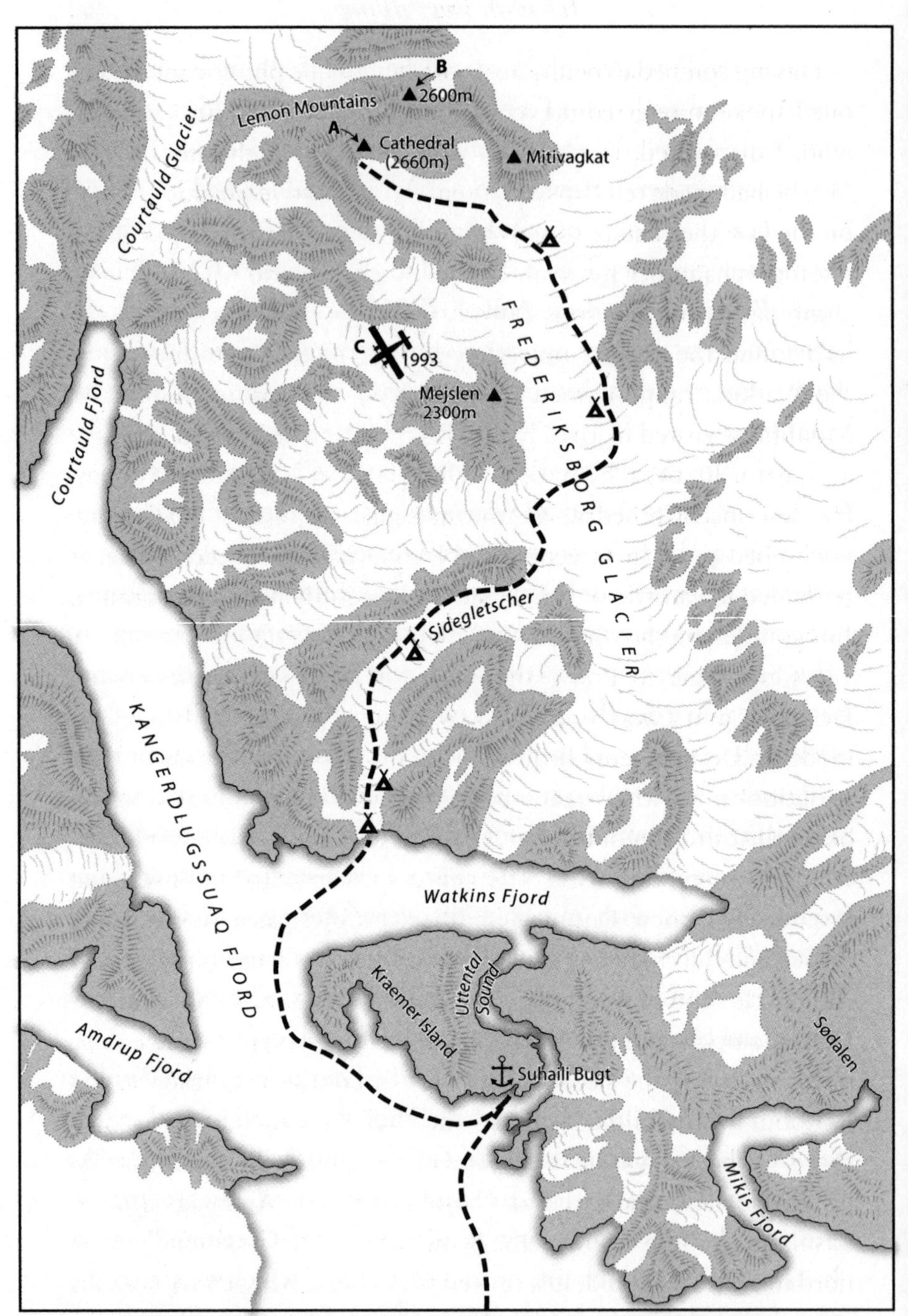

Greenland, 1991 and 1993. The route into the Lemon Mountains showing the position of the Cathedral as marked on the map that we had with us (A on map). Unfortunately the map was incorrect and it was only when we were high on the mountain that we could see clearly that the peak marked as 2,600 metres (B on map) was in fact the highest point. A and B should have been reversed – they were wrong on the map and as a result we climbed the wrong mountain.

C – In 1993 we were landed by a twin-engined Otter on the glacier below Mejslen and were climbing three days after we had set out from England. We climbed Mejslen and several other superb peaks.

Having combed expedition reports and made phone calls, everyone I spoke to referred me to a young climber called Jim Lowther, who, I discovered, lived on my doorstep. Although only twenty-five, he had made ten trips to Greenland and arrived from his home on the Lowther Estate to see me with a sheaf of maps, reports and photographs under his arm. In the secretive world of exploratory climbing, it was generous help. A few days later he called to say he'd found the perfect objective, a peak he had seen himself in the Watkins range named Cathedral. It was one of the Lemon Mountains visited in 1936 by the Everest climber Lawrence Wager and again in 1972 by another Greenland expert, Stan Woolley. He described Cathedral as 'the most attractive and challenging unclimbed peak in Greenland'. No one had been back since. It reminded me a little of the Aiguille Verte in the Chamonix range. Jim assured me the rock was granite and sound.

I soon came to know Jim better. We climbed in winter on Helvellyn and I was impressed by his competence and liked his modesty. Despite being little older than my son Joe, he was mature in outlook but with a great sense of fun, useful qualities, I imagine, being the third son of the Earl of Lonsdale, one of Cumbria's largest landowners. Jim worked for the Lowther Estate's multi-faceted businesses. I knew I needed another climber, since Robin was a novice and the challenge was immense, and Jim seemed the perfect choice. He soon proved himself immensely reliable, doing whatever I asked quickly and efficiently, assembling our supplies and equipment, including the sleds we'd use to haul our gear on the ice.

Robin meanwhile considered the challenge of the approach to shore. Cathedral was near the head of a fjord called Kangerlussuaq, just inside the Arctic Circle and halfway between Angmagssalik, or Tasiilaq as it's now known, and Scoresby Sound. The second largest fjord in east Greenland, it is tucked into a gigantic open corner that apparently held floe ice, although the most recent navigation report in the Pilot was dated 1941. Danish Navy charts for Kangerlussuaq showed white, meaning there was no data available. Weather conditions were often stormy in the Denmark Strait, between Iceland

and Greenland, but the frequency of gales increases sharply from early September, and Robin was keen to be well south before then.

We had a larger scale map showing the approaches to Cathedral. The most direct was via the Courtauld glacier, named for August Courtauld, but that was a long way up the main fjord and likely choked with ice. So we considered our best bet to be the Sidegletscher, off Watkins Fjord, more likely navigable but also a rather longer approach at forty miles. There was a final alternative, via the neighbouring Mikis Fjord, but this would add another three days to the trek. Robin at least could rely on sailors being more forthcoming than climbers with information. He read Bill Tilman's books – they were both at Berkhamsted School – although in his five voyages to the area, Tilman lost one boat off Jan Mayen Island and a second near Angmagssalik. The best authority on sailing in Arctic waters was still William Scoresby's account of whaling in the 1820s, manoeuvring wooden boats, admittedly of 400 tonnes, in the pack ice.

The Danish Polar Institute, which was, before Greenland became autonomous, tasked with approving expeditions there, took a dim view of our enterprise but Robin called Robin Duchesne, secretary-general of the Royal Yachting Association, and he called his opposite number in Denmark who then explained things to the Polar Institute and everything was sorted out. Now he needed crew. One of his regulars, Perry Crickmere, another merchant navy man, was so keen on the project that he took leave from work to come with us. A young law student called James Burdett filled the second berth, having advertised in the Royal Cruising Club's newsletter for a passage north. At twenty-three he was the youngest of the team, but admirably laid-back, almost horizontal as Robin put it, with the requisite dry sense of humour.

On 13 July, *Suhaili* left Gosport for Whitehaven, where Jim and I came on board with the climbing gear and food. It was a bit of a shock to discover that the boat had sprung a leak, but it turned out not to be a hull plank springing loose, but old electrical cable trunking in the sternpost. Robin soon had it fixed, and we filled every available space with supplies for two months, six sledges, the dinghy, climbing gear and all the myriad other things we'd need. Also along for the ride was John Dunn, the well-known Radio 2 presenter, who would leave us in Reykjavik, to be replaced by a film crew. John was six and a half feet tall, and I felt for him as he levered himself into the cramped cabin. Robin calculated that *Suhaili* had settled ten centimetres lower in the water, indicating a cargo of two tonnes.

It seemed half of Whitehaven turned out to see us off and at six o'clock on the evening of 19 July we motored out of the harbour. Among the crowd waving proudly were Mum and her partner Diana, who were now living near us in Keswick. They had made it in the nick of time. It was exciting but also unnerving, the enormity of the ocean ahead of us, the knowledge that if the wind came on the nose, it might take us two weeks to reach Iceland. Soon the slight pitching of the boat had all the newcomers feeling a little green, so Robin had us setting sail and ran through the names and functions of the boat's parts. I liked his most important advice: 'Have one hand for the boat, but always keep one for yourself.' We were split into watches, Robin took John, Perry took me, while James and Jim, the Young Turks, took the third.

I was impressed at how Robin dealt with landlubbers. He was undoubtedly the skipper and we were going to do precisely as we were told, but his way of sharing information and discussing options made it an enjoyable education. I slowly got a feel for the tiller, started to see waves coming and knew to pull it in the right direction so we didn't heel over. It was tiring work, since the weight of the tiller in heavy seas was considerable, mentally too. As a beginner, I had to focus all the time, whereas for Perry and Robin it was second nature.

Down below, we were crammed into a space three metres by two, with two bunks on each side and the floor space limited to a tiny area aft by the galley and chart table. I was used to confined spaces, being trapped in tents during mountain storms, and the consequent lack of privacy, but sailing was of a different order.

Keeping watch also took adjustment; three hours on and six off required a change in sleep patterns, but lack of sleep is something mountaineers understand.

One of the most noticeable contrasts between climbing and sailing was the difference in weather patterns. Weather changes at sea came more quickly and more often, it seemed to me, so that one moment you were wrapped up in oilskins and the next sunbathing. Perhaps it was because the weather affected the boat so intimately that you noticed it more.

The rolling and pitching of the boat, its sudden lurches and hiccups, was something altogether new. Even the simplest task took time and patience. Making tea, I was catapulted across the cabin with an open sugar bowl in my hand. Result: sugar everywhere, the cutlery drawer all over the place and the extra task of cleaning it all up before I could get back to making tea. Even so, I was enjoying myself. I welcomed the new challenges; it was what I needed. I was struck by how often things went wrong with the boat, hardly surprising given the constant wear it suffered and the corrosive environment: the Weatherfax failed, meaning we were limited to shipping forecasts; the radio stopped transmitting, and there was a leak in the loo.

The practical skills of the sailors were immensely impressive. They were constantly ingenious, prepared to take most things on. Robin took the radio apart, found a loose wire, studied the manual and reattached it. Hey presto, the radio started transmitting again. To fix the loo, the hull valve was taken out and while Robin jammed his hand over the hole to keep the Atlantic where it should be, Perry cleaned and greased it. The loo was fixed.

Robin decided these successes allowed him to declare a 'headland', a ritual born from a close encounter with one in the Shetland Islands during the 1986 Round Britain Race. Having narrowly escaped disaster, he and his crewmate, Billy King-Harman, celebrated with a nip of whisky. 'Headland' became a generic name for any bump along the way, good as well as bad, that needed acknowledging. And in his democratic way, Robin allowed three votes to decide the matter: one for the skipper, one for the crew and one for the owner. We soon had reason to declare another headland when news came on the radio that John was to become a grandfather. He'd brought along a small bottle of champagne for the occasion.

I shared my watch with Perry. He was an excellent mentor, having served four years in the merchant navy; he had the same wonderful practicality Robin shared, although Robin envied Perry's ability to roll a cigarette one-handed in all conditions. He also had a warm, twinkly sense of humour, which eased most tensions. It was interesting to compare the sorts of personalities on board. Robin had a tremendous drive, and there was no question that we wouldn't make Kangerlussuaq. When Jim said 'if we get there', Robin came straight back: 'There is no if, we're going to get there.'

The first sign of Iceland were puffins around the boat. By dinner on 28 July, after nine days at sea, we were level with Eldey Island, a seventy-seven-metre sea stack covering some seven acres and one of the largest northern gannet colonies in the world. It was a relief to see land. When the customs officer came aboard at Reykjavik Harbour he seemed amazed at the amount of booze we carried, perhaps not appreciating the number of headlands we needed to pass. It all had to be bonded for the duration of our stay, so we stowed the lot in the loo and he sealed the door. There was laundry to be done, minor repairs to the engine and a change of crew. John Dunn flew home and his berth was filled by one of our film crew, cameraman Jan Pester. Allen Jewhurst, the film's producer and director, would fly ahead to Greenland.

The entrance to Kangerlussuaq Fjord was 340 miles north-west of Reykjavik across the Denmark Strait and a nice force five was waiting for us as we emerged from the harbour. This soon faded and we motored the rest of the day with limited visibility. On 2 August we crossed the Arctic Circle, at around half past eight in the morning, too early for a headland so we settled instead for a huge fry-up. As if on cue, there was a shout from the deck that an object was in sight ahead of us: our first iceberg. It must have been a monster, because we weren't level with it for another three hours.

By then we could see the mountains, or more accurately, because we were still eighty miles away, we could see them refracted over the horizon, a phenomenon Scoresby described almost two centuries ago. Another berg appeared, this one closer and perhaps a half-mile long and sixty metres high; it must have extended below the surface almost to the ocean's floor. It had twin peaks, separated by a col, and the sides were opaque. It had broken off some northern glacier and was now drifting south. Robin kept *Suhaili* well clear knowing that a berg can roll unexpectedly but he and James dashed over in the dinghy to collect some ice to freshen up our gin.

As we approached Kangerlussuaq, a mineral exploration team confirmed on the radio there was no pack ice but warned of bergs in the entrance. We passed them cautiously, vast apartment blocks in the peaceful water, and beyond them more ice in various shapes and colours, ranging from pure white to deep blue, even mauve. Framing the horizon were brown mountains, more like the desert than the Arctic. The rocks along the shore were basalt and looked very mucky and broken but I knew the Lemon Mountains were more solid. I was filled with a sense of contentment, with the mountains ahead and the voyage behind us, having avoided getting sick and learned a little more about sailing.

Allen had met up with a team of geologists from the University of Copenhagen, led by Professor Kent Brooks from Cumbria. Kent had been coming to Greenland for twenty years and kindly lent us his aluminium-covered boat, a tremendous help in ferrying our gear ashore. With his deep local knowledge, he directed us through a narrow channel into a large sheltered bay, surrounded by hills on three sides and protected to the south by islets. Local winds would still be a risk, but Robin seemed happy and having dropped the heavy fisherman's anchor, he put the engine full astern to make sure it was firmly embedded.

Over lunch, we caught up with Allen's adventures and cross-examined Kent about conditions. After my reporting thirty years ago on the Inuit, I was riveted to hear of their camps here. Four families were expected on the coastal boat in two weeks' time. The

Inuit left their dogs marooned on an island to await their return, provided with a whole carcass for food. If the boat was delayed, then it was bad luck for the dogs. In the summer they hunted seal, but fox, narwhal and polar bear were also taken. Even though high-powered boats were available, they continued to use traditional kayaks, even if they were made from fibreglass in the UK. They had already shot an alarming number of bears that summer, which meant there were none to see, but the Danish authorities had insisted we carry firearms in case of attack. We preferred to take flares on the ice. The rifle remained on the boat, unused.

With Kent's local knowledge and Allen's view of the mountains as he flew in, we had a clearer idea of how best to approach Cathedral. The alternative routes from further up Kangerlussuaq Fjord or via Watkins Fjord were out of the question; when we came level with the mouth of Watkins, the amount of ice seemed formidable. As it was, it took us nine hours of patient work to reach the mouth of the Sidegletscher, with a man posted on the spreaders up the mast shouting directions and two 'jousters' on the bow armed with boathooks pushing off any lumps that came too close. By half past nine in the evening we were within a mile and a half of the moraine, and an hour later just off a flat ledge of rock lying at the foot of the valley.

After Robin had dropped anchor and turned off the engine, we were surrounded by a profound silence the like of which you rarely experience now in Britain. Sounds seemed to travel for miles and we unconsciously lowered our voices. Slowly other noises became apparent: the sound of two bergs grinding against each other, the quiet slop of water. We put the dinghy in the water and I waded ashore, happy to be back on land. In front of us was the wide valley leading to the entrance of the Sidegletscher, our shortcut to the huge motorway of the Frederiksborg Gletscher, or glacier, and, at its head, the Lemon Mountains. I found a good campsite and we started the laborious process of bringing our gear and supplies ashore, made much easier when Kent arrived in his boat to help. The three sailors stayed on board to cook another enormous curry;

the landlubbers were happy in their tents. I felt returned to my element: the Primus stove purring away, the mountains at my back. Robin left us in the morning for the slow passage back down the fjord to the secure anchorage.

We couldn't start hauling straightaway; the glacier no longer reached the sea and while drifts of old snow lay around, they weren't extensive enough to use. The retreat of the glacier was astonishing when compared to the ice of sixty years ago. We could see evidence of recent glaciation sixty metres above our heads. Without the ice, we had to ferry loads on our backs to where we could start pulling the sleds.

My first impression was of a bleak beauty, of stark rocks and patches of snow under grey cloud. But looking more closely I could see colour in the Arctic willow, the closest you'll get to a tree in this part of Greenland, creeping across the landscape only a few centimetres from the ground. The Inuit used it as a cure-all and in their blubber lamps. There was no wind, and yet the ice in the fjord shifted constantly, driven by ocean currents, great ocean liners of ice cruising past, with smaller chunks alongside like tugs, nudging their sides. The water in Kangerlussuaq was up to 900 metres deep, three times the depth of Denmark Strait.

I kept plodding on, slower now in my mid-fifties, more like the tortoise than the hare, but like the tortoise never stopping. We were now in a desolation of piled rocks, the dirty grey surface of the bare glacier visible ahead. I think Robin was disappointed that glaciers are grey and filthy. The walls of the valley closed in too, soaring faces of granite a thousand metres high offering more climbing than the *aiguilles* above Chamonix and yet unnamed, untouched and unexplored. Then I saw some tracks – those of a hare in the form of Jim Lowther – and I followed them to a pile of boulders by the side of the glacier. He had dumped his load.

'This should do,' he said. 'It's flat enough to start hauling here.'

We were back in camp by early afternoon, and after a brew, Jim announced he was going to make another carry. I snuggled in my sleeping bag and returned to my book. By the time he returned,

I was cooking supper and Kent's boat was approaching through the ice, with Perry, James and Robin on board. After a quick cup of tea, the two sailors, Perry and James, returned to keep watch over *Suhaili* and the land party was complete. Robin never stopped fretting about his treasure and after carrying more loads next day set up our HF radio so he could talk to the crew. The following morning we struck camp and hoisted monstrous loads onto our backs, thirty kilos or so, to complete our ferrying in one more push. I felt a little sorry for Robin, swaying under his load with his sled strapped on top. Physical activity on boats tends to be in short bursts rather than long hours.

By the time we put the tents up that evening I was heartily glad it was Jim's turn to cook. I was as tired as Robin, but couldn't resist going outside to revel in the paradise of rock that surrounded us. I started working out routes up the huge cliffs, making plans for the future. I found the experience had been deepened with how we had come here, by boat and on skis; it gave a symmetry to the adventure that you don't get arriving by aircraft, being tipped out on the snow in a blur, suddenly switching from modernity to the wilds. The approach this time had been slow; I felt better for it.

To take advantage of the cooler temperatures when the sun briefly dipped below the horizon, we holed up next day to wait for evening. Mountaineers are used to lying on their backs doing nothing; it's why we read so much. Sailors don't deal with the inactivity quite so well and Robin was restless. That day, 6 August, was my fifty-seventh birthday and I felt a little grumpy, lying in my tent, that no one had noticed, and a little homesick too. Then I heard laughter and the clearing of throats before the team broke into a discordant rendering of Happy Birthday. Sticking my head out, I saw Allen holding a miniature bottle of champagne in one hand and a tiny iced cake in the other. It was Wendy who put them up to it. I felt immensely touched. The candles were the sort that reignite after you blow them out: I took that as encouragement.

It was ten thirty in the evening when we struck the tents. The sun was just setting, bathing the rounded hump of Kraemer Island in pink light. Jim recommended crampons, since we were standing on bare ice, and I harnessed myself into my sled, known as a pulk. Mine must have held about a hundred kilos. With a ski stick in each hand, I gave an experimental heave and the pulk slid along with amazing ease. At times it would jam against one of the many flutings that criss-crossed the ice but mostly I made good progress. Eventually, we reached snow and I could start skiing. Soon I'd developed a wonderful rhythm, pushing and sliding down the pale road of the glacier trapped between the black pyramids around us.

Robin, not having skied since his honeymoon, found it harder and was soon a dot far behind us. We got out the Primus while we waited but by the time he'd arrived were eager to move on again. It's always miserable being tail-end Charlie. Gradually the sky brightened, the sun rose and the glacier became bathed in rich yellow light. The tents went up and we rested again before our second night's travel, a gentle climb to the head of the Sidegletscher and a view onto the Frederiksborg, our motorway to Cathedral. Skiing down the slope with the pulk was a lot easier than pulling it, except of course for Robin, who was mown down by his a couple of times. Not for the first time, I admired his determination. The going on the Frederiksborg wasn't much easier.

That morning, after we stopped, we gazed up the glacier towards the cirque of the Lemon Mountains, named for the man who looked after Gino Watkins's base camp. At the eastern end were two sharply pointed peaks called Mitivagkat, meaning breasts, but more in the style of Madonna's Gaultier bustier. Jim and I agreed we needed a reconnaissance to determine the best approach to Cathedral, which looked formidable. He now confessed that he had left his photographs of the mountain on *Suhaili*. At first, we didn't think it mattered. We studied the map, which showed a peak of the right height to the left of the head of the glacier. Only much later did we discover the map was wrong. Once we were looking in what we thought was the right direction, a route presented itself, up a wide gully leading to a col and then the rocky south ridge to the summit.

We had a week in which to climb the mountain but first Robin needed a bit of instruction, never having used an ice axe before. We started on the gully we intended to climb, but as soon as the sun struck it, a fusillade of stones came rattling down: not the best location for a climbing school. So we retired for a brew and then continued in a shaded gully on the other side of the cirque. I showed him how to put on his harness, how to tie a prusik knot – not one a sailor would know – and how to do an ice-axe arrest. This was very much the accelerated course. Once I had convinced him you could brake a fall with your axe he found it quite fun. We were ready to go.

I lit the stove next morning and then snuggled in my sleeping bag, reluctant to emerge into the cold. Just five more minutes. Then I unzipped the tent door and peered out. It was half past three and as far as I could tell the sky was clear. I handed hot sweet tea to Robin and Jim, followed soon after by porridge, honey and margarine, for extra calories. Then they left as I finished my cook chores. I caught them at the bottom of the slope and we tied on the rope, building a rhythm on the wide forty-degree ice leading to the col, hacking out a stance, putting in an ice screw and bringing up Robin while Jim soloed up.

We reached the top at half-past eight and gazed over the other side at the jumble of craggy peaks stretching into the distance, all of them untouched. The rocky buttress above our heads looked straightforward and I decided to ditch the ice axes for speed. I would keep Robin on a short rope while Jim scouted ahead to speed our route-finding. Robin took things steadily, unnerved a little from the exposure. Like any good sailor, he preferred to be hanging onto something with his hands, even though I kept pressing him to trust his feet more, anxious that he was tiring himself too quickly. Inevitably, we moved slowly, but if my occasional impatience flared, he remained remarkably cool and dogged.

When the rock steepened, I found Robin a belay and led the rope out for him to follow. I noticed a scum of high cloud covering the sky and grew anxious that bad weather would catch us out on the ridge. Jim seemed convinced we still had plenty of time. A particularly awkward rope length took me to the top of a tall, detached pinnacle with a drop of a hundred feet to the main mass of the mountain. There was clearly a long way still to the summit. Abseiling down would be very committing and we would still have a long way to go to the top. Worse, Robin had a real struggle joining me on top.

'I'm desperately sorry, mate,' I told him, 'but it really isn't on.' He accepted my decision without a murmur, but as Robin was photographed holding up the flag of his yacht club, I had a nagging sense of guilt. He had fulfilled his side of the bargain, getting me safely to Greenland, and I couldn't help feeling I'd let him down. I was also anxious about the length of time it would take us to descend. Soon after we started the sun broke through the clouds, bathing the surrounding peaks to the south-east in a rich but ominous gold, emphasizing the wildness of our own isolation. As the light faded, it grew colder but we couldn't rush; whenever we abseiled we had to focus on recovering the ropes efficiently or else wait patiently as Robin climbed down safely.

We didn't reach the top of the ice gully until one in the morning and then faced the wearying process of lowering first either Jim or me to cut out a belay ledge, then Robin, before whoever was left could climb down, using axes and facing the slope. We didn't reach base camp until six o'clock, twenty-six hours after setting out. Robin produced some shot glasses and a bottle of vodka, and before we collapsed into our sleeping bags toasted what had been a pretty brave effort.

Jim and I had just enough time for another attempt, while Robin, with Allen and Jan, started back to *Suhaili*. This time we had the right gear to outflank what we had dubbed Robin's Pinnacle, but abseiling into the gully I felt a stab of concern at how hard climbing out might be when we came to descend. The climbing out of the gully and back onto the ridge was superb, a full-on Scottish V that left me bubbling with pleasure. But after fourteen hours on the go, when we reached what we had thought would prove to be the summit, we saw a horizontal crest of rock gendarmes extending into the distance, with the highest, by only a few metres, 200 metres away. It would take hours to get there, and we still had the problem of reversing our route. Even worse, we could now see the shapely peak we both remembered from the pictures. We were on the wrong mountain.

It was ten in the evening when I tackled the hard climbing to get us out of the gully and regain the ridge. This time, exhausted and struggling in the half-light of the early hours, we stopped on the way down for an hour, and I managed to sleep. When I woke, I was shivering, suffering the early stages of hypothermia. We reached base camp after twenty-eight hours on the go and it was all I could do to drink the tea Jim brewed before collapsing into a deep sleep.

The following dawn we packed up and left to make our rendezvous with *Suhaili*. At first made we made good progress but then conditions got soggier as rain set in. We tried waiting it out, putting up the tent to find shelter, but it just carried on pouring and we had no choice but to go on. By the time we reached the broad col leading down to the Sidegletscher we were soaked, but stomping down the moraine and skirting the glacier, we saw a red blob on top of a boulder by the fjord. It was a duffel full of cans of beer, freshly baked bread, cheese, fresh apples and even oranges. A few hours later, we were ferrying our gear to the shoreline when we saw *Suhaili* nosing her way round the point; Robin was right on time. Back on board, Robin was in charge again for the long voyage home.

I returned to Greenland for three more adventures, perhaps most successfully, from a personal point of view, in 1993 when Jim Lowther and I were joined by Graham Little and Rob Ferguson. This time we flew in by Twin Otter, landing on the Chisel glacier, a tributary of the Frederiksborg, just south of Cathedral. We spent four weeks exploring an amazing array of steep and challenging peaks, making five first ascents between us. The highlight, I think, was a magnificent peak Graham and I dubbed The Needle.

It reminded me of the famous south-west pillar of the Petit Dru, which I had climbed more than thirty years before, 700 metres of continuously steep granite, with the crux a groove bristling with overhangs. It was the most challenging, exciting and aesthetically pleasing rock pitch I had climbed in years.

Yet that first adventure, perhaps because of the novelty and our strong sense of camaraderie, was special. Even though we had tried unsuccessfully to climb the wrong mountain, it had been one of the best and most enjoyable trips I had ever had. We'd been together for two months, with several weeks of that in the confined space of *Suhaili.* We had undeniably made some cock-ups but I don't think there was a cross word in the course of our adventure and we forged friendships that have lasted a lifetime.

Chapter Eighteen

Sacred Threads

It was warm in the little yellow tent. Both stoves were purring away, pans full of melting snow. Outside, the slopes of Panchchuli V dropped steeply away on either side from our little perch on the col; the immense gulf lay hidden in the blackness of night, although away to the east was the faintest glimmer of approaching day. Despite the hour, I was wide-awake and fully dressed; full of that excitement you feel when dread turns to relief. The summit team had been gone for twenty-four hours now, and would be incredibly parched. Nothing sucks moisture out of you like breathing hard at high altitude.

I poked a little more snow into the pan, and heard the climbers calling to each other again. They were abseiling down the rocky tower above my head, homing in on safety. I had been looking for them since before dusk, convinced that they must have been at the summit by lunchtime. The usual afternoon cloud bubbled up; the hours crept past and still no sign. What was keeping them? Then the weather worsened and my anxiety grew. Thunder boomed around the mountains and in the darkness each flash of lightning chipped away at my confidence. Here I was, in the middle of the night, alone, listening to the patter of snow on the tent, wondering what I should do if they never returned.

Half dozing in the tent, memories came crowding in, the faces of dead friends, the anguish and loss, Wendy fielding the telegrams and phone calls, as though I were rehearsing a future I could hardly tolerate imagining. Lightning flashed again, but distantly now, so that the tent was barely illuminated where before it had been, suddenly and momentarily, as bright as day. Perhaps they had bivouacked, unable to find the way down? Or perhaps one was injured and they were moving slowly? It seemed inconceivable that all four of them were gone.

Then, at around one o'clock, I heard voices and crawled a little way out of the tent, staring with renewed optimism at the black pillar in front of me. I heard nothing more. Was it the wind? Then I saw the pinprick of light from a headlamp puncturing the darkness from near the top of the pillar. It moved slightly and then another appeared above it, descending in abbreviated bursts to join the first. Whoever it was, he was abseiling. The wind had largely died away with the passing storm, and now I could hear voices again: the deeper, somewhat hesitant tones of Dick Renshaw, the lighter, clearer American accent of Steve Sustad and another very English, very cultured voice. It could be either of the others, Stephen Venables and Victor Saunders, since they sounded identical, especially on the phone. But it seemed clear all was well. Time to put the stoves on.

Watching their progress, I could appreciate why they had taken so long. Abseiling with four is a time-consuming process. The pillar had given hard climbing and while the ridge above was at an easier angle, snow conditions demanded caution. They had reached Panchchuli V's fore-summit at two o'clock and since it was so tantalizingly close, been lured on to the main top, another hour on. Of course, with every hour you add going up, you add another to come down and it was almost dark when they reached the top of the pillar. The abseils were awkward and often the ropes jammed as they tried to recover them. When they couldn't pull them free, someone would have to go back up to sort out the jam. No wonder they'd taken so long.

The lights slowly came closer; the voices became louder and more distinct. Then, as one light slid down to join the other three, it suddenly accelerated and swept briskly past the others in a great arc, accompanied by a shower of sparks and the scrape of metal on rock, and then a duller noise, a thud, the ominous sound of a human body striking the ground.

I noticed the light had gone out.

The idea of climbing in the Panchchuli range came from Harish Kapadia, the energetic and affable Mumbai cloth merchant and long-time editor of the *Himalayan Journal*. Harish not only has a passion for Himalayan exploration and an encyclopaedic memory of who had done what and where, he was also superbly connected and had already led three joint British and Indian expeditions, reaching places that British climbers could never hope to on their own. What's more, he took a more relaxed approach to operations than Indian military expeditions, which meant teams could split up and pursue their own agendas, rather like a summer Alpine meet.

We had met many times over the years and I had marvelled at his extensive knowledge about the remoter corners of the Himalaya. We had often discussed an adventure together, so when he suggested an expedition for the summer of 1992, I leapt at the chance. He proposed the Panchchuli range, which towers above the little hill station of Munsiari, in the historical district of Kumaon, not far from the north-west border of Nepal. It's a place of deep forest gorges and exquisite Alpine meadows, rich with flowers and immortalized in the writings of a host of early pioneers.

W. H. Murray, that great inspiration to my generation, was in Kumaon in 1950 and described the Panchchulis as 'the most beautiful peaks in the world'. The following year, Heinrich Harrer, author of *The White Spider* and *Seven Years in Tibet*, made the first determined effort on the highest peak in the range, Panchchuli II, almost 7,000 metres high. While he didn't make the summit, he got most of the way there, pioneering the western approach from the Goriganga valley, which would be our approach too, the first foreign climbers to attempt the Panchchuli since Harrer's day; in the interim several Indian military expeditions had climbed there.

Panch means 'five' and *chuli* means 'hearths', the hearths being those of the five Pandava brothers, heroes of the Sanskrit epic the *Mahabharata*. In Hindu mythology, these mountains are where the brothers spent their last night, their final bivouac if you like, having renounced the world and their kingdom, before their final climb up Kailas, not far across the border in Tibet. For a man approaching the end of his sixth decade, it seemed appropriate.

Harish and I agreed to bring six climbers each. His team would focus on repeating the south-west ridge of Panchchuli II, first climbed in 1973 by members of the Indo-Tibetan Border Police. His plan was to use porters and fix ropes. We would be free to tackle any of the unclimbed surrounding peaks or routes in whatever style we chose. It seemed a good opportunity to include some of the established younger stars of British climbing. I had got to know Stephen Venables when his first book won the Boardman Tasker Prize for mountain literature, set up in Pete and Joe's memory by family and friends when we returned from Everest. More recently, as president of the British Mountaineering Council (BMC), I had asked him to serve as vice president. He had only just climbed a new route on the east side of Everest and gone to the summit without oxygen, an immense effort of will and stamina that had taken him to the limits of survival. He had also recently become a father, with all the obvious conflicts between home and climbing that provoked.

Stephen had climbed a great deal with another of the Panchchuli team, Dick Renshaw, who after his stroke on Everest, was climbing again at more moderate altitudes. In the ten years since the traumatic loss of Pete and Joe, Dick had concentrated on his passion for sculpture and had recently sold his first pieces, working now in stone and bronze as well as wood. With Stephen he had made the first ascent of a difficult peak called Kishtwar Shivling in the mountains east of Srinagar and just six months before they had climbed a new route on Kusum Kanguru, in the Everest region of Nepal.

The other team-members were Victor Saunders, an architect in the process of becoming a mountain guide. His first ascent of the

Golden Pillar of Spantik had been one of the great first ascents in world mountaineering during the 1980s. He was, and remains, cultured, witty and kind, but also inscrutable and quixotic, sometimes infuriatingly so. He knew Stephen well, being his landlord, and also our fourth team-member Steve Sustad, Seattle-born but now living in mid-Wales and earning his living as a carpenter.

Steve had been on several of Doug Scott's expeditions in the early 1980s and almost climbed Makalu with him via the gigantic south-east ridge. Within two or three hundred feet of the summit, they chanced on the frozen body of the Czech climber Karel Schubert, still sitting upright in the snow where he had stopped to rest eight years before. Perhaps spooked at this encounter, their partner, French alpinist Jean Afanassieff announced he would go down, despite it now being faster to go on to the top and descend the far side. The other two had no choice but to follow. Steve has a famously dry wit and phlegmatic temperament, perfect for a mountaineer, and stamina that belies his slight frame..

I would be climbing with Graham Little, very tall, powerful and fit, someone else I had come to know while president of the BMC, since Graham performed the same role for the Mountaineering Council of Scotland at the same time. We had over the years done lots of rock and ice climbs in Scotland, where Graham has literally hundreds of first ascents to his name, especially in the Southern Highlands and the Hebrides. This was the first time we would share an expedition together.

In Mumbai, Harish and the rest of his team were there to greet us, and he whisked us home for breakfast. This exchange between British and Indian climbers was both genuine and fascinating. Harish and his wife Geeta were warmly welcoming and their perspective on the Himalaya as observant Gujarati Hindus added a spiritual dimension beyond the merely sporting. His team was a religiously and ethnically diverse group: Monesh Devjani's family had fled Sindh during Partition; Bhupesh Ashar, a timber merchant, was a Hindu Bhatia; Vijay Kothari was a Jain, and Muslim Contractor was, well, a Muslim. Victor, in his impish way, picked me up when I mentioned the latter's names. Contractor I could understand: it was like Butcher or Baker. But Muslim seemed curious to me.

'Yes ... Christian,' Victor replied. Touché.

If Harish has another passion beyond his family and the mountains, it is trains. Expeditions for him often began in an air-conditioned train compartment from Mumbai, in this case the Rajdhani Express bound for Delhi. It was rather a civilized beginning, although the continuation, on a night bus to Ranikhet, was less appealing. Expeditions in the 1950s had hired mules and set off on foot for the Panchchuli range not far beyond Ranikhet, but such romance has now faded. The forests have been cut down and a tarmac road driven through to Munsiari; the mule caravans are gone, the cool morning air shredded by the blaring of truck horns. Yet at dawn on the morning we left Munsiari, laid out before us was an enchanting view of the Panchchuli range, a crisp, jagged line of triangles against the sky, with the highest peak, Panchchuli II, towards the left-hand end, separated from us by the Goriganga river.

Another welcome aspect of climbing with Harish was his network of tried and tested contacts. No one, I would guess, has wider experience of the Indian Himalaya. His *sirdar* was Pasang Bodh, who I would meet again on adventures with Harish, resplendent in his pink pill-box hat decorated with red sequins, typical of his home town of Manali in Himachal Pradesh. He was very Tibetan-looking, unsurprisingly as he comes from one of the Bhotia groups who migrated into India. With him were two more of Harish's faithful retainers, the two Harsinhs, Harsinh Mangalsinh and Harsinh Balaksinh, the latter a shepherd with the loudest whistle I ever heard, both from Harkot in the Saryu valley. Harsinh Junior, as he was known, was formidably strong.

I knew well enough after three decades that plans in the Himalaya are susceptible to change. Harish had planned to put our base camp in a meadow some way up the Uttari Balati glacier. Our hundred or so Kumaoni porters had other ideas, downing tools at the glacier's snout, unusually low at only 3,200 metres. The summit of Panchchuli II was still more than three and a half kilometres above us, a similar height gain to Everest. A deal was worked out, and a good proportion of our supplies were moved up to an interim camp on the glacier, and then Stephen and Dick explored the top of the glacier, bypassing a couple of icefalls, for a site to put advance base. The narrow gorge of dirty ice opened out into a broad white basin surrounded by shining peaks.

We all carried a load up to the site they'd chosen but I found the effort wearying. At fifty-eight, the grind of expedition life wasn't getting any easier. The following morning, Victor spontaneously suggested that Graham and I go up to advance base and start acclimatizing, while the rest of the youngsters continued bringing up loads.

'That's really kind,' I told them. 'Thank you. I must say this is a nice team.'

I did feel a small stab of conscience two days later when Graham and I made the first ascent of the most attractive peak closest to advance base. On the other hand, you've got to grab these things while you can. At Harish's suggestion, we called it Sahadev, after one of the Pandava brothers, but it had two summits, east and west, and the one we picked was marginally lower.

The four young tyros, steeped in Alpine style, were eager to be off climbing while Harish and his team continued with their patient build-up towards Panchchuli II. Dick, while sketching the mountains, had come up with a mouth-watering challenge, a long traverse up the east ridge of the six-thousander Menaka and then traversing the ridge that joined it to the much higher Rajrambha at the head of the glacier, before descending the west ridge on the far side. They left on 1 June for what would be a five-day climb that was committing and difficult. On the third day they arrived at the summit mass of Rajrambha in the middle of an electrical storm. Victor was carrying tent poles that stuck out of his rucksack and soon became a lightning conductor. As he climbed up towards the others, they could hear him swearing from pain as each bolt of

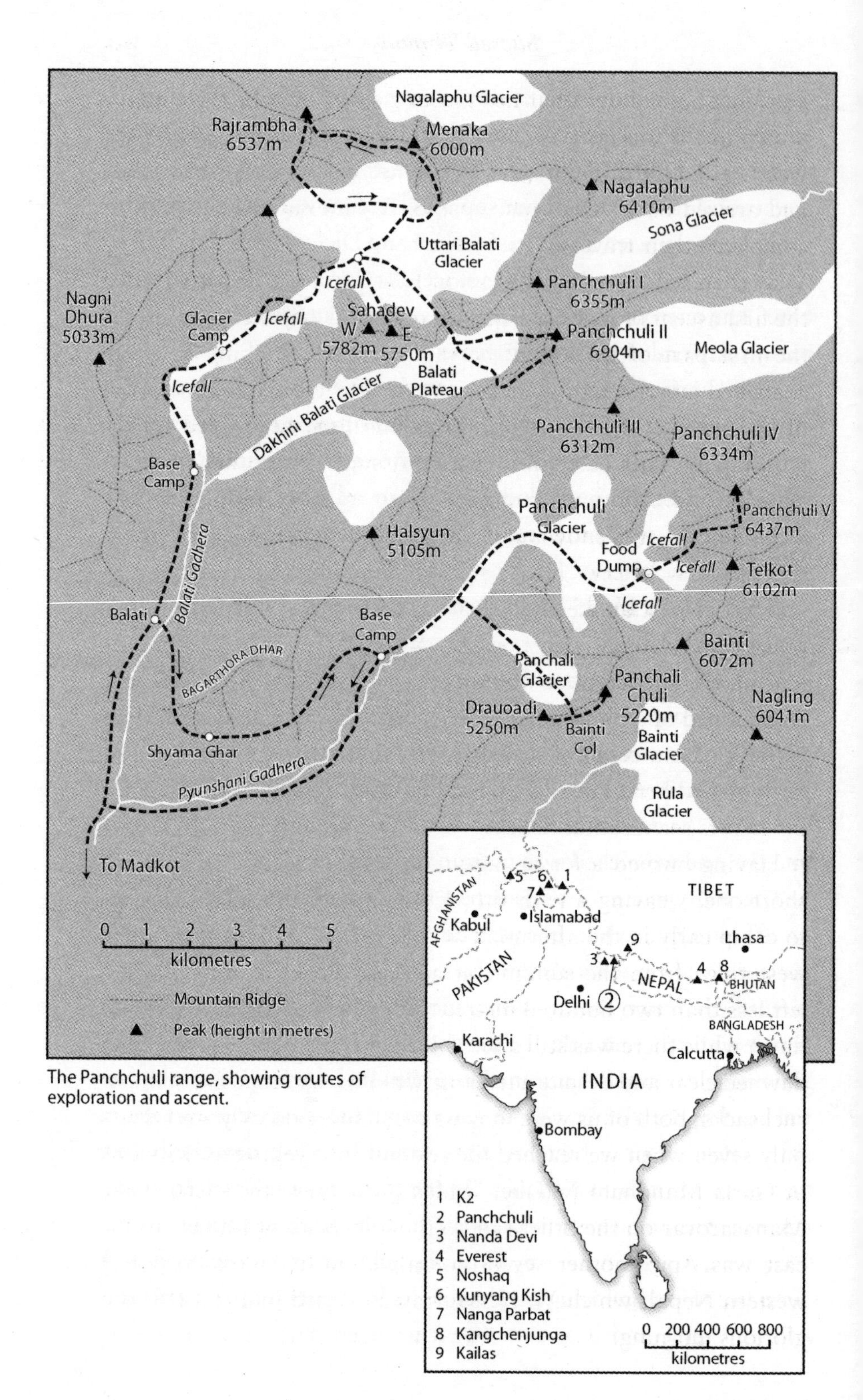

The Panchchuli range, showing routes of exploration and ascent.

lightning high above their heads sent a surge of volts through the mountain. 'It was horrible,' he said. 'Like a cattle prod.' Despite the weather and the difficult ground, they were a superbly strong team and arrived back at advance base on 5 June having successfully completed their traverse.

By then, Graham and I were on Panchchuli II, trying to make the first ascent of its west ridge. To reach our objective, we shared the first part of the route the Indians were climbing but then branched left through a complex system of crevasses to the foot of the ridge at 6,120 metres. Next morning we packed up the tent and by half past three were crossing a steep and difficult bergschrund. Above was continuous ice, made easier in places by a covering crust of snow but the ground was still too hard to move together. It was nervy, brittle ground. We moved out onto the west face to get past an ice cliff blocking the ridge and it took twelve hours of continuous effort before we found somewhere to put the tent, in the sheltered lee of another ice cliff. That night Graham complained of a blinding headache, and I became anxious he was suffering from cerebral oedema, but he explained that after suffering a bad head injury as a child he was prone to them. It made his efforts seem rather heroic.

Having burned a lot of energy, we made the following day a short one, weaving a path through more ice cliffs and crevasses to camp early in the afternoon at the bergschrund separating the west ridge from the summit, at a height of 6,730 metres. That left less than two hundred metres to the top and meant we would finish while there was still a view. It snowed heavily that night but dawned clear and despite a freezing wind we set off at six. Without rucksacks, both of us were moving much more quickly, and it was only seven when we reached the summit, marvelling at the views of Gurla Mandhata in Tibet, which rises above the sacred Lake Manasarovar on the other side to the holy peak of Kailas. To the east was Api, another seven-thousander in a remote corner of western Nepal, which W. H. Murray had tried in 1953. It was a glorious morning.

Having returned to our high camp, we dismantled the tent and traversed across to the south-west ridge and then down to the Indian camp where their summit team of Muslim Contractor, Monesh Devjani and Pasang Bodh welcomed us warmly. They had needed only one camp and very little fixed rope to reach the top, a marked contrast with the large military teams that had gone before. On the descent, we learned that Vijay Kothari, the Jain cloth merchant, had slipped and broken his ankle, sliding 200 metres. He only escaped an even longer fall after Sundersinh, one of the high-altitude Kumaon porters, had grabbed him by the collar on the way past. The mighty Harsinh Junior and Suratram had carried Vijay back to camp where our liaison officer Anil Srivastava, a wing commander in the Indian Air Force, arranged a helicopter for his evacuation.

Reunited with the others, I told them about the view I'd had of the neighbouring peaks from the summit and how interesting the Pyunshahi valley just to the east looked. 'If you are happy to miss out Panchchuli II,' Harish told us, 'we just have time to explore the Pyunshani, if we travel light.' Sustad seemed delighted, as did Venables. After their exciting traverse of Rajrambha I think another ascent of Panchchuli II would have been an anticlimax.

That night I retired early and lingered in bed the following morning. Recovering from the intense effort of climbing at altitude with a heavy pack was inevitably taking longer. Outside, the packing was already underway. Our transport would leave Munsiari in two weeks: we barely had ten days to get round to the Pyunshani and explore the peaks at its head. The bulk of our gear would now go back with Pasang and with it the main medical kit. Graham and Bhupesh were due back at work, Vijay had been evacuated and was back in Mumbai recuperating. That left eight of us, plus the Kumaoni porters, to race up the valley. Harish, Monesh and Muslim would explore and climb some of the lower peaks and were taking the barest minimum of climbing gear. Stephen and Steve sorted out enough equipment for something a little more substantial.

Three days later, having blundered through jungle in the wake of a doubtful local guide called Dhansinh, who was armed with an ancient muzzle-loading rifle and an over-optimistic sense of direction, we emerged from the foliage into a meadow at the foot of the Panchchuli glacier. The weather, co-operating for a change, cleared long enough for us to get a clear view of mighty snow peaks ahead of us. Victor and Stephen raced up the valley to find a campsite near some birches next to the river. Our porters, despite their twelve-hour day, had soon rigged a tarpaulin and set a kettle on a blazing fire that suffused the air with sweet wood-smoke. It was, as Stephen said, such a beautiful spot that you didn't want to leave.

Unfortunately we had no choice. The following day was 16 June and we had to be back in Munsiari, two days away, on 23 June. We had just five days to reconnoitre and climb an unknown Himalayan peak of around 6,500 metres. After my efforts on Panchchuli II and the difficult approach, I havered. The others had clearly built a good rapport on Rajrambha; my sudden appearance, as someone sixteen years older than Victor, the oldest of them, would be disruptive. The more cautious option was to team up with Harish and the others and explore the lower peaks. But then I thought about the mouth-watering prospect of a magnificent unclimbed summit and succumbed to temptation. We made arrangements with Harish that he would leave two porters to help us if he left the valley before us, and whatever food he didn't need. Rations were already low and we'd been hungry coming round from the other valley. He saw us off at dawn, sending two of the Kumaonis to help us with our huge loads.

That evening we explored the head of the glacier, surrounded by a treasure trove of unclimbed peaks, as though we had stumbled into a dragon's lair and couldn't believe our luck. Not surprisingly, the younger men fixed on the biggest jewel of all, Panchchuli V, the most southerly of the peaks and the most interesting. A magnificent pillar rose up to the summit from the south ridge, but how to reach it? I quietly mentioned the easier approach to Panchchuli IV, but the others were not to be dissuaded. Quickly they traced a high line from the right through the labyrinthine icefalls that guarded the approach to a gully that led on up to the ridge. It was tenuous, but it was there, and so even more attractive. It was now Wednesday: we would in theory need to reach the top by Friday, but by stretching the schedule a bit we could make that Saturday. I kept my counsel and agreed to the plan.

A storm delayed our departure next morning, but the plan unwound nicely. Stephen led us through the first icefall and then Victor, zipping himself into waterproofs, climbed a pitch of hard ice running with water that got us into a couloir up to a rocky ridge. Venables and Sustad reached its crest first, stopping for lunch and examining the upper section of a second icefall. Then the two hares rocketed ahead, picking their way through this labyrinth, while the other two youngsters kept the tortoise Bonington moving along as quickly as he could. It felt as though after Panchchuli II I had nothing left in the tank. It was obvious the others were worried about whether I could continue when I reached camp that evening.

In the morning I was all for going down, and Victor generously offered to come with me, but the others were clearly still convinced they could do the climb. If we went down now, not only would I deprive Victor of the summit, but we'd also need one of the two ropes, making things more awkward for the three who stayed. Abseiling with one rope is a time-consuming business. So I allowed myself to be persuaded and we set off after Stephen. He took a direct line, rather too close under an enormous tower of ice that was regularly spewing material onto the glacier below; we were now in the firing line. I was at the back and shouted up to the others.

'I really think we should go down. I just don't feel happy about being here.'

Stephen was at the front, 100 metres ahead of me, with the summit in his eyes.

'Well, why the fuck did you come here in the first place then?'

The heads of the other three swivelled back and forth, as though watching a particularly engaging game of tennis, as we went at each other.

'You really are incredibly self-centred, you know.'

'Well, that's pretty rich coming from you.'

The upshot was that we would continue, but up a safer line and we made it to the col on the ridge without killing one another. The col was a cramped spot and while I caught up, the others set to work building it up with loose rocks to fashion two platforms for the tents. I threw an arm around Stephen's shoulders when I arrived, and we made our apologies. He and Victor then set off to fix the first two pitches of the tower to speed progress in the morning. As they descended there was a tremendous roar and a vast cloud of white mushroomed under the ice tower we had climbed under that morning, racing across the cwm to engulf the buttress we had crossed the previous day in a shower of ice particles. It was a reminder of the threat that waited below for our descent.

While eating our meagre rations that evening, I made the obvious decision. 'I've decided that I'm not going to come with you guys to the summit. You'll be much faster without me.' They remonstrated politely, but there wasn't much need for me to argue further. It made sense that I wait at the col while they tried for the top. At three thirty in the morning, by the light of their headlamps, the four climbers disappeared along the knife-edge ridge towards the pillar and I was left on my own to wait.

A little more than twenty-four hours later, I watched in horror as one of the climbers plummeted into space. Although deeply concerned, I immediately began thinking what to do next. The hours of waiting had been much more difficult to handle. We faced a huge challenge, but it was tangible, something we could deal with, however difficult and fraught it might be. I saw a headlamp bobbing towards me: it was Sustad with news. Stephen had been last man down on the abseil and removed the back-up protection, needing gear for lower down the mountain. The peg all of them had relied on now chose its moment to fail and Stephen had fallen backwards; he had broken both his legs, the right one at his knee and the left ankle where his crampon had caught in the ice. Victor had shouted that the anchor had failed and shrewdly grabbed the ropes to stop them disappearing with Stephen. Between them, they slowed the rope sufficiently to stop Stephen, who was for a while unconscious and didn't hear the others calling to him in the dark. When he regained consciousness, it was eerily quiet; he had to call three times before they heard him.

From that moment they could go to work. Stephen, despite terrible injuries and pain, managed to get his weight off the ropes, allowing Victor and Dick to abseil down to him. When Victor reached his side, Stephen was consumed with pain and guilt about what he might have done to his family.

'If I don't get out of this alive, will you say sorry to Rosie for me?'

'Don't talk nonsense. Of course we're going to get you out of here.'

And they did, working as carefully as they could to splint Stephen's leg before starting to lower him.

After Steve came to fetch me, I boiled up the water again and made a litre of tea. The climbers had drunk almost nothing for twenty-four hours and Stephen urgently needed fluid. Then we packed up the camp into two gigantic loads and started down. I was relieved when we reached them to see Stephen smile a little and then drink something. Although he was bleeding, Victor had quickly realized there was no arterial damage and reassured Stephen that he wasn't going to bleed to death. They had already managed to lower him a hundred metres and while they carried on, Steve and I set off down to set up a camp below where Stephen could wait for a helicopter. There was no question of bringing him back across the complex icefalls we had climbed on the way up.

Under the weight of my top-heavy rucksack, climbing was awkward; we were descending powdery snow that lay a few inches deep on bullet-hard ice. A hundred metres above the cwm I felt a footstep collapse under my boot. Instinctively I grabbed my ice tools planted in the snow in front of me, but they ripped straight out. I managed to keep hold of my ice axe and tried to arrest my fall but the pick just tore through the snow and I kept gathering momentum. Then my crampons caught the slope, I flipped over and started cartwheeling out of control, vaguely aware of a mad, bouncing rush. There was a brief moment when I knew I was in mid-air, as I cleared the bergschrund at the bottom, and then I resumed bouncing and rolling as I tried to tuck my head in, in a foetal position, to protect my extremities. Steve Sustad, just above me, said it was the most horrible thing he'd ever watched and assumed I'd had it. Even if I survived what had been a 500-foot fall, how would they cope with another injured climber?

Gradually I came to a halt, upside down, head first in deep soft snow, winded and immobilized by my heavy rucksack. I flexed my arms and legs and found they were intact. Then I rolled myself upright and gazed up at the others far above me as they slowly, methodically, lowered Stephen down. I sat with my head in my hands for half an hour as Steve climbed down and collected my axes. Apart from bruises and a cut just above my left eye, likely made by my ice axe, I seemed in one piece. Stephen was confused to see my blood as Dick and Victor continued lowering him. He thought it was his.

I don't think I was in shock from my tumble. The situation we were in, Stephen's injury and the question of how we could get him out, filled my mind as I waited for the others to get down. It was all very matter of fact. Steve climbed down to me. It was obvious we couldn't set up camp where I had landed: it was much too exposed to the threat of avalanche. We'd have to go to the head of the cwm hundreds of yards away. There we dug out a platform and pitched the tents before returning to join the others who had now lowered Stephen all the way down the face. Lowering him had been the easy bit. We now had to get him up to the tents we had just pitched. Steve and I had brought down the spare tent and used this as a sled cum stretcher. Every movement of Stephen's knee was agonizing, but he was incredibly stoical. Having sent the main medical kit down, we only had paracetamol to take the edge off Stephen's pain. Victor set to work cutting off the legs of Stephen's fleece salopettes to inspect the damage.

'My god, it's as big as your head,' Victor said when he saw

Stephen's knee. There was a savage open wound that would be at severe risk of infection. Getting Stephen down from here was going to take time but with his injuries and the shortage of food there was none to waste. I felt I was best placed to exert pressure on the Indian authorities to allow a rescue flight. Steve would come with me to base camp, and then bring up whatever food was there to the spot where we'd had lunch on the first day. Victor would drop down to collect it. We left early next morning, Steve leading the way back through the labyrinthine icefall.

We reached base camp in the late afternoon, where the two Harsinhs, Senior and Junior, were waiting. They made us huge plates of rice and dal but we were both too exhausted to finish it. Next morning I carried on down the Pyunshani valley with Harsinh Senior, moving as fast as I could, covering thirty miles through the forest, rain pouring off my face, to arrive at Madkot in the mid afternoon. Harsinh found me a telephone and for the next two hours I struggled to get a message through to Harish, now at the Dak Bungalow in Munsiari. Once I got him, wheels began to turn. He talked to our liaison officer, the wing commander, who was soon in touch with the nearest air base. Harish then sent a vehicle for me.

'They're in a desperate position,' I told him when I arrived, almost at the end of my strength, my face scabby with wounds. 'The tents are pitched on a slope in an avalanche-prone basin, with steep walls all around.' I knew that the only real hope was with the helicopter. I was already exploring how we might send in a rescue party, just in case the helicopter failed, but it would take several days to put in place and carrying Stephen down through the icefall would have been agonizing and could easily have killed him.

Waiting was an anxious process but in retrospect things happened tremendously fast. The two Indian pilots, Squadron Leader P. Jaiswal and Flight Lieutenant P. K. Sharma, were in the air that day and did a reconnaissance of the range the following morning. Despite the mixed weather, despite the dangerous terrain, they managed to pluck Stephen off the mountain that Thursday, less than five days after the accident. Victor swore that the rotor blades had cut a groove in the snow slope as it hovered beside them. He and Dick left immediately for base camp, arriving that night. Two days later we were all reunited in Munsiari.

The 'tumbling Brits' might have put off some expedition leaders but Harish knew the game too well. He had suffered his own near-disaster in 1974, falling into a crevasse at over 6,000 metres while exploring the Nanda Devi region. It took his companions thirteen days to get him back to base camp where a helicopter could evacuate him and he'd spent the next two years on crutches. Yet his love of the mountains of his home country was too strong to ignore and Harish was back climbing as soon as he could walk properly.

Two years after Panchchuli, we organized another expedition together, this time to the Tirung Gad range in the southern part of Kinnaur district in Himachal Pradesh. Once again the expedition started in Mumbai, where Harish's wife Geeta organized a puja for me at their apartment in honour of my imminent sixtieth birthday, a major milestone in Hindu culture. It is at sixty that some Hindu men renounce their worldly possessions and leave their families, to wander the land almost naked begging for alms. As Graham Little pointed out, I'd been doing something similar for most of my life already. Two priests came to Geeta's home and I sat cross-legged on the floor for two hours as they burned incense. I found it a deeply moving experience.

That year we climbed in the Kinnaur range, making the first ascent of a peak called Rangrik Rang above the Tirung valley. Jim Fotheringham and I unlocked the key to the summit, climbing a steep ice face that led to a traverse that took us to a col at the base of the north-east ridge. Before the expedition we had thought we might split up into pairs, but in the end all eight of us, Indians and British together, reached the summit on the same day, our reward spectacular views of Kamet and other peaks in the Garhwal.

It was somehow fitting that my final major expedition would

be with Harish, in the summer of 2001. This time our team was truly international: Jim Lowther and I joined four Indians and two formidable Americans, Mark Richey and Mark Wilford, whom I knew well. Our objective was the Arganglas range in the Nubra valley of Ladakh, the high, arid corner of India that is in reality a corner of the Tibetan plateau. Jim and I set off to acclimatize on a nearby peak but the truth was that, at sixty-seven, I was no longer capable of carrying a heavy rucksack and climbing the sort of ground you find on that standard of challenge. I had to tell him that time had caught up with me. Jim was incredibly understanding but it was an emotional moment. We then joined Divyesh Muni and Cyrus Shroff to attempt the range's highest peak, Argan Kangri, but dangerous avalanche conditions shut us down at 6,200 metres, still 500 short of the top.

The Americans, meanwhile, climbed the stunning north buttress of a peak called Yamandaka, 1,200 metres of hard, mixed climbing that was only surpassed by the difficulty and remoteness of their descent. It took several days for them to struggle down the far side of the mountain, following a gorge of featureless slabs, loose rock and waterfalls. We had been on the point of asking the local army commander for a helicopter search when they finally emerged. Unfortunately, we had to tell them that while they were fighting for their lives on Yamandaka, two aircraft had flown into the World Trade Center towers. Harish had picked up the news trying to get cricket scores on his short-wave radio. Our base camp was only eighty miles from where Osama bin Laden was in Afghanistan.

That wasn't the end of my adventures with Harish. I might no longer be capable of high-altitude mountaineering, but I could still trek happily in the mountains and with Harish that promised a close connection to the local people. Our first trek together was in 2003, a lovely journey off the beaten track up the Sainj valley, over the Garagarasan Dhar and down the Tirthan valley in the Kullu region of India. It was a great joy that my secretary Louise and her husband Gerald could join us. I even managed a nice unclimbed peak, 5,440 metres high, with Rajal, a Gujarati who had studied in England. The following year we were in Lahaul, following the Sainchu valley in the Pangi Himal. Louise and Gerald came again, joined by Charlie Clarke and his daughter Bec, as well as our family doctor Kate and her husband Julian. And once again I managed to bag a little unclimbed peak.

Chapter Nineteen

Bonington and Sons

Joe and I had pulled ahead of the others as we plodded across the crater of Kilimanjaro. It was an almost lunar landscape, fins of ice emerging from the dark volcanic dust of the vast undulating bowl that forms the crater. Uhuru Peak, the highest point, was on the far side. We reached a slight col before the final pull to the summit and I wondered if we should wait for the others.

'Would you mind if I kept going, Dad? I'd like to spend some time on my own. I've got a lot to think about.' He wasn't exaggerating. After some pretty wild teenage years, Joe was in serious trouble. There was something forlorn but also rather brave about him as he plodded alone up that final slope before disappearing over the brow. I felt myself welling up. When your child finds himself in the kind of mess Joe was in, you feel protective and wonder what you could have done differently as a parent.

I waited for the rest of our group and we followed Joe to the top. The crowds that day had been and gone and we had the summit to ourselves to celebrate the climax of our family expedition. Joe now seemed more at ease with himself too. We couldn't know it at the time, but Kilimanjaro would be a turning point.

The idea of climbing Africa's highest mountain had started a few months before, as I contemplated climbing the highest summits on the seven continents. The first to complete the list was Dick Bass in 1985, when, thanks to Arne, he reached the summit of Everest on our permit. The 'Seven Summits' has now become quite an industry and there are several adventure travel companies to ease logistics and guide participants, but in 1991 only twelve people had completed the list, none of them British. Apart from Everest, I had, not long after the Shivling expedition, climbed Mount Vinson in Antarctica with Dick Bass and his climbing partner Frank Wells. So I already had the highest and the most expensive.

It occurred to me that Kilimanjaro would be a great objective for my extended family. Both our sons, Joe and Rupert, were keen, but I also invited my half-brother Gerald. I had first got to know Gerald and my three half-sisters when my father invited Wendy and me to their home near Bristol. Over the years, they all came to stay with us in the Lake District in order of their ages. I remember Gerald's visit particularly vividly; he was ten and arrived with a fishing rod in his hand. We were warned he was a difficult child but perhaps because of the new environment, we found him delightful. I took him on his first climb on Dow Crag, a classic easy route from the 1920s, which I found fiendishly awkward and he managed with a matter-of-fact coolness that impressed me.

After leaving school, he went to the Royal Agricultural College in Cirencester, planning to become a farm manager. One of his first jobs was managing a farm in Cumbria quite close to us at Badger Hill and we saw a lot of him and his wife Rachel. He became one of my regular climbing partners and through this we developed a strong friendship. After a few years, he joined the fertilizer division of Fisons, becoming sales manager for Northern England, Scotland and Ireland, but basing himself in Caldbeck.

Our father had died a few years before, in early 1983. After that first visit, I had seen him every year or so. He'd take me to lunch, often an oyster bar, and we'd have an enjoyable catch-up. The conversation never flagged. He was quite a small man, with small eyes, something of a Bonington trait, but despite his fascinating life, he almost never talked about himself. I gathered he kept in contact with the few survivors of that first disastrous SAS operation and with the SAS founding officer David Stirling.

Over the years, I noticed he took regular holidays alone in Eastern Europe and often wondered if he was involved in some way in working for MI6. He could pass unnoticed in any crowd, would have missed nothing with those shrewd little eyes and as a good journalist could persuade people to unburden themselves. He reminded me of a John Le Carré character, but Dad would never be drawn on what he was up to, so who knows? I did notice a lot of ageing gentlemen in dark suits, including David Stirling, at his funeral.

To prepare for Kilimanjaro, Rupert and Joe joined me for a training walk, carrying camping gear from Seathwaite over Esk Hause to drop down into upper Eskdale where we put up the tents and swam in the river's clear pools. Next morning we scrambled over Great End and along the ridge to Scafell Pike before dropping down to the Corridor Route. The weather was perfect, billowing white clouds and plenty of sunshine, and although our sacks were heavy, the boys were going strongly and we thoroughly enjoyed ourselves. I felt close to them, in a relaxed kind of way, very much three mates out in the hills.

We took our dogs with us, me with Bella, and Joe, who never did anything by halves, with his pit bull terrier Sensi, short for Sensimilla, a strain of marijuana of which Joe was rather fond, overly so in my opinion. Having been expelled from school, he failed his catering diploma in Carlisle and was renting a two-room flat in Wembley with his girlfriend Heidi, who was about to start a fashion course at St Martin's and was very focused. Joe worked a series of jobs, washing cars, driving a van, collecting and selling scrap metal. He hung out on the neighbouring council estate with his mates, some of whom were into all sorts of drugs and petty crime. Throughout his early life Joe was excited by the thrill of the illicit.

When Heidi moved out, Wendy and I worried the relationship was on the rocks. No longer able to afford the rent, he started squatting, and Wendy went down to help him move. After that, to give Joe stability, we decided to buy a flat in London. I stayed in his squat while we went flat-hunting.

I've always got on with Joe, even when things were bad. I never saw any point in lecturing him, though we had conversations about the morality of buying or selling things that had fallen off the back of a lorry. Together we found a two-bedroom flat backing onto the Grand Union Canal and reserved a bedroom for when we came to London; this way we'd stay in touch with Joe and have a London bolthole.

I asked him if he'd like to come climbing, and we drove down to Land's End where my climbing club has a hut overlooking Bosigran. I was pleased to find a welcoming group of people his age already installed and next day we did a climb. That evening Joe asked if he could borrow my car to see if there was any nightlife. He returned late next morning looking dazed and spaced out, not wanting to do anything.

As I drove Joe back to London, I fretted that he couldn't seem to go forty-eight hours without drugs. Things quickly went from bad to worse. In early 1992, he was charged with burglary. He pleaded not guilty but was committed for trial later that year. I had to tell my mother, who had always been close to Joe, what was happening; she was badly shaken. The threat of a possible custodial sentence weighed heavily on Joe; being on bail, he needed special dispensation to come with us to Kilimanjaro. I hoped the expedition would take his mind off his worries.

Rupert had also been quite a wild teenager, with his Huckleberry Finn adventures, catching the school bus on a Friday morning, but slipping away with his mates after assembly to camp out for the weekend. There was any number of pranks, which led to his exclusion in his final year, long before his final exams. Rupert was escorted into school for each exam, sat in a room on his own, and then promptly removed from the premises. Yet he had a strong sense of fairness. If he felt he was in the right he would never back down, with us, his teachers or anyone else. He was more self-possessed than Joe, and it sometimes felt there was more of a distance between us. After school he moved to London and lived with his brother for a while but always had a job, more determined to take control of his life. He worked nights in a pizza takeaway, making £12 for an eight-hour shift, before finding a job with a computer wholesaler. Still only eighteen, he was soon managing the warehouse.

From there, Rupert got onto the management training scheme for a large supermarket chain. Yet he missed Cumbria, and eventually moved home, using his hard-won IT skills, not least for me, running his own website company. His digital skills put me way ahead of the competition and played an important part in establishing me as a successful corporate speaker. He also ran a successful hip-hop magazine, called *Represent*, with Robin Clarke, his best friend from school. Some years later I mentioned this to John Peel, while doing a filming job with him, and was rather proud that he knew all about it, thinking the magazine fresh and innovative.

I had a great deal of help planning our Kilimanjaro trip from Odd Eliassen, with whom I had gone to the top of Everest in 1985. He had spent time on the flanks of Kilimanjaro building huts for the local tourist industry and recommended we avoid the popular routes by climbing the Credner glacier, which he assured me, was straightforward but rarely visited. He also recommended an experienced tour operator.

Although less challenging, Kilimanjaro was very different from any other expedition I had been on. Taking my closest family with me, I was intensely aware of my greater responsibility, but when we met at Heathrow, it felt more like a holiday than an adventure. The cabin crew on the flight to Nairobi even gave us a bottle of champagne to celebrate our presumed success. We spent a night in Nairobi at a hotel best described as full of character, in fact full of *characters*, many of them scantily clad ladies who spent the evening hanging around reception.

Next morning we climbed aboard a couple of Land Cruisers and crossed the Tanzanian border at Namanga. I found the terrain and atmosphere very different from South or Central Asia. There was a dusty brown sense of space, with Kilimanjaro slowly growing like a mushroom as we came closer.

At Kilimanjaro National Park's Marangu Gate we met our guide Hubert, who had been with Odd when he had climbed the Credner glacier back in the 1970s. He in turn introduced us to our little group of porters. The next two days were spent walking a broad trail through the forest with the sound and glimpses of birds and the occasional monkey, until the forest thinned and the battered plug of Mawenzi dominated the skyline, with the scree-clad pile of Kibo, the main summit cone, still quite distant to the left of it. Kilimanjaro may be a hike, but it's one that rises almost five kilometres into the sky with all the problems of high altitude.

Leaving our second camp at Horombo, with its wooden A-frame huts, we began our traverse round the southern flank of Kilimanjaro to reach the Credner glacier on the mountain's north-west flank. The trail became rougher and we were now camping in tents, first at Karanga Valley and then at Barranco, on the rounded crest of a ridge sparsely covered in sun-bleached grass, with a rusty tin hut, shaped like a yurt, which our porters used as a shelter. The view was dominated by Kilimanjaro's steepest rock walls and glaciers, and especially the Breach Wall, a face of overhanging rock, down which hangs an icicle of some thirty metres, like a huge yet slender stalactite. These days, because of climate change, it is rarely in condition, as Kilimanjaro's glaciated cap shrinks and fades. Reinhold Messner climbed it first in 1978 at the end of January. It was a typically bold bit of climbing, especially given how rotten the ice can be on the Breach Wall.

Sitting in the sun that evening, gazing up at the Breach Wall, I was profoundly glad we were heading for the modest Credner glacier. It was an easy walk with a gentle height gain to the Moir hut but I noticed Rupert had slowed down, which was uncharacteristic, as he was normally out in front. He complained of a headache and the whites of his eyes were bloodshot, possible symptoms of cerebral oedema. I put him on Diamox, a diuretic that would help his symptoms and resolved to stay at the hut for another day to help him acclimatize. We had a gentle walk next day and in the morning Rupert's headache had gone so we moved up to the foot of the glacier at 5,000 metres.

We pitched our tents and I cooked the team's supper of mashed potato powder with tinned sardines washed down with tea. It was a bitterly cold night, a myriad of stars glittering in an almost metallic black sky. The alarm went at half past three. I made a brew for the team before we set out for the summit. There was no need for much gear, just light instep crampons strapped to our walking boots and ski poles, with three ice axes between us just in case and a light rope for the abseil we knew we'd have to make down into the crater. The snow was frozen into crisp névé and the angle little more than twenty degrees but I was uncomfortably aware that if someone slipped it would be difficult to stop with just a ski pole. I kept a close eye as we plodded steadily up the long slope.

There was magic in the absolute silence, the pristine trackless snow and the knowledge that we were on our own, even though on the other side of the mountain, on the regular routes, there must be hundreds plodding in files towards the summit. By the time we reached the crater rim, the sun had crept above the slope in front of us casting long shadows across the plains below. We were looking down on the crater of Kilimanjaro, a great bowl of brown volcanic ash with gleaming white *penitentes*, icy fingers reaching towards the sky.

Immediately below us was a sheer ice wall of some twenty metres dropping down into the crater. Joe's friend Denis Murtagh had never abseiled before: it was quite something to start near the top of Kilimanjaro. I gave him a top rope and he managed it very coolly. Once down we trekked across the main bowl to the small subsidiary Rausch crater, site of the last eruption some 200,000 years ago, a blink of an eye in geological terms. Kilimanjaro is not extinct, merely dormant; once we stood on the Rausch crater's rim we could smell pungent sulphur fumes and the volcanic ash was hot to the touch.

From there we continued to the highest point on the main crater's rim, Uhuru Peak, with Joe a little ahead of us, contemplating his future. He seemed much more relaxed in the mountains. Though we had the summit to ourselves, there were too many traces of human activity for my taste: signposts, tattered flags and traces of rubbish. We hugged and took photos, and the team was in great shape as we headed down the standard route to Kibo hut, racing down pumice scree in giant bounds. I was well aware that our porters had worked even harder than we had, bringing our gear round to meet us there: I don't think the thousands who climb Kilimanjaro appreciate how tough the porters' lives can be.

With the climb over we were in holiday mode; we camped on the edge of the Ngorongoro Crater and watched lions and hyena basking in the sun within yards of herds of wildebeest and zebra quietly grazing, prey and predator living cheek by jowl. We had close views of elephant, rhinoceros and hippopotami wallowing in the water. For me, the next day was most satisfying of all. After driving past Lake Natron with its clouds of pink flamingo, we left the track and drove through a sea of long grass towards Ol Donyo Lengai, an active volcano on the edge of the Rift valley. It was a perfect cone and we left the Land Cruisers at its base to plod up the final few hundred feet of volcanic ash and debris to the rim of a crater filled with molten lava covered with thin crust so it resembled a frozen pond, albeit one pulsating with heat.

I couldn't resist trying to circle the crater, though the others left me to it. As I reached the other side, the rim became more fragile with fumaroles pumping out noxious gases. It brought echoes of exploring South America with Sebastian Snow. Completing the circumnavigation satisfied my almost childish appetite for mild risk and competition. Yet it made for a perfect day, all of us reaching the top of this pristine volcano from whose summit we could see only rolling hills of grass without any sign of human intervention anywhere, beyond our two vehicles at the base. The imprint of their tyres would vanish in a matter of hours.

It had been a good trip for all of us, but especially for Joe. He faced another five months of waiting before a trial that lasted three days. The delay was nerve-racking and because I had a public profile we came under the full scrutiny of the media, something Wendy dreaded. They snooped around Caldbeck and Nether Row trying to pick up extra background and gossip. Our neighbours simply stonewalled.

I was uncertain whether to attend the trial. I desperately wanted to support Joe, but knew if I showed up the media's interest would be much greater. In the end, I was there for the final day and to our immense relief Joe was acquitted. He emerged from the experience with new resolve and absolute integrity.

Heidi had supported Joe through the trial, but they split amicably soon afterwards. Then he met Jude. She was very different, a little shy, but beautiful and elfin; she brought out the best in Joe. They fell deeply in love and because she was Australian and her work permit had nearly expired they got married in Chelsea Register Office in the spring of 1994. It was a lovely wedding. They arrived at the reception in a white Cadillac convertible. Beth, Jude's mum, and her brother Dave came over and at the reception Beth said how happy she was for them, but couldn't help being a little sad at losing a daughter to London.

The tables turned a few years later when Joe, having fallen in love with Sydney's exceptional lifestyle, persuaded Jude to return to her home country. By then he was working successfully in the music business but still hadn't really found himself. In Australia, after a year working outdoors in conservation, he switched paths, running an ultra-marathon and qualifying as a fitness trainer. He was finding the sense of direction that had eluded him. Jude continued in the music industry, working for Sony.

Rupert had his own brush with the law, in wholly different circumstances. His expanding web design business led to him starting an online travel agency handling bookings for ski chalets. This was at the very start of the internet business boom. Thanks to his energy and vision, the company did well but the majority shareholders became greedy. At an acrimonious meeting to discuss buying Rupert out, they concocted a story accusing Rupert of assault. Luckily, another director had recorded the meeting and

Rupert's solicitor was able to demolish the case. Rupert and his family had to endure years of legal wrangling before they could agree a fair price for his shares. He was then able to start a new business, called Mountain Fuel, with Darren Foote, a sports nutritionist, manufacturing energy and recovery drinks. Their products are used by some of the country's leading mountain runners and have already been to the summit of Everest.

Rupert met Ann when she was still in the sixth form. Her parents, Robert and Carol Dewhurst, were hairdressers in Keswick. She was rather shy with dark straight hair framing the kind of regular, expressive features that keep their beauty. She eventually went to university and qualified as a primary school teacher, finding a job in a small village school just outside Aspatria, ten miles west of Keswick. She's a devoted and effective teacher, as I've witnessed for myself when visiting the school to talk to the children. Ann and Rupert married at the lovely St Bega's Church on the shores of Lake Bassenthwaite in 1998. They are settled in Keswick and share a passion for the outdoors.

Wendy and I sometimes wondered if the boys would ever start having children but Ann gave birth to Emily on my birthday in 2002, a wonderful present. It seemed to be catching, because next to arrive in Sydney was Edie, closely followed by Will in Keswick and then Honor back in Sydney. They don't see each other often but get on wonderfully well together.

The year after Kilimanjaro, in 1993, I continued my Seven Summits campaign, going for Mount Elbruz but making it a Caucasus climbing holiday with friends. My climbing partner was Jim Fotheringham, with whom I had had so many good adventures. I also invited my loyal secretary Louise with her husband Gerry; Jim Curran, who came to shoot some film, said it was rather like seeing Miss Moneypenny in the field with Bond. I'm afraid I hardly resemble 007, but Louise had been such a rock-solid presence at home, I did wonder who would get us out of trouble.

It was huge fun, and I was deeply impressed with the Caucasus:

stunningly beautiful and relatively unspoilt, beyond some ugly and crumbling Soviet-era infrastructure. Jim and I came within a whisker of climbing the stunning peak of Ushba North, a much more desirable objective than Elbruz, despite being a little lower in altitude. We set out with Vokka, an experienced Ukrainian climber, but the weather deteriorated into a storm as we reached the North Summit. After a hairy descent we reached easier ground but Vokka admonished us: 'Be careful, the adventure is not yet over.' It became my mantra in any number of situations.

Kilimanjaro and Elbruz were thoroughly enjoyable experiences as holidays with family and friends. Yet I found myself losing interest in the Seven Summits. I still had Denali, the Carstensz Pyramid and Aconcagua to do, but the prospect of repeating a well-known route where logistics could be bought off the shelf didn't inspire me much. I couldn't find a new route up any of them and even if there were such a thing, it would probably be beyond me. What I had come to love most in my climbing was the lure of exploration and of the unknown. I found myself drawn into an ever-expanding number of pioneering expeditions, which excited me a lot more. The Seven Summits was put on a backburner and stayed there.

Climbing with my family, on the other hand, had been a great experience. I had long dreamed of sharing my passion for exploration with my nearest and dearest, and wondered about mounting a family expedition to an unclimbed peak. I knew Joe would be all for it. We had been ice-climbing together and he was longing to go to the Himalaya. Rupert, on the other hand, had never had a good head for heights and while he had enjoyed our Kilimanjaro trip, it hadn't moved him in the way it had Joe. He was not at all keen on the thought of a Himalayan expedition. Gerald, meanwhile, was up for anything.

I researched objectives and asked friends for advice. I wanted an unclimbed peak, ideally over 6,000 metres somewhere I hadn't been before that looked reasonably safe. Julian Freeman-Attwood came up with a mountain of around 6,200 metres called Danga, close to Kangchenjunga. I'd never been to eastern Nepal, so it was immediately attractive. He sent me a photograph. It wasn't particularly beautiful or dramatic, was in fact a bit of a hump, but it looked reasonably straightforward and free from danger, and those were the main things. Doug Scott also sent me some pictures. He had passed below Danga on his way up the Ghunsa Khola to the north side of Kangchenjunga, to make his remarkable first ascent of its west ridge with Pete Boardman and Joe Tasker.

We planned the trip for the spring of 2000. Joe wanted to bring along Jude and her brother Dave, while Gerald asked if his son James, a law student at Liverpool University, could join us. I also felt we needed a doctor, so invited a friend from the village surgery, Rupert Bennett, who was also a keen climber. Organizing the trip was easy; Bikrum Pandey, founder and owner of Himalaya Expeditions, was a good friend who had looked after the logistics for all my expeditions into Tibet. Danga wasn't on the list of peaks available from the Nepali government, but Bikrum assured me he could get a permit.

A few days before departure I met Gerald in our village pub, the Old Crown. Rachel, Gerald's wife, looked hard at me, and said, 'Take good care of him. I couldn't live without him.' She had reason to be concerned. A few weeks earlier Gerald and I had one of the closest calls I've ever experienced, climbing a route called *Parallel Gully B* on Lochnagar, a fine peak on the Queen's Balmoral Estate.

All had gone well and I completed the final serious pitch above a snow bay. I had been going well and so only inserted a single piece of protection into a crack about halfway up. I couldn't find a belay in the snow slope at the top and so, when I ran out of rope, simply belayed off the blades of my ice axes, having cut a thin ledge for my boots and crampons. Then I called Gerald up. The first moves out of the snow bay were up an icy bulge but the snow above it was broken; his ice axes pulled out simultaneously and he fell. I was pulled straight off my inadequate axe belays and catapulted into space, headfirst down the pitch I had just led.

Looking straight down the cliff, in mid-air, I had just enough time to realize I was about to die and to wonder if it was going to hurt. Then my headlong fall stopped abruptly, and I found myself lying on the steep snow of the little bay, held by that single running belay above me. Gerald, who had slid some twenty metres down the snow bay, acting as an involuntary counterweight, was wondering why he hadn't been held when he fell. We'd probably been very lucky that I hit the steep snow before our combined weight came onto that little runner, reducing the impact of the fall.

Inevitably the story of our adventure reached our wives. Apart from anything else I had to explain some broken ribs; then the story reached the local press. I'm not sure how shaken Gerald was by our narrow escape. He's a very reserved, cool customer in the most difficult of circumstances. I'm less so, but I have found that in the many extreme crises and near misses I have faced over the years, the misadventure focuses the mind and there is no time for fear. I've often been asked how it is I've survived when so many of my climbing friends have died and the answer must be plain luck. I'm also asked how I justified it when I had a wife and two sons. There is no justification; it was my thirst for adventure, undoubtedly selfish, that drove me on. Rachel's words made me intensely aware of my responsibility, not just to Gerald, James and Joe, but also to their wives.

No matter how many times I've been to Kathmandu, there is always a frisson of excitement as the plane flies in over the rim of the Kathmandu valley and touches down. In the 1960s, the runway seemed far from town. Now the city has surrounded it, a breaking wave of humanity filling up the vast bowl with concrete houses and dusty streets full of garbage and old vehicles belching smoky exhaust fumes. Yet I still loved it and the welcome was as warm as ever. Pulling into the forecourt of the Marshyangdi Hotel, we were greeted with a huge blue banner welcoming Sir Chris Bonington and his expedition.

We had a full week in Kathmandu, catching up with old friends, particularly Pertemba and his family. James designed some Danga Expedition T-shirts and had them stitched in one of the workshops in Thamel. Joe ran up the steep hill to the temple and stupa at Swayambhu overlooking the haze of smog trapped in the valley. I fretted about getting the permission we needed, even though Bikram assured me it was all in hand. I wanted to hear it from the minister himself and managed to get a meeting on the afternoon of our planned departure. The rest of the team caught an earlier flight and I followed on the last plane to Biratnagar on the plains, clutching our precious permit.

We were up early for our flight to the mountains but the clouds were already piling up when our Twin Otter took off. It was among the most spectacular and scary flights I have ever had, picking our way between huge cumulonimbus mushrooming around us. We caught glimpses of Everest, Makalu and Kangchenjunga through the narrow cloud canyons leading towards them. Then, as we came closer, the clouds closed around us, pulsating with light and terrifying power. Our pilot suddenly dropped the nose of the aircraft and we dived for the grass strip at Suketar airport perched on top of a hill. Buzzing with adrenalin, we unloaded all our baggage and a team of waiting porters ferried them down to the village of Taplejung. We spent the night camped outside the school.

It was a delightful trek to base camp, reminiscent of what it had been like on our way to Annapurna II and Nuptse in the 1960s. We met very few trekkers. The houses were thatched and the little fields were planted with potatoes and barley, to be harvested in June. Then we were walking up forested slopes with glimpses of snow peaks drawing near. It took six days to reach Ghunsa, the start of Sherpa country. The houses were of typical Sherpa design with stone walls and big granite slabs on their roofs, the women in traditional dress, the men in jeans and down jackets.

At sixty-five, I was pleased to find I was going well. My little family expedition seemed relaxed and happy and it was heart-warming to see how Joe looked after Jude. We were now in the shadow of Kangchenjunga, following the river across a series of steep scree slopes, the most dangerous ground of the entire expedition. As Jude was in the middle, big blocks came tumbling down.

You couldn't predict their trajectory; it was simply a matter of luck if anything hit you. Jude just kept moving across the shifting scree as we watched helplessly. She made it, seemed a little shaken, but then just determinedly carried on.

That night, at Kambachen, Joe announced it was Anzac Day, one of the most important anniversaries in the Australian calendar, commemorating the disastrous Gallipoli campaign in the Great War. It was a rather romantic gesture, typical of Joe, who wanted our own little ceremony for the sake of Dave and Jude. We finished with a toast from bottles of beer.

It took ten days to reach base camp at Lhonak, a place for grazing yaks in the summer at around 4,750 metres. I now had to marry up what we saw on the ground with the pictures Julian and Doug had given us; we weren't sure how accurate our maps were or of the best approach to Danga. Early in the morning, I climbed the hill behind base camp to get a more distant view. I was troubled by what I saw. I wasn't at all sure that the valley leading up from Lhonak reached our mountain, and the icefall at its head looked dangerous. Even more disturbing, I realized the mountain we had chosen as our objective, the mountain in the photographs Doug and Julian had sent us, was not Danga at all but a nameless peak of 6,194 metres. Danga was a sharp-pointed peak to its immediate north-west.

That same day, our capable *sirdar* Phurtenji Sherpa had walked up the Danga glacier to check out a site for advance base. He reported that it was hard going over broken moraines but that it led all the way to the foot of the Danga icefall and that from close up it looked reasonably safe. Next day, we went up to take a look and agreed with Phurtenji's assessment. The climb was on.

Now we faced another problem. I had packed some lightweight tents in a duffel bag at Badger Hill but they were nowhere to be found. I remembered our hurried departure, the dash for the train and the chaos at Euston. I'd left the tents on the train. The rest of the team found this very funny, especially Joe, whom I have at times berated for being forgetful. No matter. With the help of our patient crew, we moved some of our base camp tents up the mountain and early on 4 May we set out for the summit.

The first 300 metres led up a dry glacier with a light dusting of snow. There was the odd steep little step and narrow crevasse, but we didn't need the rope until the glacier opened up into a wide snow-covered basin. Tying on, I led up firm névé, picking my way around big crevasses. This led us to the upper part of the icefall, where a series of ice shelves led to an easy slope and a col between the real Danga and our own peak. It was only seven o'clock and we looked at Danga's more appealing summit some distance away across a snow-covered glacier. Gerald was immediately interested, suggesting we might go for it, but I was all too aware of the mixed abilities of our team and our responsibility for our sons. So we stuck to our peak, now dubbed Danga II.

Phurtenji and I took turns breaking trail and we gained height steadily, crossing a dodgy snow bridge over a huge crevasse and heading for what appeared to be the summit, a huge fin of ice jutting out of the rounded ridge. This proved rather dangerous, but I quickly realized it wasn't the summit at all; the true top was a rounded mound about half a mile away. We resumed our plod and reached the top at around one o'clock. It was an emotional moment: four Boningtons and our good friend Phurtenji on top of an unclimbed peak with a magnificent vista around us, the huge sprawling mass of Kangchenjunga and the shapely peak of Jannu with its huge north face. In the distance to the west were Makalu and Everest. I felt very content and great love for my family.

We had been incredibly lucky, having the best and clearest day of the entire expedition for our summit bid. The visibility was still perfect when we got back to advance base at half past four. Next day we made it all the way back to Ghunsa, where James played volleyball with the porters against the local village team. Then we set out on the return trek, skirting the western flank of Jannu. At the Mergan La we were overtaken by a blizzard. We ransacked our gear to loan our porters clothing; the following day we got below the snow line, turning back east across the grain of the land, up through dense jungle, over ridges, down the other side: six hard days back to the air strip at Suketar. There we discovered we couldn't fly because of bad visibility. We faced another long hike down the valley and a crowded night bus to Biratnagar for the morning flight to Kathmandu. The discomfort didn't matter; it had been a wonderful adventure, made even better by being a family affair.

The expedition to Danga was pivotal for Joe. Having got himself fit over the previous few years, he now realized he wanted to help others do the same. The world of commercial adventure was growing fast and he saw an opportunity, opening Joe's Basecamp in Sydney, a unique gym that trains athletes for outdoor and adventure sports. Over the years he has coached Everest summiteers, Channel swimmers, ultra-runners and adventure racers. He also set up a trekking company, bringing me in on some of his adventures in Nepal and Bhutan. I watched him earning the loyalty and affection of his clients. I'm immensely proud of both my sons, but Joe's journey has been a revelation.

Chapter Twenty

Sepu Kangri

At dusk we drove into Diru, around 300 miles north-east of Lhasa, a grubby, institutional town of barracks and government buildings patrolled by packs of mangy dogs. None of us wanted to stay there, but there was nothing beyond it and the teeming rain made camping unappealing. The post office had a guesthouse whose guardian was the friendly postmistress Mrs Donkar. She showed us to a simple room with a wood stove, beds and blankets. We were woken in the middle of the night when all the dogs of Diru started howling at once. It was so loud the windows rattled and both Charlie Clarke and I started laughing helplessly. We recorded it on tape as a sound effect.

At breakfast we explained our plans to Mrs Donkar and pulled out our only picture of Sepu Kangri, the mysterious mountain we had come to find.

'Ah yes,' she said at once, 'that's above my home village. I went on a picnic there with my family several years ago.' She disappeared to her room and came back with her handbag. 'Here it is,' she said, producing a photograph of herself with Sepu Kangri in the background. 'The road from here crosses a pass and then after a couple of hours drops down into a valley. You go to the village of Senza and from there it's a two-day walk. And don't bother to ask anyone else in Diru, they won't know, they never go there.'

It was extraordinary but we had solved the problem of our route to Sepu Kangri in the space of a few minutes. It seems the secret to exploration is to get close and then ask your landlady.

Our fascination with the enigma of Sepu Kangri dated back fifteen years to our flight from Chengdu to Lhasa, on our way to the north-east ridge of Everest. Through the scratched, blurry windows of our old Russian turbo-prop we saw a vast range of mountains none of us knew anything about: jagged peaks, sinuous ridges and glaciers stretching away to the northern horizon. All we knew was our rough location: north and east of Lhasa.

'They must be at least six thousand metres.'

'Look at that peak over there, it could be even higher.'

'I wonder if anyone has ever been into them?'

Then the peaks were behind us and we started our descent into Lhasa's Gonggar airport. The challenge of Everest filled our minds and the vision of those endless peaks faded. Two years later I received an intriguing letter from armchair traveller and map enthusiast Frank Boothman. He was fascinated by the geography of Tibet and had noticed on an US air force chart a range of peaks topping 7,000 metres north-east of Lhasa. The highest was marked as 7,350 metres, which would make it the highest point on the Tibetan plateau, although Frank warned me heights on the map would likely be on the high side.

Other projects intervened, but Frank kept feeding me odd nuggets of information and in 1987 the Royal Geographical Society published a gazetteer and map of mountains in Central Asia. I asked Jim Fotheringham, my partner from Shivling and our first trip to Menlungtse, if he would be interested in exploring the area in 1989. We secured backing and after a lot of enquiries found a travel agent in Hong Kong who assured us they could arrange permission with the Tibet Mountaineering Association, the organization that we thought, after Menlungtse, was in charge. With our bags packed, a fax arrived from the TMA saying that it couldn't after all give us the necessary permit for the area we wanted to visit but we could choose from a list of other peaks authorized by the Chinese Mountaineering Association. None of them had anywhere near the same appeal so we abandoned our plans and went to Scotland instead. Our remote hidden peak faded from view again.

Market reforms changed Tibetan tourism in the 1990s; I learned of a new travel and trekking agency in Lhasa that seemed reliable, was polite and answered my faxes promptly. Tempted again, I gathered a team of four for the summer of 1996: Jim Fotheringham, Graham Little and Jim Lowther. Charlie Clarke would be our doctor and old friends Jim Curran and Paul Nunn, who had both been on Rangrik Rang in 1994, planned to come in support. Sadly, Paul was killed in an avalanche in the Karakoram in the summer of 1995.

Then my ambitions took a swerve. I became involved in a Norwegian expedition to Antarctica later in 1996 and while in theory I could do both, my friendly new travel agent in Lhasa suddenly stopped answering my messages. It seemed as though we might not even get permission to go to Tibet. What's more, the Antarctic expedition would involve hard big-wall climbing and I felt I needed to focus all my efforts on that if I was to be anything more than a passenger. I took the difficult decision to withdraw from the Tibetan venture.

It didn't take me long to realize I'd made the wrong choice. The prospect of living for two weeks on a featureless rock tower, sleeping on a 'portaledge' with people I didn't know at all well, left me feeling increasingly uneasy. Meanwhile, the remaining members of the Tibet expedition had struggled to raise sponsorship or secure permission and had decided to postpone for a year. I invited the two Jims and Graham round for dinner to see if they would have me back for 1997; it was a delightful evening and I was reminded of what really mattered: working with friends whom one knows and trusts.

Even so, I'd gone from having had two expeditions planned for 1996 to none, and it occurred to me that I could organize a fast reconnaissance of the peak, to find out where exactly it was and how best to approach it. Charlie was the only team-member who could get time off, so we decided to go out as a pair early in August.

I was also put in touch with a Tibetan fixer based in Kathmandu called Tse Dorje who promised he could get us the necessary permits, a jeep and a guide for $5,000 per head.

We also discovered our mountain's name. My old friend Mac, Ian McNaught-Davis, after a long career in computing, had recently become president of the international climbing body, the UIAA. At a conference in Seoul the Chinese delegation had given him a new book as a gift: *Immortal Mountains in the Snow Region.* Suddenly we had pictures from our unknown range, which we now knew as the Nyenchen Tanglha, including one of our mountain, which we now learned was called Sepu Kangri, the White Snow God in Tibetan, and wasn't over 7,000 metres but 6,956 metres. I felt a small stab of disappointment that a little of the mystery of our journey had been taken away. On the other hand, we were off to explore an area the size of the Swiss Alps to survey a peak that no Western explorer had seen and at least we now knew what our objective looked like. And while it looked a complex snow peak, it did look climbable.

One of the great pleasures of the reconnaissance was spending time with Charlie. We had known each other for over twenty years; he'd been doctor on four of my expeditions and had collaborated on a book about the tragedy on Everest in 1982, but there is an elusive quality about him. He's urbane, worldly and has a playful sense of humour but there's a reserve as well. Perhaps it's his decades as a consultant neurologist, a life spent considering the mind from a scientific perspective. His wife Ruth, an eminent consultant psychiatrist who never thought twice about puncturing the egos of self-satisfied mountaineers, dropped him outside Wembley Conference Centre where I'd been giving a lecture prior to departure. My son Rupert was giving us a lift to Heathrow and as always I was fretting about missing the flight.

Charlie emerged from the car, looking rather elegant in jeans and a striped blazer – 'bought from Oxfam, useful for upgrades' – smiling in his charming way. I had a wonderful sense of freedom and anticipation. There had been no great effort of planning or organization; it was like going on our holidays. The blazer worked, and we were soon sitting in some luxury in the executive lounge of British Airways, reflecting on the fact that we had almost no idea where we were going, save for a longitude and latitude, and drawing up a list of all the things we did not know. It was a long list.

The mysterious Tse Dorje, our Tibetan Mr Fixit, wasn't in Kathmandu when we arrived: 'He's gone to Lhasa,' we were told. When we followed on a crowded Boeing a couple of days later, we saw little of Everest, locked away behind monsoon cloud, but when we cleared immigration there was a young Tibetan standing at the exit with a large sign that read: 'BONINGTON'. He introduced himself as our guide, Pasang Choephel. We would come to rely heavily on him in the next few weeks and indeed in the coming years as a wily supporter of our enterprise. Lhasa had changed out of all recognition from my first visit in the drab days of 1982. Now we were staying at the Holiday Inn, eating in the hotel's Tibetan-themed restaurant, wearing traditional Tibetan coats. Charlie produced a bottle of champagne from beneath his to celebrate my birthday. I had almost forgotten. I was sixty-two. It hardly seemed possible.

Two days later we pulled out of the Holiday Inn in a Jinbei pick-up truck with all our kit bouncing around in the back. Tse Dorje had made the briefest appearance to trouser his ten grand and our team had assembled. Pasang we knew, but we also met his entrancingly beautiful wife Yishi; Mingma was the cook, his only qualifications for this responsibility being his recent unemployment and the fact that Pasang was his next-door neighbour. His culinary skills were that of any other average eighteen-year-old male: zero. Happily, Tsering, the driver and, as it turned out, new owner of the Jinbei, was a careful, quiet and sober man. For the duration of the expedition he wore a gabardine golfing jacket, a trilby and pointed black shoes, which only emphasized his city origins. But he was a good and careful driver and we felt safe in his hands.

Our principal map was the cheap tourist version we'd bought at the airport. The road to Nakchu was clear, a grim new Chinese city of garish high-rises already looking threadbare plonked like a sore in the beautiful expanse of the plateau. Yet nomads swaggered down the main street, the women with their turquoise jewellery adding a splash of romance. That was a day's drive from Lhasa. Diru too was marked. After that, we had our photograph to rely on. What bothered us about Mrs Donkar's photo was that it looked a lot like the one from the book Mac had given us, taken from a similar angle. We had assumed this was of the south face because of the rather baffling caption: an example of what I think is sometimes called Chinglish. 'Azimuth for taking picture: north-east.' We assumed this meant that the photographer was facing north-east but if so, what was Mrs Donkar doing on the south side of the mountain? Charlie thought about it laterally for a moment, and then looked up a mountain aspect we both knew well: the north side of Everest. The caption read, 'Azimuth for taking picture: north.' We were clearly looking at the north face of Sepu Kangri, not the south.

Two days later we crossed a high pass and dropped down into the fertile Yu-chong valley, very different from the arid plateau. The pick-up truck parked in a meadow by a suspension bridge that crossed the river to the village of Khinda. This was as far as we could drive. There were still no mountains over 5,000 metres in sight: no wonder those who had travelled this way before had not commented on Sepu Kangri. Pasang warned us it would take time to rustle up some yaks to carry our gear; it was ploughing season and local farmers needed them. Yet it didn't take long at all. When we got back from our stroll the next day, he told us we would leave at eleven next morning with four yaks and two herders. At exactly five minutes to the hour, bang on time, four yaks crossed the meadow, driven by a smiling man on horseback with a long pig-tail tied with a bright red ribbon. There was a silver-handled dagger at his waist. This was Tembe.

'He has three fathers,' Pasang explained. 'One here in Khinda, and two more up the valley.' Polyandry was clearly still common, with brothers often marrying the same woman.

Picture two happy men of a certain age walking up a glorious valley. The grass was lush and green under fragrant juniper and willow, the clouds white and billowing against a cobalt sky and everywhere were flowers: primroses, gentians, small roses, blue, yellow, red and purple. It was so much richer and more verdant than I had imagined. The hillsides were closely cropped grass and reminded me of the over-grazed uplands of the Lake District. We passed the occasional *ba*, or yak-hair herder's tent, and on the second day reached Samda monastery, undergoing renovation and devoid of senior monks who were said to be away for the summer. A skeleton crew of young lamas had been left in charge and were suspicious and hostile. Pasang told them they weren't police and should get on with their praying.

We beat a hasty retreat and turned up a wide, rather barren valley that we were told led to Sepu Kangri. There was still no sign of our mountain. Then a final, tedious slope led suddenly to the top of a moraine and a view of the mountains as abrupt and spectacular as reaching a summit, an extravaganza of ice peaks, glaciers and below the sacred waters of Samtso Taring, stretching into the distance for eight kilometres and ending in a vast glacial amphitheatre. Towering to the right was the vastness of Sepu Kangri's north face. It was some time before either of us could assimilate the complexity and scale of the landscape. Neither the photo in the book or Mrs Donkar's snap had captured the magic of this magnificent mountain view. Tembe knelt and pressed his forehead on the grassy shore. Pasang and Mingma did the same. We pitched camp on the shore and went to bed very happy.

In the morning we watched the sun light up the distant eastern peaks with gold and as the minutes passed, Sepu Kangri blushed pink, reflected perfectly in the still waters of the lake. Before leaving us for a few days, Tembe pointed out the names of Sepu's neighbours: Chomo Mangyal, Sepu's wife, to the east; Gosham Taktso, the son and prime minister of Sepu; Seamo Uylmitok, the turquoise flower, or Sepu's daughter. Sepu Kangri he called Sepu Kunglha Karpu. Neither of us mentioned that we'd left our tourist map behind in the vehicle. We could, however, remember a 5,600-metre pass east of the lake's southern end called the Sa La and though we couldn't yet see it, guessed there might be an easy summit above it. Tembe had told Pasang that the local yak-herders sometimes took their animals over it. So in the afternoon Pasang and Mingma helped us carry a tent and food round to the far end of Samtso Taring.

Next day, hiking up to the col, two ferocious dogs guarding two small yak-herder tents raced to intercept us, happily going around me to get at Charlie. Presumably brain surgeons make better eating. He fended them off with his ski stick. There was some poetic justice in this; Charlie had breezily waved away my suggestion we get rabies jabs. 'Just commercial medicine from the travel clinics.' Happily, this time, we escaped unharmed. I would not be so lucky in the future.

The weather was grey, the mountains coming and going through the mist. The trail seemed to cross some distance from the col, which seemed strange, so we struck off towards the low point. There was a little snow slope just below, so we got out the ice axes. At the top we could look down the far side into a rotten gully that was impassable; now the higher path made sense. Across the valley, Sepu Kangri swam out of the mist and I photographed it, now just eight kilometres away, and recorded my thoughts, picking out possible lines for the following year. Then I bagged the summit just south of the col, and we bounded down to camp, dodging the dogs again, in just a couple of hours. Next morning we packed up the gear and started hiking back to our base camp at the northern end of the lake, intercepted by Pasang and Mingma who helped us with our loads.

Time was running short, and if we were to approach Sepu Kangri from another direction we had to leave immediately. Tembe was due back next morning, and since we still felt strong, spent the afternoon climbing the peak to the south-west of the lake. In a little over three hours we were a thousand metres higher on a shoulder at 5,700 metres and looking straight on to Sepu Kangri's north face, bristling with its seracs and crevasses. We pressed on towards the summit but the snow was chest-deep and I eventually followed Charlie in turning back to base camp, both of us still revelling in the luminous beauty around us.

On cue, as we finished our fried eggs next morning, there was the distant jingling of a bridle and a figure in a red headband, zigzagging behind his yaks, came into view. We said goodbye to Norge, a grandmother with a wry, toothless smile who lived in a stone hut a hundred yards from base camp with her granddaughter. Ringma, a nun of about sixteen, was staying with them. Mingma and Pasang had made friends while we were away; apparently the women were worried, seeing our ice axes, that we were mineral prospectors; mining had ruined plenty of Tibetan valleys. We persuaded them to let us take their photograph, the argument swayed by the Polaroid of Tembe they'd seen, and they disappeared back to their hut to do their hair and put on jewellery. Pasang pointed out that I was exactly the same age as the 'very old lady'. Norge was unimpressed with Charlie's status as a doctor, having been told the year before she would soon be dead.

'And here I am,' she cackled. 'What do you doctors know?'

Within the hour we were gone and in two wearying days were back at Mrs Donkar's guesthouse in Diru, showering in icy cold water and, since Mingma made it clear he'd had enough of cooking, gorging at a Sichuan restaurant in a shack on the main street. Walking in, Charlie said he felt the same incongruity as one did entering a Chinese takeaway in a small Welsh town. There was a poster of a Caribbean beach on the wall, all palm trees and golden sand but the floor was mud. The wife recognized immediately that trade might be a little brisker than usual, and sent out a long sequence of increasingly hot dishes and a steady supply of beer in brown bottles. The dogs of Diru did not keep us awake that night.

Having seen Sepu Kangri from the north, which we had supposed was the south, we had just enough time to do the opposite. Driving back to Nakchu, we took a side road we'd spotted on our way through to Chali, or Lhari town, birthplace of the two rival Panchen Lamas. It was a seedy place with not a mountain in sight.

The local police told us there were no yaks and that anyway we didn't have time to reach Sepu Kangri. So we doubled back and took a rough track that took us, after Mingma had the pick-up truck dragged out of the Jiali river, to within seventy kilometres. We had four days to cover the ground and return. After the first two hours walking, a yak caravan passed us, with several riderless saddled ponies. We could not believe our luck.

I hadn't ridden a horse since Patagonia with Wendy in 1963 and while these ponies were small they had tiny wooden saddles and stirrups for someone the size of a Newmarket jockey. The caravan barely stopped to accommodate us, but we were soon trotting along. The leader Temba called to us.

'He says sit up straight and hold the reins like this, in one hand,' Pasang shouted, looking himself like a natural. Temba, who had purloined Charlie's ski stick, was soon waving it at his men to bring back wandering yaks. Soon he had us doing it. The landscape, vast and open, was very different from the wooded gorges further north. In two hours we'd travelled twenty kilometres and Temba and his crew disappeared up a side valley. But as if by magic another yak caravan appeared, and they took us another twenty kilometres, dropping us at the head of our valley where we could see a steep slope and a col. Here we camped, and the following day dropped down into the Yapu valley, and we got a clear view of the Sepu Kangri massif from the south, the other side of the jigsaw.

Compared to the northern approach, this side of the mountain looked steep and complex. There was no obvious way to approach it, and it would take a longer and detailed reconnaissance of the side valleys carved by its glaciers. We certainly didn't have time to do that; Charlie had patients booked in his London surgery in a week's time. Still, we had seen the massif and got a strong impression of the mountain's southern challenges. Now we had to retrace our steps leaving enough time in Lhasa to convince the authorities to give us permission to climb the following year. It seemed impossible that we would have the same luck coming out that we had going in; while we didn't find any yak caravans to whisk us along, on the plain below was the incongruous sight of a large green truck. On board was a nomad's wife who had newly given birth; the nomad had sent for the truck to save his wife from riding a pony home. Pasang rushed ahead to negotiate our passage, and we were soon rolling across the grasslands to Jiali. Mingma and Tsering were astonished to see us back so quickly, mission accomplished.

Our reconnaissance to Sepu Kangri was one of the best trips I had ever undertaken. Not since my first expedition to the Himalaya, to Annapurna II more than thirty-five years before, had I enjoyed the same spirit of exploratory adventure. Everything about it had been fresh and full of surprises, a real venture into the unknown. With just two of us, the experience had been enhanced; decision-making was simpler and it was easier to get to know the people we met along the way.

The full expedition to Sepu Kangri the following year would be very different. Graham Little's partner Christine was about to have a baby and so to take his place I invited John Porter, who lived in Caldbeck, the village below my home. Born in New Hampshire, John, like so many, had been opposed on principle to the Vietnam War and fled to Britain, continuing his studies at Leeds University, where he met the brilliant young alpinist Alex MacIntyre. They had teamed up with some of the stars of Polish mountaineering in the mid 1970s and made a number of impressive first ascents. John was relaxed and affable, with a laconic sense of humour. I'd also asked Jim Curran along to make a film, just as he had on Kongur.

Six months after flying home, I was back at Lhasa airport, scanning the exit for Pasang. His face looked puffier than when I had last seen him and he had a fresh scar on his face; he was quick to tell us he had been in a fight. This time we had brought our own cook, Nawang, one of three Sherpas who joined us from Nepal. He and Charlie, with *sirdar* Dawa and his assistant Pemba, trailed through the markets buying fresh food to boost our rations. He even found bananas from Ecuador. It was a far cry from our experience on Everest just fifteen years before. The other astonishing change was our communications equipment, satellite phones the size of a laptop that you opened to take out the receiver. Standing on the roof of our hotel I could phone Wendy and talk to her as she woke in the morning; no big deal to the Skype generation but to us it was a marvel.

Even in late April, the valley to the sacred lake of Samtso Taring was still frozen hard. Jim Fotheringham, as a dedicated Buddhist, decided he would visit a hermit who, we were told, lived at the foot of Sepu Kangri, and then continue up the valley to see if there was a feasible route round the back of the mountain. The home of the hermit was at the base of a long ridge extending from the Turquoise Flower; clusters of willow, still bare of leaves, surrounded two flat-roofed huts. He was waiting for us, long dark ringlets framing his narrow face and moustache. Pasang had come with us, and after Jim offered gifts of butter, sugar and *tsampa*, or barley flour, we were invited to sit down. His name was Samten Tsokpu, roughly translated 'seated in concentration', and he came from Chali, where we'd been the year before. He had lived alone here for four years, ate no meat, took no stimulants – not even tea – and relied for food on the generosity of locals. There was a gap in the wall of his little courtyard where he sat meditating, contemplating the family and court of Sepu Kangri.

We continued up the valley a little, crossing a second ice-bound lake into which flowed the Thong Wuk glacier. Crossing it, we got a clearer perspective of the west side of the peak and there seemed to be a feasible route rising to the crest of the north-west ridge. It warranted a closer inspection, so we came back a couple of days later, weighed down with tents and gear, and in the thin air this approach swiftly lost its appeal. Cloud rolled in, bringing flurries of snow. The ridge itself seemed narrow and rocky, while the glacier basin below the west face of Turquoise Flower was an ominous maze of seracs and crevasses. The north ridge, which we could see in profile, was beginning to look more attractive. Even so, as we took the decision to focus our efforts there, I had a feeling of disquiet, that we hadn't pushed our recce far enough.

We dubbed the north ridge the Frendo Spur after the popular challenge above Chamonix. Jim Fotheringham led a difficult pitch to gain access to the spur proper, scratching his way up a rocky gully when the ice ran out. Jim Lowther and I dug out a snow cave at camp two while the others pushed the route up the spur. All of us took a turn in front and my optimism grew that we might get a chance at the top. It was not to be. Having planned our summit bid, I awoke to the sound of snow pattering on the walls of our tent at camp two and listened to the wind roaring across the spur. I heard someone emerge from our snow hole; it was John, telling us he was sick and thinking of going down.

'I've been coughing up a lot of gunge and my lungs feel full of fluid,' John said. 'It feels like pulmonary oedema to me.' He thought if he went down he should be able to shake it off and return. I wasn't happy with him going alone, and since we were a group of friends working together, it felt right we should all go down, rest and then return. The weather had other ideas. We remained locked in cloud and heavy snow and as the days passed, it became clear our chances were fading.

Charlie was preoccupied with treating Tsini, a beautiful young woman who lived in a modest hut close to our base camp and was suffering from an ectopic pregnancy; her husband Karte had arrived in camp to seek our help. Charlie used the satellite phone to call a gynaecologist friend in London to confirm the diagnosis. Tsini was in terrible pain, but thanks to Charlie's intervention she was made comfortable and the danger passed. The rest of us played bridge, wrote emails and gossiped. When the weather cleared we recovered our gear from the mountain, now buried in snow. We left base camp two days later in a blizzard. Prayer flags were rustling in the wind. Tsini and her mother-in-law Orsa stood on the hillside above the camp, their hair and clothing fluttering in the wind.

'Well done, you old bugger,' Jim Curran said to Charlie.

'Oh, it was only nature and a few painkillers,' he replied, but I could see Charlie was crying.

We were both already planning to return; some useful research in the Tibet Meteorological Office, poring over weather maps and rainfall data, suggested that the optimum date to reach the summit of Sepu Kangri would be 1 October. I applied for a climbing permit for the following year and Charlie went off to talk to our agent about making a longer exploratory trek on the eastern side of the massif. Charlie's plan was to meet us at the end of his trek just as we arrived.

Early in the next September, I was rattling across the Tibetan plateau again, mouth covered with a bandanna against the dust, sharing a Land Cruiser with Graham Little and his young friend Scott Muir, drafted in at the last minute to replace Jim Lowther who had pulled out when his mother fell ill. Scott turned off the driver's Tibetan pop music and slotted in a tape of The Doors he had borrowed from his father.

'This must have been your kind of music,' he said with a grin. I didn't dare tell him I was probably older than his father.

The Land Cruiser wound over the last pass and we dropped down into the Salween valley. The year before the road had been paved with ice, but now it was fringed with grass. It was harvest time, and there was a festival on, the locals in their best clothes, old women flicking through their rosaries as they muttered prayers, the young *Khamba* men, with red cord woven in their hair, merry with drink and swaggering around. In Diru, we ate at our old restaurant, now partly developed into a Western-style nightclub. But the village still felt like a film set, hardly real; the bridge had been swept away in heavy summer rains, reinforcing the impression of impermancence.

Next morning we set out for the Yuchong valley and our rendezvous with Charlie. The bridge was down here too; I could pick out Charlie's tents on the far bank and then I saw Charlie, suspended upside down on a wire across the river, pulling himself across. It was wonderful seeing him again and hearing of his adventures. He'd been travelling with a young friend of his daughter's, Elliot Robertson. I couldn't help envying him and comparing the freedom and lightness of his mountain travels with the complexities of a climbing expedition.

At the lake of Samtso Taring, Karte and Tsini, fully recovered, welcomed us warmly, and I walked through the lush grass up to their house for Tibetan tea and yoghurt. Although we were a team of four climbers, we soon split into two: Graham and Scott were the hares, Victor Saunders and I were the tortoises. It was fun climbing with Victor again. There were moments when I was feeling my age, wondering if I still had it in me, when Victor's conversation would lift my spirits. He shared my enthusiasm for exploring the side valley under the Turquoise Flower, the approach Jim had favoured and which we had failed to explore properly the year before. We spent a rewarding time together hunting down a route Victor had spotted on an acclimatization climb with Charlie. This bypassed the horrendous lower icefall and brought us eventually to the upper Thong Wuk glacier under the final summit mass of Sepu Kangri. It was safer than the Frendo Spur route of the previous year with the added bonus that we weren't required to traverse the Turquoise Flower before getting to grips with the main summit.

On our first attempt on the summit, we reached camp two, at a height of 6,350 metres, no more than a day's climbing from the top. I lay in my sleeping bag too excited to sleep, listening to the patter of snow accumulating on the tent. We planned to leave at one o'clock in the morning but kept postponing as the snow continued. When I woke at dawn to silence, I wondered if this heralded good weather and poked the sides of the tent. There was a 'swoosh' as inches of snow slid off, followed by the gentle patter of more falling snow. I stuck my head out to discover we were in a whiteout. Graham came over to explain that he and Scott had got soaked in their single-skin tent and had dug a snow hole.

Graham crammed into our tent and we spent the day playing bridge as the snow carried on falling. I became anxious that we'd walked into a trap, cut off from retreat by the avalanche threat behind us as our fuel and food dwindled. When Graham and Scott woke next morning they both felt ill, either from a blown can of fish, or else carbon monoxide poisoning from their stove. It was a fine morning and the rest of us could still have gone for the summit, and yet I agreed to all of us going down together; I felt we were a single team and should stick together. I'm not sure the younger Bonington would have done that. It showed a change in my priorities; the wellbeing and inclusiveness of the group were as important to me as success. Was this a growing maturity on my part? Or was it my own failing stamina, part of the ageing process, working on my subconscious?

We spent a week resting at base camp, in quite good weather, but on the way back up I fell behind almost immediately. I couldn't help wondering about my chances. Then Victor caught me up, and as we plodded upwards chatting I began to forget my fatigue. Yet it was slow-going. The snow that had fallen in the last few days was deep and felt dangerous. It dawned on me that snowshoes were the key to making progress on such wearying terrain but we only had three pairs between five of us.

A decision had to be made. Since I had been going the slowest, it made sense I should go down, and as the junior partner, Elliot joined me. I tried to do a piece to camera for the news reports we were sending ITN, but couldn't control my emotions and slumped down in the snow. The others patted me on the back and then began climbing into the swirling cloud as Elliot and I prepared to descend. In spite of my emotion I had no regrets; given the situation, it made sense for the strongest three to go on. I did feel sorry for Elliot though, who remained silent and thoughtful; I knew how I would have reacted at his age.

In the end Victor and Scott came agonizingly close to the summit. They could see the summit, just 150 metres above their heads, but wisely turned back as the weather closed in. Finding their way back in a whiteout from close on 7,000 metres was just too risky; anyway, finding the highest bump on what we knew was a plateau would have been impossible in heavy cloud. Graham had decided that instead of joining them on their summit bid, he would climb the Turquoise Flower, at 6,650 metres a significant and beautiful summit and our only major success of the expedition. The reconnaissance with Charlie had been magical, but on our two main attempts I had found myself struggling to keep up and needing extra rest days. I suspect this was also affecting my judgement as leader. Even so, I think I was still in denial; it was only two years later on the Arganglas expedition that I was forced to recognize that my hard Himalayan climbing days were over.

Chapter Twenty-One

A Strange Retirement

How far are we driven by ego? How much does the approval of our peers mean to us? Or fame in the wider world? I certainly had an ego and enjoyed recognition, but I don't think I was ever consumed by it. In those early days, when I discovered my passion for climbing, there was a thrill in the risk, and a satisfaction in finding an activity I was good at, but above all I treasured the actual sensation of climbing for its own sake. I was ambitious, but only for those things just in front of me. My challenges were both measurable and attainable. I dreamed of what I would do in Wales next spring or the Northern Highlands or Skye in the long summer holidays, of my first Very Severe, and on up the grades. The Alps and the Himalaya were beyond the horizon.

The same applied when I was able finally to reach the Alps. Attempting the north wall of the Eiger as my first Alpine route was Hamish MacInnes's choice, not mine. My subsequent attempts with Don Whillans were for the quality of the challenge rather than fame and fortune. Yet it was in this period that the media started coming to us in search of a story, and since we were utterly broke, I saw in them a means to an end. It was only when Ian Clough and I made the first British ascent that I fully understood the opportunities the media offered, not only in funding my climbing but also as a way of making a living.

In the struggle to write my first book, to lecture in front of an audience, to take better pictures and tell a story, I discovered I was pretty good at storytelling. I drew satisfaction not only from being creative, but also entrepreneurial in securing funding for my expeditions. When I started lecturing, the hatted ladies who attended my presentations at luncheon clubs expressed a motherly concern about what I would do when I got older and mountaineering was no longer possible. Business-minded friends, like my agent George Greenfield, Bob Stoodley and Graham Tiso, expressed the same concern. They all tried to involve me in various business initiatives. Yet my heart wasn't in it and I could never really commit myself. Consequently I never become rich. Here I am, at the age of eighty-two, doing much the same as I have always done, not simply to top up my pension, but because I still enjoy all aspects of my working life, even if I have gently moved back down the grades in climbing, or cut back the number of lectures I give. The past has never much concerned me; I never kept scrapbooks or dwelt on my climbing career. Curiosity and enthusiasm are what drive me: the joy and pleasure of new paths.

The allure of fame, of being in the public eye, crept up on me. My first glimpse of it was after our ascent of the Central Pillar of Frêney in 1961, and then to a much greater extent after the Eiger. It became a fixture after the big expeditions of the 1970s, to Annapurna and Everest. And yes, I enjoyed the recognition, but I wasn't going for any of those objectives in search of it. The driving forces were still the core ones, the thrill of risk, the fascination of the unknown, of solving problems of increasing scale and complexity, which in a way came to a climax with the south-west face of Everest. They are the same reasons I continued my climbing adventures deep into my seventies. Wherever I went, whatever I did, I always tried to squeeze in a climb.

There was an element of good timing. My skills suited public taste at that time: the boom in outdoor education in the 1960s and 1970s, the arrival of colour supplements, the new possibilities of travel. These days, young climbers are still doing incredible things in the best possible style all over the Himalaya but the public pays no attention. Someone like Bear Grylls has a set of attributes that better suits the media as it is now, seeing the potential of fast-moving reality television and making the most of it. The world has changed, for better or worse. If Mum had grown up in the world today she would have faced none of the hindrances that undercut her writing ambitions, both as a single mother and as a woman in the workplace. What she did achieve, given her era, was incredible: a senior advertising executive long before the time of *Mad Men*, and a much-loved teacher.

Fame meant being approached by complete strangers. You're travelling on a train and you want to read your book and then someone starts talking to you. Sometimes, if they're interesting, it's a welcome interruption. Sometimes you feel trapped. Mostly they want to say things or ask questions you've heard before, but they don't know that. You just have to be friendly; it's common courtesy. Of course, this was in the era before social media, although I'm quite happy to do selfies in my eighties. Fame had a downside of course, especially for our children. There are consequences to having a famous parent. Joe has spoken of being both proud of his dad, but also resenting me for the pressure he felt. I think after Kilimanjaro that dissipated.

My first formal recognition came from the Royal Geographical Society when in 1974 they gave me the Founder's Gold Medal, their foremost award 'for mountain explorations'. I was on Changabang at the time of the presentation, and so it was Mum, still living in London, who went along to Kensington Gore to collect my medal and read out my speech. It meant a lot to us both. The Society had been at the forefront of exploration through the Victorian era and had an equal place with the Alpine Club in organizing and planning all the pre-war Everest expeditions and the successful ascent of 1953. From that success the Mount Everest Foundation was formed, with the profits from John Hunt's book, film rights and official lectures, to fund exploratory mountaineering and scientific expeditions. I was very grateful that the MEF underwrote our expedition to the south face of Annapurna, though I am glad to say we managed to make a profit for them.

In early 1976, after the south-west face of Everest, an official-looking letter, marked official, arrived at Badger Hill, telling me I had been nominated to become a Commander of the British Empire for services to mountaineering. Would I accept? The announcement was made in the Queen's Birthday Honours List that June with the investiture later that summer. Wendy wasn't able to come down to London for the ceremony, so once again Mum stepped in and accompanied me to Buckingham Palace.

Though I missed having Wendy with me, it was good to share the experience with Mum. At that stage I was only just beginning to appreciate how much she had done for me; our day at the Palace was very special. I spent the night in my club, the Army and Navy, known as the Rag, on the corner of Pall Mall and St James's Square. Mum came over from Hampstead and we walked together to Buckingham Palace through the park, I slightly self-conscious in a morning suit, Mum smiling proudly for the cameras in a rather jaunty hat.

I didn't fully understand how much she had sacrificed. A few years later, I appeared on the BBC Radio 4 programme *In the Psychiatrist's Chair* and spoke to Anthony Clare a little about my father, and the role of fathers. Mum wrote me a heartfelt letter wondering why I hadn't spoken more about her, and the role of mothers. I couldn't help feeling a stab of conscience, given just how much she had done to help me achieve success.

Mum had left advertising in the 1960s, changing to a career she had long aspired to, teaching English in a secondary school. Her first job was in a comprehensive in Barnet but she then moved to a Catholic high school for girls in Highgate where she stayed until retirement. She then moved back to her native Cheshire, before I bought her a house in Keswick to be nearer to the family. When I was giving public lectures around the UK and even in the United States or Australia, there would be former pupils of hers in the audience, telling me what a wonderful teacher Mum had been. She became something of a character, riding a Vespa to school, and then a Reliant Robin three-wheeler, which she could drive with her motorcycle licence, having failed her full driving test. It was a great comfort, in her last years, that she was near us where we could support her.

With success and a public profile comes responsibility. In the aftermath of Everest in the mid-1970s, a steady stream of individuals or charities began to approach me. In 1976 I accepted an invitation to become vice president of the British Mountaineering Council (BMC), climbing's representative body. Climbing politics is often fractious, and these were stirring times. A ferocious conflict had arisen between the more anarchic wing of the climbing world and the educators, led by Sir Jack Longland, a brilliant climber of the pre-war era who had been to Everest in 1933 and as Derbyshire's director of education was a leading thinker and mover in outdoor education. He had also played an important role in setting up the BMC.

High-profile fatal climbing accidents, particularly the deaths of six young people in the Cairngorms in 1971, prompted calls for more regulation and better training. A lot of climbers were suspicious of this. The whole premise of climbing is freedom: to go where you want and choose your own level of risk. The very word 'certificate' is anathema and many still prefer to learn through clubs or friends. Educational types, on the other hand, need to keep risk to a minimum, because of their professional duty of care.

The training debate of that era was a good grounding for when I became BMC president in 1988. I was a strong believer in keeping meetings moving, giving members time to express differing views but driving things on if the argument started to go round in circles. If I wanted to get agreement over something I felt was important, I would spend hours on the phone beforehand, talking to people whose agreement I felt was important and who had influence on the committee.

Our general secretary was Dennis Gray, one of the great names of post-war working-class British climbing and the BMC's first employee; he had been in the post since the mid-1970s, steering the organization as it grew in importance. When Dennis decided to move on during my presidency, my old friend Derek Walker replaced him. After Paine in 1963, he had continued his career as a teacher, as headmaster of the English School in Punta Arenas before returning to England to teach history in a Cheshire comprehensive school. Derek was an outstanding general secretary, immensely good at getting people to work together. It is quite a political role, yet he never had an enemy.

I had just become vice president of the BMC for the second time, to prepare for my presidency, when Francis Harris, director of the charity Lepra, asked if he could come and see me. Slightly built, wearing glasses and a tweed suit, he had the look of a gentle academic yet the story he told me about the work Lepra was doing to combat leprosy was deeply impressive. I had seen sufferers on my visits to Nepal, all too often begging in the streets with disfigured faces or amputated limbs. He wanted me to become president, and while I was already stretched, on impulse, I agreed, performing the role for almost thirty years until I finally stepped down in 2014.

Leprosy is caused by bacteria spread through close and repeated contact with nose and mouth droplets from someone with untreated severe leprosy. It's a problem of the developing world, where families share small huts or rooms and medical care is limited or non-existent. It starts by damaging small nerves on the skin's surface resulting in loss of sensation. Unnoticed burns or ulcers become infected, leading to permanent disability, amputation and disfigurement. Sufferers have been stigmatized throughout history and often forcibly isolated from society. In the 1940s drugs were discovered that alleviate symptoms but only in 1981 did a multi-drug treatment offering a total cure become available, provided the symptoms are discovered early.

At that time Lepra was most active in Malawi, on the principle that it was best to focus on a country that experienced a high level of leprosy and where its efforts would make the biggest difference, even possibly eradicate the disease. This needed a properly structured health system to educate the population about early symptoms, regular health inspections from aid posts and distribution of drugs.

I had a fascinating visit to Malawi in September 1985 to see for myself and enable me to speak more effectively back in the UK. This beautiful country flanks the western shore of Lake Malawi, formerly known as Lake Nyasa, at the southern end of the Rift valley. It gained independence from Britain in 1963. Dr Hastings Banda was the first prime minister, declaring himself president for life in 1970. He was a dictator, but the country was relatively prosperous, stable and sufficiently compact to allow Lepra to introduce an effective drug treatment regime throughout the country. They also did research into the new antibiotic cocktail to combat the disease. I was taken around in a four-wheel drive, over bumpy tracks to isolated villages, to see all aspects of their work, the assistants on bicycles pedalling to a track junction where they would find waiting in the shade of a tree some of their patients awaiting their ration of pills. They'd also inspect the lesions on their skin to check for any change.

My reward at the end of the tour was the chance to climb Chambe Peak, a granite dome in the Mulanje Massif that reaches over 3,000 metres. The Malawi Mountain Club maintains a hut there, and when I reached it I was introduced to Gordon Craig who was to be my partner the following morning. We climbed a route called *Devil's Staircase*, starting up wonderfully rough granite slabs, too easy to need a rope. Then, imperceptibly, the angle steepened and the drop below suddenly became daunting. We stopped to tie on but there were no obvious cracks, just tufts of grass whose roots stretched in thin tentacles across the rock. We used these as running belays, looping a sling round a big clump and hoping they would hold in the event of a fall. An occasional stunted vellozia, a sort of cactus-like shrub, offered a dubious belay. This was not Borrowdale.

As the sun dropped towards the far horizon we reached the top, parched with thirst, faces smeared with dirt, exhausted, to see the rock lit with a wonderful rich glow, which then quickly died. Under a darkening, starlit sky, I felt a mixture of exhilaration and alarm. How the hell were we going to get down in the dark? We had no extra clothes, it was getting cold and our throats were raw. Then we saw two head-torches bobbing up the ridge below us. They belonged to two young porters sent to guide us down the vague path that led back to the hut. An hour or so later we were downing a beer and waiting for dinner after an amazing eighteen hours. Gordon had been the perfect companion, totally cool and efficient throughout.

In the early nineties I was approached by Amanda Nobbs, the director of what is now the Campaign for National Parks (CNP), which represents the voluntary side of the national park movement, to see if I'd become their president. It had an instant appeal, just because I'd done so much of my climbing in our National Parks. In theory it was a figurehead role but in practice I became closely involved. I was taken along to numerous meetings with ministers and senior civil servants to strengthen our case. This involved a fair amount of homework to ensure I knew what I was talking about.

As I came to know about the issues and the workings of government, I found myself drawn in more deeply. I became chair of the corporate forum, comprising representatives of companies having an impact on the parks, from the quarrying industry to utilities like water companies. I quickly discovered this wasn't a PR exercise: we had a useful influence on their conduct in the parks. Their environmental officers had a genuine concern for what they were doing. Mike Crabtree, for example, environmental officer for North West Water, had an evangelical zeal for conservation that certainly put me to shame.

By far the most rewarding of my duties was to visit the National Parks themselves. This was usually over two or three days and Wendy always came with me. I never ceased to wonder at the beauty and variety of the parks: the extraordinary sky and cloudscapes of the Norfolk Broads; the rounded hills of the Brecon Beacons; the moorland of the artillery ranges in the Northumberland National Park that had become unofficial nature reserves for wildlife. I also made a host of friends among the dedicated staff of CNP who escorted me and among the staff and volunteers of the National Parks and various park societies.

It was during my time with CNP, in 1996, that another official letter came from the Cabinet Office. I was away at the time but

Wendy phoned to say it was asking if I would accept a knighthood. I should say so. The knighthoods John Hunt and Edmund Hillary received after the 1953 Everest expedition had been for the climb alone: that achievement had been so huge in every respect. I understood very well that mine was made not just for mountaineering achievement but also for what I had put back. This time I had my whole family with me, Wendy, Joe, Jude, Rupert and Ann, though unfortunately we were only allotted three seats, which went to Wendy and the boys, while Ann and Jude had to wait outside the railings of Buckingham Palace. We then all went for a superb lunch.

Luckily for me, most of my friends have been climbers and one or two adventurers and that sort don't let you get away with swanking around. They treat you as being perfectly ordinary, and that's precisely what I wanted. I still feel very much at home among my peers, which has made for a hugely enjoyable non-retirement.

After my last real expedition, to Arganglas in 2001, I filled the gap with some wonderful treks with Harish Kapadia and with my son Joe on his treks to Nepal and Bhutan. Yet I still felt hungry for the sort of exploratory climbing that I had loved best throughout my life. I couldn't have anticipated I would experience the greatest pleasure and purest enjoyment of my climbing life in the Anti Atlas of Morocco. Throughout my late sixties and deep into my seventies, I made almost annual trips, exploring, prospecting for new routes, climbing for the sheer fun of it in great company and staying in a comfortable hotel – what more could one ask?

Derek Walker got me into it. We'd climbed together in the UK since Patagonia and both been involved in climbing politics at the BMC. Staying at his home in Frodsham, he'd spoken of how much he enjoyed visiting Morocco with Joe Brown and a small group of friends. It sounded brilliant fun; I told Derek I'd love to join him. He warned me it was very much invitation only; he'd have to check with the others. Fortunately they approved.

The Anti Atlas, well to the south of the main Atlas range, was then barely known as a climbing venue. Les Brown and Trevor

Jones, with whom I'd climbed on Nuptse in 1961, discovered the potential of the Jebel el Kest group almost by chance in 1991 while on holiday with their wives. They had originally planned to visit Wadi Rum in Jordan, but the first Gulf War put a stop to that, so they changed their destination to Morocco, climbing and walking in the Todra Gorge of the Atlas before driving down to the Anti Atlas, for sightseeing more than anything else. As they drove round the north side of the Jebel el Kest they immediately recognized the immense potential. They stayed briefly in the only hotel in Tafraoute with a licence to sell alcohol, the Hotel Les Amandiers, but were short of time and so completed just one route on the most conspicuous crag.

Back in Britain, Les told Claude Davies, who was a close friend and regular climbing partner of Joe Brown. The following spring, this small group returned to the climbing paradise of Tafraoute and started developing its huge potential. They managed to keep it a secret, inviting just a few more friends to join them over the years, putting up new routes, rarely, if ever, repeating one and always from the Hotel Les Amandiers. When I joined them in 2001, there were just six of us, Joe Brown, Les Brown, Claude Davies, Pete Turnbull, Derek Walker and myself. We saw no other climbers throughout the two weeks.

The hotel was on top of a small hill an easy walk from the town and looked like a Moroccan fort, three storeys, a flat roof and small external windows and two internal quadrangles. The bedrooms were Spartan but comfortable, and there was a bar and swimming pool. Each day's climbing followed a similar pattern: an excellent breakfast of boiled eggs, bread rolls and coffee, and then jump in our little fleet of rented Fiats, stopping at a shop on the way for sardines, oranges and local bread for lunch.

Sometimes we knew the way to the crag, if one of the team had been there before; sometimes we didn't and had to figure it out. It was all part of the adventure. The villages clinging to the slopes of the Jebel el Kest were up winding rutted tracks and paths defended by savage shrubs, like the thorny argan trees, that flourished in poor soil and arid conditions. The kernel inside its berries provided oil excellent for cooking as well as a moisturizer. Its sharp thorns weren't enough to deter the goats that seemed to live in the trees, grazing the foliage, watched by old and wizened goatherds or those so young they should have been in school.

Nearer the villages we passed womenfolk in their voluminous dark dresses, hair covered by the *haik*, a form of headscarf, carrying huge loads of fodder. The Berbers, who live in these mountains, are a proud race and held out against the French colonists for a long time. There are signs of how much more fertile the land around the Jebel el Kest was in past times from the extensive terracing on all the easier slopes, like that found in Nepal. Once on the crag we could hear the amplified call to prayer throughout the day from the mosques in the villages below. We were sometimes invited into Berber homes for a glass of mint tea, particularly when we had been climbing in sight of their houses and they had been watching us.

Jebel el Kest had an extraordinary beauty and character. In the morning or late-afternoon light, the quartzite rock assumed a range of rich and warm colours from light brown that verged on pink in full sunlight, through gold to reds of every hue reaching a dark purple that reduced to black silhouettes against the star-studded blue-black sky of night. It also provided the perfect climbing medium. Even on what seemed the blankest rock there were just enough cracks in which to place protection although at times the climbing could get very scary. Yet almost every time you reached what seemed a dead end, you could pull round a corner and find a solution.

There was little sense of competition. We had such a huge expanse of superb unclimbed rock at every kind of level and near perfect conditions most of the time that competition was pointless. We'd get back to the hotel on an absolute high from a day of fun, sometimes demanding, occasionally terrifying climbing: the high was the highest when we had suffered a bit of an epic. And the evenings were a very important part of the overall experience. That first beer when we got back to the hotel, sharing what we had done that day with whoever was back, then a hot bath, dinner and a keenly fought game of bridge. Joe, Claude and Pete were quite a bit cannier than me but we had some good contests.

The number of climbers steadily increased as we told our friends about how delectable the area was. We soon needed a longer table to sit down together at dinner. It became like the pre-Great War climbing parties based at the Pen y Pass Hotel in Snowdonia or the Wasdale Head Inn in the Lakes. Joe was undoubtedly the unofficial president of the group, simply by his presence, with his big broad smile, his ability as a raconteur and the warmth of manner, quite apart from the way he had dominated British climbing through his sheer ability and the quality of routes he put up. He is among the best-loved of all our leading climbing personalities. I might have the knighthood, but drinking gin and tonic in the Hotel Les Amandiers, Joe was still 'Baron Brown', our benign patriarch.

Although I had known him since 1961 on the first ascent of *Trango* in North Wales and afterwards climbing in the Alps with Tom Patey as well as various television climbs, I had never really got to know Joe. Now on our regular Moroccan holidays, often on the same rope, I came much closer. It was not so much any reserve: Joe is very open in his manner. It was more a complete confidence, a sense of being at home with himself and his choices, which act almost as a shield. He is a master of one-upmanship, taking the piss gently with that broad smile. He almost never gave offence. And his self-confidence wasn't assertive or in any way boastful; he could fit into any group. Perhaps that's why he'd been invited to join the expedition to Kangchenjunga back in 1955 and why he is still admired with such affection today.

Conversation ranged from what we'd been doing that day or planned for tomorrow, or stories from the past; some even discussed current affairs or art. There was little on climbing ethics: we were all committed trad climbers although most of us were pragmatic and tolerant about what people got up to back in Europe and even the Todra Gorge. None of us wanted bolts in the Anti Atlas; that would kill something very special. In my ten years, I saw the Anti

Atlas change from being an exclusive playground for a small group of friends to a popular climbing destination. The trad-climbing ethos, however, remains strong.

I measured the effects of my own ageing in that decade. In 2001 at sixty-seven I was still going strong, operating at a level British climbers grade at E1, the mildest of the Extremes and respectable enough. I'd dropped a little from my early fifties when I was leading E2 and even E3. I could still swing leads with friends like Jim Fotheringham and Graham Little, some fifteen years younger than me. I remember Joe Brown warning me over a pre-dinner gin in 2004, the year I turned seventy: 'Make the most of it now; once you're seventy it's downhill all the way.' Joe is four years older than me and I'd noticed in 2001 how his rheumatism was giving him some trouble. Even so the magic in his climbing was still there. Perhaps that's why the quartzite and the warm dry weather of Morocco were so attractive. It made us a little younger again.

I couldn't stop the clock for ever. As I moved into my late seventies I found myself handing over the lead more frequently to Graham Little and Mike Mortimer, and needing a good tight rope on some of their harder leads. It didn't worry me. I simply loved being there, loved their company and revelled in the glorious unspoilt freedom of the mountains. That last year, 2012, my Norwegian friends Odd and Ralph came to Morocco too, our friendship as strong as ever. Odd was still using the Berghaus windshirt he'd worn on Menlungtse almost twenty-five years earlier. Berghaus first sponsored me on Everest in 1985 and I've enjoyed a happy commercial connection with them ever since, not only using Berghaus gear on my expeditions, but also becoming non-executive chairman in 1997, involved in the board's decisions. We've had some great adventures together, particularly when Andy Rubin, chair of Berghaus' parent company, asked me to join the heads of the group's other brands on an ascent of Kilimanjaro. None of them had done anything like it before, but they all got to the top.

I had been involved with Outward Bound periodically ever since my two years as an instructor at the Army Outward Bound School.

During the 1970s, when each Outward Bound Centre was semi-autonomous with its own board of local directors, Roger Putnam, the principal at Eskdale, asked me to come on the board. It was a delight, very friendly and informal and Roger was an excellent leader, listening and consulting with his instructors yet taking clear decisions. Sadly the entire organization was centralized and the school boards were terminated.

It was in 1997 that the new director of Outward Bound, Major-General Sir Michael Hobbs, approached me to see if I would come onto the main board as a trustee. I'd seen for myself the life-changing impact Outward Bound could make in a young person's development and was happy to accept. Meetings were held at Buckingham Palace in a large room opulently decorated in Chinese style with a huge mahogany table in the middle. The Duke of Edinburgh was in the chair; he let everyone have their say provided they kept to the point, summed up discussion and decisions succinctly and leavened it all with a good dry humour, all the better at times for being politically incorrect. He was the best committee chairman I have ever served under.

I also became chair of the safety committee, my first step being to change its name to the risk-management commitment on the premise that Outward Bound must have adventure and without risk there could be no adventure. The satisfaction comes in managing that risk well. All the members were professionals and I made sure I had my biannual risk management meetings at Outward Bound Centres. The winter meeting was at Loch Eil in the Highlands so I could grab a winter route on Ben Nevis with Tony Shepherd, the centre's head. I observed that the best instructors were not only good at instructing but had also retained their passion for adventure.

The retirement age for trustees was seventy-five but the board graciously elevated me to the role of deputy patron so I could still participate. I was also bestowed with a final, totally unexpected but gratifying honour, Commander of the Royal Victorian Order, in the gift of the Queen for services to the Royal Family, in this case my contribution to Outward Bound. Wendy and my entire Keswick family were able to attend and the following day we were given an individual tour of the Tower of London with my good friend Bill Callaghan, a yeoman warder who took us into all kinds of interesting places the general public wouldn't see, followed by a wild trip on an RNLI boat up and down the Thames.

Outward Bound has gone from strength to strength with the appointment as chief executive of Nick Barrett, a keen hill walker and former deputy director of Voluntary Service Overseas and director of the Ramblers' Association. Nick believes passionately in bringing back adventure into Outward Bound. The Duke of York has succeeded his father as chair. At a meeting in 2011, when we were all brainstorming how we could raise a very large sum for a capital investment, the Duke, who was striding up and down near the window, suddenly pointed and said: 'That's what we can do – a charity abseil down the Shard.'

The UK's tallest building was in its final stages of construction and since the Duke had connections with its owners, the Kuwaiti royal family, he managed to clinch the deal. Most of our trustees did the 1,000-foot abseil, raising the necessary £100,000 or putting it up themselves. I'm afraid I didn't quite manage that much but was allowed to abseil the first top section for the photo opportunity. I must confess to a few butterflies before setting off: I always do on any abseil. But it was an extraordinary experience, with the whole of London beneath my feet, and raised a lot of money for Outward Bound.

Perhaps the most satisfying role I performed in the last few years was as Chancellor of Lancaster University. I hadn't been to university myself, although I'd acquired several honorary degrees along the way, and the role allowed me to discover something of that world and engage with young people, perhaps even offer them something from a lifetime of experience that is a little unusual. It started with a phone call from the vice-chancellor Paul Wellings, who had taken over in 2002 and was rapidly boosting the university's reputation and league table position. Princess Alexandra, who had been the university's first and in fact only chancellor, had decided after forty-five years' devoted service it was time to stand down; Paul was looking for someone with charity experience and a media profile who was local, with a direct connection to the university's constituency. Would I mind if he came to talk to me about it? We agreed that I'd do five years, and if we still liked each other, I'd do five more.

Thus began ten very happy and interesting years as chancellor. Because of royal protocol, Princess Alexandra was limited in her role, so I started more or less with a blank sheet of paper. I addressed the students at their graduation ceremonies and took full advantage; I had enough experience in my life of things not going to plan, especially when I was young. Don't be afraid of mistakes and don't be afraid of change, I told them. I went walking with the hiking club, and climbing with the climbing club. I also took an interest in student politics, and would invite the Students Union officials around for lunch at Badger Hill each year; I'd get the Old Crown in Hesket Newmarket to open early so I could buy them a pint after walking round High Pike. And while I had no executive power, when I saw plans for the new sports centre, with an architecturally pleasing but practically useless climbing wall, I intervened to get a proper climbing wall manufacturer involved. There were famous encounters too on the croquet lawns between me and my opposite number at York University, another War of the Roses. The role always gave me plenty of scope to mix business with pleasure, and so when my term of office ended, I was delighted to become an ambassador for the university, meaning that I've never really retired at all.

Chapter Twenty-Two

The Cruellest Challenge

We were never ones for lying on a beach. When the boys grew up and left home, Wendy would book activity holidays. She discovered a company offering bike or canoe trips in France, delivering your luggage each night to a comfortable *auberge*, leaving you to navigate your own way. We canoed down the River Creuse, a sleepy tributary of the Loire, with kingfishers flashing across the sun-dappled water and the occasional otter peering at us inquisitively. The following year we cycled through Provence.

Our final holiday of this kind was a celebration for Wendy's seventieth birthday organized by Maria Coffey, who had been Joe Tasker's partner. After Joe's death she had emigrated to Canada and fallen in love with a vet and passionate sea canoeist. They started a boutique ethical adventure travel company, Hidden Places, offering trips around the world, including the Galápagos. We had Maria and a knowledgeable ecologist to guide us as we sailed each night from island to island, during the day watching wildlife or snorkelling alongside seals and myriad exotic fish. At the end of the tour we took off for a week in the Ecudorean hills above Quito staying at an eco-lodge and watching the hummingbirds. On the night of President Obama's first election we caught a cab into town and watched the results come in. Both of us felt a tremendous wave of optimism that night.

Wendy had retired from teaching the Alexander Technique and

was now deeply into photography. It was fascinating to compare our approaches. I already knew I was a happy snapper: that's what a photojournalist or expedition photographer is. You are taking a series of pictures to illustrate a story. Wendy was an artist, interested in shapes, textures and colours, fascinated by detail and the beauty of nature. She'd spend an hour composing a single picture. I tended to take my Kindle with me on walks so I could park myself in the shade of a tree and read.

She was still playing golf with her great friends Gill and Dennis Clarke, even when they retired to Catalonia. We began visiting twice a year, Wendy playing a round most days. We would spend a couple of days doing something together, but otherwise it was up to me to find people to climb with. One special old friend was José Anglada whom I've known since the 1970s when we were living in Bowdon. His father, a businessman in Barcelona, had sent him to Manchester to improve his English. José was a brilliant climber, pioneering hard new routes on the conglomerate pillars of Montserrat, just twenty minutes from the centre of Barcelona. He also became one of Spain's best-known expedition leaders, inviting me to Barcelona to give lectures and taking me climbing with his Catalan friends. With Gill and Den in L'Escala this became a twice-yearly event.

Another regular visit was to Sydney to spend time with our Australian family. Once Joe and Jude's children Edie and Honor were born we would rent a nearby apartment. As usual I combined work, play and family, doing speaking engagements around Australia, visiting Berghaus's agents and enjoying weekend climbing with friends in the Blue Mountains. In 2011, I joined Joe in Bhutan for a trek he was leading while Wendy helped transform Jude's kitchen; it was a hands-on effort, sanding and staining a wooden floor, putting in new shelves and cupboards and redecorating. It was typically determined of her: Wendy had needed keyhole surgery on a painful knee only a few days before flying out to Sydney.

The following year, Wendy began tripping over, on kerbs or rocky steps. Our doctor, Kate, referred Wendy to the neurologist at Cumberland Infirmary in Carlisle. He diagnosed a dropped foot caused by a damaged nerve in the lower leg and recommended corrective footwear. I don't think either of us was convinced. We were becoming increasingly worried, not just by Wendy's falls but her pronounced loss of energy and general unsteadiness.

In early August 2012 we drove down to Bryn Mel, where Charlie Clarke has a lovely holiday home perched above the Menai Straits. In the past I had relied on him as an expedition doctor; now I needed his professional skill as a neurologist. With Wendy's blessing, I asked him to assess her. Charlie saw her on her own, spent a good hour with her, then asked me in, and told us he felt we should have a second opinion. He knew just the man, a consultant called Tim Williams at the Royal Victoria Infirmary in Newcastle. Then we simply got on with our holiday.

Earlier that summer I had been invited to carry the Olympic Torch to the top of Snowdon as part of the preamble to London 2012. It wasn't part of the relay, more a photo opportunity than anything else, or so it seemed. I drove down from Cumbria and stayed with my nephew Liam who was converting a huge Baptist railway station the following morning dressed in a smart white Olympic tracksuit. I did ask whether I shouldn't be carrying it on foot but there were, apparently, security issues, so I boarded the train with a little body of minders and Olympic officials with Liam and Sylvan, another of my nephews.

I felt a bit of a fraud watching streams of people walking and running to the summit. One of them was even carrying a torch; presumably he had taken part in the actual relay. Yet I was having fun and my minders, both police officers in tracksuits, were great company. At the top station my torch was ignited and I joined the cheering crowd packed around the summit of Snowdon. I did my best to run athletically to the top and with a bit of help from my police escort clambered onto the trig point to wave my torch. Suddenly, I was almost in tears. It was intensely emotional. What really hit me was being transported back to my roots, to where it had all started for me as a young lad of sixteen.

I couldn't help regretting that I hadn't brought Wendy and my Keswick family with me so I decided we should have our own family ceremony. I had brought the torch with us to Bryn Mel for a repeat performance. Charlie, his partner Marcela, Sepu, his endearingly mad Tibetan terrier, Rupert and Ann raced up the track from Pen y Pass. Wendy and I took our grandchildren Will and Emily on the train, carrying the torch with us. Marcela and Charlie arrived long after Rupert and Ann, having carried Sepu most of the way in a rucksack.

Life went on. That September we had another trip to Australia, as usual via Hong Kong, staying with friends above Sheko Bay. James Riley was finance director of Jardines and chairman of the Hong Kong section of the Royal Geographical Society. He and his wife Georgie were warm-hearted hosts, providing Wendy with a peaceful haven in their beautiful house to recover from the flight as I carried out a series of commitments for Berghaus and Lancaster University. In Sydney, as well as spending time with Joe and the family, we drove up to Forster, where Jude's mum Beth lived on a bluff high above the ocean. We sat watching whales from her house and walked along the pristine beaches far below.

I had to leave early for Lancaster University events in Singapore and Kuala Lumpur. That meant Wendy would have to travel on her own as far as Hong Kong, where I would catch up with her. I couldn't help worrying how she would cope, but it all went smoothly. After we got home I drove her over to Newcastle for tests, including electrocardiograms, and then life went on as usual, with me rushing around giving lectures and cramming in other engagements before flying to Spain for a short break with Gill and Den.

The winter Lancaster University degree ceremony was coming up, a special one for Wendy, since Geraldine, one of her closest friends, was receiving her doctorate. I would be making the presentation. The day before, we had our follow-up appointment in Newcastle with Tim Williams. I think we were both a bit apprehensive as we drove over. We hadn't talked much about it to each other; I think we didn't want to worry each other. We were shown into his rooms and Tim got straight to the point. He had bad news. Wendy had motor neurone disease.

It was like being hit very hard in the stomach. Both of us burst into tears and fell into one another's arms and clung to each other. Tim had a box of tissues handy and we slowly composed ourselves. Wendy told me afterwards she had wondered if she might have multiple sclerosis, having seen a friend suffer from it. We had never thought of MND. Tim was sympathetic, explained to us no one knew the cause, that it was fatal and there was no cure. He thought it likely Wendy could have between two and five years, but couldn't be certain.

That catastrophic moment of diagnosis was strangely inconclusive. Everything had changed and nothing had. We still had lives to live. I drove us back to Cumbria, having planned to stay with Geraldine in Ulverston. When we told her our news, we all wept, but felt an immense love, something we were to experience again and again as we told our nearest and dearest. The vice-chancellor's driver picked me up next morning and Wendy followed with Geraldine later. The very normality of it all and the celebration of Geraldine's achievement somehow made things more bearable.

Wendy had an immense strength of character, and a philosophy of living in the present, of looking practically into the future, always thinking of others before herself, always in command of herself. It was simply a matter of focusing on priorities. At first our lives continued as before, although I cut down on my engagements. We had a visit from Yvette, the specialist MND nurse Tim Williams sent as part of his clinic. She was full of warmth and confidence, answering all our questions and assuring us that she or a colleague would always be at the end of the phone. It was a luxury having Kate, our doctor, just half a mile down the track at Potts Ghyll. She told us we could phone at any time, day or night. We already knew Joyce, our district nurse. She would be our point of contact for social services and all the other experts available to us. She was matter-of-fact but had a warm heart and proved an invaluable ally in the months ahead.

We had an early appointment at Cumberland Infirmary to fit Wendy for an electric wheelchair. It seemed huge, rather intimidating in fact, with a finger controller to allow her to steer it around furniture. The technician explained they didn't want to keep changing it; this model would suit Wendy as her illness progressed. I didn't need the reminder. I understood all too well the inevitable outcome and simply tried to give all the support I could. Wendy, on the other hand, read everything she could about the disease.

In February we were back at L'Escala, Wendy playing nine holes of golf with me as her caddy. Walking through woodland to the ninth tee, holding onto my arm, she tripped on a root and I was unable to prevent her falling. What was worse, she landed on her coccyx and bruised it badly. After that we went for gentle walks and played a lot of bridge. The advance of the disease was gradual. Wendy's speech became slightly slurred. She found the stairs more difficult and the occupational therapist suggested an extra banister and grab rail but we were still sleeping on the first floor.

At the end of March, Joe and the family, the 'Sydney Bons', came over to stay with us and Wendy tried out a little wheelie trolley so she could keep going out for walks. She kept challenging her limits. She set out with some of her golfing friends one day to walk up Latrigg, the hill above Keswick. The path was marked as wheelchair-friendly but she soon discovered otherwise as she pushed her wheeled trolley along. There was lots of laughter as she struggled up and down the hill; such challenges could be joyous, even against the inexorable development of the disease. We were involved in a fight, sharing moments of intense joy at minor victories, making the most of every moment of happiness.

Walking slowly became more difficult, as did the stairs. We decided it was time to get a more practical vehicle and traded in Wendy's Subaru for a bright red Renault Kangoo. It had a tailgate and the controls could be hand-operated so Wendy could drive. In the back was an equally red three-wheel scooter. Wendy took to this immediately, accelerating down the lane, round the corner and out of sight before reappearing with a delighted smile on her face. She had some independence back. We drove to Keswick to show our new vehicles off to Rupert and Ann. Walking beside Derwentwater, Wendy pulled away from us and the children chased after her.

That summer of 2013 we moved our bedroom downstairs to what had been Wendy's teaching studio. She loved that she could see the squirrel feeder from our new bed. We adapted the adjacent bathroom to suit her needs and altered her old pottery workshop into a snug, with remote-controlled French windows so she could be as independent as possible, able to drive her scooter out into the garden. Various devices were delivered to help her upright and into her wheelchair. At least we had the space. I couldn't help wondering how someone in a small flat would cope.

Rupert gave me incredible support, which became increasingly vital as Wendy's illness developed. Another wonderful friend was Vera, from Wendy's golf club in Keswick. She was a farmer's daughter, strong and practical, as well as a sportswoman and made her living painting and decorating. Vera had decorated Badger Hill, inside and out. As Wendy's illness developed she helped in so many different ways that we asked if we could employ her, and she agreed. We had help too from Hospice at Home, who came in once a week to bathe Wendy and give me the chance of a full night's sleep. Crossroads, now the Carers Trust, came for half a day once a week to give me a bit of a rest.

I was still trying to keep up with my other commitments, attending Berghaus meetings, going on a short lecture tour and keeping up my voluntary work. I needed to, not only to keep money coming in, but also as an outlet for the pressure I felt at home. I found the role of carer challenging; everything took so long, requiring immense patience on my part, a quality I have always rather lacked. I experienced fatigue too, a problem that became more acute as Wendy's condition worsened and she needed more physical help.

Her speech was becoming more slurred. I have never been the

best of listeners and was sometimes driven to an exasperated outburst because I couldn't understand. Then I would be engulfed with guilt and regret, profuse with apologies, even tears as I regained my composure and sought to reassure her. At this stage we only had partial support, so there were a lot of times when we were on our own, particularly at night. I loved her so much, was, deep down, so terrified of losing her, and yet felt so inadequate in the practical expression of that love.

Christmas was something we could look forward to; Joe and his family were flying into Manchester. Vera was hard at work in Wendy's office upstairs, storing all the records of her widely varied interests. Rupert's family arrived and Emily tasked herself with transforming Badger Hill into an animal hospital, with notices stuck everywhere. My picture library became the animals' ward; the main office was the consulting room. The Sydney Bons reached Badger Hill late on Christmas Eve. It was a shock for them to see just how much Wendy's illness had taken from her, but it was joyous as well, having the whole family with us. I had ordered a goose, and Joe, with his love of cooking, was in his element on Christmas Day, the rest of us helping as his sous-chefs.

After a walk down the lane, with Wendy in the lead on her scooter, she was able to join us for dinner though only able to spoon down soft foods; then she retreated to her recliner chair in front of the fire, where some of us kept her company through the rest of the meal. The Keswick Bons came in the early evening with Ann's parents and family. The children were delighted to see each other. Will and Edie, who are close in age and have similar senses of humour, got on particularly well. They dragged Wendy and me into their games. Every one of the ten days Joe and Jude stayed was precious.

Wendy had been finding it increasingly difficult to swallow for some time with food often going down the wrong way into her lungs leading to painful paroxysms of coughing and choking. Tim Williams, our consultant, had warned us of this and suggested that at some point Wendy might be better off with a tube going straight into her stomach through the skin and stomach wall, what's called a percutaneous endoscopic gastrostomy tube, or peg-tube. Wendy had thought it through carefully, as she always did, and suggested it at the MND clinic we attended just before Christmas.

I drove her across to Newcastle in January and since she was going to be in hospital for a week booked myself into a local hotel so I could be with her as much as possible. She was in the neurological ward and had a room to herself yet it was all very open and friendly. I was told I could stay day and night, as long as I wanted. Once she'd had the operation I had to learn how to feed her, using the peg. It made a huge difference; she was no longer choking and coughing when eating, and once we had learned the routine, it was easy to deliver.

She was discharged quite late in the day and by the time we got back to Badger Hill it was dark and raining heavily. There was no one at home. To get her into the house as quickly as possible I used the wheeled walking frame but it kept getting stuck in our muddy parking area as the rain lashed down and the wind buffeted us. I felt alone and vulnerable; Wendy was quietly stoical but tiring fast. We barely made it to the kitchen door and into the warm safe shelter of our home. I got Wendy settled in our big comfy recliner armchair and for the first time fed her through the peg without anyone nearby to call for help or advice.

At last, in bed, I could snuggle up against her, getting every bit as much assurance from her as I could give to her, by our close physical contact. Her illness was biting harder and harder. She could no longer talk; indeed barely make a sound. Wendy would ring a little bell to get attention and then write down whatever she wanted to say. She tried an application on her iPad, which synthesized her typed notes into speech, but it didn't suit her. Her handwriting was clear, easy to read and expressive. I have kept dozens of reporter's notebooks recording her needs and her side of conversations.

She suffered also from something called restless leg syndrome, a neurological condition not necessarily associated with her MND. It's like an uncomfortable itch but experienced inside your legs, so scratching does nothing to help. The reflex response was to kick, but that did nothing either. It made sleep very difficult; Wendy found it hard to lie or sit comfortably. Walking helped, as did some drugs, but it took a while to control. I find it difficult to conceive what it must have been like for her, facing this relentless decline and increasing dependence. She never complained and, right to the end, was always thinking of others, gesturing to remind me to offer one of our carers and visitors a cup of tea or a comfortable seat.

We got more help from social services, with a carer coming in four times a day, but they were on a tight schedule and out in the country that was difficult. If the carer hadn't been to us before, they had a job to find us. It meant you could never be sure just when they would turn up. At this stage it wasn't critical because I could do everything on my own without support, but it became increasingly tiring, particularly when she needed to get up during the night; she needed help to get out of bed and back in again.

Things came to a head in mid April 2014. I had dozed off but was as usual on edge in case she needed me. I was suddenly aware that something was wrong: she wasn't lying beside me. I hurled myself out of bed but she ran out of strength before I could reach her, slumping to the floor from her walking frame. I wasn't strong enough to get her back into bed on my own and had to phone my brother Gerald in the village. He managed the task easily. It was good to snuggle close to her and drift off to sleep.

Next day, we held a big meeting in our living room with Joyce, our district nurse, in the chair, one of the other nurses, and someone from social services. Rupert, who had already done so much, was there too. Joyce said we definitely qualified for full twenty-four-hour NHS home care. We understood it would take a little time to arrange everything and in the meantime Wendy could stay in our local hospice in Carlisle for a week or so. Wendy had a big room with French windows through which she could drive her scooter and see green fields. I was allowed to stay all day and as long into the night as I wanted. We had plenty of visitors and could go out for walks in the park next door.

Then we had the next crisis. The nurse reported one morning that there was blood in Wendy's urine. The hospice could only give palliative care so she had to go into hospital. We both hated that idea but discussing it was obviously difficult with Wendy having to write down her thoughts. We accepted the decision. At first, it wasn't too bad. She was in the gastric ward and had a nice single room but next morning I discovered she'd been moved to a crowded open ward. The beds were close together and it was incredibly noisy. The nurses were obviously stretched and I found it difficult to find anyone to answer my questions though I could see for myself Wendy was on a drip. I was also told I would have to observe visiting hours. When I returned that afternoon I was told they were deciding whether to examine Wendy by endoscope and until they decided weren't feeding her: hence the drip. I returned home in an agony of worry.

Next day there was still no information and Wendy was looking very pale and wan. She had not been fed for two days. I was frantic but did what I should have done in the hospice: I phoned Yvette, our MND nurse in Newcastle. When I explained what was happening, she immediately said that an endoscopy might well kill her. There was no point in her being in hospital: any surgical intervention would be fatal.

I made my mind up immediately, explained to Wendy what Yvette had said, found the ward sister and told her I was taking Wendy home. It took another couple of hours to sort out the paperwork and then I drove Wendy home in the Kangoo. We both resolved she would never again leave home. Our full support system was nearly in place, although it still needed me or a family member, usually Rupert, to be available at all times since we now needed two people to help Wendy move.

She now slept in a hospital bed, installed in our downstairs bedroom; I had a single bed beside it. I could no longer snuggle up close to her but at least I was there, could hold her hand and help in the night. If Rupert or a friend were staying I'd sometimes slip upstairs to get a full night's sleep. I still kept up with some of my work. I needed to, to keep my own balance. Even now I feel guilty about needing those breaks.

We got to know our carers, learned about their lives, offered them lunch or supper; we became like a family. There were also all the other specialists and our dear friend Vera doing regular slots, although she now had to be employed directly by the care contractor. There was no time for sadness or reflection. My richest memories were our walks, exploring the tracks and quiet roads within half an hour's drive or so. We often went up to the Solway; the nature reserves had scooter-friendly paths and there was a wealth of birdlife. We could watch waders feeding on the mud flats and gulls wheeling in the sky with such effortless freedom to the other side of the firth. Behind the shore were the Galloway hills where we had wandered so often in the past.

In early summer Wendy became weaker. We decided to get Joe over from Australia as soon as possible. He arrived in June and though he could manage only a few days it was important to them both. He was devoted to his mum, yet on the other side of the world had inevitably felt isolated and out of touch. Even the practical actions of feeding through the peg or helping her out of her chair had to be learned when the rest of us were doing it all with the ease of practice. Yet his presence and love meant a huge amount and his departure was a sad one, for they both knew they were unlikely to see each other again. It was so hard on him.

I had always found it difficult to talk with Wendy about her approaching death; early on in her illness she indicated she wanted to be cremated and her ashes to be scattered to the winds on top of High Pike. Shortly after Joe's visit she wrote she wanted to have her funeral in our village church and be buried in the churchyard. Her dad, Les, had died in his early nineties and had his funeral service there too. His vicar, Colin Reid, was a friend. He and Les regularly went walking together and had long discussions on philosophy and religion. Wendy and Colin planned a church service for Les with poetry and songs rather than psalms and hymns. It had been a celebration of a long and at times difficult life, which, in its last twenty years in Caldbeck, had been happy and fulfilling. I'm sure Wendy was thinking of a service along the same lines for herself.

I called Malcolm, our current vicar, and he came up to see us the following morning. Malcolm has a warm, energetic manner and he sat beside Wendy, who was lying on the couch, held her hand and spoke to her. I told him of the funeral service we had planned for Les. He responded gently but firmly that he would have to observe the Church of England ritual, but there were plenty of readings from the Bible, psalms and hymns he was sure Wendy would approve. He couldn't have been kinder, but he was insistent. He asked Wendy how she felt. She wrote: 'I will think.'

We didn't talk about it that day, but next morning she indicated she had something to tell me and wrote: 'Marie-Elsa.' I understood at once. Why hadn't I thought of it? Marie-Elsa is Melvyn Bragg's daughter. He had been brought up in Wigton and had a holiday home near by. Marie-Elsa had been close to her grandparents growing up and Wendy had known her since her childhood. They had become especially close in the last couple of years, when a close friend of Wendy's was dying in London. Wendy would stay with Marie-Elsa in Hampstead Garden Suburb when she came down to visit. They shared the same philosophical and spiritual curiosity, often talking long into the night; Marie-Elsa was also a Church of England priest. I phoned her that morning and explained the situation, asking if she'd be prepared to conduct Wendy's funeral. She consented immediately, provided she was available and of course that Malcolm was happy about it.

It was turning into a humid summer and it became ever more difficult to get Wendy comfortable and to move her from one resting place to another. Her snug, at the end of the house, with its French windows and daybed, was a peaceful room. But she was getting so terribly weak. We had to use the hoist more and more to move her, a relentless loss of independence. She was having increasing difficulty in writing, her notes becoming shorter and more difficult to decipher.

Rupert was now staying at Badger Hill most of the time, as

Wendy's condition worsened. On 21 July there was another meeting with Joyce, the district nurse, Louise, the manager at her care company and other specialists, standing around Wendy, seated in her armchair in the living room, able to understand every single word and nuance of conversation, but unable to take part. Some of the group made the effort to involve her, but all too easily it slipped into a conversation over her head. There was talk of moving her hospital bed into the living room, of fitting a catheter, of using the hoist at all times. Then the meeting dispersed and we were left feeling a little stunned.

Next morning Wendy indicated she'd like to go outside and look at the garden. We sat her in her big electric wheel chair. Rupert needed to help her operate the finger control and we carefully navigated our way through the living room and snug, out onto the patio and into the garden, up onto the lawn where she went slowly from plant to plant, gazing intensely at each one. She seemed to be saying goodbye. I think we both had to hide our tears.

We spent the rest of the day quietly, carers coming and going, feeding Wendy through the peg, Rupert and I doing what we could to help her get comfortable. That night it took her a long time to settle but eventually Wendy sank into a fitful sleep. Around midnight she woke up again. The carer and I did what we could to make her comfortable and she fell asleep again but her breathing was now very shallow. She seemed to be slipping away. I told the carer to wake Rupert and he came down quickly. I also phoned our doctor Kate to tell her I thought Wendy was dying. She said she'd come straightaway.

Then I crouched on my single bed holding Wendy's hand; Rupert was on the other side holding her other hand. I can remember very little of the detail of those moments. I don't think we were in tears at that time, but united in intense love for Wendy, trying to protect and shelter her, as her breathing grew weaker and weaker and finally became imperceptible. Did she hear our words? Feel our hands on hers, our arms around her? I want to think she did.

*

The week after Wendy's death was filled with preparations and getting Joe and the Sydney family back to the UK. There was no time for grief. Marie-Elsa, though recovering from a bout of illness, came straight up to help plan the funeral. She was a wonderful, soothing, compassionate and practical presence. Malcolm, our vicar, was helpful in every way. Rupert sorted out all the many arrangements, with help from my wonderful secretary Margaret Trinder, and Frances Daltrey, who has run my photo library for so many years. Joe, Jude, Edie and Honor flew in from Australia and stayed at Badger Hill.

The undertakers arrived and took Wendy's body to Carlisle but Marie-Elsa suggested she be brought home the day before the funeral. The coffin was opened and placed on supports in the snug, surrounded by her things. It was good having her there, lying so still and reposed, home for one last night. The hospital bed was taken away and I had our big double bed reassembled; all I could think was how empty it was without her beside me.

The morning of the funeral dawned cloudy; rain fell throughout the day. You could barely see High Pike. The hearse arrived, the coffin was closed and we carried it out to the hearse, Rupert and Joe in front, Rob and Marcus, their childhood friends, in the middle, my brother Gerald and I bringing up the rear. Once the coffin was in the hearse we led it on foot with the rest of the family to the beech tree at the end of the track and then drove to the Oddfellows Arms in Caldbeck where friends were waiting. Together we led the hearse to the church.

Marie-Elsa was there to greet us and guide us through the service. All of us took part: I gave the eulogy; Rupert and Joe talked of their mum and the four grandchildren read a poem they had composed, each taking a verse at a time. Wendy's oldest friend Rosemary spoke, as did Paul Ross, who ran the Lamp Lighter coffee bar when she started folk singing, and Stephen Bolger, one of Wendy's professional colleagues. Dave Goulder, folk singer, old friend and neighbour sang 'The Carter', and Margaret Walker, from our Bowdon days, played the harp, and we took Wendy on her final journey to her grave close to the church wall, as we listened to a recording of her singing, all of us in tears.

Gathering at the village hall to drink and reminisce, I found myself in shock, unable to get around to thank the so many people for their support and kindness. I just sat in a corner with a few close family and friends. The first real agony of grief hit me when Joe and the family went back to Australia and I was at Badger Hill on my own. I can remember walking 'round the block' howling. The decision to climb the Old Man of Hoy was to give my mind something else to focus on. On getting back from the Orkneys I began trying to meet my usual commitments but the effects of my prolapsed discs were biting hard. I had to move into our bungalow in Keswick, where Rupert could care for me. Things got so bad I was put on morphine and could only sleep on my left side lying against pillows with a hot water bottle pressing against my lower back.

Normally, in the summer, I would have led an annual walk for Berghaus, the 'Bonington walk', a bit of fun and to raise awareness among the staff. Wendy's final illness made that impossible. It was postponed to October but now I was laid up and couldn't make it. A scan showed how badly the discs had been compressed and the radiologist suggested a spinal injection of slow-release anaesthetics and steroids to reduce the pain. Rupert drove me to Newcastle and I hobbled into the operating theatre in my surgical gown, lying face down on the operating table. The radiologist was looking at an X-ray image to identify a spot as close as possible to the trapped nerves, and I experienced a sudden agonizing stabbing pain that almost made me leap into the air.

'Bingo!' the radiologist exclaimed. 'Spot on!'

Rupert drove me back to Keswick and my back improved until I was able to take short walks down to the shores of Derwentwater. Finally, I drove myself back to Badger Hill. It was a bittersweet experience, getting back to the house where I had known so much love and which I loved so much, yet empty of the woman I loved. I walked around the familiar block, the track to Potts Ghyll, dropping down to the little stream that joins the Caldew that in turn joins the Eden to flow out into the Solway Firth.

Beyond Potts Ghyll I walked up onto the open fell, skirting the drystone walls leading back to the mine track from Nether Row. I found myself weeping as I walked the old familiar trail, the memories too painful to bear, big gasping retching sobs, but then I stopped and became aware of the quiet soothing beauty, on this border between field and fell, the sheep quietly munching the grass, the scattered houses of Nether Row partly hidden by the trees growing among them, my own Badger Hill barely visible. I was glad to be home again, even as I felt its emptiness.

Conclusion

Love after Love

In February 2014, as Wendy's MND was starting to bite hard, I made a flying visit down to London for my old friend Charlie Clarke's seventieth birthday. Charlie had lost his own wife Ruth to cancer a couple of years before, but had recently met the very beautiful Marcela Contreras, a highly respected consultant haematologist. Marcela was hosting a big party for Charlie at her house in Hampstead Garden Suburb with friends from all the various aspects of his life. I found myself on a table with old climbing chums Jim Curran and Henry Day, who had led the first British expedition to climb Annapurna.

Sitting next to me was Loreto Herman, the wife of my old friend Ian McNaught-Davis. Like Marcela, Loreto is Chilean, and they are close friends. Mac had been suffering from Alzheimer's for several years and was now seriously ill with cancer so Loreto had come by herself. It was the first time I had talked with her at any length. I think before I had almost been frightened by her extraordinary beauty and self-confidence. Yet talking with her that night I thoroughly enjoyed her company. Mac died shortly after but I couldn't go down to his funeral: Wendy's condition was deteriorating so quickly.

I next saw Loreto at a retrospective exhibition of Jim Curran's work in Sheffield that November after Wendy had died; she came up from London with Charlie and Marcela. In February she was at the Royal Geographical Society for a kind of 'This is Your Life' with climbing mates and Rupert, with the author Julie Summers interviewing us on stage to raise funds for the Mountain Heritage Trust. The following night she was giving a dinner party at her home to celebrate Charlie's birthday and I sat next to her, once again delighted by her company.

We began to run into each other more often, partly, I suspect, through the designs of close friends. In April I was at the Piolet d'Or in Chamonix, an annual award launched by the elite Groupe de Haute Montagne. Each year a panel of judges give awards deemed to the boldest and most ethically pure ascents in the greater ranges. I was being given a lifetime achievement award, only the seventh person to be thus honoured. Loreto had been skiing at Leysin with Doug and Trish Scott, who had given both Loreto and Mac terrific support throughout his illness. Doug had received the lifetime award the previous year and was going to present me with mine.

During our few days in Chamonix, we bumped into each other at various social functions, which culminated at the Montenvers Hotel. A special train had been laid on to take us up to the closing party. My first visit had been in 1958 climbing with Hamish, when we dossed in a little hut just beyond the hotel and were so broke that whenever we needed provisions we walked down to Chamonix and back. The hotel hasn't changed, in fact has never been done up. The furnishings are the same as they were in the nineteenth century. Loreto and I explored the old rooms, enjoyed more food and wine, listened to the lugubrious notes of the long Alpine horn. Spontaneously, I invited Loreto to the Alpine Club's dinner later that month. She accepted, and offered me her spare room for the night.

I travelled down that morning, expecting to have lunch with a friend at the Athenaeum but my friend had forgotten, phoning to apologize after I'd sat waiting for an hour. Feeling a little bruised, I arrived at Loreto's door and told her my sad story over a cup of tea. She commiserated, saying she'd cheer me up, which she already had. I told her I'd been invited to Chile on a lecture tour the following year and without thinking I asked her 'Would you like to come?' She replied, without hesitation, 'I'd love to.'

That's really where it all started. It was a tsunami of joyous emotion. We arrived at the Alpine Club dinner, which happened to be at my club, the Army and Navy, arm in arm. That raised a few eyebrows. We remained engrossed in each other throughout dinner, raising a few more. We left the club hand in hand, heading for the bus stop just past the Ritz Hotel, and as we waited for the No.9, I kissed her for the first time, and we continued kissing until the bus arrived and then kissed all the way back to Kensington High Street. Waking up in the morning, entwined in each other's arms, I studied her beautiful face: Loreto has sparkling eyes and wonderful cheekbones, but behind those features is a lively, warm intelligence. She is very decisive, even impulsive, can be fiery but doesn't hold grudges. She is also intensely loyal, always prepared to go out of her way to help and support those she loves.

In many ways we are very different. If Loreto is decisive, I undoubtedly dither a bit, can be influenced, yet get back on to the right track in the end. She is essentially gregarious and sociable, while I have a limited social stamina. Yet in the important things we have the same values. Neither of us lives in the past. We try to learn from it but don't regret. We found we could laugh together easily. We knew from that very first night we had found the person we wanted to share the rest of our lives with, an understanding and love that has only grown.

Of course, we still had our own lives to lead, which kept us apart for a while, but we talked on the phone several times a day. A fortnight after that fateful Alpine Club dinner, I had a dinner at Lancaster University, standing in for the busy new chancellor Alan Milburn in my new role as the university's ambassador. It was great having Loreto with me; so wonderfully good at the social bit, charming everyone. The following day I was giving a lecture in Keswick, an obvious opportunity to introduce Loreto to my family over tea with Rupert, Ann, Emily and Will.

I was very aware they might find it difficult to understand how

I'd fallen so deeply in love only eight months after the death of Wendy but they greeted us warmly. As we were about to walk down to the climbing wall where the lecture was taking place, Will went up to his mum and said softly: 'I like Loreto.' Ann told him to go and tell her. Will, always quite shy, was happy to do so. It was a nice start.

When Loreto left for her house in France, leaving me in London to give a lecture, her daughter Elvira took the opportunity to invite me to supper. As I walked up to the front door, it flew open and Elvira's four children Luca, Matteo, Livia and Filippo burst out and jumped into my arms. Elvira followed, smiling warmly, and gave me a hug. Elvira is very like her mother, extrovert and beautiful, with those striking cheekbones and a mane of long blonde hair. She'd worked for Condé Nast before marrying Nick Hurrell, a former chief executive of Saatchi and Saatchi now running his own advertising agency. He's also chair of the Groucho Club. They made me feel part of their family from that very first night.

After the lecture, I travelled with Doug and Trish out to La Loma, which Loreto and Mac had bought in the late 1990s. It's some twelve miles north of St Tropez in forested hills below the village of La Garde-Freinet, traditionally designed and with an amazing view across low wooded hills and vineyards to a forested range of hills that stretch across the horizon, hiding all but a few glimpses of the Mediterranean. Over the last couple of years I have come to love this house and its view. Loreto and I have walked almost all the hills we can see and quite a few more.

Getting home to Badger Hill, I faced a difficult decision. I had arranged to go out and see Joe and his family for a holiday lasting six weeks. My first inclination was to take Loreto with me, but worried that, with the sense of distance and separation Joe had experienced throughout Wendy's illness, I needed to be there entirely for them. So I decided I should go on my own. Those six weeks apart were difficult. We missed each other intensely. What would we have done without WhatsApp? But if anything, the separation strengthened our attachment, bringing home how much we needed each other. It made us determined never be parted for more than a few days at a time in the future.

We spent most of the summer in the Lakes, sharing my love of its hills with Loreto and she joined me in the autumn for as many of my lecture and charity commitments as she could. Equally I wanted to share with her as much of the things that were important to her. She is a committed Roman Catholic and always tries to make it to Mass on Sunday at Our Lady of Victories in Kensington. I started joining her and still do. I'm essentially an agnostic, probably always will be, but I find a real peace and reassurance in church, a time to meditate. Loreto's priest, Monsignor Jim Curry, had become a good friend of Loreto and I immediately warmed to his great compassion and sense of humour.

That September I gave a lecture in Oxford celebrating the fortieth anniversary of our ascent of the south-west face of Everest. We were put up in a room in Wadham College and when I woke the following morning, I snuggled up to Loreto and just knew I wanted to be more than her partner. The words just burst out of me.

'Let's get married.'

Loreto smiled sleepily. 'People as old as us don't bother to get married. I'll think about it.' And then a few minutes later, she kissed me for a long time and then with that wonderful smile of hers said: 'Okay.'

We didn't tell anyone else for some time. Our previous marriages had been in register offices, but Loreto wanted to be married in church by Monsignor. I liked the idea, so Monsignor was the first person we told. He was delighted and when I mentioned that Mum had had me baptized at St Mary's Catholic Church in Holly Place, Hampstead, he was even more delighted, saying it would make things much easier. When I told my Keswick family, Emily was pleased, saying she had always wanted to be a bridesmaid. From there it all escalated. Rupert, Ann and Elvira very much took over, and since the Sydney Bons were flying over, we needed to find jobs for four grandsons and four granddaughters, who all became bridesmaids and pages, with each one of them reading a line of one of the lessons. Elvira, looking more like sister than daughter, was giving her mother away.

My good old friend Charlie was best man. I stayed with him at his house in Angel the night before the wedding, and then we caught the bus to Notting Hill, walking through Kensington Gardens to the church after a light lunch. Loreto was radiant in a white trouser suit, looking lovelier than I had ever seen her as she walked up the aisle with Elvira and her faithful pages and bridesmaids, the best behaved I'd ever seen them. It was one of the most wonderful days of our lives, finishing with all sixty of us, guests and all, piling into a coach to take us to the Groucho Club, where we had a brilliant reception that stretched into the earlier hours, the children doing impromptu congas through the rooms and a wedding cake formed of a magnificent slender pyramid of profiteroles.

A few days later we caught the Eurostar to Paris for a long weekend, and then very shortly after drove down to La Loma, my trusty Subaru packed with my entire archive to help me write this book. A corner of our bedroom has become my office, and exploration of the wooded hills around us has been our escape after a day's literary struggle. I know I wouldn't have made it through without Loreto's loving support and the occasional kick up the backside when I've had a bit of a tantrum with writer's block.

Writing these words, looking back over all the years, has been a challenging exercise of introspection, reliving the joy and despair. But that is now all in the past. What I value above all is finding, for the second time, a deep passionate joyous love that fills my whole being, and the love also for our families and friends – and making the absolute most of whatever time we have left on this earth.

Author's Note

Covering eighty-three years of life and researching my immediate ancestors to explore possible influences on my own character, thinking about and talking to the people who have affected my life as a son, a husband and father, a fellow climber or colleague means I have a lot of people to thank in telling my story. I thank them all for the richness of life that I have experienced.

In particular I owe my mum a special gratitude for the letters she wrote to me, all of which I have kept, and for keeping the ones that I wrote to her; she also kept copious diaries and an unfinished autobiography, which filled in much of my early upbringing. Wendy, my wife of fifty-two years, kept up the family tradition as diligent archivist, storing family papers which I was able to find and use after her tragic death. My half-brother Gerald, and Rosemary, my half-sister, have let me have documents and pictures belonging to our father and grandfather. Louise Boxhall gave me a very useful Doran family tree and other information. I also owe a great deal to my sons, Joe and Rupert, who confided in me the stories of their early lives and misadventures, all of which formed the foundations of the successful lives they are now leading as loving husbands, parents and entrepreneurs.

Many thanks to Iain MacGregor, Non-fiction Publishing Director at Simon & Schuster UK, who commissioned the book and has since kept a very supportive and patient interest in its progress. Ed Douglas has done a wonderful job as my editor, improving my prose, firmly cutting where necessary and giving me steady support and advice throughout. Jo Whitford, the project editor, has been terrific, particularly in slotting in last-minute changes at the proof stage. Frances Daltrey, who has run my picture library for thirty years, helped with research, selected all the pictures used in the book and worked closely with Martin Lubikowski of ML Design, who devised the maps and diagrams.

The following were also invaluable for background information and short quotes: Peter and Leni Gillman, *Extreme Eiger* (Simon & Schuster, 2015); Stephen Venables, *A Slender Thread* (Hutchinson, 2000) and thanks for the map; Victor Saunders, *No Place to Fall*, (Hodder & Stoughton, 1994); Jeff Connor, *Dougal Haston: The Philosophy of Risk* (Canongate, 2002); Jim Curran, *High Achiever: The Life and Climbs of Chris Bonington* (Constable, 1999). I also drew heavily from the online back issues of the *Alpine Journal*. It's great these journals are now so widely available through the internet.

Jude Beveridge, my personal assistant, has ably held the fort, fielding my phone calls and emails, enabling me to focus on the book. Most important of all, I could never have undertaken and written it without the love and support of my wife Loreto, who has been with me throughout, patiently understanding why I can't just go out for a walk, kicking me out of writer's block and making me laugh with her joyous sense of humour.

Index

(the initials CB refer to Chris Bonington)